Webster's

Speller

The WEBSTER'S SPELLER is designed for use as a handbook in the office, and in the home, as a Quick Reference Guide to spelling, and proper word hyphenation.

Words that contain double dashes (=) between indicate where a hyphenated word should either be, when syllable division, or...

This book was not published by the original publishers of the Webster's Dictionaries, or by any of their successors.

® Landoll, Inc.
© 1997 Landoll, Inc.
Ashland, Ohio 44805

WEBSTER'S SPELLER

This WEBSTER'S SPELLER is designed for use in the school, in the office, and in the home, as a Quick Referance Guide to spelling and proper word hyphenation.

Words that contain double dashes (--) between letters indicates a hyphenated word. Single dashes (-) show syllabic division.

A

aard-vark
a-back
ab-a-cus
  ab-a-cus-es
  ab-a-ci
a-baft
  abaft-ment
  abaft-ed
ab-a-lo-ne
a-ban-don
  aban-doned
  aban-don-er
  aban-don-ment
a-base
  a-based
  a-bas-ing
  a-base-ment
a-bash
  a-bash-ment
a-bate
  a-bat-ed
  a-bat-ing
  a-bat-a-ble
  a-bate-ment
aba-tis
ab-at-oir
ab-ba-cy
  ab-ba-tial
ab-bess
ab-bey
  ab-beys
ab-bot
ab-bre-vi-a-tion
  ab-bre-vi-ate
  ab-bre-vi-at-ed
  ab-bre-vi-at-ing
  ab-bre-vi-a-tor
ab-di-cate
  ab-di-cat-ed
  ab-di-cat-ing
  ab-di-ca-tion
ab-do-men
  ab-dom-i-nal
  ab-dom-i-nal-ly
ab-duce
ab-duct
  ab-duc-tion
  ab-duc-tor
  ab-duct-ing
a-beam
a-bed
ab-er-rance
  ab-er-ran-cy

ab-er-rant
  ab-er-rant-ly
ab-er-ra-tion
  ab-er-ra-tion-al
a-bet
  a-bet-ted
  a-bet-ting
  a-bet-ment
  a-bet-tor
  a-bet-ter
a-bey-ance
ab-hor
  ab-horred
  ab-hor-ring
  ab-hor-rence
  ab-hor-er
ab-hor-rence
ab-hor-rent
  ab-hor-rent-ly
a-bide
  a-bid-er
  a-bi-ded
  a-bid-ing
  a-bid-ance
a-bid-ing
  a-bid-ing-ly
a-bil-i-ty
  a-bil-i-ties
ab-ject
  ab-ject-ly
  ab-ject-ness
  ab-jec-tion
ab-jure
  ab-jured
  ab-jur-ing
  ab-ju-ra-tion
  ab-jur-er
ab-late
  ab-lat-ed
  ab-lat-ing
  ab-la-tion
  ab-la-tive
ab-laut
a-blaze
a-ble
  a-bler
  a-blest
  a-bly
a-ble-bod-ied
a-bloom
ab-lu-tion
  ab-lu-tion-ar-y
ab-ne-gate

a-broad
ab-ro-gate
  ab-ro-gat-ed
  ab-ro-gat-ing
  ab-ro-ga-tion
ab-rupt
  abrupt-ness
  abrupt-ly
ab-scess
  ab-scessed
ab-scis-sa
  ab-scis-sas
  ab-scis-sae
ab-scis-sion
ab-scond
  ab-scond-er
ab-sence
ab-sent
  ab-sent-ly
ab-sen-tee
  ab-sen-tee-ism
ab-sent-mind-ed
  ab-sent-mind-ed-ly
ab-sinthe
ab-so-lute
  ab-so-lute-ly
  ab-so-lu-tion
  ab-so-lut-ism
  ab-so-lut-ist
ab-solve
  ab-solved
  ab-solv-ing
ab-sorb
  ab-sorb-er
  ab-sorb-a-bil-i-ty
  ab-sorb-a-ble
  ab-sorb-tive
ab-stain
  ab-stain-er
  ab-sten-tion
  ab-sti-nence
  ab-sti-nent
ab-ste-mi-ous
  ab-ste-mi-ous-ly
ab-stract
  ab-stract-ly
  ab-strac-tion
  ab-strac-tive
ab-stract-ed
  ab-stract-ed-ly
ab-strac-tion-ism
  ab-strac-tion-ist
ab-struse

ab-ne-gat-ed
ab-ne-gat-ing
ab-ne-ga-tor
ab-ne-ga-tion
ab-nor-mal
ab-nor-mal-ly
ab-nor-mal-i-ty
ab-nor-mal-i-ties
a-board
a-bode
a-boil
a-bol-ish
a-bol-ish-a-ble
a-bol-ish-er
a-bol-ish-ment
a-b-oma-sum
a-b-oma-sal
a-bom-i-na-ble
a-bom-i-na-bly
a-bom-i-nate
a-bom-i-nat-ed
a-bom-i-na-tion
a-bom-i-na-tor
ab-o-rig-i-ne
ab-o-rig-i-nal
ab-o-rig-i-nal-ly
a-born-ing
a-bort
a-bort-er
a-bor-ti-fa-cient
a-bor-tion
a-bor-tion-ist
a-bor-tive
a-bor-tive-ness
a-bor-tive-ly
a-bout-face
a-bove-board
ab-ra-ca-dab-ra
abrad-ant
a-brade
a-brad-ed
a-brad-er
a-bra-sion
a-bra-sive
a-bra-sive-ly
ab-re-act
a-breast
a-bridge
a-bridged
a-bridg-ing
a-bridg-ment
a-bridge-ment
a-broach

ab-struse-ly
ab-surd
ab-surd-i-ty
ab-surd-ly
a-bub-ble
a-build-ing
a-bud-dance
a-bun-dant
a-bun-dant-ly
a-buse
a-bused
a-bus-ing
a-bus-er
a-bu-sive
a-bu-sive-ly
a-but
a-but-ter
a-but-ted
a-but-ting
a-but-ment
a-but-tals
a-but-ting
a-buzz
a-bye
a-bysm
a-bys-mal
a-bys-mal-ly
a-byss
a-bys-sal
a-ca-cia
ac-a-deme
ac-a-dem-ic
ac-a-dem-i-cal-ly
ac-a-dem-i-cal
acad-e-mi-cian
a-cad-e-my
a-cad-e-mies
a-can-thus
a-can-thus-es
a-can-thi
a cap-pel-la
ac-cede
ac-ced-ed
ac-ced-ing
ac-ce-le-ran-do
ac-cel-er-ate
ac-cel-er-at-ed
ac-cel-er-at-ing
ac-cel-er-a-tive
ac-cel-er-at-ing-ly
ac-cel-er-a-tion
ac-cel-er-a-tor
ac-cel-er-om-e-ter

a-ce-ti-fi-er
ac-e-tone
ac-e-ton-ic
ac-e-to-phe-net-i-din
a-ce-tous
a-cet-y-late
a-cet-y-lat-ing
a-cet-y-lat-ed
a-cet-y-la-tion
a-cet-y-la-tive
a-ce-tyl-cho-line
a-ce-tyl-cho-lin-ic
a-cet-y-lene
a-cet-y-le-nic
ache
ached
ach-ing
a-chene
a-chieve
a-chiev-ed
a-chiev-ing
a-chiev-a-ble
a-chiev-er
a-chieve-ment
a-chla-myd-e-ous
a-chlor-hy-dric
a-chon-drite
a-chon-drit-ic
ach-ro-mat-ic
ach-ro-ma-tic-i-ty
ach-ro-ma-tize
a-cic-u-la
a-cic-u-late
a-cic-u-lar
ac-id
ac-id-ness
ac-id-ly
ac-id-ic
a-cid-i-fy
a-cid-i-fied
a-cid-i-fy-ing
a-cid-i-fi-ca-tion
a-cid-i-fi-er
a-cid-i-ty
ac-i-do-phile
ac-i-do-phil-ic
ac-i-do-sis
ac-i-dot-ic
a-cid-u-late
a-cid-u-lat-ed
a-cid-u-lat-ing
a-cid-u-la-tion
a-cid-u-lent

4

ac-cul-tur-a-tion-al
ac-cul-tur-a-tive
ac-cum-u-late
ac-cum-u-lat-ed
ac-cum-u-lat-ing
ac-cum-u-la-tion
ac-cu-mu-la-tive
ac-cu-mu-la-tive-ly
ac-cum-u-la-tor
ac-cu-ra-cy
ac-cu-ra-cies
ac-cu-rate
ac-cu-rate-ly
ac-cu-rate-ness
ac-curs-ed
ac-curst
ac-curs-ed-ly
ac-cus-al
ac-cu-sa-tion
ac-cu-sa-tive
ac-cuse
ac-cus-er
ac-cus-ed
ac-cus-ing
ac-cu-sa-tion
ac-cu-sa-to-ry
ac-cus-tom
ac-cus-tom-a-tion
ac-cus-tomed
ac-cus-tomed-ness
ace-dia
a-cel-da-ma
a-cel-lu-lar
a-ce-quia
a-cerb
a-cer-bi-ty
ac-er-o-la
ac-er-vate
ac-er-vate-ly
ac-er-va-tion
ac-e-tab-u-lar-ia
ac-e-tab-u-lum
ac-e-tab-u-lar
ac-et-al-de-hyde
ac-et-amide
ac-et-amin-o-phen
ac-et-an-i-lide
ac-e-tate
a-ce-tic
a-cet-i-fy
a-cet-i-fied
a-cet-i-fy-ing
a-ce-ti-fi-ca-tion

ac-com-mo-dat-er
ac-com-mo-da-tion
ac-com-pa-ni-ment
ac-com-pa-nist
ac-com-pa-ny
ac-com-pa-nied
ac-com-pa-ny-ing
ac-com-pa-nies
ac-com-plice
ac-com-plish
ac-com-plish-a-ble
ac-com-plish-ment
ac-com-plish-er
ac-com-plished
ac-cord
ac-cord-ance
ac-cord-ing
ac-cord-ing-ly
ac-cor-dant
ac-cor-dant-ly
ac-cor-di-on
ac-cor-di-on-ist
ac-cost
ac-couche-ment
ac-cou-cheur
ac-count
ac-count-a-ble
ac-count-a-bil-i-ty
ac-count-a-bly
ac-count-an-cy
ac-count-ant
ac-coun-tant-ship
ac-count-ing
ac-cou-tre-ment
ac-cred-it
ac-cred-i-table
ac-cred-i-ta-tion
ac-crete
ac-creting
ac-creted
ac-cre-tion
ac-cre-tive
ac-cre-tion-ary
ac-cru-al
ac-crue
ac-crued
ac-cru-ing
ac-cru-a-ble
ac-crue-ment
ac-cul-tur-ate
ac-cul-tur-ating
ac-cul-tur-ated
ac-cul-tur-a-tion

ac-cent
ac-cent-less
ac-cen-tu-al
ac-cen-tu-al-ly
ac-cen-tu-ate
ac-cen-tu-at-ed
ac-cen-tu-at-ing
ac-cen-tu-a-tion
ac-cept
ac-cept-ing-ly
ac-cept-ance
ac-cept-er
ac-cept-or
ac-cept-a-ble
ac-cept-a-bil-i-ty
ac-cept-a-bly
ac-cept-a-ble-ness
ac-cept-ed
ac-cept-ed-ly
ac-cess
ac-ces-si-ble
ac-ces-si-bil-i-ty
ac-ces-si-bly
ac-ces-sion
ac-ces-sion-al
ac-ces-so-ry
ac-ces-so-ri-ly
ac-ci-dent
ac-ci-dent-ly
ac-ci-den-tal
ac-ci-den-tal-ly
ac-ci-dent--prone
ac-cip-i-ter
ac-cip-i-trine
ac-claim
ac-claim-er
ac-cla-ma-tion
ac-clam-a-to-ry
ac-cli-mate
ac-cli-mat-ed
ac-cli-mat-ing
ac-cli-ma-tion
ac-cli-ma-tize
ac-cli-ma-tized
ac-cli-ma-tiz-er
ac-cli-ma-tiz-ing
ac-cliv-i-ty
ac-cliv-i-ties
ac-co-lade
ac-com-mo-date
ac-com-mo-dat-ed
ac-com-mo-dat-ing
ac-com-mo-da-tive

a-cid-u-lous
ac-i-nar
ac-i-nus
  ac-i-nous
ac-knowl-edge
  ac-knowl-edged
  ac-knowl-edg-ing
ac-me
ac-ne
  ac-ned
ac-o-lyte
ac-o-nite
a-corn
a-cous-tic
  a-cous-ti-cal
  a-cous-ti-cal-ly
a-cous-tics
ac-quaint
ac-quaint-ance
  ac-quaint-ance-ship
ac-qui-esce
  ac-qui-esc-ed
  ac-qui-esc-ing
  ac-qui-es-cence
  ac-qui-es-cent
  ac-qui-es-cent-ly
ac-quire
  ac-quired
  ac-quir-ing
  ac-quir-er
ac-quit
  ac-quit-ted
  ac-quit-ting
  ac-quit-tal
a-cre
a-cre-age
ac-rid
  acrid-i-ty
ac-ri-mo-ni-ous
  ac-ri-mo-ni-ous-ly
ac-ri-mo-ny
ac-ro-bat
  ac-ro-bat-ic
ac-ro-nym
ac-ro-pho-bi-a
a-crop-o-lis
a-cros-tic
  a-cros-ti-cal-ly
a-cryl-ic
ac-ry-lo-ni-trile
act-ing
ac-tin-ia
  ac-tin-i-an

ac-tin-ic
  ac-tin-i-cal-ly
ac-tin-ism
ac-tin-i-um
ac-ti-nom-e-ter
  ac-ti-nom-e-try
ac-ti-no-mor-phic
  ac-ti-no-mor-phy
ac-ti-no-my-ces
  ac-ti-no-my-ce-tal
ac-ti-no-my-co-sis
  ac-ti-no-my-cot-ic
ac-ti-non
ac-ti-no-zo-an
ac-tion
  ac-tion-a-ble
  ac-tion-a-bly
ac-ti-vate
  ac-ti-vat-ed
  ac-ti-vat-ing
  ac-ti-va-tion
  ac-ti-va-tor
ac-tive
  ac-tive-ly
ac-tiv-ism
  ac-tiv-ist
ac-tiv-i-ty
  ac-tiv-i-ties
ac-tor
ac-tress
ac-tu-al
  ac-tu-al-ly
ac-tu-al-i-ty
  ac-tu-al-i-ties
ac-tu-al-ize
  ac-tu-al-ized
  ac-tu-al-iz-ing
  ac-tu-al-i-za-tion
ac-tu-ar-y
  ac-tu-ar-ies
  ac-tu-ar-i-al
ac-tu-ate
  ac-tu-at-ed
  ac-tu-at-ing
  ac-tu-a-tion
  ac-tu-a-tor
a-cu-i-ty
  a-cu-i-ties
a-cu-men
a-cu-mi-nate
ac-u-punc-ture
a-cute
  a-cute-ly

a-cut-er
a-cy-clic
ac-yl
ad-age
a-da-gio
ad-a-mant
  ad-a-mant-ly
ad-a-man-tine
a-dapt
  a-dapt-er
  a-dapt-ed-ness
a-dapt-a-ble
  a-dapt-a-bil-i-ty
ad-ap-ta-tion
  ad-ap-ta-tion-al
  ad-ap-ta-tion-al-ly
a-dap-tive
  a-dap-tive-ly
  a-d-ap-tiv-i-ty
add
  add-a-ble
  add-i-ble
ad-dax
  ad-dax-es
ad-dend
ad-den-dum
  ad-den-da
ad-der
ad-dict
  ad-dic-tion
ad-dict-ed
ad-dic-tive
ad-di-tion
  ad-di-tion-al
  ad-di-tion-al-ly
ad-di-tive
  ad-di-tive-ly
  ad-di-tiv-i-ty
ad-dle
ad-dress
  ad-dress-er
  ad-dress-ee
  ad-dress-a-ble
ad-duce
  ad-duc-ing
  ad-duced
  ad-duc-er
ad-duct
  ad-duc-tion
  ad-duc-tive
a-de-lan-ta-do
a-demp-tion
ad-e-nine

ad-e-ni-tis
ad-e-no-car-ci-no-ma
ad-e-no-hy-poph-y-sis
ad-e-noid
ad-e-noi-dal
ad-e-no-ma
aden-o-sine
a-dept
a-dept-ly
ad-e-qua-cy
ad-e-quate
ad-e-quate-ly
ad-here
ad-hered
ad-her-ing
ad-her-ence
ad-her-ent
ad-her-ent-ly
ad-he-sion
ad-he-sion-al
ad-he-sive
ad-he-sive-ly
ad-he-sive-ness
ad hoc
ad ho-mi-nem
ad-i-a-bat-ic
a-dieu
ad in-fi-ni-tum
a-di-os
ad-i-pose
ad-i-pos-i-ty
ad-ja-cen-cy
ad-ja-cen-cies
ad-ja-cent
ad-ja-cent-ly
ad-jec-tive
ad-jec-ti-val
ad-join
ad-join-ing
ad-journ
ad-journ-ment
ad-judge
ad-judged
ad-judg-ing
ad-ju-di-cate
ad-ju-di-cat-ed
ad-ju-di-cat-ing
ad-ju-di-ca-tion
ad-ju-di-ca-tor
ad-junct
ad-junc-tive
ad-jure
ad-jured

ad-jur-ing
ad-ju-ra-tion
ad-ju-ra-to-ry
ad-jur-er
ad-just
ad-just-a-ble
ad-just-er
ad-jus-tor
ad-just-ment
ad-ju-tan-cy
ad-ju-tant
ad lib
ad libbed
ad lib-bing
ad-man
ad-men
ad-min-is-ter
ad-min-is-ter-ing
ad-min-is-tered
ad-min-is-trate
ad-min-is-trat-ing
ad-min-is-trated
ad-min-is-tra-tion
ad-min-is-tra-tive
ad-min-is-tra-tor
ad-mi-ral
ad-mi-ral-ty
ad-mire
ad-mired
ad-mir-ing
ad-mi-ra-tion
ad-mi-rer
ad-mis-si-ble
ad-mis-si-bil-i-ty
ad-mis-sion
ad-mis-sive
ad-mit
ad-mit-ted
ad-mit-ting
ad-mit-ted-ly
ad-mit-tance
ad-mix
ad-mix-ture
ad-mon-ish
ad-mon-ish-er
ad-mo-ni-tion
ad-mon-i-to-ry
ad-mon-ish-ing-ly
ad-mon-ish-ment
a-do
a-do-be
ad-o-les-cence
ad-o-les-cent

ad-o-les-cent-ly
a-dopt
a-dopt-a-ble
a-dop-tion
a-dop-tive
a-dore
a-dored
a-dor-ing
a-dor-a-ble
ad-o-ra-tion
a-dorn
a-dorn-ment
a-doze
ad-re-nal
ad-re-nal-ly
a-dren-a-line
a-drift
a-droit
a-droit-ly
ad-sorb
ad-sor-bent
ad-sorp-tion
ad-u-late
ad-u-lat-ed
ad-u-lat-ing
ad-u-la-tor
ad-u-la-to-ry
a-dult
a-dult-hood
a-dul-ter-ate
a-dul-ter-at-ed
a-dul-ter-at-ing
a-dul-ter-ant
a-dul-ter-a-tion
a-dul-ter-y
a-dul-ter-ies
a-dul-ter-er
a-dul-ter-ous
ad-um-brate
ad-um-brat-ed
ad-um-brat-ing
ad va-lo-rem
ad-vance
ad-vanced
ad-vanc-ing
ad-vance-ment
ad-van-tage
ad-van-taged
ad-van-tag-ing
ad-van-ta-geous
ad-van-ta-geous-ly
ad-vent
ad-ven-ti-tious

7

ad-ven-tive
ad-ven-ture
ad-ven-tured
ad-ven-tur-ing
ad-ven-tur-er
ad-ven-ture-some
ad-verb
ad-ver-bi-al
ad-ver-sar-y
ad-ver-sar-ies
ad-verse
ad-verse-ly
ad-verse-ness
ad-ver-sj-ty
ad-ver-si-ties
ad-vert
ad-vert-ence
ad-vert-ent
ad-ver-tise
ad-ver-tised
ad-ver-tis-ing
ad-ver-tis-er
ad-ver-tise-ment
ad-vice
ad-vise
ad-vised
ad-vis-ing
ad-vis-a-bil-i-ty
ad-vi-sor
ad-vis-ed-ly
ad-vise-ment
ad-vi-so-ry
ad-vo-ca-cy
ad-vo-ca-cies
ad-vo-cate
ad-vo-cat-ed
ad-vo-cat-ing
ad-vo-ca-tion
ae-gis
ae-on
aer-ate
aer-at-ed
aer-at-ing
aer-a-tion
aer-a-tor
aer-en-chy-ma
aer-i-al
aer-i-al-ly
aer-i-al-ist
aer-ie
aer-i-fy
aer-i-fi-ca-tion
aer-obe

aero-me-chan-ics
aero-naut-ics
aero-nau-ti-cal
aero-nau-tic
aero-pause
aer-o-plane
aer-o-sol
aero-sol-ize
aero-sol-iza-tion
aero-sol-iz-ing
aero-sol-ized
aer-o-space
aero-sphere
aero-stat
aero-stat-ics
aes-thete
aes-thet-ic
aes-thet-i-cal-ly
aes-thet-i-cal
afar
afeard
af-fa-ble
af-fa-bil-i-ty
af-fa-bly
af-fair
af-fect
af-fect-ing
af-fect-ing-ly
af-fect-ive
af-fec-ta-tion
af-fect-ed
af-fect-ed-ly
af-fect-ed-ness
af-fec-tion
af-fec-tion-ate
af-fec-tion-ate-ly
af-fer-ent
af-fer-ent-ly
af-fi-ance
af-fi-anced
af-fi-anc-ing
af-fi-da-vit
af-fil-i-ate
af-fil-i-at-ed
af-fil-i-at-ing
af-fin-i-ty
af-fin-i-ties
af-firm
af-firm-a-ble
af-firm-a-bly
af-fir-ma-tion
af-firm-a-tive
af-fix

af-fix-a-ble
af-fix-ment
af-fix-a-tion
af-fla-tus
af-flict
af-flic-tion
af-flu-ence
af-flu-ent
af-flu-ent-ly
af-fray
af-fri-cate
af-fric-a-tive
af-fri-ca-tion
af-front
af-ghan
afield
afire
aflame
af-la-tox-in
afloat
aflut-ter
afoot
afore
afore-men-tioned
afore-said
afore-thought
a for-ti-o-ri
afoul
afraid
afreet
afresh
af-ter
af-ter-ef-fect
af-ter-glow
af-ter--hours
af-ter-life
af-ter-most
af-ter-noon
af-ter-taste
af-ter-thought
af-ter-time
af-ter-ward
af-ter-wards
again
against
agape
aga-pe-ic
agar
ag-ate
ag-ate-ware
aga-ve
agaze
age

aged
ag-ing
age-ing
aged
age-less
age-long
agen-cy
agen-cies
agen-da
agen-da-less
agent
agen-tial
ag-glom-er-ate
ag-glom-er-at-ed
ag-glom-er-at-ing
ag-glom-er-a-tion
ag-glom-er-a-tive
ag-glu-ti-nate
ag-glu-ti-nat-ed
ag-glu-tin-at-ing
ag-glu-ti-na-tion
ag-glu-ti-na-tive
ag-gran-dize
ag-gran-dized
ag-gran-diz-ing
ag-gran-dize-ment
ag-gran-diz-er
ag-gra-vate
ag-gra-vat-ed
ag-gra-vat-ing
ag-gra-va-tion
ag-gre-gate
ag-gre-gat-ed
ag-gre-gat-ing
ag-gre-ga-tion
ag-gre-ga-tive
ag-gress
ag-gress-ive
ag-gress-ive-ly
ag-gress-ive-ness
ag-gres-sor
ag-gres-sion
ag-grieve
ag-grieved
ag-griev-ing
aghast
ag-ile
ag-ile-ly
agil-i-ty
agin-ner
agio
ag-i-tate
ag-i-tat-ed

ag-i-tat-ing
ag-i-tat-ed-ly
ag-i-ta-tion
ag-i-ta-tor
ag-i-ta-tion-al
agleam
aglow
agly-con
ag-nail
ag-nate
ag-na-tion
ag-nat-i-cal-ly
ag-nat-ic
ag-nize
ag-niz-ing
ag-nized
ag-no-men
ag-nom-i-na
ag-nos-tic
ag-nos-ti-cism
agog
ag-o-nal
agon-ic
ag-o-nist
ag-o-nis-tic
ag-o-nis-ti-cal-ly
ag-o-nis-ti-cal
ag-o-nize
ag-o-nized
ag-o-niz-ing
ag-o-niz-ing-ly
ag-o-ny
ag-o-nies
ag-o-ra-pho-bia
ag-o-ra-pho-bic
ag-o-ra-pho-bi-ac
agrar-i-an
agrar-i-an-ism
agree
agreed
agree-ing
agree-a-bil-i-ty
agree-a-ble
agree-a-ble-ness
agree-a-bly
agree-ment
ag-ri-busi-ness
ag-ri-cul-ture
ag-ri-cul-tur-al
ag-ri-cul-tur-ist
agron-o-my
ag-ro-nom-ic
ag-ro-nom-i-cal

agron-o-mist
ag-ro-nom-i-cal-ly
aground
ague
agu-ish-ly
agu-ish
aha
ahead
ahem
ahoy
aide-de-camp
ai-grette
ai-guille
ai-guil-lette
ai-ki-do
ail
ail-ing
ail-ment
ai-lan-thus
ai-ler-on
aim-less
air-less
air-less-ness
air-borne
air-brush
air-con-di-tion
air-con-di-tioned
air con-di-tion-er
air con-di-tion-ing
air-craft
air-field
air-mail
air-man
air-men
air-plane
air-port
air pres-sure
air-sick-ness
air-space
air-wave
airy
air-i-er
air-i-est
air-i-ness
air-i-ly
aisle
ajar
akim-bo
akin
al-a-bas-ter
al-a-bas-trine
a la carte
alack

alac-ri-ty
 alac-ri-tous
alarm
 alarm-ing
 alarm-ing-ly
 alarm-ist
 alarm-ism
alas
alate
 alat-ed
al-ba-core
 al-ba-cores
al-ba-tross
 al-ba-tross-es
al-be-do
al-be-it
al-bi-no
 al-bi-nos
 al-bi-nism
al-bum
al-bu-men
al-bu-min
 al-bu-mi-nous
al-che-my
 al-che-mist
 al-che-mize
 al-che-miz-ing
 al-che-mized
al-co-hol
 al-co-hol-ic
 al-co-hol-ism
 al-co-hol-i-cal-ly
al-cove
al-de-hyde
 al-de-hy-dic
al-der
 al-der-man
 al-der-man-ic
ale-a-to-ry
alee
alert
 alert-ness
 alert-ly
ale-wife
 ale-wives
al-ex-an-drine
al-ex-an-drite
alex-ia
al-fal-fa
al-fil-a-ria
al-for-ja
al-fres-co
al-ga

al-gae
al-gal
al-goid
al-ge-bra
 al-ge-bra-ic
 al-ge-bra-ic-al
 al-ge-bra-ic-al-ly
 al-ge-bra-ist
al-go-rithm
 al-go-rith-mic
ali-as
 ali-as-es
al-i-bi
 al-i-bi-ing
 al-i-bied
alien
 alien-a-ble
 alien-a-bil-i-ty
alien-ate
 alien-at-ed
 alien-at-ing
 alien-ator
alien-ist
 alien-ism
ali-form
alight
 alight-ed
 alit
 alight-ing
 alight-ment
align
 align-ment
alike
al-i-ment
 al-i-men-tal
 al-i-men-tal-ly
 al-i-men-ta-tion
 al-i-men-ta-ry
 al-i-men-ta-ry ca-nal
al-i-mo-ny
 al-i-mo-nies
aline-ment
al-i-quant
al-i-quot
alive
 alive-ness
al-ka-li
 al-ka-lies
 al-ka-lis
 al-ka-line
 al-ka-lin-i-ty
 al-ka-lize
 al-ka-lized

al-ka-liz-ing
al-ka-li-za-tion
al-ka-loid
 al-ka-loi-dal
all-Amer-i-can
all-a-round
al-lay
 al-layed
 al-lay-ing
 al-lay-er
al-le-ga-tion
al-lege
 al-leged
 al-leg-ing
 al-lege-a-ble
 al-leg-ed-ly
al-le-giance
al-le-go-ry
 al-le-go-ries
 al-le-gor-ic
 al-le-gor-i-cal
 al-le-gor-i-cal-ly
 al-le-gor-ist
al-le-gret-to
al-le-gro
 al-le-gros
al-ler-gen
 al-ler-gen-ic
al-ler-gy
 al-ler-gies
 al-ler-gic
 al-ler-gist
al-le-vi-ate
 al-le-vi-at-ed
 al-le-vi-at-ing
 al-le-vi-a-tion
 al-le-vi-a-tor
 al-le-vi-a-tive
 al-le-vi-a-to-ry
al-ley
 al-leys
al-li-ance
al-lied
al-li-ga-tor
all--in-clu-sive
 all--in-cul-sive-ness
al-lit-er-ate
 al-lit-er-at-ed
 al-lit-er-at-ing
 al-lit-er-a-tive
 al-lit-er-a-tive-ly
 al-lit-er-a-tive-ness
 al-lit-er-a-tion

al-lo-ca-ble
al-lo-cate
al-lo-cat-ed
al-lo-cat-ing
al-lo-ca-tion
al-lo-cu-tion
al-log-a-mous
al-log-a-my
al-lo-ge-ne-ic
al-lo-graph
al-lo-graph-ic
al-lom-er-ism
al-lom-er-ous
al-lo-path
al-lop-a-thy
al-lo-path-ic
al-lo-path-i-cal-ly
al-lop-a-thist
al-lo-phone
al-lo-phon-ic
al-lo-pu-ri-nol
al-lo-ste-ric
al-lo-ste-ri-cal-ly
al-lot
al-lot-ted
al-lot-ting
al-lot-ment
al-lot-ta-ble
al-lot-ter
al-lo-trope
al-lo-trop-ic
al-lo-trop-cal-ly
al-lot-ro-py
al-lot-ro-pism
al-lo-trope
al-lo-trop-ic
al-lo-trop-i-cal-ly
al-low
al-low-a-ble
al-low-a-bly
al-low-ed-ly
al-low-ance
al-low-anced
al-low-anc-ing
al-loy
all--pow-er-ful
all--pur-pose
all right
all-spice
al-lude
al-lud-ed
al-lud-ing
al-lure

al-lured
al-lur-ing
al-lure-ment
al-lur-er
al-lur-ing-ly
al-lu-sion
al-lu-sive
al-lu-sive-ly
al-lu-sive-ness
al-lu-via
al-lu-vi-al
al-lu-vi-um
al-lu-viums
al-ly
al-lies
al-lied
al-ly-ing
al-ma mat-er
al-ma-nac
al-man-dine
al-man-dite
al-mighty
al-mighti-ness
al-mond
al-mo-ner
al-most
alms-giv-er
alms-giv-ing
alms-house
al-ni-co
al-oe
aloft
alo-ha
alone
alone-ness
along
along-shore
along-side
aloof
aloof-ly
aloof-ness
al-o-pe-cia
al-paca
al-pen-glow
al-pen-stock
al-pes-trine
al-pha
al-pha-bet
al-pha-bet-ic
al-pha-bet-i-cal
al-pha-bet-i-cal-ly
al-pha-bet-i-za-tion
al-pha-bet-ize

al-pha-bet-ized
al-pha-bet-iz-ing
al-ready
al-so
al-tar
al-ter
al-ter-a-bil-ity
al-ter-a-ble
al-ter-ant
al-ter-a-tion
al-ter-a-tive
al-ter-cate
al-ter-cat-ing
al-ter-cat-ed
al-ter-ca-tion
al-ter e-go
al-ter-nate
al-ter-nat-ed
al-ter-nat-ing
al-ter-nate-ly
al-ter-na-tion
al-ter-na-tive
al-ter-na-tive-ly
al-ter-na-tive-ness
al-ter-na-tor
al-though
al-tim-e-ter
al-tim-e-try
al-ti-pla-no
al-ti-tude
al-to
al-to-cu-mu-lus
al-to-gether
al-to-re-lie-vo
al-to-stra-tus
al-tru-ism
al-tru-is-tic
al-tru-is-ti-cal-ly
al-tru-ist
al-lu-mi-na
alu-mi-nate
alu-mi-nif-er-ous
al-u-min-i-um
alu-mi-nous
alu-mi-num
alum-na
alum-nae
alum-nus
alum-ni
al-ve-o-lar
al-ve-o-lus
al-ve-o-li
al-ways

11

alys-sum
amain
amal-gam
  amal-gam-a-ble
  amal-gam-ate
  amal-gam-at-ed
  amal-gam-at-ing
  amal-gam-a-tion
aman-u-en-ses
  aman-u-en-ses
am-a-ryl-lis
amass
  amass-ment
  amass-er
am-a-teur
  am-a-teur-ism
  am-a-teur-ish
  am-a-teur-ish-ly
  am-a-teur-ish-ness
am-a-tive
  am-a-tive-ness
  am-a-tive-ly
am-a-to-ry
am-au-ro-sis
amaze
  amazed
  amaz-ing
  amaz-ed-ly
  amaz-ed-ness
  amaze-ment
  amaz-ing-ly
am-bas-sa-do-ri-al
am-ber
amber-gris
am-ber-jack
am-bi-dex-trous
  am-bi-dex-trous-ly
  am-bi-dex-ter-i-ty
am-bi-ance
  am-bi-ence
am-bi-ent
am-big-u-ous
  am-big-u-ous-ly
  am-big-u-ous-ness
am-bi-gu-i-ty
am-bit
am-bi-tion
  am-bi-tion-less
am-bi-tious
  am-bi-tious-ly
  am-bi-tious-ness
am-biv-a-lence
  am-biv-a-lent

am-biv-a-lent-ly
am-bi-ver-sion
  am-bi-ver-sive
am-bi-vert
am-ble
  am-bled
  am-bling
  am-bler
am-blyg-o-nite
am-bly-opia
am-bo-cep-tor
am-bro-sia
  am-bro-sial-ly
  am-bro-sial
am-bro-type
ambs-ace
am-bu-la-crum
am-bu-lance
am-bu-la-to-ry
am-bu-lant
am-bu-late
  am-bu-lat-ed
  am-bu-lat-ing
  am-bu-la-tion
am-bus-cade
  am-bus-cad-ed
  am-bus-cad-ing
  am-bus-cad-er
am-bush
  am-bush-ment
  am-bush-er
ameba
amel-io-rate
  amel-io-rat-ed
  amel-io-rat-ing
  amel-io-ra-ble
  amel-io-ra-tion
  amel-ior-a-tive
  amel-io-ra-tor
amen
ame-na-ble
  ame-na-bil-i-ty
  ame-na-ble-ness
  ame-na-bly
amend
  amend-a-ble
  amend-er
  amend-ment
  amends
amend-i-ty
  amend-i-ties
amerce
  amerced

amerc-ing
amerce-a-ble
amerce-ment
amerce-er
Amer-i-ca
Amer-i-can
Amer-i-cana
Amer-i-can-ism
am-e-thyst
  am-e-thys-tine
am-e-tro-pia
ami-a-ble
  ami-a-bil-i-ty
  ami-a-bly
  ami-a-ble-ness
ami-ca-ble
  am-i-ca-bil-i-ty
  am-i-ca-bly
  am-i-ca-ble-ness
am-ice
amid
  amidst
am-ide
  amid-ic
amid-ships
ami-go
amine
amino acid
ami-no-ac-id-uria
ami-no-py-rine
amir
amiss
am-i-to-sis
  am-i-tot-ic
  am-i-tot-i-cal-ly
am-i-ty
am-me-ter
am-mi-no
am-mon-nia
am-mon-ic
am-mo-ni-ac
am-mo-ni-um
am-mo-ni-un chlo-ride
am-mu-ni-tion
am-ne-sia
  am-ne-sic
  am-nes-tic
am-nes-ty
am-ni-on
  am-ni-ons
  am-ni-on-ic
  am-nia
  am-ni-ot-ic

12

a-moe-ba
a-moe-bae
a-moe-bas
a-moe-bic
a-moe-ban
a-moe-boid
a-mok
a-mong
a-mongst
a-mon-til-la-do
a-mor-al
a-mo-ral-i-ty
a-mor-al-ism
a-mor-al-ly
amo-ret-to
am-or-ist
am-o-rous
am-o-rous-ly
am-o-rous-ness
a-mor-phism
a-mor-phous
a-mor-phous-ness
a-mor-phous-ly
am-or-tize
am-or-tized
am-or-tiz-ing
am-or-ti-za-tion
am-or-tiz-able
a-mount
a-mour
am-per-age
am-pere
am-per-sand
am-phet-a-mine
am-phib-ia
am-phib-i-an
am-phib-i-ous
am-phib-i-ous-ly
am-phib-i-ous-ness
am-phi-the-a-ter
am-phi-the-at-ric
am-pho-ra
am-phe-rae
am-phe-ras
am-ple
am-pler
am-plest
am-ple-ness
am-ply
am-pli-fy
am-pli-fied
am-pli-fy-ing
am-pli-fi-ca-tion

am-pli-fi-er
am-pli-tude
am-pul
am-pu-tate
am-pu-tat-ed
am-pu-tat-ing
am-pu-ta-tion
am-pu-tee
a-muck
am-u-let
a-muse
a-mused
a-mus-ing
a-muse-ment
a-mus-ed
am-yl-ase
a-nach-ro-nism
a-nach-ro-nis-tik
a-nach-ro-nis-ti-cal-ly
a-nach-ro-nous
an-a-con-da
an-aer-obe
an-aes-the-sia
an-aes-thet-ic
an-a-gram
an-a-gram-mat-ic
an-a-gram-mat-i-cal
ana-gram-ma-tize
ana-gram-ma-tized
ana-gram-ma-tiz-ing
a-nal
an-a-lects
an-al-ge-sic
al-a-log
an-a-log-i-cal
an-a-log-i-cal-ly
a-nal-o-gize
a-nal-o-gized
a-nal-o-giz-ing
a-nal-o-gy
a-nal-o-gies
a-nal-o-gous
a-nal-y-sis
a-nal-y-ses
an-a-lyst
an-a-lyt-ic
an-a-lyt-ics
an-a-lyze
an-a-lyzed
an-a-lyz-ing
an-a-lyz-a-ble
an-a-ly-za-tion
an-a-lyz-er

an-a-pest
an-a-pes-tic
an-ar-chism
an-ar-chis-tic
an-ar-chy
an-ar-chic
an-ar-chi-cal
a-nath-e-ma
a-nath-e-mas
a-nath-e-ma-tize
a-nath-e-ma-tized
a-nath-e-ma-tiz-ing
a-nath-e-mat-iz-a-tion
a-nat-o-mize
a-nat-o-mized
a-nat-o-mizing
a-nat-o-mi-za-tion
a-nat-o-my
a-nat-o-mies
an-a-tom-i-cal
an-a-tom-i-cal-ly
a-nat-o-mist
an-ces-tor
an-ces-tral
an-ces-tress
an-ces-try
an-chor
an-chor-age
an-cho-ress
an-cho-rite
an-cho-vy
an-cient
an-cient-ly
an-cient-ness
an-cil-lary
an-dan-te
and-i-ron
an-dro-gen
an-drog-y-nous
an-drog-y-ny
an-dros-ter-one
an-ec-dote
an-ec-dot-age
an-ec-do-tal
an-ec-dot-ist
a-ne-mia
a-ne-mic
an-e-mom-e-ter
an-e-mom-e-try
a-nem-o-ne
an-er-oid
an-es-the-sia
an-es-thet-ic

an-es-the-tize
an-es-the-tized
an-es-the-tiz-ing
an-eu-rysm
an-eu-rism
an-eu-rys-mal
a-new
an-ga-ry
an-gel
an-gel-ic
an-gel-i-cal
an-gel-i-cal-ly
an-gel-i-ca
an-ger
an-gi-na
an-gi-na pec-to-ris
an-gi-o-sperm
an-gi-o-sper-mous
an-gle
an-gler
an-gle-worm
an-gling
an-go-ra
an-gos-tu-ra bark
an-gry
an-gri-ly
an-gri-ness
ang-strom u-nit
an-guish
an-gu-lar
an-gu-lar-i-ty
an-gu-lar-ly
an-hy-dride
an-hy-drous
an-i-line
an-i-mad-vert
an-i-mad-ver-sion
an-i-mal
an-i-mal-cule
an-i-mal-cu-lar
an-i-mal-ism
an-i-mal-i-ty
an-i-mal-ize
an-i-mal-ized
an-i-mal-iz-ing
an-i-mate
an-i-mat-ed
an-i-mat-ing
an-i-ma-tion
a-ni-ma-to
an-i-mism
an-i-mis-tic
an-i-mos-i-ty

an-i-mus
an-i-on
an-ise
an-i-seed
an-i-sette
an-kle
an-kle-bone
an-klet
an-ky-lose
an-ky-losed
an-ky-los-ing
an-ky-lo-sis
an-ky-lot-ic
an-nal-ist
an-nal-is-tic
an-nals
an-neal
an-ne-lid
an-nel-i-dan
an-nex
an-nex-a-tion
an-nex-a-tion-ist
an-ni-hi-late
an-ni-hi-lat-ed
an-ni-hi-lat-ing
an-ni-hi-la-tion
an-ni-hi-la-tor
an-ni-ver-sa-ry
an-ni-ver-sa-ries
an-no Dom-i-ni
an-no-tate
an-no-tat-ed
an-no-tat-ing
an-no-ta-tion
an-no-ta-tor
an-nounce
an-nounced
an-nounc-ing
an-nounce-ment
an-nounc-er
an-noy
an-noy-ance
an-noy-er
an-nu-al
an-nu-i-ty
an-nu-i-tant
an-nul
an-nulled
an-nul-ling
an-nul-ment
an-nu-lar
an-nu-lar-i-ty
an-nu-lar-ly

an-nu-late
an-nu-let
an-nu-lus
an-nu-lus-es
an-nun-ci-a-tion
an-nun-ci-ate
an-nun-ci-at-ed
an-nun-ci-at-ing
an-nun-ci-a-tor
an-ode
an-od-ic
an-o-dyne
a-noint
a-noint-er
a-noint-ment
a-nom-a-ly
a-nom-a-lism
a-nom-a-lous
a-nom-a-lous-ly
an-o-mie
an-o-my
an-o-nym
a-non-y-mous
a-non-y-nym-i-ty
a-non-y-mous-ly
a-noph-e-les
an-oth-er
an-ox-ia
an-ser-ine
an-swer
an-swer-a-ble
ant-ac-id
an-tag-o-nist
an-tag-o-nism
an-tag-o-nis-tic
an-tag-o-nis-ti-cal-ly
an-tag-o-nize
an-tag-o-nized
an-tag-o-niz-ing
ant-arc-tic
an-te
an-ted
an-te-ing
ant-eat-er
an-te--bel-lum
an-te-ced-ence
an-te-ced-ent
an-te-cede
an-te-ced-ed
an-te-ced-ing
an-te-cham-ber
an-te-choir
an-te-date

an-te-dat-ed
an-te-dat-ing
an-te-di-lu-vi-an
an-te-lope
an-te-lopes
an-te me-rid-i-em
an-ten-na
an-ten-nae
an-ten-nas
an-te-pe-nult
an-te-pe-nul-ti-mate
an-te-ri-or
an-te-room
an-them
an-ther
an-ther-id-i-um
an-thol-o-gy
an-thol-o-gies
an-thol-o-gist
an-thol-o-gize
an-thol-o-giz-ing
an-tho-zo-an
an-thra-cene
an-thra-cite
an-thra-cit-ic
an-thrax
an-thra-ces
an-thro-po-cen-tric
an-thro-po-gen-e-sis
an-thro-poid
an-thro-pol-o-gy
an-thro-po-log-ic
an-thro-po-log-i-cal
an-thro-pol-o-gist
an-thr-pom-e-try
an-thro-po-met-ric
an-ti-air-craft
an-ti-bi-o-sis
an-ti-bi-ot-ic
an-ti-bod-y
an-ti-bod-ies
an-tic
an-ti-christ
an-tic-i-pate
an-tic-i-pat-ed
an-tic-i-pat-ing
an-tic-i-pa-tion
an-tic-i-pa-tive
an-tic-i-pa-to-ry
an-ti-cler-i-cal
an-ti-cler-i-cal-ism
an-ti-cli-max
an-ti-cli-mac-tic

an-ti-cli-nal
an-ti-cline
an-ti-cy-clone
an-ti-dote
an-ti-dot-al
an-ti-fed-er-al
an-ti-fed-er-al-ist
an-ti-fed-er-al-ism
an-ti-freeze
an-ti-gen
an-ti-he-ro
an-ti-his-ta-mine
an-ti-log-a-rithm
an-ti-ma-cas-sar
an-ti-mis-sile
an-ti-mo-ny
an-ti-pas-to
an-tip-a-thy
an-ti-phon
an-tiph-o-nal
an-ti-pode
an-ti-quar-i-an
an-ti-quar-y
an-ti-quar-ies
an-ti-quate
an-ti-quat-ed
an-ti-quat-ing
an-ti-quat-ed
an-tique
an-tiqed
an-tiq-uing
an-tique-ly
an-tiq-ui-ty
an-tiq-ui-ties
an-ti-Sem-i-tism
an-ti-sep-sis
an-ti-sep-tic
an-ti-se-rum
an-ti-slav-er-y
an-ti-so-cial
an-tith-e-sis
an-tith-e-ses
an-ti-thet-i-cal
an-ti-tox-in
an-ti-tox-in
an-ti-trust
ant-ler
ant-ler-ed
an-to-nym
an-trum
an-tra
a-nus
an-vil

anx-i-e-ty
anx-i-e-ties
anx-ious
an-y
an-y-bod-y
an-y-bod-ies
an-y-how
an-y-more
an-y-one
an-y-place
an-y-thing
an-y-way
an-y-where
an-y-wise
a-or-ta
a-or-tas
a-or-tae
a-or-tal
a-or-tic
a-pace
a-pache
a-part
a-part-heid
a-part-ment
ap-a-thy
ap-a-thet-ic
ap-a-thet-i-cal-ly
ape
a-per-ri-tif
ap-er-ture
a-pex
a-pex-es
a-pi-ces
ap-i-cal
a-pha-sia
a-phe-li-on
a-phe-lia
a-phid
a-phis
a-phi-des
aph-o-rism
aph-o-rist
aph-ro-dis-i-ac
a-pi-an
a-pi-ar-i-an
a-pi-a-rist
a-pi-ary
a-pi-ar-ies
a-pi-cul-ture
a-pi-cul-tur-al
a-pi-cul-tur-ist
a-piece
ap-ish

ap-ish-ly
ap-ish-ness
a-plomb
a-poc-a-lypse
a-poc-a-lyp-tic
a-poc-o-pe
a-poc-ry-phal
ap-o-gee
a-po-lit-i-cal
a-pol-o-get-ics
a-pol-o-gist
a-pol-o-gize
a-pol-o-gized
a-pol-o-giz-ing
a-pol-o-gy
a-pol-o-gies
ap-o-plec-tic
ap-o-plex-y
a-port
a-pos-ta-sy
a-pos-ta-sies
a-pos-tate
a-pos-ta-tize
a-pos-ta-tized
a-pos-to-tiz-ing
a pos-te-ri-o-ri
a-pos-tle
a-pos-tle-ship
a-pos-to-late
ap-os-tol-ic
ap-os-tol-i-cal
a-pos-tro-phe
a-poth-e-cary
a-poth-e-car-ies
ap-o-thegm
ap-o-phthegm
ap-o-theg-mat-ic
a-poth-e-o-sis
a-poth-e-o-ses
a-poth-e-o-size
a-poth-e-o-sized
ap-pall
ap-palled
ap-pal-ling
ap-pa-rat-us
ap-pa-rat-us-es
ap-par-el
ap-par-ent
ap-pa-ri-tion
ap-pa-ri-tion-al
ap-peal
ap-peal-a-ble
ap-peal-er

ap-pear
ap-pear-ance
ap-pease
ap-peased
ap-peasing
ap-pease-ment
ap-peas-a-ble
ap-peas-er
ap-pel-lant
ap-pel-late
ap-pel-la-tion
ap-pel-la-tive
ap-pend
ap-pen-dage
ap-pend-ant
ap-pen-dec-to-my
ap-pen-di-ci-tis
ap-pen-dix
ap-pen-dix-es
ap-pen-di-ces
ap-per-cep-tion
ap-per-cep-tive
ap-per-tain
ap-pe-tite
ap-pe-tiz-er
ap-pe-tiz-ing
ap-plaud
ap-plause
ap-ple
ap-ple-jack
ap-pli-ance
ap-pli-ca-ble
ap-pli-ca-bil-i-ty
ap-pli-ca-ble-ness
ap-pli-cant
ap-pli-ca-tion
ap-pli-ca-tive
ap-pli-ca-to-ry
ap-pli-ca-tor
ap-plied
ap-ply
ap-ply-ing
ap-point
ap-point-a-ble
ap-point-ee
ap-point-er
ap-point-ment
ap-por-tion
ap-por-tion-ment
ap-pose
ap-posed
ap-pos-ing
ap-po-site

ap-po-si-tion
ap-po-si-tion-al
ap-pos-i-tive
ap-praise
ap-prais-al
ap-praised
ap-praiser
ap-prais-ing
ap-pre-ci-a-ble
ap-pre-ci-a-bly
ap-pre-ci-ate
ap-pre-ci-at-ed
ap-pre-ci-at-ing
ap-pre-ci-a-tion
ap-pre-ci-a-tive
ap-pre-hend
ap-pre-hen-si-ble
ap-pre-hen-sion
ap-pre-hen-sive
ap-pren-tice
ap-pren-tic-ed
ap-pren-tic-ing
ap-pre-tice-ship
ap-prise
ap-prised
ap-pris-ing
ap-prize
ap-proach
ap-proach-a-bil-i-ty
ap-proach-a-ble
ap-pro-ba-tion
ap-pro-ba-tive
ap-pro-ba-to-ry
ap-pro-pri-ate
ap-pro-pri-at-ed
ap-pro-pri-at-ing
ap-pro-pri-ate-ly
ap-pro-pri-a-tor
ap-pro-pri-a-tion
ap-pro-pri-a-tive
ap-prox-i-mate
ap-prox-i-mate-ly
ap-prox-i-ma-tion
ap-pur-te-nance
ap-pur-te-nant
ap-ri-cot
a-pri-o-ri
a-pron
ap-ro-pos
apt
apt-ly
apt-ness
ap-ter-ous

ap-ti-tude
aq-ua
  aq-uas
  aq-uae
a-qua-cul-ture
aq-ua-ma-rine
aq-ua-naut
aq-ua-plane
aquar-ia
aquar-i-um
  aquar-i-ums
a-quat-ic
aq-ua-tint
aq-ue-duct
a-que-ous
aq-ui-line
ar-a-besque
ar-a-ble
a-rach-nid
  a-rach-ni-dan
ar-ba-lest
  ar-ba-lest-er
  ar-ba-list
ar-bi-ter
  ar-bi-tral
ar-bit-ra-ment
ar-bi-trar-y
  ar-bi-trar-i-ly
ar-bi-trate
  ar-bi-trat-ed
  ar-bi-trat-ing
  ar-bi-tra-ble
  ar-bi-tra-tor
  ar-bi-tra-tion
ar-bor
ar-bo-re-al
ar-bo-res-cent
ar-bo-re-ta
  ar-bo-re-tum
  ar-bo-re-tums
ar-bor-vi-tae
ar-bu-tus
arc
  arced
  arc-ing
ar-cade
ar-cane
arch
  arch-ly
ar-cha-ic
ar-cha-ism
ar-cha-ist
ar-cha-is-tic

arch-du-cal
arch-duke
arch-en-e-my
  arch-en-e-mies
arch-er
  ar-cher-y
ar-che-type
  ar-che-typ-al
  ar-che-typ-i-cal
arch-fiend
ar-chi-e-pis-co-pal
  ar-chi-e-pis-co-pate
ar-chi-pel-a-goes
  ar-chi-pel-a-gos
ar-chi-tect
  ar-chi-tec-ton-ic
  ar-chi-tec-ture
  ar-chi-trave
ar-chive
  ar-chi-val
  ar-chi-vist
ar-chon
arch-priest
arch-way
arc-tic
ar-dent
  ar-dent-ly
ar-dor
ar-du-ous
  ar-du-ous-ly
ar-e-a
  ar-e-al
ar-e-a-way
a-re-na
a-re-o-la
  a-re-o-lae
  a-re-o-las
ar-gent
ar-gen-tine
ar-gil
ar-gon
ar-go-sy
  ar-go-sies
ar-got
  ar-got-ic
ar-gue
  ar-gued
  ar-gu-ing
  ar-gu-a-ble
  ar-gu-er
  ar-gu-ment
  ar-gu-men-ta-tion
  ar-gu-men-ta-tive

ar-gyle
  ar-gyll
a-ri-a
ar-id
  a-rid-i-ty
a-right
a-rise
  a-rose
  a-ris-en
  a-ris-ing
ar-is-toc-ra-cy
  ar-is-toc-ra-cies
  aris-to-crat
  aris-to-crat-ic
a-rith-me-tic
  a-rith-met-i-cal
  a-rith-me-ti-cian
ar-ma-da
ar-ma-dil-lo
ar-ma-ment
ar-ma-ture
ar-mi-stice
ar-moire
ar-mor
ar-mor-er
ar-mor-y
  ar-mor-ies
arm-pit
ar-my
  ar-mies
ar-ni-ca
a-ro-ma
ar-o-mat-ic
  ar-o-mat-i-cal
a-round
a-rouse
  a-roused
  a-rous-ing
ar-peg-gi-o
  ar-peg-gi-os
ar-raign
  ar-raign-ment
ar-range
  ar-ranged
  ar-rang-er
  ar-rang-ing
  ar-range-ment
ar-rant
  ar-rant-ly
ar-ras
ar-ray
ar-rear
ar-rest

ar-rest-er
ar-rest-or
ar-ri-val
ar-rive
ar-rived
ar-riv-ing
ar-ro-gant
ar-ro-gat-ed
ar-ro-gat-ing
ar-ro-ga-tion
ar-row
ar-row-head
ar-row-root
ar-roy-o
ar-roy-os
ar-se-nal
ar-se-nate
ar-se-nic
ar-son
ar-son-ist
ar-te-ri-al
ar-te-ri-o-scle-ro-sis
ar-ter-y
ar-ter-ies
ar-te-sian well
art-ful
art-ful-ly
ar-thri-tis
ar-thrit-ic
ar-thro-pod
ar-throp-o-dal
ar-throp-o-dous
ar-ti-choke
ar-ti-cle
ar-tic-u-lar
ar-tic-u-late
ar-tic-u-lat-ed
ar-tic-u-lat-ing
ar-tic-u-late-ly
ar-tic-u-lar-tor
ar-tic-u-la-tion
ar-te-fact
ar-ti-fact
ar-ti-fice
ar-tif-i-cer
ar-ti-fi-cial
ar-ti-fi-ci-al-i-ty
ar-ti-fi-cial-ly
ar-til-ler-y
ar-til-ler-ist
ar-ti-san
art-ist
ar-tiste

ar-tis-tic
ar-tis-ti-cal-ly
art-ist-ry
art-y
as-bes-tos
as-bes-tus
as-cend
as-cend-ance
as-cend-ence
as-cend-an-cy
as-cend-en-cy
as-cend-ant
as-cend-ent
as-cen-sion
as-cent
as-cer-tain
as-cer-tain-a-ble
as-cer-tain-ment
as-cet-ic
as-cet-is-al
as-cet-i-cism
as-cot
as-cribe
as-cribed
as-crib-ing
as-crib-a-ble
a-sep-sis
a-sep-tic
a-sex-u-al
a-sex-u-al-i-ty
a-sex-u-al-ly
a-shamed
a-sham-ed-ly
ash-en
ash-lar
ash-ler
a-shore
ash-y
a-side
as-i-nine
a-skance
a-skew
a-slant
a-slope
a-so-cial
as-par-a-gus
as-pect
as-pen
as-per-i-ty
as-perse
as-persed
as-pers-ing
as-per-sion

as-phalt
as-phal-tic
as-pho-del
as-phyx-ia
as-phyx-i-ate
as-phyx-i-at-ed
as-phyx-i-a-tion
as-pic
as-pi-dis-tra
as-pir-ant
as-pi-rate
as-pi-rat-ed
as-pi-rat-ing
as-pi-ra-tion
as-pi-ra-tor
as-pire
as-pired
as-pir-ing
as-pir-er
as-pi-rin
as-sail
as-sail-a-ble
as-sail-ant
as-sas-sin
as-sas-si-nate
as-sas-si-nat-ed
as-sas-si-na-tion
as-sault
as-say
as-say-er
as-sem-blage
as-sem-ble
as-sem-bled
as-sem-bling
as-sem-bler
as-sem-bly
as-sem-blies
as-sem-bly-man
as-sem-bly-men
as-sent
as-sent-er
as-sert
as-sert-er
as-ser-tion
as-ser-tive
as-ser-tive-ly
as-sess
as-sess-a-ble
as-sess-ment
as-sess-or
as-set
as-si-du-i-ty
as-sid-u-ous

as-sid-u-ous-ly
as-sid-u-ous-ness
as-sign
as-sign-a-bil-i-ty
as-sign-a-ble
as-sign-a-bly
as-sig-na-tion
as-sign-ee
as-sign-ment
as-sist
as-sist-ance
as-sis-tant
as-size
as-so-ci-ate
as-so-ci-at-ed
as-so-ci-at-ing
as-so-ci-a-tion
as-so-nance
as-sort
as-sor-ted
as-sort-ment
as-sume
as-sumed
as-sum-ing
as-sump-tion
as-sur-ance
as-sure
as-sured
as-sur-ing
as-sur-er
as-sur-ed-ly
as-ter
as-ter-isk
a-stern
as-ter-oid
as-ter-oi-dal
asth-ma
asth-mat-ic
a-stig-ma-tism
as-tig-mat-ic
a-stir
as-ton-ish
as-ton-ish-ing
as-ton-ish-ment
as-tound
as-tound-ing
a-strad-dle
as-tra-khan
as-tral
a-stray
a-stride
as-trin-gent
as-trin-gen-cy

as-tro-dome
as-tro-labe
as-trol-o-gy
as-trol-o-ger
as-tro-log-ic
as-tro-log-i-cal
as-tro-naut
as-tro-nau-tics
as-tro-nau-ti-cal
as-tro-nom-ic
as-tro-nom-i-cal-ly
as-tron-o-my
as-tron-o-mer
as-tro-phys-ics
as-tro-phys-i-cist
as-tute
as-tute-ly
a-sun-der
a-sy-lum
a-sym-me-try
asym-met-ric
asym-met-ri-cal
asym-met-ri-cal-ly
at-a-vism
at-a-vist
at-a-vis-tic
a-tax-ia
a-tax-ic
at-el-ier
a-thirst
ath-lete
ath-let-ic
ath-let-ics
a-thwart
a-tilt
at-las
at-las-es
at-mos-phere
at-oll
at-om
ato-nal-i-ty
ato-nal
a-tone
a-toned
a-top
a-tri-um
a-tro-cious
a-tro-cious-ly
a-troc-i-y
a-troc-i-ties
at-ro-phy
at-ro-phies
at-ro-phied

at-ro-pine
at-tach
at-tach-a-ble
at-tach-ment
at-tack
at-tain
at-tain-a-ble
at-tain-a-bil-i-ty
at-tain-ment
at-tain-der
at-taint
at-tar
at-tempt
at-tempt-a-ble
at-tend
at-tend-ance
at-tend-ant
at-ten-tion
at-ten-tive
at-ten-u-ate
at-ten-u-at-ed
at-ten-u-at-ing
at-ten-u-a-tion
at-test
at-tes-ta-tion
at-tic
at-tire
at-tired
at-tir-ing
at-ti-tude
at-ti-tu-di-nize
at-ti-tu-di-nized
at-tor-ney
at-tract
at-trac-tive
at-tract-or
at-trac-tion
at-tri-bute
at-tri-but-ed
at-tri-but-ing
at-tri-bu-tion
at-trib-u-tive
at-tri-tion
at-tune
at-tuned
at-tun-ing
a-typ-i-cal
a-typ-ic
a-typ-i-cal-ly
au-burn
au cou-rant
auc-tion
auc-tion-eer

au-da-cious
au-dac-i-ty
au-di-ble
au-di-bly
au-di-ence
au-di-o
au-di-o-vis-u-al
au-dit
au-di-tion
au-dit-or
au-di-to-rium
au-di-to-ry
au-ger
aug-ment
aug-ment-a-ble
aug-men-ta-tion
aug-ment-a-tive
au-grat-in
au-gur
au-gu-ry
au-gu-ries
au-gust
au-gust-ly
auk
aunt
au-ra
au-ras
au-rae
au-ral
au-ral-ly
au-re-ate
au-re-ole
au-re-voir
au-ri-cle
au-rif-er-ous
au-ro-ra
au-ro-ra bor-e-al-is
aus-cul-tate
aus-cul-tat-ed
aus-cul-tat-ing
aus-cul-ta-tion
aus-tere
aus-ter-i-ty
aus-ter-i-ties
aus-tral
au-then-tic
au-then-ti-cat-ed
au-then-ti-cat-ing
au-then-ti-ca-tion
au-thor
au-thor-i-tar-i-an
au-thor-i-tar-i-an-ism
au-thor-i-ta-tive

au-thor-i-ty
au-thor-i-ties
au-thor-ize
au-thor-ized
au-thor-iz-ing
au-thor-i-za-tion
au-thor-ship
au-to
au-to-bi-og-ra-phy
au-to-bi-og-ra-phies
au-to-bi-og-ra-pher
au-toc-ra-cy
au-toc-ra-cies
au-to-crat
au-to-crat-ic
au-to-crat-i-cal
au-toc-ra-cy
au-toc-ra-cies
au-to-graph
au-to-mat
au-to-mat-ic
au-to-ma-tion
au-to-mate
au-to-mat-ed
au-to-mat-ing
au-tom-a-tism
au-tom-a-ton
au-tom-a-tons
au-tom-a-ta
au-to-mo-bile
au-to-mo-tive
au-to-nom-ic
au-to-nom-i-cal-ly
au-ton-o-mous
au-ton-o-mous-ly
au-ton-o-my
au-ton-o-mies
au-ton-o-mist
au-top-sy
au-to-sug-ges-tion
au-tumn
au-tum-nal
aux-il-ia-ry
aux-il-ia-ries
a-vail
a-vail-a-bil-i-ty
a-vail-ably
av-a-lanche
av-a-lanched
av-a-lanch-ing
a-vant-garde
av-a-rice
av-a-ri-cious

av-a-ri-cious-ly
a-vast
av-a-tar
a-ve
a-venge
a-venged
a-veng-ing
a-veng-er
av-e-nue
a-ver
a-verred
a-ver-ment
av-er-age
av-er-aged
av-er-ag-ing
a-verse
a-verse-ly
a-ver-sion
a-vi-a-tion
a-vi-a-tor
av-id
a-void
a-vow
a-wait
a-wake
a-wak-en
awe
awe-some
awe-struck
aw-ful
aw-ful-ly
aw-ful-ness
awhile
awk-ward
awk-ward-ly
awn
awned
awn-ing
awry
ax
ax-es
ax-i-al
ax-i-al-ly
ax-i-om
ax-i-o-mat-ic
ax-i-o-mat-i-cal
ax-is
ax-es
ax-le
azal-ea
az-i-muth
az-i-muth-al
az-ure

B

bab-bitt
bab-ble
  bab-bled
  bab-bling
  bab-bler
ba-bel
ba-boon
ba-bush-ka
ba-by
  ba-bies
  ba-bied
  ba-by-ing
bac-ca-lau-re-ate
bac-ca-rat
bac-cha-nal
  bac-cha-na-li-an
bac-chant
bac-chant-te
bach-e-lor
  bach-e-lor-hood
bac-il-lar-y
bac-cil-lus
  bac-cil-li
back-bite
  back-bit
  back-bit-ten
  back-bit-er
back-board
back-fire
  back-fired
  back-fir-ing
back-gam-mon
back-ground
back-hand
  back-hand-ed
back-ing
back-lash
back-log
back-slide
  back-slid
  back-slid-den
  back-slid-ing
  back-slid-er
back-spin
back-stop
back-stroke
back-talk
back-up
back-ward
  back-wards
back-wash
back-water
back-woods

  back-woods-man
ba-con
bac-ter-ia
  bac-ter-i-um
  bac-te-ri-al
  bac-te-ri-al-ly
bac-te-ri-cide
  bac-te-ri-ci-dal
bac-te-ri-ol-o-gy
  bac-te-ri-ol-o-gist
  bac-te-ri-o-log-i-cal
bac-te-ri-o-phage
bad
bade
badge
  badged
  badg-ing
badg-er
bad-i-nage
bad-land
  bad-lands
bad-ly
bad-min-ton
bad-tem-pered
baf-fle
  baf-fled
  baf-fling
  baf-fler
bag
  bagged
  bag-ging
ba-gasse
bag-a-telle
ba-gel
bag-gage
bag-gy
  bag-gi-er
  bag-gi-est
bag-man
bagn-io
bag-pipe
  bag-pi-per
bah
bail
bail-iff
bail-i-wick
bails-man
  bails-men
bairn
bait
bake
  baked
  bak-ing

bak-er
  bak-er-y
  bak-er-ies
bak-ing pow-der
bak-ing so-da
bak-sheesh
  bak-shish
bal-a-lai-ka
bal-ance
  bal-anced
  bal-anc-ing
  bal-anc-er
bal-brig-gan
bal-co-ny
  bal-co-nies
bald
  bald-ness
bal-der-dash
bald-head
bal-dric
bale
  baled
  bal-ing
ba-leen
bale-ful
  bale-ful-ly
balk
  balk-er
bal-kan-ize
  bal-kan-ized
  bal-kan-iz-ing
  bal-kan-i-za-tion
balk-y
  balk-i-er
  balk-i-est
bal-lad
  bal-lade
  bal-lad-eer
  bal-lad-ry
bal-last
ball-bear-ing
bal-le-ri-na
bal-let
bal-lis-tic
  bal-lis-tics
  bal-lis-ti-cian
bal-loon
bal-lot
  bal-lot-ed
  bal-lot-ing
ball-room
bal-ly-hoo
balm

balm-y
  balm-ier
  balm-i-est
  balm-i-ly
ba-lo-ney
bal-sa
bal-sam
bal-us-ter
bal-us-trade
bam-bi-no
  bam-bi-nos
bam-boo
ban
  banned
  ban-ning
ba-nal
  ba-nal-i-ty
ban-nan-a
band-age
  band-aged
  band-ag-ing
ban-dana
  ban-dan-na
ban-deau
  ban-deaux
ban-de-role
ban-dit
  ban-dits
  ban-dit-ti
  ban-dit-ry
band-mas-ter
band-o-leer
  ban-do-lier
bands-man
  bands-men
band-stand
band-wa-gon
ban-dy
  ban-died
  ban-dy-ing
ban-dy--leg-ged
bane-ful
  ban-ful-ness
ban-gla-desh
ban-gle
ban-ish
  ban-ish-ment
ban-i-ster
ban-jo
bank
bank-er
bank-ing
bank-note

bank-rupt
  bank-rupt-cy
  bank-rupt-cies
ban-ner
banns
ban-quet
  ban-quet-ter
ban-quette
ban-tam
ban-tam-weight
ban-ter
  ban-ter-er
  ban-ter-ing-ly
ban-yan
ban-zal
ba-o-bab
bap-tism
  bap-tis-mal
bap-tist
  bap-tist-ery
  bap-tis-ter-ies
bap-tize
  bap-tized
  bap-tiz-er
  bap-tiz-ing
bar
  barred
  bar-ring
bar-bar-ic
bar-ba-rism
bar-bar-i-ty
  bar-bar-i-ties
bar-ba-rize
  bar-ba-rized
  bar-ba-riz-ing
bar-ba-rous
bar-be-cue
  bar-be-cued
  bar-be-cu-ing
bar-ber
bar-ber-ry
  bar-ber-ries
bar-ber-shop
bar-bi-tal
bar-bi-tu-rate
  bar-bi-tur-ic
bar-busse
bar-ca-role
bard
bare
  bar-er
  bar-est
bare-back

bare-faced
bare-foot
bare-hand-ed
bare-ly
bar-gain
  bar-gain-er
barge
  barg-ed
  barg-ing
bar-i-tone
bar-i-um
bar-keep-er
bar-ken-tine
bark-er
bar-ley
bar-maid
bar-man
  bar-men
bar-mitz-vah
barm-y
bar-na-cle
barn-storm
  barn-storm-er
  barn-storm-ing
barn-yard
bar-o-graph
ba-rom-et-er
  bar-o-met-ric
  bar-o-met-ric-al
bar-on
  ba-ro-ni-al
bar-on-age
bar-on-ess
bar-on-et
  bar-on-et-age
  bar-on-et-cy
bar-o-ny
  bar-o-nies
ba-roque
barque
bar-quen-tine
bar-rack
bar-ra-cu-da
  bar-ra-cu-das
bar-rage
  bar-raged
  bar-rag-ing
bar-ra-try
  bar-ra-tries
  bar-ra-tor
  bar-ra-trous
bar-rel
  bar-reled

22

bar-relled
bar-rel-ling
bar-ren
bar-ren-ly
bar-ren-ness
bar-rette
bar-ri-cade
bar-ri-cad-ed
bar-ri-cad-ing
bar-ri-er
bar-ring
bar-ri-o
bar-ri-os
bar-ris-ter
bar-room
bar-row
bar-ten-der
bar-ter
bar-ter-er
ba-sal
ba-salt
base-ment
bash-ful
bash-ful-ly
ba-sic
ba-si-cal-ly
ba-sil
ba-sil-i-cia
bas-i-lisk
ba-sin
ba-sis
bas-ket
bas-ket-ball
bas-ket-ry
bas-re-lief
bas-si-net
bas-tard
baste
bast-ed
bast-ing
bas-tille
bas-ti-on
bas-ti-oned
bat
bat-ted
bat-ting
bat-ter
batch
bate
bat-ed
bat-ing
bathe
bathed

bath-ing
bath-er
bath-i-nette
ba-thos
bath-y-scaphe
bath-y-sphere
ba-tik
ba-tiste
bat-on
bat-ten
bat-ter
bat-tery
bat-tle
bat-tled
bat-tling
bat-tle dore
bat-tle-field
bat-tle-ment
bat-ty
bat-ti-er
bat-ti-est
bau-ble
bawd-y
bawd-i-er
bawd-i-est
bay-o-net
bay-o-net-ted
bay-o-net-ing
bay-ou
ba-zaar
ba-zoo-ka
beach
bea-con
bead
bead-ed
bead-like
bead-y
bead-i-er
bead-i-est
beak
beaked
beak-er
beam
beam-ed
bear
bear-ing
bear-a-ble
bear-a-bly
bear-er
beard
beard-ed
beard-less
bear-skin

beast
beast-li-ness
beast-ly
beast-li-er
beast-li-est
beat
beat-en
beat-ing
beat-er
be-a-tif-ic
be-at-i-fy
be-at-i-fied
be-at-i-fi-ca-tion
be-at-i-tude
beat-nik
beau
beaus
beaux
beau geste
beau-te-ous
beau-te-ous-ly
beau-ti-cian
beau-ti-fy
beau-ti-fied
beau-ti-fy-ing
beau-ti-fi-ca-tion
beau-ti-fi-er
beau-ti-ful
beau-ty
beaux-arts
bea-ver
be-calm
beck-on
be-cloud
be-come
be-com-ing
be-com-ing-ly
bed
bed-ded
bed-ding
be-daub
be-daz-zle
be-daz-zled
be-daz-zling
be-daz-zle-ment
bed-bug
bed-clothes
be-deck
be-dev-il
be-dev-iled
be-dev-il-ing
be-dev-il-ment
be-dew

bed-fast
bed-fel-low
be-dim
  be-dimmed
  be-dim-ming
bed-lam
bed-pan
be-drag-gle
  be-drag-gled
  be-drag-gling
bed-rid-den
bed-rock
bed-room
bed-sore
bed-spread
bed-spring
bed-time
bee-bread
beech
beef
beef-eat-er
beef-steak
beef-y
  beef-i-er
  beef-i-est
bee-hive
bee-line
beer-y
  beer-i-er
  beer-i-est
beest-ings
bees-wax
bee-tle
  bee-tled
  bee-tling
bee-tle-browed
be-fall
  be-fall-en
  be-fall-ing
be-fit
  be-fit-ted
  be-fit-ting
be-fog
  be-fogged
  be-fog-ging
be-fore
be-fore-hand
be-foul
be-friend
be-fud-dle
  be-fud-dled
  be-fud-dling
beg

beg-ged
beg-ging
be-get
  be-get-ten
  be-got
  be-got-ten
beg-gar
  beg-gar-dom
  beg-gar-hood
  beg-gar-ly
be-gin
  be-gan
  be-gun
  be-gin-ning
  be-gin-ner
be-go-ni-a
be-grime
  be-grimed
  be-grim-ing
be-grudge
  be-grudged
  be-grudg-ing
  be-grudg-ing-ly
be-guile
  be-guiled
  be-guil-ing
  be-guil-er
be-half
be-have
  be-haved
  be-hav-ing
be-hav-ior
  be-hav-ior-ism
  be-hav-ior-ist
  be-hav-ior-is-tic
be-head
be-he-moth
be-hest
be-hind
be-hind-hand
be-hold
  be-hold-ing
  be-hold-er
  be-hold-en
be-hoove
  be-hooved
  be-hoov-ing
beige
be-ing
be-la-bor
be-lat-ed
  be-lat-ed-ly
  be-lat-ed-ness

be-lay
  be-lay-ed
  be-lay-ing
belch
bel-dam
be-lea-quer
bel-fry
  bel-fries
be-lie
  be-lied
  be-ly-ing
be-lief
be-lieve
  be-lieved
  be-liev-ing
  be-liev-a-ble
  be-liev-er
be-lit-tle
  be-lit-tled
  be-lit-tling
bel-la-don-na
bell-boy
bell bouy
belle
belles let-tres
bell-hop
bel-li-cose
  bel-li-cos-i-ty
bel-lig-er-ence
  bel-lig-er-en-cy
  bel-li-ger-ent
  bel-lig-er-ent-ly
bel-low
  bel-lows
bell-weth-er
bel-ly
  bel-lies
  bel-lied
  bel-ly-ing
bel-ly-ache
  bel-ly-ach-ing
bel-ly-but-ton
be-long
  be-long-ings
be-loved
be-low
belt
  belt-ed
belt-way
be-lu-ga
be-mire
  be-mired
  be-mir-ing

be-moan
be-muse
  be-mused
  be-mus-ing
bench
bend
  bend-ing
  bend-er
be-neath
ben-e-dict
ben-e-dic-tion
ben-e-fac-tion
ben-e-fac-tor
  ben-e-fac-tress
ben-e-fice
  ben-e-ficed
  ben-e-fic-ing
be-nef-i-cence
be-nef-i-cent
be-ne-fi-cial
  ben-e-fi-cial-ly
  ben-e-fi-ci-ar-ies
ben-e-fit
  ben-e-fit-ed
  ben-e-fit-ing
be-nev-o-lence
  be-nev-o-lent
  be-nev-o-lent-ly
be-night-ed
be-nign
  be-nig-ni-ty
  be-nig-ni-ties
  be-nign-ly
be-nig-nant
  be-nig-nan-cies
  be-nig-nan-cy
ben-i-son
ben-ny
  ben-nies
be-numb
bent
ben-zene
ben-zine
ben-zo-ate
ben-zo-in
ben-zol
be-queath
be-quest
be-rate
  be-rat-ed
  be-rat-ing
be-reave
  be-reaved

be-reav-ing
be-reft
be-ret
ber-ga-mot
ber-i-ber-i
berke-li-um
ber-ry
  ber-ries
  ber-ried
  ber-ry-ing
ber-serk
berth
ber-tha
ber-yl
be-ryl-li-um
be-seech
  be-seeched
  be-seech-ing
  be-seech-ing-ly
be-set
  be-set-ting
be-shrew
be-side
  be-sides
be-siege
  be-sieged
  be-sieg-ing
  be-sieg-er
be-smear
be-smirch
bes-om
be-sot
  be-sot-ted
  be-sot-ting
be-spat-ter
be-speak
  be-speak-ing
best
bes-tial
  bes-tial-ly
  bes-ti-al-i-ty
  bes-ti-al-i-ties
be-stir
  be-stirred
  be-stir-ring
be-stow
  be-stow-al
be-strew
be-stride
  be-strid-den
  be-strid-ing
bet
  bet-ted

bet-ting
be-ta
be-take
  be-tak-en
  be-tak-ing
be-ta rays
be-ta-tron
be-tel
beth-el
be-tide
  be-tid-ed
  be-tid-ing
be-to-ken
be-tray
  be-tray-al
  be-tray-er
be-troth
  be-troth-al
  be-troth-ed
bet-ter
bet-ter-ment
bet-tor
be-tween
be-twixt
bev-el
  bev-eled
  bev-el-ing
bev-er-age
bev-y
  bev-ies
be-wail
be-ware
be-wil-der
  be-wil-der-ing-ly
  be-wil-der-ment
be-witch
  be-witch-er
  be-witch-ery
  be-witch-ing
  be-witch-ing-ly
  be-witch-ment
be-yond
be-zique
bi-an-nu-al
bi-as
  bi-ased
  bi-as-ing
bi-ax-i-al
  bi-ax-i-al-ly
bi-be-lot
Bi-ble
  Bib-li-cal
  Bib-li-cal-ly

bib-li-og-ra-phy
  bib-li-og-ra-phies
  bib-li-o-graphic
bib-li-o-ma-ni-a
  bib-li-o-ma-ni-ac
bib-li-o-phile
bib-u-lous
bi-cam-er-al
bi-car-bo-nate
bi-ce-te-nary
  bi-cen-te-nar-ies
bi-cen-ten-ni-al
bi-ceps
bi-chlo-ride
bick-er
bi-con-cave
bi-con-vex
bi-cus-pid
  bi-cus-pi-dal
  bi-cus-pi-date
bi-cy-cle
  bi-cy-cled
  bi-cy-cling
  bi-cy-cler
  bi-cy-clist
bid
  bid-den
  bid-da-ble
  bid-der
bid-dy
  bid-dies
bide
  bid-ed
  bid-ing
bi-en-ni-al
  bi-en-ni-al-ly
bier
bi-fid
bi-fo-cal
  bi-fo-cals
bi-fur-cate
  bi-fur-cat-ed
  bi-fur-cat-ing
  bi-fur-ca-tion
big
  big-ger
  big-gest
big-a-my
  big-a-mies
  big-a-mist
  big-a-mous
big-heart-ed
big-horn

bight
big-no-ni-a
big-ot
  big-ot-ed
  big-ot-ed-ly
  big-ot-ry
  big-ot-ries
bi-jou
  bi-joux
bi-ju-gous
bi-ki-ni
bi-lat-er-al
  bi-lat-er-al-ly
bil-ber-ry
  bil-ber-ries
bilge
bil-i-ary
bi-lin-gual
bil-ious
bilk
bill
  bil-led
  bil-ling
bil-la-bong
bill-board
bil-let
bil-let-doux
bill-fold
bill-hook
bil-liards
bil-lings-gate
bil-lion
  bil-lion-are
  bil-lionth
bil-low
  bil-low-y
  bil-low-ier
  bil-low-i-est
bil-ly goat
bi-met-al-lism
  bi-met-al-list
  bi-me-tal-lic
bi-month-ly
  bi-month-lies
bi-na-ry
bi-nate
bin-au-ral
bind
  bind-ing
bind-er
bind-ery
  bind-er-ies
binge

bin-go
bin-na-cle
bi-noc-u-lar
bi-no-mi-al
bio-chem-is-try
  bio-chem-i-cal
  bio-chem-ist
bi-o-cide
bi-o-e-col-o-gy
bi-o-en-gi-neer-ing
bi-o-gen-e-sis
  bi-o-ge-net-ic
bi-og-ra-phy
  bi-og-ra-pher
  bi-o-graph-ic
  bi-o-graph-i-cal
  bi-o-graph-i-cal-ly
bi-ol-o-gy
  bi-o-log-i-cal
  bi-ol-o-gist
bi-o-met-rics
bi-o-nom-ics
bi-o-phys-ics
  bi-o-phys-i-cal
  bi-o-phys-i-cist
bi-op-sy
  bi-op-sies
bi-o-sphere
bi-o-tin
bi-par-ti-san
bi-par-tite
  bi-par-ti-tion
bi-ped
  bi-ped-al
bi-plane
bi-po-lar
  bi-po-lar-i-ty
birch
  birch-en
bird-bath
bird-brain
  bird-brained
bird-call
bird-ie
bird-lime
bird-man
bird's-eye
bi-ret-ta
birth-day
birth-mark
birth-place
birth-right
birth-stone

bis-cuit
bi-sect
  bi-sec-tion
  bi-sec-tor
bi-sex-u-al
bish-op
  bish-op-ric
bis-muth
bi-son
bisque
bis-ter
  bis-tered
bis-tro
  bis-tros
bi-sul-fide
bitch
bite
  bit-ten
  bit-ing
  bit-ing-ly
bit-stock
bit-ter
  bit-ter-ish
  bit-ter-ly
  bit-ter-ness
bit-tern
bit-ter-root
bit-ters
bit-ter-sweet
bi-tu-men
bi-tu-mi-nous coal
bi-va-lent
  bi-va-lence
bi-valve
  bi-val-vu-lar
biv-ou-ac
  biv-ou-acked
  biv-ou-ack-ing
bi-week-ly
  bi-week-lies
bi-year-ly
bi-zarre
  bi-zarre-ly
  bi-zarre-ness
blab
  blab-bed
  blab-bing
  blab-ber
  blab-ber-mouth
black-ball
black-ber-ry
  black-ber-ries
black-bird

black-board
black-en
black-guard
black-head
black-ing
black-jack
black-list
black-mail
black-out
black-smith
black-snake
black-top
blad-der
blade
  blad-ed
blame
  blamed
  blam-ing
  blam-a-ble
  blame-a-ble
  blame-ful
  blame-less
  blame-less-ly
  blame-less-ness
blame-wor-thy
  blame-wor-thi-ness
blanch
  blanc-er
  blanch-ing
blanc-mange
bland
  bland-ly
  bland-ness
blan-dish
  blan-dish-er
  blan-dish-ment
blank
  blank-ly
  blank-ness
blan-ket
blare
  blared
  blar-ing
blar-ney
blas-pheme
  blas-phemed
  blas-phem-ing
  blas-phem-er
  blas-phem-ies
blas-phe-my
blast-ed
bas-tu-la
blat

blat-ted
blat-ting
bla-tant
  bla-tan-cy
  bla-tant-ly
blath-er
blaze
  blazed
  blaz-ing
bla-zer
bleach
  bleach-er
bleak
  bleak-ly
  bleak-ness
blear
  bleary
  blear-i-ness
bleed
  bleed-ing
  bleed-er
blem-ish
blench
blend
  blend-ed
  blend-ing
  blend-er
bless
  bless-ed
  bles-sing
  bless-ed-ness
blind
  blind-ing
  blind-ing-ly
  blind-ly
  blind-ness
blind-fold
blind-man's bluff
blink-er
bliss
  bliss-ful
  bliss-ful-ly
  bliss-ful-ness
blis-ter
  blis-ter-y
blithe
  blithe-ly
blithe-some
  blithe-some-ly
blitz-krieg
bliz-zard
block
  block-er

block-ade
block-ad-ed
block-ad-ing
block-ad-er
block-bus-ter
block-head
block-house
block-ish
block-ish-ly
blocky
blond
blood-curd-ling
blood bank
blood-ed
blood-hound
blood-less
blood-less-ly
blood-less-ness
blood-let-ting
blood pres-sure
blood re-la-tion
blood-shed
blood-shot
blood-stone
blood-suck-er
blood-thirst-y
blood-thirst-i-ly
bloody
blood-i-er
blood-i-est
blood-ied
blood-y-ing
blood-i-ly
blood-i-ness
bloom-ers
bloom-ing
bloom-ing-ly
bloop-er
blos-som
blot
blot-ted
blot-ting
blotch
blotchy
blot-ter
blow
blown
blow-ing
blow-er
blow-fly
blow-flies
blow-gun
blow-hole

blow-out
blow-pipe
blow-torch
blow-up
blow-y
blowz-y
blub-ber
blub-bery
blu-cher
bludg-eon
blue
blu-er
blu-est
blue-ness
blue-bell
blue-ber-ry
blue-ber-ries
blue-bird
blue-blood-ed
blue-bon-net
blue-coat
blue-col-lar
blue-fish
blue-grass
blue-jac-ket
blue-nose
blue-pen-cil
blue-print
blu-et
blu-ing
blun-der
blun-der-er
blun-der-ing-ly
blun-der-buss
blunt
blunt-ly
blunt-ness
blur
blur-red
blur-ring
blur-ry
blush
blushed
blush-ing
blush-ing-ly
blus-ter
blus-ter-er
blus-ter-ing-ly
blus-ter-ous
blus-ter-y
bo-a
board-er
board-walk

boast
boas-ter
boast-ful
boast-ful-ness
boast-ing-ly
boat-house
boat-man
boat-swain
bob
bob-bed
bob-bing
bob-bin
bob-ble
bob-bled
bob-bling
bob-by-pin
bob-cat
bob-o-link
bob-sled
bob-tail
bob-white
bock
bode
bod-ed
bod-ing
bod-ice
bod-i-ly
bod-kin
bod-y
bod-ied
bod-y-ing
bod-y-guard
bog
bog-gy
bog-ging
bo-gey
bog-gle
bog-gled
bog-gling
bog-gler
bo-gus
bo-gy
boil-er
bois-ter-ous
bois-ter-ous-ly
bois-ter-ous-ness
bo-la
bo-las
bold
bold-ly
bold-ness
bold-face
bo-le-ro

28

bol-lix
boli-worm
boll weevil
bo-lo
bo-lo-gna
bo-lo-ney
bol-ster
  bol-ster-er
bolt
  bolt-ed
  bolt-er
bom-bard
  bom-bard-ment
bom-bar-dier
bom-bast
  bom-bas-tic
  bom-bas-ti-cal-ly
bomb-er
bomb-proof
bomb-shell
bomb-sight
bo-na fide
bo-nan-za
bon-bon
bond-age
bond-ed
bond-man
  bond-men
bonds-men
bone
  boned
  bon-ing
bone-head
bon-er
bon-fire
bon-go
  bon-gos
  bon-gies
bon-ho-mie
bo-ni-to
bon-net
bon-ny
bon-sai
bo-nus
  bo-nus-es
bon voy-age
bon-y
  bon-i-er
  bon-i-est
boo
  booed
  boo-ing
boo-by

boo-bies
boo-by trap
boo-dle
boo-hoo
  boo-hooed
  boo-hoo-ing
book
  book-bind-er
book-case
book-end
book-ie
book-ish
  book-ish-ness
book-keep-ing
  book-keep-er
book-let
book-mak-er
book-mark
book-mo-bile
book-plate
book-sell-er
  book-sell-ing
book-stall
book-worm
boo-me-rang
boon docks
boon-dog-gle
boor
  boor-ish
  boor-ish-ness
boost
  boost-er
boot-black
boot-ee
boot-jack
boot-leg
  boot-legged
  boot-leg-ging
  boot-leg-ger
boot-less
  boot-less-ly
  boot-less-ness
boot-lick
  boot-lick-er
boo-ty
  boo-ties
booze
  booz-er
  booz-y
  booz-i-er
  booz-i-est
bo-rax
bor-der

bor-der-ed
bor-der-ing
bor-der-land
bor-der-line
bore
  bored
bor-ing
bor-er
bo-re-al
bore-dom
bo-ric
bo-ron
bor-ough
bor-row
  bor-row-er
borsch
bosh
bosk-y
bos-om
boss-ism
boss-y
  boss-i-er
  boss-i-est
bo-sun
bot-a-ny
  bo-tan-i-cal
  bot-a-nist
  bot-a-nize
botch
  botchy
  botch-i-er
  botch-i-est
both-er
  both-er-some
bot-tle
  bot-tled
  bot-tling
  bot-tle-ful
  bot-tler
bot-tle-neck
bot-tom
  bot-tom-less
bot-u-lism
bou-doir
bouf-fant
bough
bought
bouil-lon
boul-der
boul-e-vard
bounce
  bounced
  bounc-ing

bound
bound-a-ry
  bound-a-ries
bound-er
bound-less
  bound-less-ness
boun-te-ous
  boun-te-ous-ness
boun-ti-ful
boun-ty
  boun-ties
bou-quet
bour-bon
bour-geois
bour-geoi-sie
bou-tique
bou-ton-niere
bo-vine
bow-el
bow-ery
bow-ie
bow-ing
bowl
bow-leg
  bow-leg-ged
bowl-er
bow-line
bow-ling
bow-man
  bow-men
bow-string
box
  box-ful
  box-fuls
box-car
box-er
box-ing
box of-fice
boy
  boy-hood
  boy-ish
  boy-ish-ly
boy-cott
boy-friend
boy-sen-ber-ry
  boy-sen-ber-ries
brace
  bra-ced
  brac-ing
brace-let
brac-er
bra-ces
brack-en

brack-et
brack-ish
  brack-ish-ness
bract
brae
brag
  brag-ged
  brag-ging
brag-gart
braid
  braid-er
  braid-ing
braille
brain-child
brain-less
brain-pow-er
brain-storm
  brain-storm-ing
brain-wash-ing
brain-y
  brain-i-er
  brain-i-est
braise
  braised
  brais-ing
bram-ble
  bram-bly
branch
  branch-ed
brand
  brand-er
brand-ish
brand-new
bran-dy
  bran-dies
  bran-died
  bran-dy-ing
bra-sier
bras-se-rie
  bras-se-ries
bras-siere
brassy
  brass-i-er
  brass-i-est
brat
  brat-tish
  brat-ty
bra-va-do
brave
  braved
  brav-ing
  brav-ery
bra-vo

bra-vos
bra-vu-ra
brawl
  braw-ler
brawn
  brawny
  brawn-i-er
bra-zen
bra-zier
breach
bread
  bread=ed
breadth-ways
break
  break-ing
  break-a-ble
break-age
brak-er
breath
breathe
  breathed
  breath-ing
breath-er
breath-ing
breath-tak-ing
  breath-tak-ing-ly
breathy
  breath-i-er
  breath-i-est
breech-es
breech-load-er
bred
breed
  breed-ing
breeze
  breezy
  breez-i-er
  breez-i-est
breth-ren
bre-vet
  bre-vet-ted
  bre-vet-ting
bre-vi-a-ry
  bre-vi-a-ries
brev-i-ty
bri-ar
  bri-ary
bribe
  bribed
  brib-ing
  brib-a-ble
birb-ery
  brib-er-ies

30

bric-a-brac
brick-lay-er
 brick-lay-ing
brick-work
bride
 brid-al
bride-groom
brides-maid
bridge
bri-dle
 bri-dled
 bri-dling
brief
 brief-ly
 brief-ing
bri-er
bri-gade
bri-a-dier
brig-an-tine
bright
 bright-ly
 bright-en
bril-liance
 bril-lian-cy
 bril-liant
brim
 brimmed
 brim-ming
brim-stone
brine
briny
bring
 bring-ing
brink
bri-oche
bri-quet
 bri-quette
brisk
 brisk-ly
bris-ket
bris-tle
 bris-tled
britch-es
brit-tle
broach
 broached
 broach-ing
broad-cast
 broad-cast-ed
 broad-cast-ing
broad-cloth
broad-mind-ed
broad-side

bro-cade
 bro-cad-ed
 bro-cad-ing
broc-co-li
bro-chure
broil-er
bro-ken
bro-ker
bro-ker-age
bro-mide
bro-mine
bron-chi
 bron-chi-al
 bron-chi-tis
 bron-chue
bron-co
 bron-cos
bron-to-saur
bronze
 bronz-ed
 bronz-ing
brooch
brood
 brood-ing
brook
broom-stick
broth-el
broth-er
broth-er-in-law
 broth-ers-in-law
broth-er-ly
brow-beat
 brow-beat-en
 brow-beat-ing
brown
 brown-ie
browse
 browsed
 brows-ing
bru-in
bruise
 bruis-ed
 bruis-er
 bruis-ing
brunch
bru-net
brusque
bru-tal
 bru-tal-i-ty
 bru-tal-ize
 bru-tal-ized
 bru-tal-iz-ing
 bru-tal-i-za-tion

brut-ish
bub-ble
 bub-bled
 bub-bling
 bub-bler
bu-bon-ic plague
buc-ca-neer
buck-board
buck-et
 buck-et-ed
 buck-et-ing
buck-eye
buck-le
buck-tooth
 buck-teeth
 buck-toothed
buck-wheat
bu-col-ic
bud
 bud-ded
 bud-ding
bud-dy
budge
budg-et
buff-er
buf-fet
 buf-fet-ed
 buf-fet=ing
bug-a-boo
bug-gy
 bug-gi-er
 bug-gi-est
bu-gle
 bu-gled
 bu-gling
 bu-gler
build
 build-er
 build-ing
built--in
built-up
bulb
bul-ba-ceous
bul-bar
bul-bous
bulge
 bulged
 bulg-ing
 bulgy
bulk-head
bulk-y
 bulk-i-er
 bulk-i-est

bulk-i-ly
bul-let
bul-le-tin
bul-let-proof
bull-fight
  bull-fight-er
  bull-fight-ing
bull-finch
bul-lion
bull-pen
bull's-eye
bul-ly
  bul-lies
  bul-lied
  bul-ly-ing
bul-rush
bul-wark
bum
  bum-mer
  bum-mest
bum-ble-bee
bump-er
bump-kin
bump-tious
bump-y
  bump-i-er
  bump-i-est
bunch
  bunchy
bun-co
bun-combe
bun-dle
  bun-dled
  bun-dling
bun-ga-low
bun-gle
  bun-gled
  bun-gling
  bun-gler
bun-ion
bunk-er
bunk-house
bun-ko
bun-kum
bun-ny
  bun-nies
bun-ting
bu-oy
buoy-an-cy
  buoy-ant
  buoy-ant-ly
bur-ble
bur-den

bur-den-some
bur-dock
bu-rette
burg-er
bur-gess
bur-glar
  bur-glar-ize
  bur-glar-ized
  bur-glar-iz-ing
  bur-gla-ries
  bur-gla-ry
bur-gle
  bur-gled
  bur-gling
bur-i-al
bur-lap
bur-lesque
  bur-lesqued
  bur-les-quing
  bur-les-quer
bur-ly
  bur-li-er
  bur-li-est
burn
  burn-ed
  burnt
  burn-ing
  burn-a-ble
burn-er
bur-nish
  bur-nish-er
bur-noose
burn-sides
burp
burr
  burred
  bur-ring
bur-ro
  bur-ros
bur-row
  bur-row-er
bur-sa
  bur-sae
  bur-sal
bur-sar
  bur-sa-ri-al
  bur-sa-ry
  bur-sa-ries
bur-si-tis
burst
  burst-ing
  burst-er
bur-y

bur-ied
bur-y-ing
bus-boy
bus-by
  bus-bies
bushed
bu-shi-do
bush-ing
bush-man
  bush-men
bush-mas-ter
bush-whack
  bush-whack-er
  bush-whack-ing
bush-y
  bush-i-er
  bush-i-est
bus-i-ly
busi-ness
busi-ness-like
busi-ness-man
  busi-ness-men
  busi-ness-wom-an
bus-kin
  bus-kined
bus-tard
bus-tle
  bus-tled
  bus-tling
  bus-tler
bus-y
  bus-i-er
  bus-i-est
  bus-ied
  bus-y-ing
bu-ta-di-ene
bu-tane
butch-er
butch-ery
  butch-er-ies
but-ler
butte
but-ton
but-tress
bu-ty-ric
bux-om
buy
  bought
  buy-ing
buz-zard
by-gong
by-law
byte

C

ca-bal
 ca-balled
 ca-ball-ing
cab-a-la
 cab-a-lis-tic
 cab-a-lis-ti-cal
ca-bal-le-ro
ca-ba-na
cab-a-ret
ca-ble
 ca-bled
 ca-bling
ca-ble-gram
cab-o-chon
ca-boo-dle
ca-boose
cab-ri-o-let
cach-a-lot
cache
 cached
 cach-ing
ca-chet
ca-cique
cack-le
ca-coph-o-ny
 ca-coph-o-nies
cac-tus
 cac-tus-es
cac-ti
cad
 cad-dish
ca-dav-er
 ca-dav-er-ous
cad-die
 cad-died
cad-dis fly
cad-dy
 cad-dies
ca-dence
ca-den-za
ca-det
cadge
 cadged
 cadg-ing
cad-mi-um
ca-dre
ca-du-ce-us
 ca-du-cei
cea-su-ra
 cae-su-rae
ca-fe
caf-e-te-ria
caf-feine

caf-tan
cage
 caged
cai-man
cairn
cais-son
cai-tiff
ca-jole
cake
 caked
cal-a-bash
cal-a-boose
cal-a-mine
ca-lam-i-ty
 ca-lam-i-ties
 ca-lam-i-tous
cal-cic
cal-ci-fy
 cal-ci-fied
 cal-ci-fy-ing
 cal-ci-fi-ca-tion
cal-ci-mine
cal-cite
cal-ci-um
cal-cu-la-ble
 cal-cu-la-bil-i-ty
cal-cu-late
 cal-cu-lat-ed
 cal-cu-lat-ing
 cal-cu-la-tion
cal-cu-la-tor
cal-cu-lus
 cal-cu-lus-es
cal-dron
cal-en-dar
cal-i-ber
cal-i-brate
 cal-i-brat-ed
 cal-i-brat-ing
 cal-i-bra-tion
cal-i-co
 cal-i-coes
cal-i-per
ca-liph
 cal-iph-ate
cal-is-then-ics
cal-lig-ra-pher
 cal-lig-ra-phy
call-ing
cal-li-o-pe
cal-lous
 cal-loused
cal-low

cal-lus
 cal-lus-es
calm
ca-lor-ic
cal-o-rie
 cal-o-ries
cal-o-rif-ic
cal-u-met
cal-um-ny
calve
 calved
ca-lyp-so
 ca-lyp-sos
ca-lyx
 ca-lyx-es
cal-y-ces
ca-ma-ra-de-rie
cam-ber
cam-bi-um
cam-bric
cam-el
cam-era
cam-i-sole
cam-ou-flage
 cam-ou-flaged
 cam-ou-flag-ing
cam-paign
cam-pa-ni-le
 cam-pa-ni-les
camp-er
cam-phor
cam-pus
 cam-pus-es
camp-y
cam-shaft
can
 canned
 can-ning
ca-nal
 ca-naled
 ca-nal-ing
ca-nard
ca-nar-y
can-can
can-cel
 can-celed
 can-cel-ing
 can-cel-la-tion
can-cer
can-de-la-brum
can-did
can-di-da-cy
 can-di-da-cies

can-di-date
can-died
can-dle
can-dor
can-dy
  can-dies
  can-dy-ing
cane
ca-nine
can-is-ter
can-ker
  can-ker-ous
can-na-bis
canned
can-ner
can-nery
  can-ner-ies
can-ni-bal
can-non
can-not
can-ny
  can-nier
ca-noe
can-on
ca-non-i-cal
can-on-ize
  can-on-ized
  can-on-i-za-tion
can-o-py
can-ta-loup
  can-ta-loupe
  can-ta-lope
can-tan-ker-ous
can-ta-ta
can-teen
can-ti-cle
can-ti-lev-er
can-to
  can-tos
can-ton
can-tor
can-vas
can-yon
ca-pa-bil-i-ty
  cap-pa-bil-i-ties
ca-pa-ble
  ca-pa-bly
ca-pa-cious
ca-pac-i-tate
  ca-pac-i-tat-ed
  ca-pac-i-tat-ing
ca-pac-i-ty
  ca-pac-i-ties

ca-per
ca-pi-as
cap-il-lar-i-ty
cap-il-lar-y
  cap-il-lar-ies
cap-i-tal
cap-i-ta-tion
ca-pit-u-late
  ca-pit-u-lat-ed
  ca-pit-u-lat-ing
  ca-pit-u-la-tor
ca-pon
ca-pote
ca-price
  ca-pri-cious
  ca-pri-cious-ly
cap-ri-ole
  cap-ri-oled
  cap-ri-ol-ing
cap-size
cap-stone
cap-sule
  cap-su-lar
cap-tain
  cap-tain-cy
cap-tion
cap-tious
  cap-tious-ness
cap-ti-vate
cap-tive
  cap-tiv-i-ty
  cap-tiv-i-ties
cap-tor
cap-ture
  cap-tured
  cap-tur-ing
  cap-tur-er
car-a-cole
  car-a-coled
  car-a-col-ing
car-a-cul
ca-rafe
car-a-van
car-a-van-sa-ry
  car-a-van-sa-ries
car-a-vel
car-a-way
car-bide
car-bo-hy-drate
car-bo-lat-ed
car-bol-ic
car-bon
car-bo-na-ceous

car-bo-nate
  car-bo-na-tion
car-bon di-ox-ide
car-bon-if-er-ous
car-bon-ize
  car-bon-ized
  car-bon-iz-ing
  car-bon-i-za-tion
car-bon mon-ox-ide
car-boy
car-bun-cle
car-bu-re-tor
car-cass
car-cin-o-gen
  car-cin-o-gen-ic
car-ci-no-ma
  car-ci-no-mas
  car-ci-no-ma-ta
car-da-mom
car-di-ac
car-di-gan
car-di-nal
car-di-o-graph
  car-di-og-ra-phy
ca-reen
ca-reer
care-ful
  care-ful-ly
care-less
  care-less-ly
  care-less-ness
ca-ress
  ca-ress-ing-ly
car-et
care-worn
car-go
  car-gos
car-hop
car-i-bou
car-i-ca-ture
  car-i-ca-tured
  car-i-ca-tur-ing
  car-i-ca-tur-ist
car-ies
car-il-lon
  car-il-lonned
  car-i-lon-ning
car-mine
car-nage
car-nal
  car-nal-i-ty
  car-nal-ly
car-na-tion

car-nel-ian
car-ni-val
car-ni-vore
  car-niv-o-rous
  car-niv-o-rous-ly
car-om
ca-rot-id
ca-rous-al
ca-rouse
  ca-roused
  ca-rous-ing
  ca-rous-er
car-ou-sel
car-pen-ter
  car-pen-try
car-pet
car-pet-ing
car-pus
car-riage
car-ri-ole
car-rot
car-roty
car-ry
  car-ried
  car-ry-ing
cart
cart-age
carte-blanche
car-tel
car-ti-lage
  car-ti-lag-i-nous
car-tog-ra-phy
  car-tog-ra-pher
  car-to-graph-ic
car-ton
car-toon
  car-toon-ist
car-tridge
cart-wheel
car-vel
car-y-at-id
  car-y-at-ids
  car-y-at-i-des
ca-sa-ba
cas-cade
  cas-cad-ed
  cas-cad-ing
ca-sein
case-mate
  case-mat-ed
case-ment
  case-ment-ed
case-work

case-work-er
cash-ew
cash-mere
cas-ing
ca-si-no
cas-ket
cas-sette
cas-si-no
cas-sock
  cas-socked
cas-so-wary
  cas-so-war-ies
cast
  cast-ing
cas-ta-net
cast-a-way
caste
cas-tel-lat-ed
cast-er
cas-ti-gate
  cas-ti-gat-ed
cast i-ron
cas-tle
cas-tor
cas-trate
  cas-trat-ed
  cas-trat-er
  cas-tra-tion
cas-u-al
cas-u-al-ty
  cas-u-al-ties
cas-u-ist
  cas-u-ist-ic
  cas-u-ist-ry
  cas-u-ist-ries
cat-a-clysm
  cat-a-cly-mal
cat-a-comb
cat-a-falque
cat-a-lep-sy
  cat-a-lep-tic
cat-a-log
  cat-a-loged
  cat-a-log-ing
  cat-a-log-er
ca-tal-pa
ca-tal-y-sis
  ca-tal-y-ses
  cat-a-lyt-ic
cat-a-lyst
cat-a-lyze
  cat-a-lyzed
  cat-a-lyz-ing

cat-a-ma-ran
cat-a-pult
ca-tarrh
ca-tas-tro-phe
  cat-as-troph-ic
catch
  caught
  catch-ing
catch-er
catch-up
cat-e-chism
  cat-e-chis-mal
cat-e-chiz
cat-e-chu-men
cat-e-gor-i-cal
  cat-e-gor-i-cal-ly
cat-e-go-ry
  cat-a-go-ries
  cat-e-gor-ize
  cat-e-gor-ized
  cat-e-gor-iz-ing
ca-ter
ca-ter-er
cat-er-pil-lar
ca-ter-waul
cat-fish
  cat-fish-es
cat-gut
ca-thar-sis
  ca-thar-ses
ca-thar-tic
ca-the-dral
cath-e-ter
cat-i-on
cat-nap
  cat-napped
  cat-nap-ping
cat-nip
cat's-paw
cat-sup
cat-tail
cat-tle
cat-ty
  cat-tier
  cat-ti-est
  cat-ti-ly
  cat-ti-ness
cat-ty-cor-ner
cau-cus
  cau-cus-es
  cau-cused
  cau-cus-ing
cau-dal

cau-date
  cau-dat-ed
cau-dle
caul-dron
cau-li-flow-er
caulk
  caulk-er
caus-al
  caus-al-ly
cau-sal-i-ty
  cau-sal-i-ties
cause-way
caus-tic
  caus-ti-cal-ly
cau-ter-ize
  cau-ter-ized
  cau-ter-iz-ing
  cau-ter-i-za-tion
cau-ter-y
  cau-ter-ies
cau-tion
  cau-tion-ary
cau-tious
cav-al-cade
cav-a-lier
  cav-a-lier-ly
cav-al-ry
cave
ca-ve-at
cav-ern
  cav-ern-ous
cav-ier
cav-il
  cav-iled
  cav-il-ing
cav-i-ty
  cav-i-ties
ca-vort
cay-enne
cay-man
  cay-mans
cay-use
ce-cum
ce-dar
cede
  ced-ed
  ced-ing
ce-dil-la
ceil-ing
cel-an-dine
cel-a-brant
cel-e-brate
  cel-e-brat-ed

cel-e-brat-ing
cel-e-bra-tion
cel-e-bra-tor
ce-leb-ri-ty
  ce-leb-ri-ties
ce-ler-i-ty
cel-er-y
ce-les-tial
ce-li-ac
cel-i-ba-cy
  cel-i-bate
cel-lar
cel-lo
  cel-los
  cel-list
cel-lo-phane
cel-lu-lar
cel-lule
cel-lu-lose
ce-ment
cem-e-ter-y
ce-no-bite
cen-o-taph
cen-ser
cen-sor
  cen-so-ri-al
  cen-sor-ship
cen-so-ri-ous
  cen-so-ri-ous-ly
  cen-so-ri-ous-ness
cen-sure
  cen-sured
  cen-sur-ing
  cen-sur-er
cen-sus
  cen-sus-es
  cen-sused
  cen-sus-ing
cen-tare
cen-taur
cen-te-nar-i-an
cen-te-na-ry
  cen-te-nar-ies
cen-ten-ni-al
cen-ter
cen-ti-are
cen-ti-grade
cen-ti-gram
cen-ti-li-ter
cen-ti-me-ter
cen-tral
  cen-tral-ize
  cen-tral-ized

cen-tral-iz-ing
cen-trif-u-gal
cen-tri-fuge
cen-trip-e-tal
cen-tu-ri-an
cen-tu-ry
  cen-tu-ries
ce-ram-ic
  ce-ram-ics
ce-re-al
cer-e-bel-lum
cer-e-bral
cer-e-brum
cer-e-mo-ni-al
  cer-e-mo-no-al-ism
cer-e-mo-ny
  cer-e-mo-nies
ce-rise
ce-ric
  ce-ri-um
cer-tain
cer-tain-ty
  cer-tain-ties
cer-tif-i-cate
  cer-tif-i-ca-tion
cer-ti-fy
  cer-ti-fied
  cer-ti-fy-ing
cer-ti-tude
ce-ru-le-an
cer-vi-cal
cer-vix
  cer-vix-es
  cer-vi-ces
ces-sa-tion
ces-sion
cess-pool
ce-ta-cean
  ce-ta-ceous
chafe
  chafed
  chaf-ing
chaf-er
chaff
  chaf-fer
  chaff-er-er
cha-grin
  cha-grined
  cha-grin-ing
chain re-ac-tion
chair-man
  chair-men
chaise-longue

chal-et
chal-ice
chalk
 chalky
chal-lenge
 chal-lenged
 chal-leng-ing
cham-ber
cham-ber-maid
cha-me-le-on
cham-ois
cham-pagne
cham-pi-on
 cham-pi-on-ship
chance-ful
chan-cel-lor
chanc-y
 chanc-i-er
 chanc-i-est
chan-de-lier
change
 changed
 chang-ing
 chang-a-ble
chan-nel
chan-ti-cleer
cha-os
cha-ot-ic
cha-pa-re-jos
chap-ar-ral
cha-peau
 cha-peaux
chap-el
chap-e-ron
chap-fall-en
chap-lain
chap-let
chap-ter
char
 charred
 char-ring
char-ac-ter
char-ac-ter-is-tic
 char-ac-ter-is-ti-cal-ly
char-ac-ter-ize
 char-ac-ter-ized
 char-ac-ter-iz-ing
 char-ac-ter-i-za-tion
 char-ac-ter-iz-er
cha-rade
char-coal
charge
 charged

 charg-ing
 charg-er
char-i-ot
 char-i-ot-eer
cha-ris-ma
char-i-ta-ble
 char-i-ta-ble-ness
 char-i-ta-bly
char-i-ty
 char-i-ties
cha-riv-a-ri
char-la-tan
 char-la-tan-ism
char-ley horse
°harm
char-nel
char-ter
char-treuse
char-wom-an
chary
 char-i-er
 char-i-est
chase
 chased
 chas-ing
 chas-er
chasm
chas-sis
chaste
 chaste-ly
chas-ten
chas-tise
 chas-tised
 chas-tis-ing
 chas-tis-ment
 chas-tis-er
 chas-ti-ty
chat
 chat-ted
 chat-ting
cha-teau
 cha-teaux
chat-e-laine
chat-tel
chat-ter
chat-ter-box
chat-ty
 chat-ti-er
 chat-ti-est
 chat-ti-ly
 chat-ti-ness
chauf-feur
chau-vin-ist

chau-vin-ism
 chau-vin-is-tic
cheap
 cheap-ly
 cheap-ness
 cheap-en
cheap-skate
cheat
check-er-board
check-list
check-mate
 check-mat-ed
 check-mat-ing
check-out
check-point
check-room
check-up
ched-dar
cheek-bone
cheek-y
 cheek-i-er
 cheek-i-est
 cheek-i-ness
cheer-ful
 cheer-ful-ly
 cheer-ful-ness
cheer-lead-er
cheer-less
 cheer-less-ly
 cheer-less-ness
chee-y
 cheer-i-er
 cheer-i-est
 cheer-i-ly
 cheer-i-ness
cheese-burg-er
cheese-cake
cheese-cloth
chees-y
 chees-i-er
 chees-i-est
 chees-i-ness
chee-tah
chem-i-cal
 chem-i-cal-ly
che-mise
chem-ist
chem-is-try
chem-o-ther-a-py
che-nille
cher-ish
che-root
cher-ry

cher-ries
cher-ub
  cher-ubs
  cher-u-bim
  che-ru-bic
cher-vil
chess-man
  chess-men
chest-nut
chest-y
  chest-i-er
  chest-i-est
chev-ron
chew
  chew-er
chi-a-ro-scu-ro
chi-can-ery
  cha-can-er-ies
chi-chi
chick-a-dee
chic-ken
chic-ken-heart-ed
chic-le
chic-o-ry
  chic-o-ries
chide
  chid-ed
chief
  chief-ly
chief-tain
chif-fon
chif-fo-nier
chi-gnon
chil-blain
chil-dren
child-bear-ing
child-birth
child-hood
child-ish
  child-ish-ly
  child-like
chili
  chil-ies
chill
  chill-ing-ly
chill-y
  chill-i-er
  chill-i-est
  chill-i-ness
chi-me-ra
chi-mer-ic
  chi-mer-i-cal
  chi-mer-i-cal-ly

chi-mer-i-cal-ness
chim-ney
chim-pan-zee
chin
  chinned
  chin-ning
chi-na
chi-no
  chi-nos
chi-noi-se-rie
chintz-y
  chintz-i-er
  chintz-i-est
chip
  chipped
  chip-ping
chip-munk
chip-per
chi-rog-ra-pher
chi-rog-ra-phy
chi-rop-o-dist
chi-ro-prac-tic
chi-ro-prac-tor
chis-el
  chis-eled
  chis-el-ing
  chis-el-er
chit-chat
chi-tin
chit-ter-ling
chiv-al-ry
  chiv-al-ries
  chiv-al-ric
  chiv-al-rous
  chiv-al-rous-ly
  chiv-al-rous-ness
chlo-rine
chlo-ro-form
clo-ro-phyll
chock-full
choc-o-late
choice
  choice-ly
  choice-ness
choir-boy
choke
  choked
  chok-ing
  chok-er
chol-er
chol-era
chol-er-ic
cho-les-te-rol

choose
  chose
  cho-sen
  choos-ing
choos-y
  choos-i-er
  choos-i-est
chop
  chopped
  chop-ping
chop-per
  chop-pi-ness
chop-py
  chop-pi-er
  chop-i-est
chop-sticks
chop su-ey
cho-ral
  cho-ral-ly
cho-rale
chord
  chord-al
cho-rea
cho-re-og-ra-phy
  cho-re-og-ra-pher
  cho-re-o-graph-ic
cho-ric
chor-is-ter
chor-tle
  chor-tled
  chor-tling
cho-rus
  cho-rus-es
  cho-rused
  cho-rus-ing
chos-en
chow-der
chow mein
chrism
Christ
chris-ten
  chris-ten-ing
Chris-tian
Chris-ti-an-i-ty
  Chris-ti-an-i-ties
Christ-mas
chro-mate
chro-mat-ic
  chro-mat-i-cal-ly
chro-mat-ics
chro-ma-tin
chro-mic
chro-mi-um

chro-mo
  chro-mus
chro-mo-lith-o-graph
chro-mo-some
chro-mo-sphere
chron-ic
  chron-i-cal-ly
chron-i-cle
  chron-i-cled
  chron-i-cling
  chron-i-cler
chron-o-log-i-cal
  chron-o-log-i-cal-ly
chro-no-lo-gy
  chro-nol-o-gies
  chro-nol-o-gist
chro-nom-e-ter
  chron-o-met-ric
chrys-a-lis
  chry-sa-lis-es
  chry-sal-i-des
chry-san-the-mum
chrys-o-lite
chub-by
  chub-bi-er
  chub-bi-est
  chub-bi-ness
chuck-full
chuck-le
  chuck-led
  chuck-ling
chuk-ker
chum-my
  chum-mi-er
  chum-mi-est
chunk
  chunky
  chunk-i-er
  chunk-i-est
church
  church-li-ness
  church-ly
church-go-er
church-man
  church-men
church-war-den
church-yard
churl-ish
  churl-ish-ly
  churl-ish-ness
churn-er
chut-ney
chutz-pah

ci-bo-ri-um
  ci-bo-ria
ci-ca-da
  ci-ca-das
  ci-ca-dea
cic-a-trix
  cic-a-tri-ces
  cic-a-trize
  cic-a-trized
  cic-a-triz-ing
cic-e-ro-ne
ci-der
ci-gar
cig-a-rette
cil-ia
  cil-i-ar-y
cil-i-ate
cin-cho-na
cinc-ture
cin-der
cin-e-ma
  cin-e-mas
  cin-e-mat-ic
cin-e-ma-to-graph
  cin-e-ma-tog-ra-phy
cin-e-rar-i-um
cin-na-bar
cin-na-mon
cinque-foil
ci-on
ci-pher
cir-ca
cir-ca-di-an
cir-cle
  cir-cled
  cir-cling
cir-clet
cir-cuit
  cir-cu-i-tous
  cir-cu-i-tous-ly
  cir-cu-i-tous-ness
cir-cu-lar
  cir-cu-lar-ize
  cir-cu-lar-ized
  cir-cu-lar-iz-ing
  cir-cu-lar-i-za-tion
cir-cu-la-tion
  cir-cu-late
  cir-cu-lat-ed
  cir-cu-lat-ing
  cir-cu-la-tive
  cir-cu-la-tor
  cir-cu-la-to-ry

cir-cum-am-bi-ent
cir-cum-cise
  cir-cum-cised
  cir-cum-cis-ing
  cir-cum-cis-er
  cir-cum-ci-sion
cir-cum-fer-ence
  cir-cum-fer-en-tial
cir-cum-flex
cir-cum-flu-ent
cir-cum-fuse
  cir-cum-fus-ing
  cir-cum-fu-sion
cir-cum-lo-cu-tion
  cir-cum-lo-cu-to-ry
cir-cum-nav-i-gate
  cir-cum-nav-i-gat-ed
  cir-cum-nav-i-gat-ing
  cir-cum-nav-i-ga-tion
  cir-cum-nav-i-ga-tor
cir-cum-scribe
  cir-cum-scribed
  cir-cum-scrib-ing
  cir-cum-scrib-er
  cir-cum-scrip-tion
  cir-cum-scrip-tive
cir-cum-spect
cir-cum-stance
  cir-cum-stan-tial
  cir-cum-stan-ti-al-i-ty
  cir-cum-stan-ti-at-ed
  cir-cum-stan-ti-at-ing
  cir-cum-stan-ti-a-tion
cir-cum-vent
  cir-cum-ven-tion
  cir-cum-ven-tive
cir-cus
  cir-cus-es
cir-rho-sis
  cir-rhot-ic
cir-rus
cis-tern
cit-a-del
cite
  cit-ed
  cit-ing
ci-ta-tion
cith-a-ra
cit-i-zen
  cit-i-zen-ship
cit-i-zen-ry
  cit-i-zen-ries
cit-rate

cit-ric
cit-ron
cit-ron-el-la
cit-rus
cit-tern
city
  cit-ies
ci-ty-state
civ-et
civ-ic
  civ-ics
civ-il
ci-vil-ian
ci-vil-i-ty
  ci-vil-i-ties
civ-i-li-za-tion
civ-i-lize
  civ-i-lized
  civ-i-liz-ing
clab-ber
claim
  claim-a-ble
  claim-ant
  claim-er
clair-voy-ance
  clair-voy-ant
clam
  clammed
  clam-ming
clam-bake
clam-bar
clam-my
  clam-mi-er
  clam-mi-est
  clam-mi-ly
  clam-mi-ness
clam-or
  clam-or-ous
clan
  clan-nish
clan-des-tine
clang-or
  clang-or-ous
clans-man
  clans-men
clap
  clapped
  clap-ping
clap-board
clap-per
clap-trap
claque
clar-et

clar-i-fy
  clar-i-fied
  clar-i-fy-ing
  clar-i-fi-ca-tion
clar-i-net
  clar-i-net-ist
clar-i-on
clar-i-ty
class-a-ble
clas-sic
  clas-si-cal
  clas-si-cal-ly
clas-si-cism
  clas-si-cist
clas-si-fy
  clas-si-fied
  clas-si-fy-ing
  clas-si-fi-er
  clas-si-fi-ca-tion
class-mate
class-room
class-y
  class-i-er
  class-i-est
clat-ter
clause
  claus-i-cle
claus-tro-pho-bia
clav-i-chord
clav-i-cle
cla-vier
clay
  clay-ey
clay-more
clean-cut
clean-er
clean-ly
  clean-li-er
  clean-li-est
  clean-li-ness
cleanse
  cleansed
  cleans-ing
  cleans-er
clean-up
clear
  clear-ly
  clear-ness
clear-ance
clear-cut
clear-ing
clear-sight-ed
cleav-age

cleave
  cleaved
  cleav-ing
cleav-er
clef
cleft
clem-en-cy
  clem-ent
clere-sto-ry
  clere-sto-riees
cler-gy
  cler-gies
cler-gy-man
  cler-gy-men
cler-ic
  cler-i-cal
  cler-i-cal-ism
  cler-i-cal-ist
clev-er
  clev-er-ly
  clev-er-ness
clev-is
  clev-is-es
clew
cli-ent
cli-en-tele
cliff-hang-er
cli-mac-ter-ic
cli-mate
  cli-mat-ic
  cli-mat-i-cal
climb
  climb-a-ble
  climb-er
clinch-er
cling
  cling-ing
  cling-ing-ly
  cling-er
clin-ic
  clin-i-cal
  clin-i-cal-ly
clink-er
clip
  clipped
  clip-ping
clip-per
clique
  cliqu-ey
  cliqu-ish
clit-o-ris
clo-a-ca
  clo-a-cae

clo-a-cal
clob-ber
clock-wise
clock-work
clod
  clod-dish
  clod-dy
clog
  clog-ged
  clog-ging
clois-ter
  clois-tral
close
  closed
  clos-ing
  clos-est
  close-ly
  close-ness
close-fist-ed
close-mouthed
clos-et
  clos-et-ed
  clos-et-ing
close-up
clo-sure
clot
  clot-ted
  clot-ting
clothe
  clothed
  cloth-ing
clothes-horse
clothes-line
clothes-pin
cloth-ier
cloth-ing
clo-ture
cloud-burst
cloud-y
  cloud-i-er
  cloud-i-est
  cloud-i-ly
  cloud-i-ness
clo-ven
clo-ver
clo-ver-leaf
clown
  clown-ish
cloy
  cloy-ing-ly
club
  clubbed
  club-bing

club-foot
club-house
clump
  clumpy
clum-sy
  clum-si-er
  clum-si-est
  clum-si-ly
  clum-si-ness
clus-ter
coach-man
  coach-men
co-ag-u-late
  co-ag-u-lat-ed
  co-ag-u-lat-ing
  co-ag-u-la-tion
co-a-lesce
  co-a-lesced
  co-a-les-cing
  co-a-les-cence
  co-a-les-cent
co-a-li-tion
coarse
  coars-er
  coars-est
  coars-en
  coarse-ly
coast-er
coast-line
coat-ing
co-au-thor
coax
  coax-ing-ly
co-balt
cob-ble
  cob-bled
  cob-bling
cob-bler
cob-ble-stone
co-bra
cob-web
  cob-webbed
  cob-web-by
co-ca
co-caine
coc-cyx
  coc-cy-ges
  coc-cyg-e-al
coch-le-a
cock-ade
cock-a-too
cock-crow
cock-er span-iel

cock-eyed
cock-fight
cock-le
cock-le-bur
cock-le-shell
cock-ney
  cock-neys
cock-pit
cock-roach
cocks-comb
cock-sure
cock-tail
cocky
  cock-i-er
  cock-i-est
  cock-i-ness
co-coa
co-co-nut
co-coon
cod
  cod-fish
cod-dle
  cod-dled
  cod-dling
code
  cod-ed
  cod-ing
co-deine
codg-er
cod-i-cil
cod-i-fy
  cod-i-fied
  cod-i-fy-ing
  cod-i-fi-ca-tion
cod-liv-er oil
co-ed
co-ed-u-ca-tion
coe-len-ter-ate
co-e-qual
co-erce
  co-erced
  co-er-cing
  co-er-ci-ble
  co-er-cion
  co-er-cive
co-ex-ist
  co-ex-ist-ence
  co-ex-ist-ent
cof-fee
cof-fee-house
cof-fee-pot
cof-fer
cof-fin

co-gent
co-gen-cy
co-gent-ly
cog-i-tate
cog-i-tat-ed
cog-i-tat-ing
cog-i-ta-ble
cog-i-ta-tive
cog-nac
cog-nate
cog-ni-tion
cog-ni-tive
cog-ni-zance
cog-ni-zant
cog-wheel
co-hab-it
co-hab-i-ta-tion
co-here
co-hered
co-her-ing
co-her-ent
co-her-ence
co-her-en-cy
co-her-ent-ly
co-he-sion
co-he-sive
co-hes-sive-ly
co-hes-sive-ness
co-hort
coif-feur
coif-fure
coif-fured
coif-fur-ing
coin-age
co-in-cide
co-in-cid-ed
co-in-cid-ing
co-in-ci-dence
co-in-ci-den-tal
co-in-ci-den-tal-ly
co-i-tion
co-i-tus
co-i-tal
coke
coked
cok-ing
co-la
col-an-der
cold-blood-ed
cole-slaw
col-ic
col-icky
col-i-se-um

co-li-tis
col-lab-o-rate
col-lab-o-rat-ed
col-lab-o-rat-ing
col-lab-o-ra-tion
col-lab-o-ra-tor
col-lage
col-lapse
col-lapsed
col-laps-ing
col-lap-si-ble
col-lar
col-lar-bone
col-late
col-lat-ed
col-lat-ing
col-la-tion
col-la-tor
col-lat-er-al
col-league
col-lect
col-lect-i-ble
col-lec-tor
col-lect-ed
col-lec-tion
col-lec-tive
col-lec-tive-ly
col-lec-tiv-i-ty
col-lec-tiv-ism
col-lec-tiv-ize
col-lec-tiv-iz-ing
col-lec-tiv-i-za-tion
col-lege
col-le-gi-al
col-le-gian
col-le-giate
col-lide
col-lid-ed
col-lid-ing
col-li-sion
col-li-mate
col-li-mat-ed
col-li-mat-ing
col-li-ma-tion
col-lo-cate
col-lo-cat-ed
col-lo-cat-ing
col-lo-ca-tion
col-loid
col-lo-qui-al
col-lo-qui-al-ly
col-lo-qui-al-ism
col-lo-quy

col-lo-quies
col-lu-sion
col-lu-sive
co-logne
co-lon
colo-nel
co-lo-ni-al
co-lo-ni-al-ism
co-lo-ni-al-ist
col-o-nist
col-o-nade
col-o-ny
col-o-nies
col-o-nize
col-o-nized
col-o-niz-ing
col-o-niz-er
col-o-ni-za-tion
col-or
col-or-er
col-or-less
col-or-a-tion
col-or-blind
col-or-blind-ness
col-or-cast
col-ored
col-or-fast
col-or-ful
col-or-ing
co-los-sal
co-los-sus
co-los-si
colt-ish
col-um-bine
col-umn
co-lum-nar
co-lumned
col-um-nist
co-ma
co-mas
co-ma-tose
com-bat
com-bat-ed
com-bat-ing
com-bat-ant
com-ba-tive
comb-er
com-bi-na-tion
com-bi-na-tion-al
com-bi-na-tive
com-bine
com-bined
com-bin-ing

com-bin-a-ble
com-bin-er
com-bo
com-bos
com-bust-ti-ble
com-bus-ti-bil-i-ty
con-bus-tion
com-bus-tive
come
com-ing
come-back
co-me-di-an
co-me-di-enne
come-down
com-e-dy
com-e-dies
come-ly
come-li-ness
come-on
com-er
com-et
come-up-pance
com-fort
com-fort-a-ble
com-fort-a-bly
com-fort-er
com-fy
com-fi-er
com-fi-est
com-ic
com-i-cal
com-ing
com-i-ty
com-i-ties
com-ma
com-mas
com-mand
com-man-dant
com-man-deer
com-mand-er
com-mand-er-ship
com-mand-ment
com-man-do
com-man-dos
com-mem-o-rate
com-mem-o-rat-ed
com-mem-o-rat-ing
com-mem-o-ra-ble
com-mem-o-ra-tion
com-mem-o-ra-tive
com-mem-o-ra-to-ry
com-mence
com-menced

com-menc-ing
com-mence-ment
com-mend
com-mend-a-ble
com-mend-a-bly
com-men-da-tion
com-mend-a-to-ry
com-men-su-rate
com-men-su-rate-ly
com-men-su-ra-tion
com-ment
com-men-tary
com-men-tar-ies
com-men-ta-tor
com-merce
com-mer-cial
com-mer-cial-ism
com-mer-cial-ize
com-mer-cial-ized
com-mer-cial-iz-ing
com-mie
com-mis-er-ate
com-mis-er-at-ed
com-mis-er-at-ing
com-mis-er-a-tion
com-mis-er-a-tive
com-mis-sar
com-mis-sar-y
com-mis-sar-ies
com-mis-sion
com-mis-sioned
com-mis-sion-er
com-mit
com-mit-ted
com-mit-ting
com-mit-ment
com-mit-tee
com-mit-tee-man
com-mit-tee-wo-man
com-mode
com-mo-di-ous
com-mod-i-ty
com-mod-i-ties
com-mo-dore
com-mon
com-mon-al-ty
com-mon-al-ties
com-mon-place
com-mons
com-mon-wealth
com-mo-tion
com-mu-nal
com-mu-nal-i-ty

com-mune
com-muned
com-mun-ing
com-mu-ni-cant
com-mu-ni-cate
com-mu-ni-cat-ed
com-mu-ni-cat-ing
com-mu-ni-ca-ble
com-mu-ni-ca-tive
com-mu-ni-ca-tion
com-mun-ion
com-mun-ism
com-mun-ist
com-mu-ni-ty
com-mu-ni-ties
com-mu-nize
com-mu-nized
com-mu-niz-ing
com-mu-ta-tion
com-mu-ta-tor
com-mute
com-mut-ed
com-mut-ing
com-mut-a-ble
com-mut-er
com-pact
com-pan-ion
com-pan-ion-a-ble
com-pan-ion-ship
com-pa-ny
com-pa-nies
com-par-a-ble
com-par-a-bil-ity
com-par-a-tive
com-pare
com-pared
com-par-ing
com-par-i-son
com-part-ment
com-part-men-tal
com-part-ment-ed
com-part-men-tal-ize
com-pass
com-pas-sion
com-pas-sion-ate
com-pat-ible
com-pat-i-bly
com-pat-i-bil-i-ty
com-pa-tri-ot
com-peer
com-pel
com-pelled
com-pel-ling

com-pem-di-ous
com-pen-di-um
com-pen-sate
com-pen-sat-ed
com-pen-sat-ing
com-pen-sa-tive
com-pen-sa-tor
com-pen-sa-to-ry
com-pen-sa-tion
com-pete
com-pet-ed
com-pet-ing
com-pet-i-tor
com-pe-tence
com-pe-ten-cy
com-pe-tent
com-pe-ti-tion
com-pet-i-tive
com-pile
com-piled
com-pil-ing
com-pi-la-tion
com-pla-cence
com-pla-cen-cy
com-pla-cent
com-plain
com-plain-ant
com-plaint
com-plai-sance
com-plai-sant
com-plect-ed
com-ple-ment
com-ple-men-tal
com-ple-men-ta-ry
com-plete
com-plet-ed
com-plet-ing
com-plet-a-ble
com-ple-tion
com-plex
com-plex-ion
com-plex-ioned
com-plex-i-ty
com-plex-i-ties
com-pli-ance
com-pli-an-cy
com-pli-ant
com-pli-cate
com-pli-cat-ed
com-pli-cat-ing
com-pli-ca-tion
com-plic-i-ty
com-plic-i-ties

com-pli-ment
com-pli-men-ta-ri-ly
com-ply
com-plied
com-ply-ing
com-po-nent
com-port
com-port-ment
com-pose
com-posed
com-pos-ing
com-pos-er
com-pos-ite
com-po-si-tion
com-post
com-po-sure
com-pote
com-pound
com-pre-hend
com-pre-hend-i-ble
com-pre-hen-si-ble
com-pre-hen-si-bly
com-pre-hen-sion
com-pre-hen-sive
com-press
com-presed
com-press-i-ble
com-press-i-bil-ity
com-pres-sion
com-pres-sor
com-prise
com-prised
com-pris-ing
com-pro-mise
com-pro-mised
com-pro-mis-ing
comp-trol-ler
com-pul-sion
com-pul-sive
com-pul-so-ry
com-punc-tion
com-pute
com-put-ed
com-put-ing
com-pu-ta-tion
com-pu-ter
com-put-er-ize
com-put-er-ized
com-put-er-iz-ing
com-put-er-i-za-tion
com-rade
com-rade-ship
com-sat

con
conned
con-ning
con-cave
con-ceal
con-ceal-a-ble
con-ceal-ment
con-cede
con-ced-ed
con-ced-ing
con-ceit
con-ceit-ed
con-ceive
con-ceived
con-ceiv-ing
con-ceiv-a-ble
con-ceiv-a-bly
con-cen-trate
con-cen-tra-ted
con-cen-trat-ing
con-cen-tra-tive
con-cen-tra-tion
con-cen-tric
con-cen-tri-cal
con-cen-tric-i-ty
con-cept
con-cep-tu-al
con-cep-tion
con-cep-tive
con-cep-tu-al-ize
con-cep-tu-al-ized
con-cep-tu-al-iz-ing
con-cern
con-cerned
con-cern-ing
con-cert
con-cert-ed
con-cer-ti-na
con-cert-mas-ter
con-cer-to
con-ces-sion
con-ces-sion-aire
conch
conchs
con-cil-i-ate
con-cil-i-at-ed
con-cil-i-at-ing
con-cil-i-a-tion
con-cil-i-a-to-ry
con-cise
con-cise-ness
con-cise-ly
con-clave

con-clude
con-clud-ed
con-clud-ing
con-clu-sion
con-clu-sive
con-coct
con-coc-tion
con-com-i-tant
con-com-i-tance
con-cord
con-cord-ance
con-cord-ant
con-course
con-crete
con-cret-ed
con-cret-ing
con-cre-tion
con-cre-tive
con-cu-bine
con-cur
con-curred
con-cur-ring
con-cur-rence
con-cur-rent
con-cus-sion
con-cus-sive
con-demn
con-dem-na-ble
con-dem-na-tion
con-dem-na-to-ry
con-dense
con-densed
con-dens-ing
con-den-sa-ble
con-den-sa-tion
con-dens-er
con-de-scend
con-de-scend-ing
con-de-scen-sion
con-di-ment
con-di-tion
con-di-tion-al
con-di-tion-er
con-di-tion-ed
con-dole
con-doled
con-dol-ing
con-do-la-to-ry
con-do-ler
con-do-lence
con-dom
con-do-min-i-um
con-done

con-doned
con-don-ing
con-do-na-tion
con-dor
con-duce
con-duced
con-duc-ing
con-duct
con-duct-i-bil-i-ty
con-duct-i-ble
con-duct-ance
con-duc-tion
con-fer-ence
con-fer-en-tial
con-fess
con-fess-ed-ly
con-fes-sion
con-fes-sion-al
con-fes-sor
con-fet-ti
con-fi-dant
con-fi-dante
con-fide
con-fid-ed
con-fid-ing
con-fi-dence
con-fi-dent
con-fi-den-tial
con-fig-u-ra-tion
con-fig-u-ra-tion-al
con-fine
con-fined
con-fin-ing
con-fine-ment
con-firm
con-firm-a-ble
con-fir-ma-tion
con-fir-ma-tive
con-fir-ma-to-ry
con-fir-med
con-firm-ed-ly
con-firm-ed-ness
con-fis-cate
con-fis-cat-ed
con-fis-cat-ing
con-fis-ca-tion
con-fis-ca-tor
con-fis-ca-to-ry
con-fla-gra-tion
con-flict
con-flict-ing
con-flic-tive
con-flic-tion

con-flu-ence
con-flu-ent
con-flux
con-form
con-form-ist
con-form-ism
con-form-a-ble
con-form-a-bly
con-form-ance
con-for-ma-tion
con-form-i-ty
con-form-i-ties
con-found
con-found-ed
con-found-ed-ly
con-front
con-fron-ta-tion
con-fuse
confused
con-fus-ing
con-fus-ed-ly
con-fus-ed-ness
con-fu-sion
con-fute
con-futed
con-fut-ing
con-fu-ta-tion
con-ga
con-gas
con-geal
con-geal-ment
con-gen-ial
con-ge-ni-al-i-ty
con-gen-ial-ly
con-gen-i-tal
con-ger
con-ge-ries
con-gest
con-ges-tion
con-ges-tive
con-glom-er-ate
con-glom-er-at-ing
con-glom-er-a-tion
con-grat-u-late
con-grat-u-lat-ed
con-grat-u-lat-ing
con-grat-u-la-tor
con-grat-u-la-to-ry
con-grat-u-la-tion
con-gre-gate
con-gre-gat-ed
con-gre-gat-ing
con-gre-ga-tion

con-gre-ga-tion-al
con-gress
con-gres-sion-al
con-gress-man
con-gress-men
con-gress-wom-an
con-gress-wom-en
con-gru-ent
con-gru-ent-ly
con-gru-ence
con-gru-en-cy
con-gru-en-cies
con-gru-i-ty
con-gru-i-ties
con-gru-ous
con-gru-ous-ly
con-ic
con-i-cal
co-ni-fer
con-jec-ture
con-jec-tured
con-jec-tur-ing
con-jec-tur-al
con-join
con-joint
con-joint-ly
con-ju-gal
con-ju-gal-ly
con-ju-gate
con-ju-gat-ed
con-ju-gat-ing
con-ju-ga-tion
con-ju-ga-tive
con-junc-tion
con-junc-tive
con-jur-a-tion
con-jure
con-jured
con-jur-ing
con-jur-er
con-nect
con-nec-tor
con-nec-tion
con-nec-tive
con-nip-tion
con-nive
con-nived
con-niv-ing
con-niv-ance
con-nois-seur
con-note
con-not-ed
con-not-ing

con-no-ta-tion
con-no-ta-tive
con-nu-bi-al
con-ni-bi-al-ly
con-quer
con-quer-a-ble
con-quer-or
con-quest
con-quis-ta-dor
con-quis-ta-dors
con-quis-ta-dor-es
con-san-quin-e-ous
con-san-quin-i-ty
con-science
con-sci-en-tious
con-sci-en-tious-ly
con-scious
con-scious-ly
con-scious-ness
con-script
con-scrip-tion
con-se-crate
con-se-crat-ed
con-se-crat-ing
con-se-cra-tive
con-se-cra-tion
con-sec-u-tive
con-sec-u-tive-ly
con-sen-sus
con-sent
con-sent-er
con-se-quence
con-se-quent
con-se-quent-ly
con-se-quen-tial
con-se-quen-ti-al-i-ty
con-se-quen-tial-ly
con-ser-va-tion
con-ser-va-tion-al
con-ser-va-tion-ist
con-serv-a-tive
con-serv-a-tism
con-ser-va-tive-ly
con-serv-a-to-ry
con-serv-a-to-ries
con-serve
con-served
con-serv-ing
con-serv-a-ble
con-serv-er
con-sid-er
con-sid-er-a-ble
con-sid-er-a-bly

con-sid-er-ate
con-sid-er-a-tion
con-sid-er-ing
con-sign
con-sign-er
con-sign-or
con-sign-ment
con-sign-ee
con-sist
con-sist-en-cy
con-sist-en-cies
con-sist-ence
con-sist-ent
con-sist-ent-ly
con-sis-to-ry
con-sis-to-ries
con-so-la-tion
con-sol-a-to-ry
con-sole
con-soled
con-sol-ing
con-sol-a-ble
con-sol-i-date
con-sol-i-dat-ed
con-sol-i-dat-ing
con-sol-i-da-tion
con-so-nant
con-so-nance
con-so-nant-ly
con-so-nan-tal
con-sort
con-sor-ti-um
con-sor-tia
con-spic-u-ous
con-spic-u-ous-ly
con-spic-u-ous-ness
con-spire
con-spired
con-spir-ing
con-spir-a-cy
con-spir-a-cies
con-spir-a-tor
con-spir-a-to-ri-al
con-spir-er
con-spir-ing-ly
con-sta-ble
con-sta-ble-ship
con-stab-u-lar-y
con-stab-u-lar-ies
con-stant
con-stan-cy
con-stant-ly
con-stel-la-tion

con-ster-na-tion
con-sti-pate
  con-sti-pa-tion
con-stit-u-en-cy
  con-stit-u-en-cies
con-stit-u-ent
con-sti-tute
con-sti-tu-tion
  con-sti-tu-tion-al
  con-sti-tu-tion-al-i-ty
  con-sti-tu-tion-al-ly
con-strain
  con-strain-a-ble
  con-strained
con-straint
con-strict
  con-stric-tive
  con-stric-tion
con-stric-tor
con-struct
  con-struc-tor
con-struc-tion
  con-struc-tion-al
con-struc-tive
  con-struc-tive-ly
  con-struc-tive-ness
con-strue
  con-strued
  con-stru-ing
  con-stru-a-ble
  con-stru-er
con-sul
  con-su-lar
  con-sul-ship
con-su-late
con-sult
  con-sul-ta-tion
con-sult-ant
con-sume
  con-sumed
  con-sum-ing
  con-sum-a-ble
con-sum-er
con-sum-mate
  con-sum-mat-ed
  con-sum-mat-ing
  con-sum-mate-ly
  con-sum-ma-tion
con-sump-tion
com-sump-tive
con-tact
con-ta-gion
  con-ta-gious

con-ta-gious-ness
con-tain
  con-tain-a-ble
con-tain-er
con-tain-ment
con-tam-i-nate
  con-tam-i-nat-ed
  con-tam-i-nat-ing
  con-tam-i-nant
  con-tam-i-na-tion
  con-tam-i-na-tive
  con-tam-i-na-tor
con-tem-plate
  con-tem-plat-ed
  con-tem-plat-ing
  con-tem-pla-tion
  con-tem-pla-tive
con-tem-po-ra-ne-ous
con-tem-po-rar-y
  con-tem-po-rar-ies
con-tempt
  con-tempt-i-ble
  con-tempt-i-bly
con-temp-tu-ous
  con-temp-tu-ous-ly
con-tend
  con-tend-er
con-tent
  con-tent-ment
con-tent-ed
  con-tent-ed-ly
  con-tent-ed-ness
con-ten-tion
con-ten-tious
  con-ten-tious-ly
  con-ten-tious-ness
con-ter-mi-ous
con-test
  con-test-a-ble
  con-test-er
con-test-ant
con-text
con-tig-u-ous
  con-ti-gu-i-ty
  con-ti-gu-i-ties
  con-tig-u-ous-ly
  con-tig-u-ous-ness
con-ti-nence
  con-ti-nen-cy
con-ti-nent
  con-ti-nent-ly
  con-ti-nen-tal
con-tin-gent

con-tin-gen-cies
con-tin-gent-ly
con-tin-u-al
  con-tin-u-al-ly
con-tin-u-ance
con-tin-ue
  con-tin-ued
  con-tin-u-ing
  con-tin-u-a-tion
  con-tin-u-er
con-ti-nu-i-ty
  con-ti-nu-i-ties
con-tin-u-ous
  con-tin-u-ous-ly
con-tin-u-um
  con-tin-ua
con-tort
  con-tor-tion
  con-tor-tive
  con-tor-tion-ist
con-tour
con-tra-band
can-tra-cep-tive
  con-tra-cep-tion
con-tract
  con-tract-ed
  con-tract-i-ble
  con-trac-tu-al
con-trac-tion
  con-trac-tive
  con-trac-tile
con-trac-tor
con-tra-dict
  con-tra-dict-a-ble
  con-tra-dic-tion
  con-tra-dic-to-ry
con-tra-dis-tinc-tion
con-trail
con-tral-to
  con-tral-tos
  con-tral-ti
con-trap-tion
con-tra-pun-tal
con-tra-ri-wise
con-tra-ry
  con-tra-ries
  con-tra-ri-ly
  con-tra-ri-ness
con-trast
  con-trast-a-ble
  con-trast-ing-ly
con-tra-vene
  con-tra-vened

con-tra-ven-ing
con-tra-ven-er
con-tra-ven-tion
con-trib-ute
con-trib-ut-ed
con-trib-ut-ing
con-trib-ut-a-ble
con-trib-u-tor
con-trib-u-tory
con-tri-bu-tion
con-trite
con-trite-ly
con-trite-ness
con-tri-tion
con-trive
con-triv-ed
con-triv-ing
con-triv-ance
con-trol
con-trolled
con-trol-ling
con-trol-la-ble
con-trol-ler
con-trol-ler-ship
con-tro-ver-sy
con-tro-ver-sies
con-tro-ver-sal
con-tro-ver-sial-ly
con-tro-vert
con-tu-me-ly
con-tu-me-lies
con-tuse
con-tused
con-tus-ing
con-tu-sion
co-nun-drum
cov-va-lesce
con-va-lesced
con-va-les-cing
con-va-les-cence
con-va-les-cent
con-vec-tion
con-vene
con-vened
con-ven-ing
con-ven-er
con-ven-ience
con-ven-ient
con-ven-ient-ly
con-vent
con-ven-tion
con-ven-tion-al
con-ven-tion-al-ism

con-ven-tion-al-ist
con-ven-tion-al-i-ty
con-ven-tion-al-i-ties
con-ven-tion-al-ize
con-ven-tion-al-ized
con-ven-tion-al-iz-ing
con-verge
con-verged
con-verg-ing
con-ver-gence
con-ver-gen-cy
con-ver-gent
con-ver-sant
con-ver-sa-tion
con-ver-sa-tion-al
con-ver-sa-tion-al-ist
con-verse
con-versed
con-vers-ing
con-verse-ly
con-ver-sion
con-vert
con-vert-er
con-vert-i-ble
con-vert-i-bil-i-ty
con-vert-i-bly
con-vex
con-vex-ly
con-vex-i-ty
con-vey
con-vey-a-ble
con-vey-ance
con-vey-er
con-vey-or
con-vict
con-vic-tion
con-vic-tion-al
con-vince
con-vinced
con-vinc-ing
con-vinc-er
con-vinc-i-ble
con-viv-i-al
con-viv-i-al-i-ty
con-viv-i-al-ly
con-vo-ca-tion
con-vo-ca on-al
con-voke
con-voked
con-vok-ing
con-vok-er
con-vo-lute
con-vo-lut-ed

con-vo-lut-ing
con-vo-lute-ly
con-vo-lu-tion
con-voy
con-vulse
con-vulsed
con-vuls-ing
con-vul-sion
con-vul-sive
con-vul-sive-ly
co-ny
coo
cooed
coo-ing
coo-ing-ly
cook-book
cook-er-y
cook-e-ries
cook-out
cool
cool-ish
cool-ly
cool-ness
cool-ant
cool-er
coo-lie
coo-lies
coon-skin
coop-er
coop-er-age
co-op-er-ate
co-op-er-at-ed
co-op-er-at-ing
co-op-er-a-tion
co-op-er-a-tive
co-op-er-a-tive-ly
co-opt
co-op-ta-tion
co-or-di-nate
co-or-di-nat-ed
co-or-di-nat-ing
co-or-di-nate-ly
co-or-di-na-tor
co-or-di-na-tion
coo-tie
cop
copped
cop-ping
cope-stone
co-pi-lot
co-pi-ous
co-pi-ous-ly
co-pi-ous-ness

cop-out
cop-per
  cop-per-y
cop-per-head
cop-per-plate
cop-pice
cop-ra
copse
cop-u-la
  cop-u-las
  cop-u-lae
  cop-u-lar
cop-u-late
  cop-u-lat-ed
  cop-u-lat-ing
  cop-u-la-tion
cop-u-la-tive
  cop-u-la-tive-ly
copy
  cop-ies
  cop-ied
  cop-y-ing
cop-y-book
cop-y-cat
cop-y-ist
cop-y-right
co-quet
  co-quet-ted
  co-quet-ting
co-quet-ry
  co-quet-ries
co-quette
  co-quet-tish
  co-quet-tish-ly
cor-a-cle
cor-al
cor-bel
cord-age
cor-date
  cor-date-ly
cor-dial
  cor-dial-i-ty
  cor-dial-ness
  cor-dial-ly
cor-dil-le-ra
cord-ite
cor-don
cor-do-van
cor-du-roy
cord-wood
core
  cored
  cor-ing

co-re-la-tion
co-re-spond-ent
co-ri-an-der
cor-ker
cork-screw
corn-cob
cor-nea
  cor-ne-al
cor-ner
cor-ner-stone
cor-net
  cor-net-ist
corn-flow-er
cor-nice
corn-starch
cor-nu-co-pi-a
corn-y
  corn-i-er
  conr-i-est
co-rol-la
cor-ol-lar-y
  cor-ol-lar-ies
co-ro-na
  co-ro-nas
  co-ro-nae
cor-o-nar-y
cor-o-na-tion
cor-o-ner
  cor-o-ner-ship
cor-o-net
  cor-o-net-ed
cor-po-ral
cor-po-rate
  cor-po-rate-ly
  cor-po-ra-tive
cor-po-ra-tion
cor-po-rat-ism
cor-po-re-al
  cor-po-re-al-i-ty
  cor-po-re-al-ness
corps
corpse
corps-man
  corps-men
cor-pu-lent
  cor-pu-lence
  cor-pu-len-cy
cor-pus
cor-pus-cle
  cor-pus-cu-lar
cor-ral
  cor-ralled
  cor-ral-ling

cor-rect
  cor-rect-a-ble
  cor-rect-i-ble
  cor-rect-ness
  cor-rec-tor
cor-rec-tion
  cor-rec-tion-al
cor-rec-tive
cor-re-late
  cor-re-lat-ed
  cor-re-lat-ing
cor-re-la-tion
cor-rel-a-tive
cor-re-spond
  cor-re-spond-ing
  cor-re-spond-ing-ly
cor-re-spond-ence
cor-re-spond-ent
cor-ri-dor
cor-ri-gi-ble
  cor-ri-gi-bil-i-ty
  cor-ri-gi-bly
cor-rob-o-rate
  cor-rob-o-rat-ed
  cor-rob-o-rat-ing
  cor-rob-o-ra-tion
  cor-rob-o-ra-tive
  cor-rob-o-ra-to-ry
cor-rode
  cor-rod-ed
  cor-rod-ing
  cor-rod-i-ble
cor-ro-sion
cor-ro-sive
cor-ru-gate
  cor-ru-gat-ed
  cor-ru-gat-ing
  cor-ru-ga-tion
cor-rupt
  cor-rupt-er
  cor-rup-ti-ble
  cor-rup-ti-bil-i-ty
  cor-rupt-ly
  cor-rupt-ness
  cor-rup-tion
cor-sage
cor-sair
cor-set
  cor-set-ed
cor-tex
  cor-ti-ces
cor-ti-cal
cor-ti-sone

co-run-dum
co-sig-na-to-ry
cos-met-ic
cos-mic
  cos-mi-cal-ly
cos-mog-o-ny
  cos-mog-o-nies
  cos-mo-gon-ic
  cos-mog-o-nist
cos-mog-o-ny
  cos-mog-o-nist
cos-mog-ra-phy
  cos-mog-ra-phies
  cos-mog-ra-pher
  cos-mo-graph-ic
cos-mol-o-gy
  cos-mol-o-gies
  cos-mo-log-ic
  cos-mol-o-gist
cos-mo-naut
cos-mo-pol-i-tan
  cos-mo-pol-i-tan-ism
cos-mop-o-lite
cos-mos
cost-ly
  cost-li-er
  cost-li-est
  cost-li-ness
cost--plus
cos-tume
  cos-tumed
  cos-tum-ing
cos-tum-er
co-sy
  co-si-er
  cos-i-est
co-te-rie
co-ter-mi-nous
co-til-lion
cot-tage
cot-ter
cot-ton
  cot-ton-y
cot-ton-mouth
cot-ton-seed
cot-ton-tail
cot-ton-wood
couch
coun-cil
  coun-cil-or
  coun-cil-man
  coun-cil-lor-ship
count

count-a-ble
count-down
coun-te-nance
  coun-te-nanced
  coun-te-nanc-ing
  coun-te-nanc-er
count-er
coun-ter-act
  coun-ter-ac-tion
  coun-ter-ac-tive
coun-ter-at-tack
coun-ter-charge
  coun-ter-charged
  coun-ter-char-ging
coun-ter-claim
  coun-ter-claim-ant
coun-ter-clock-wise
coun-ter-cul-ture
coun-ter-es-pi-o-nage
coun-ter-feit
  coun-ter-feit-er
coun-ter-in-tel-li-gence
coun-ter-mand
coun-ter-meas-ure
coun-ter-of-fen-sive
coun-ter-pane
coun-ter-part
coun-ter-point
coun-ter-poise
  coun-ter-poised
  coun-ter-pois-ing
coun-ter-rev-o-lu-tion
coun-ter-sign
  coun-ter-sig-na-ture
coun-ter-sink
  coun-ter-sank
  coun-ter-sunk
coun-ter-spy
  coun-ter-spies
coun-ter-weight
coun-tees
  count-less
coun-tri-fied
coun-try
  coun-tries
coun-try-man
  coun-try-men
  coun-try-wom-an
  coun-try-wom-en
coun-try-side
coun-ty
  coun-ties
coup

coups
coup-le
  coup-led
  coup-ling
coup-ler
cou-pon
cour-age
  cou-ra-geous
cour-i-er
course
  coursed
  cours-ing
cours-er
cour-te-ous
  cour-te-ous-ly
cour-te-sy
  cour-te-sies
court-house
cour-ti-er
court-ly
  court-li-er
  court-li-est
court-mar-tial
  courts-mar-tial
  court-mar-tialed
court-room
court-ship
cous-in
  cous-in-hood
  cous-in-ly
cou-tu-rier
cov-e-nant
  cov-e-nan-ter
  cov-e-nan-tor
cov-er-age
cov-er-all
cov-er-let
cov-ert
  cov-ert-ly
  cov-ert-ness
cov-er-up
cov-et
  cov-et-a-ble
  cov-et-er
cov-et-ous
  cov-et-ous-ly
cov-ey
cow-ard
  cow-ard-ly
  cow-ard-ice
cow-boy
cow-er
  cow-er-ing-ly

cow-hide
cowl
  cowled
cow-lick
cow-man
  cow-men
co-work-er
cow-poke
cow-ry
  cow-rie
  cow-ries
cox-swain
coy
  coy-ly
coy-o-te
coz-en
  coz-en-age
  coz-en-er
crab
  crabbed
  crab-bing
  crab-by
crack-down
crack-er
crack-ing
crack-le
  crack-led
  crack-ling
crack-up
cra-dle
  cra-dled
  cra-dling
crafts-man
  crafts-man-ship
crafty
  craft-i-er
  craft-i-est
  craft-i-ly
  craft-i-ness
crag
  crag-ged
  crag-gy
  crag-gi-ness
cram
  crammed
  cram-ming
  cram-mer
cran-ber-ry
  cran-ber-ries
crane
  craned
  cran-ing
cra-ni-um

cra-ni-ums
cra-nia
cra-ni-al
cra-ni-ate
cra-ni-al-ly
crank-case
crank-shaft
crank-y
  crank-i-er
  crank-i-est
  crank-i-ly
  crank-i-ness
cran-ny
  cran-nies
  cran-nied
crash-land
crass
  crass-ly
  crass-ness
crate
  crat-ed
  crat-ing
cra-ter
  cra-ter-al
  cra-tered
cra-vat
crave
  craved
  crav-ing
  crav-er
  crav-ing-ly
craw-fish
crawl
  crawl-y
  crawl-ing-ly
crawl-er
cray-fish
cray-on
craze
  craz-ing
cra-zy
  cra-zi-er
  cra-zi-est
  cra-zi-ly
cream-er
cream-er-y
  cream-er-ies
cre-ate
  cre-at-ed
  cre-at-ing
cre-a-tion
  cre-a-tion-al
cre-a-tive

  cre-a-tive-i-ty
cre-a-tor
crea-ture
cre-dence
cre-den-za
cred-i-ble
  cred-i-bil-i-ty
  cred-i-bly
cred-it
  cred-it-a-ble
  cred-it-a-bil-i-ty
  cred-it-a-bly
cred-i-tor
cre-do
  cre-dos
cred-u-lous
creek
creel
cre-ma-to-ry
  cre-ma-to-ri-um
cre-o-sote
crepe
  creped
  crep-ing
cre-pus-cu-lar
cres-cen-do
cres-cent
crest
  crest-ed
  crest-less
crest-fall-en
cre-tin-ism
cre-tonne
crev-ice
crew-el
crib
  cribbed
  crib-bing
  crib-ber
crib-bage
crick-et
crim-i-nal
  crim-i-nal-i-ty
  crim-i-nal-ly
crim-i-nol-o-gy
  crim-i-nol-o-gist
crimpy
  crimp-i-er
  crimp-i-est
crim-son
cringe
  cringed
  cring-ing

crin-kle
 crin-kled
 crin-kli-est
crip-ple
 crip-pled
 crip-pling
cri-sis
 cri-ses
criss-cross
cri-te-ri-on
cri-te-ria
crit-ic
crit-i-cal
 crit-i-cal-ly
 crit-i-cal-ness
crit-i-cism
crit-i-cize
 crit-i-cized
 crit-i-ciz-ing
 crit-i-ciz-a-ble
cri-tique
crit-er
croak-y
 croak-i-er
 croak-i-est
crois-sant
cro-ny
 cro-nies
crook-ed
croon-er
crop
 cropped
 crop-ping
 crop-per
cro-quette
cross-bar
cross-bow
cross-bred
 cross-breed
 cross-breed-ing
cross-coun-try
cross-cut
cross-ex-am-ine
 cross-ex-am-ined
 cross-ex-am-in-ing
cross-fer-ti-li-za-tion
cross-ing
cross-pol-li-na-tion
 cross-pol-li-nate
cross-pur-pose
cross-ref-er-ence
cross-stitch
cross-ways

crotch-ety
 crotch-et-i-ness
crouch
croup
 croupy
crou-pi-er
crou-ton
crow-bar
crow's--foot
 crow's--feet
crow's--nest
cru-cial
 cru-ci-al-i-ty
 cru-cial-ly
cru-ci-ble
cru-ci-fix
cru-ci-fix-ion
cru-ci-form
cru-ci-fy
 cru-ci-fied
 cru-ci-fy-ing
crude
 crud-er
 crud-est
 crude-ly
 crude-ness
cru-di-ty
cru-di-ties
cru-el
 cru-el-ly
cru-et
cruise
 cruised
 cruis-ing
cruis-er
crul-ler
crum-ble
 crum-bled
 crum-bling
 crum-bly
crunchy
 crunch-i-er
 crunch-i-est
cru-sade
 cru-sad-er
crush-er
 crush-ing
 crush-ing-ly
crus-ta-cean
crust-y
 crust-i-er
cry
 cried

cry-ing
cry-ba-by
cry-o-gen-ics
cry-o-sur-gery
crypt
 crypt-al
crypt-a-nal-y-sis
crypt-ic
 cryp-ti-cal
 cryp-ti-cal-ly
cryp-to-gram
cryp-to-graph
 cryp-tog-ra-phy
 cryp-to-graph-ic
 cryp-tog-ra-pher
crys-tal
crys-tal-line
crys-tal-lize
 crys-tal-lized
 crys-tal-liz-ing
 crys-tal-liz-er
 crys-tal-liz-a-ble
 crys-tal-li-za-tion
cub-by
 cub-bies
cu-bic
cu-bi-cle
cu-bit
cuck-old
 cuck-old-ry
cudg-el
 cudg-eled
 cudg-el-ing
cui-sine
cul-de-sac
 culs-de-sac
cu-li-nary
cul-mi-nant
cul-mi-nate
 cul-mi-nat-ed
 cul-mi-nat-ing
 cul-mi-na-tion
cu-lottes
cul-pa-ble
 cul-pa-bil-i-ty
 cul-pa-bly
cul-prit
cult
 cul-tic
cul-ti-vate
 cul-ti-vat-ed
 cul-ti-vat-ing
 cul-ti-va-tion

52

cul-ti-va-ble
cul-ti-vat-a-ble
cul-ti-va-tor
cul-tur-al
cul-ture
cul-tured
cul-tur-ing
cul-vert
cum-ber
cum-ber-some
cum-brance
cum lau-de
cum-mer-bound
cum-mu-late
cum-mu-lat-ed
cum-mu-lat-ing
cum-mu-la-tion
cum-mu-la-tive
cu-ne-i-form
cum-ni-lin-gus
cun-ning
cun-ning-ly
cup-board
cup-ful
cup-fuls
cu-pid-i-ty
cu-po-la
cur-a-ble
cur-a-bil-i-ty
cur-a-bly
cu-rate
cur-a-tive
cu-ra-tor
cu-ra-to-ri-al
cu-ra-tor-ship
curb-ing
curb-stone
cur-dle
cur-dled
cur-dling
cure
cured
cur-ing
cure-all
cur-few
cu-ria
cu-ri-ae
cu-ri-al
cu-rie
cu-ri-o
cu-ri-os
cu-ri-os-i-ty
cu-ri-os-i-ties

cu-ri-ous
cu-ri-um
curl
curl-er
curl-i-cue
curly
curl-i-er
curl-i-est
cur-rant
cur-ren-cy
cur-ren-cies
cur-rent
cur-ric-u-lum
cur-ric-u-lums
cur-ric-u-la
cur-ri-c-u-lar
cur-rish
cur-ry
cur-ries
cur-ri-er
cur-ry-comb
curse
cur-sive
cur-sive-ly
curt
cur-tail
cur-tail-ment
cur-tain
curt-sy
curt-sies
curt-sied
curt-sy-ing
cur-va-ceous
cur-va-ture
curve
cruved
curv-ing
curv-ed-nesss
cur-vi-lin-e-ar
cush-ion
cush-y
cush-i-er
cush-i-est
cus-pid
cus-pi-dal
cus-pi-date
cus-pi-dor
cuss-ed
cuss-ed-ly
cuss-ed-ness
cus-tard
cus-to-dian
cus-to-di-an-ship

cus-to-dy
cus-to-dies
cus-to-di-al
cus-tom
cus-tom-ary
cus-tom-ar-ies
cus-tom-ar-i-ly
cus-tom-ar-i-ness
cus-tom-built
cus-tom-er
cus-tom-ize
cus-tom-ized
cus-tom-iz-ing
cus-tom-made
cu-ta-ne-ous
cu-ti-cle
cut-lery
cut-let
cut-ting
cut-ting-ly
cut-tle
cut-up
cy-an-ic
cy-cle
cy-clic
cy-cli-cal
cy-cli-cal-ly
cy-clom-e-ter
cy-clone
cy-clo-rama
cy-clo-ram-ic
cy-clo-tron
cyg-net
cyl-in-der
cy-lin-dric
cy-lin-dri-cal
cym-bal
cym-bal-ist
cyn-ic
cyn-i-cism
cyn-i-cal
cyn-i-cal-ly
cy-no-sure
cy-pher
cy-press
cyst
cys-tic
cys-tic fi-bro-sis
cy-tol-o-gy
cy-tol-o-gist
czar
czar-e-vitch
cza-ri-na

D

dab
 dabbed
 dab-bing
dab-ble
 dab-bled
 dab-bing
 dab-bler
dac-tyl
 dac-tyl-ic
dad-dy--long-legs
daf-fo-dil
daf-fy
 daf-fi-er
 daf-fi-est
dag-ger
da-guerre-o-type
dahl-ia
dai-ly
 dai-lies
dain-ty
 dain-ti-er
 dain-ti-est
 dain-ties
 dain-ti-ly
dai-qui-ri
dair-y
 dair-ies
dair-y-man
 dair-y-men
da-is
dai-sy
 dai-sies
dal-ly
 dal-lied
 dal-ly-ing
 dal-li-ance
dam-age
 dam-aged
 dam-ag-ing
 dam-age-a-ble
dam-a-scene
 dam-a-scened
 dam-a-scen-ing
dam-ask
damn
dam-na-ble
 dam-na-ble-ness
 dam-na-bly
dam-na-tion
damned
damp-en
damp-er
dam-sel

dam-son
dan-de-li-on
dan-der
dan-dle
 dan-dled
 dan-dling
dan-druff
dan-dy
 dan-dies
 dan-di-er
 dan-di-est
 dan-dy-ism
dan-ger
dan-ger-ous
 dan-ger-ous-ly
dan-gle
 dan-gled
 dan-gling
 dan-gler
dank
 dank-ly
 dank-ness
dan-seuse
 dan-seus-es
dap-per
dap-ple
 dap-pled
 dap-pling
dare
 dared
 dar-ing
dare-dev-il
 dar-ing-ly
dark
 dark-ish
 dark-ly
dark-en
dark-ling
dark-room
dar-ling
 dar-ling-ly
darn-er
dart-er
dash-board
dash-ing
das-tard
 das-tard-li-ness
 das-tard-ly
da-ta
date
 dat-ed
 dat-ing
 dat-a-ble

dat-er
date-less
date-line
da-tive
da-tum
daub
 daub-er
daugh-ter
 daugh-ter-ly
daugh-ter--in--law
 daugh-ters--in--law
daunt-less
 daunt-less-ly
 daunt-less-ness
dau-phin
dav-en-port
dav-it
daw-dle
 daw-dled
 daw-dling
 daw-dler
dawn
day-break
day-dream
 day-dream-er
day-light
day-time
daze
 dazed
 daz-ing
 daz-ed-ly
daz-zle
 daz-zled
dea-con
 dea-con-ry
 dea-con-ship
dea-con-ess
dead-beat
dead-en
 dead-en-er
dead-end
dead-line
dead-lock
dead-ly
 dead-li-er
 dead-li-est
 dead-li-ness
dead-pan
dead-wood
deaf
 deaf-ly
 deaf-ness
deaf-en

54

deaf-en-ing-ly
deaf-mute
deal
dealt
deal-ing
deal-er
dean-ship
dear
dear-ly
dearth
death
death-less
death-ly
death-blow
death-trap
death-watch
de-ba-cle
de-bar
de-barred
de-bar-ring
de-bar-ment
de-bark
de-bar-ka-tion
de-base
de-based
de-bas-ing
de-base-ment
de-bas-er
de-bate
de-bat-ed
de-bat-ing
de-bat-a-ble
de-bat-er
de-bauch
de-bauch-er
de-bauch-ment
de-bauch-ery
de-bauch-er-ies
deb-au-chee
de-ben-ture
de-bil-i-tate
de-bil-i-tat-ed
de-bil-i-tat-ing
de-bil-i-ta-tion
de-bil-i-ty
de-bil-i-ties
deb-it
deb-o-nair
de-bris
debt-or
de-bunk
de-bunk-er
de-but

deb-u-tante
de-cade
dec-a-dent
dec-a-dence
dec-a-dent-ly
dec-a-gon
dec-a-gram
dec-a-he-dron
dec-a-he-drons
de-cal
de-camp
de-camp-ment
de-cant
de-cant-er
de-cap-i-tate
de-cap-i-tat-ed
de-cap-i-tat-ing
de-cap-i-ta-tion
dec-a-pod
de-cath-lon
de-cay
de-crease
de-creased
de-ceit
de-ceit-ful
de-ceit-ful-ly
de-ceit-ful-ness
de-ceive
de-ceived
de-ceiv-ing
de-ceiv-er
de-ceiv-ing-ly
de-ceiv-a-ble
de-cel-er-ate
de-cel-er-at-ed
de-cel-er-at-ing
de-cel-er-a-tion
de-cen-cy
de-cen-cies
de-cen-ni-al
de-cen-ni-al-ly
de-cent
de-cent-ly
de-cen-tral-ize
de-cen-tral-ized
de-cen-tral-iz-ing
de-cen-tral-i-za-tion
de-cep-tion
de-cep-tive
de-cep-tive-ly
de-cep-tive-ness
dec-i-bel
de-cide

de-cid-ed
de-cid-ing
de-cid-a-ble
de-cid-ed-ly
de-cid-u-ous
de-cid-u-ous-ly
dec-i-mal
dec-i-mate
dec-i-mat-ed
dec-i-mat-ing
dec-i-ma-tion
de-ci-pher
de-ci-pher-a-ble
de-ci-sion
de-ci-sive
de-ci-sive-ly
de-ci-sive-ness
deck-le edge
de-claim
dec-la-ma-tion
de-clam-a-tory
de-clas-si-fy
de-clas-si-fied
de-clas-si-fy-ing
de-clen-sion
dec-li-na-tion
de-cline
de-clined
de-clin-ing
de-clin-a-ble
de-cliv-i-ty
de-cliv-i-ties
de-code
de-cod-ed
de-cod-ing
de-cod-er
de-com-pose
de-com-posed
de-com-pos-ing
de-com-po-si-tion
de-com-press
de-com-pres-sion
de-con-tam-i-nate
de-con-tam-i-nat-ed
de-con-tam-i-nat-ing
de-con-tam-i-na-tion
de-con-trol
de-con-trolled
de-con-trol-ling
de-cor
dec-o-rate
dec-o-rat-ed
dec-o-rat-ing

dec-o-ra-tion
dec-o-ra-tive
dec-o-ra-tive-ly
dec-o-ra-tor
dec-o-rous
dec-o-rous-ly
de-co-rum
de-coy
de-crease
de-creased
de-creas-ing
de-creas-ing-ly
de-cree
de-creed
de-cree-ing
de-crep-it
de-crep-i-tude
de-crep-it-ly
de-cre-scen-do
de-cre-scen-dos
de-cry
de-cried
de-cry-ing
de-cri-al
ded-i-cate
ded-i-cat-ed
ded-i-cat-ing
ded-i-ca-to-ry
ded-i-ca-tive
ded-i-ca-tion
de-duce
de-duc-i-ble
de-duct
de-duct-i-ble
de-duc-tion
de-duc-tive
de-duc-tive-ly
deep
deep-ly
deep-ness
deep-en
deep-root-ed
deep-seat-ed
deer-skin
de-es-ca-late
de-es-ca-lat-ed
de-es-ca-lat-ing
de-es-ca-la-tion
de-face
de-faced
de-fac-ing
de-face-ment
de-fac-er

de fac-to
de-fame
de-famed
de-fam-ing
def-a-ma-tion
de-fam-a-to-ry
de-fam-er
de-fault
de-fault-er
de-feat
de-feat-ism
de-feat-ist
def-e-cate
def-e-cat-ed
def-e-cat-ing
def-e-ca-tion
de-fect
de-fec-tion
de-fec-tor
de-fec-tive
de-fec-tive-ly
de-fec-tive-ness
de-fend
de-fend-er
de-fend-ant
de-fense
de-fense-less
de-fense-less-ly
de-fense-less-ness
de-fen-si-ble
de-fen-si-bil-i-ty
de-fen-si-bly
de-fen-sive
de-fen-sive-ly
de-fer
de-ferred
de-fer-ring
de-fer-ment
def-er-ence
def-er-en-tial
def-er-en-tial-ly
de-fi-ance
de-fi-ant
de-fi-ant-ly
de-fi-cient
de-fi-cien-cy
de-fi-cien-cies
de-fi-cient-ly
def-i-cit
de-file
de-filed
de-fil-ing
de-fine

de-fined
de-fin-ing
de-fin-er
de-fin-a-ble
de-fin-a-bly
def-i-nite
def-i-nite-ly
def-i-nite-ness
def-i-ni-tion
de-fin-i-tive
de-fin-i-tive-ly
de-flate
de-flat-ed
de-flat-ing
de-fla-tion
de-fla-tion-ary
de-flect
de-flec-tion
de-flec-tive
de-flec-tor
de-flow-er
de-fo-li-ate
de-fo-li-at-ed
de-fo-li-at-ing
de-for-est
de-for-est-a-tion
de-form
de-for-ma-tion
de-formed
de-form-i-ty
de-form-i-ties
de-fraud
de-fray
de-fray-al
de-fray-ment
de-fray-a-ble
de-frost
de-frost-er
deft
deft-ly
deft-ness
de-funct
de-fy
de-fied
de-fy-ing
de-fi-er
de-gen-er-ate
de-gen-er-at-ed
de-gen-er-at-ing
de-gen-er-ate-ly
de-gen-er-a-cy
de-gen-er-a-tion
de-gen-er-a-tive

56

de-grade
  de-graded
  de-grad-ing
  deg-ra-da-tion
de-gree
de-his-cence
  de-his-cent
de-hy-drate
  de-hy-drat-ed
  de-hy-drat-ing
  de-hy-dra-tion
de-i-fy
  de-i-fied
  de-i-fy-ing
  de-i-fi-ca-tion
  de-i-fi-er
deign
de-ist
  de-ism
  de-is-tic
  de-is-ti-cal
de-i-ty
  de-i-ties
de-ject-ed
  de-jec-ted-ly
  de-jec-tion
de ju-re
de-lay
  de-lay-er
de-lec-ta-ble
  de-lec-ta-ble-ness
  de-lec-ta-bly
  de-lec-ta-tion
del-e-gate
  del-e-gat-ed
  del-e-gat-ing
del-e-ga-tion
de-lete
  de-let-ed
  de-let-ing
  de-le-tion
del-e-te-ri-ous
de-lib-er-ate
  de-lib-er-at-ed
  de-lib-er-at-ing
  de-lib-er-ate-ly
  de-lib-er-ate-ness
  de-lib-er-a-tion
  de-lib-er-a-tive
  de-lib-er-a-tor
del-i-ca-cy
  del-i-ca-cies
del-i-cate

del-i-cate-ly
del-i-cate-ness
del-i-ca-tes-sen
de-li-cious
  de-li-cious-ly
  de-li-cious-ness
de-lim-it
  de-lim-i-ta-tion
de-lin-e-ate
  de-lin-e-at-ed
  de-lin-e-at-ing
  de-lin-e-a-tion
  de-lin-e-a-tor
de-lin-quent
  de-lin-quen-cy
  de-lin-quen-cies
de-lir-i-um
  de-lir-i-ums
  de-lir-ia
  de-lir-i-ous
  de-lir-i-ous-ly
de-liv-er
  de-liv-er-a-ble
  de-liv-er-er
de-liv-er-ance
de-liv-ery
  de-liv-er-ies
de-louse
  de-loused
  de-lous-ing
del-phin-i-um
del-ta
del-toid
de-lude
  de-lud-ed
  de-lud-ing
  de-lud-er
  de-lu-sive
  de-lu-so-ry
  de-lu-sive-ly
del-uge
  del-uged
  del-ug-ing
de-lu-sion
de-luxe
delve
  delved
  delv-ing
dem-a-gogue
  dem-a-gogu-ery
  dem-a-gog-ic
  dem-a-gog-i-cal
de-mand

  de-mand-er
de-mar-ca-tion
de-mean
  de-mean-or
de-ment-ed
de-men-tia
de-mer-it
dem-i-god
de-mise
  de-mised
  de-mis-ing
dem-i-tasse
de-mo-bi-lize
  de-mo-bi-lized
  de-mo-bi-liz-ing
  de-mo-bi-li-za-tion
de-moc-ra-cy
  de-moc-ra-cies
dem-o-crat
dem-o-crat-ic
  dem-o-crat-i-cal-ly
de-moc-ra-tize
  de-moc-ra-tized
  de-moc-ra-tiz-ing
  de-moc-ra-ti-za-tion
de-mog-ra-phy
  de-mog-ra-pher
  dem-o-graph-ic
de-mol-ish
  de-mol-ish-er
  dem-o-li-tion
de-mon
  de-mon-ic
de-mon-e-tize
  de-mon-e-tized
  de-mon-e-tiz-ing
  de-mon-e-ti-za-tion
de-mo-ni-ac
  de-mo-ni-a-cal
de-mon-ol-o-gy
  de-mon-ol-o-gist
dem-on-strate
  dem-on-strat-ed
  dem-on-strat-ing
  de-mon-stra-ble
  de-mon-stra-bly
  dem-on-stra-tion
de-mon-stra-tive
  de-mon-stra-tive-ly
  de-mon-stra-tive-ness
  dem-on-stra-tor
de-mor-al-ize
  de-mor-al-ized

de-mor-al-iz-ing
de-mor-al-i-za-tion
de-mor-al-iz-er
de-mote
de-mot-ed
de-mot-ing
de-mo-tion
de-mur
de-murred
de-mur-ring
de-mur-ral
de-mur-er
de-mur-est
de-mure-ly
de-mure-ness
de-mur-rage
de-nat-u-ral-ize
de-nat-u-ral-ized
de-nat-u-ral-iz-ing
de-nat-u-ral-i-za-tion
de-na-ture
de-na-tured
de-na-tur-ing
den-drite
den-dro-lite
den-drol-o-gy
den-e-ga-tion
de-ni-al
de-ni-er
den-im
den-i-zen
de-nom-i-nate
de-nom-i-nat-ed
de-nom-i-nat-ing
de-nom-i-na-tion
de-nom-i-na-tion-al
de-nom-i-na-tion-al-
ism
de-nom-i-na-tive
de-nom-i-na-tor
de-note
de-not-ed
de-not-ing
de-no-ta-tion
de-noue-ment
de-nounce
de-nounced
de-noun-cing
de-nounce-ment
de-nun-ci-a-tion
de-nun-ci-a-to-ry
dense
den-ser

den-sest
dense-ly
dense-ness
den-si-ty
den-si-ties
den-tal
den-tate
den-ti-frice
den-tin
den-tist
den-tist-ry
den-ti-tion
den-ture
de-nude
de-nud-ed
de-nud-ing
den-u-da-tion
de-nun-ci-ate
de-nun-ci-at-ed
de-nun-ci-at-ing
de-nun-ci-a-tion
de-nun-ci-a-to-ry
de-ny
de-nied
de-ny-ing
de-o-dor-ant
de-o-dor-ize
de-o-dor-ized
de-o-dor-iz-ing
de-part
de-part-ed
de-part-ment
de-part-men-tal
de-par-ture
de-pend
de-pend-ence
de-pend-a-ble
de-pend-a-bly
de-pend-a-bil-i-ty
de-pend-en-cy
de-pend-en-cies
de-pend-ent
de-pict
de-pic-tion
de-pil-a-to-ry
de-pil-a-to-ries
de-plete
de-plet-ed
de-plet-ing
de-ple-tion
de-plor-a-ble
de-plor-a-bly
de-plore

de-plored
de-plor-ing
de-ploy
de-ploy-ment
de-po-nent
de-pop-u-late
de-pop-u-lat-ed
de-pop-u-lat-ing
de-pop-u-la-tion
de-port
de-por-ta-tion
de-port-ment
de-pose
de-posed
de-pos-ing
de-pos-a-ble
de-pos-it
de-pos-i-tor
dep-o-si-tion
de-pos-i-to-ry
de-pot
de-prave
de-praved
de-prav-ing
de-prav-i-ty
dep-re-cate
dep-re-cat-ed
dep-re-cat-ing
dep-re-cat-ing-ly
dep-re-ca-tion
dep-re-ca-to-ry
de-pre-ci-ate
de-pre-ci-at-ed
de-pre-ci-at-ing
de-pre-ci-a-tion
de-pre-ci-a-to-ry
de-pre-ci-a-tor
dep-re-date
dep-re-dat-ed
dep-re-dat-ing
dep-re-da-tion
de-press
de-pres-sant
de-pressed
de-pres-sion
de-prive
de-prived
de-priv-ing
dep-ri-va-tion
depth
dep-u-ta-tion
de-pute
de-put-ed

de-put-ing
dep-u-tize
  dep-u-tized
  dep-u-tiz-ing
dep-u-ty
  dep-u-ties
  dep-u-ty-ship
de-rail
  de-rail-ment
de-range
  de-ranged
  de-rang-ing
  de-range-ment
der-e-lict
  der-e-lic-tion
de-ride
  de-rid-ed
  de-rid-ing
de-ri-sion
de-ri-sive
  de-ri-sive-ly
  de-ri-so-ry
der-i-va-tion
de-riv-a-tive
de-rive
  de-rived
  de-riv-ing
  de-riv-a-ble
der-ma
  der-mal
der-ma-tol-o-gy
  der-ma-to-log-i-cal
  der-ma-tol-o-gist
der-mis
der-o-gate
  der-o-gat-ed
  der-o-gat-ing
  der-o-ga-tion
de-rog-a-to-ry
  de-rog-a-to-ri-ly
der-rick
der-rin-ger
der-vish
des-cant
de-scend
  de-scend-a-ble
de-scend-ant
de-scent
de-scribe
  de-scribed
  de-scrib-ing
  de-scriba-ble
  de-scrib-er

de-scrip-tion
  de-scrip-tive
  de-scrip-tive-ly
  de-scrip-tive-ness
de-scry
  de-scried
  de-scry-ing
des-e-crate
  des-e-crat-ed
  des-e-crat-ing
  des-e-cra-tion
de-seg-re-gate
  de-seg-re-gat-ed
  de-seg-re-gat-ing
  de-seg-re-ga-tion
des-ert
de-sert
  de-sert-er
  de-ser-tion
des-ha-bille
des-ic-cate
  des-ic-cat-ed
  des-ic-cat-ing
  des-ic-ca-tion
  des-ic-ca-tive
de-sid-er-a-tum
de-sign
des-ig-nate
  des-ig-nat-ed
  des-ig-nat-ing
  des-ig-na-tion
  des-ig-na-tive
  des-ig-na-tor
de-sign-ed-ly
de-sign-er
de-sign-ing
de-sire
  de-sired
  de-sir-ing
  de-sir-a-ble
  de-sir-a-bil-i-ty
  de-sir-a-bly
  de-sir-ous
de-sist
des-o-late
  des-o-lat-ed
  des-o-lat-ing
  des-o-late-ly
  des-o-la-tion
de-spair
  de-spair-ing
  de-spair-ing-ly
des-per-a-do

des-per-a-does
des-per-ate
  des-per-ate-ly
  des-per-ate-ness
  des-per-a-tion
des-pi-ca-ble
  des-pi-ca-bly
de-spise
  de-spised
  de-spis-ing
de-spite
de-spoil
  de-spoil-er
  de-spo-li-a-tion
de-spond
  de-spond-en-cy
  de-spond-ence
  de-spond-ent
  de-spond-ent-ly
des-pot
  des-pot-ic
  des-pot-i-cal-ly
des-pot-ism
des-sert
des-ti-na-tion
des-tine
  des-tined
  des-tin-ing
des-ti-ny
  des-ti-nies
des-ti-tute
  des-ti-tu-tion
de-stroy
de-stroy-er
de-struc-tion
  de-struct-i-ble
  de-struct-i-bil-i-ty
de-struc-tive
  de-struc-tive-ly
  de-struc-tive-ness
des-ue-tude
des-ul-to-ry
  des-ul-to-ri-ly
de-tach
  de-tach-a-ble
de-tached
de-tach-ment
de-tail
  de-tailed
de-tain
  de-tain-ment
  de-tain-er
de-tect

de-tect-a-ble
de-tec-tion
de-tec-tive
de-tec-tor
de-ten-tion
de-ter
de-terred
de-ter-ring
de-ter-gent
de-te-ri-o-rate
de-te-ri-o-rat-ed
de-te-ri-o-rat-ing
de-te-ri-o-ra-tion
de-ter-mi-na-ble
de-ter-mi-nant
de-ter-ni-nate
de-ter-mi-na-tion
de-ter-mi-na-tive
de-ter-mine
de-ter-mined
de-ter-min-ing
de-ter-min-er
de-ter-mined
de-ter-mined-ly
de-ter-min-ism
de-ter-min-ist
de-ter-rent
de-ter-rence
de-test
de-test-a-ble
de-test-a-bly
de-tes-ta-tion
de-throne
de-throned
de-thron-ing
de-throne-ment
de-tour
de-tract
de-trac-tion
de-trac-tor
det-ri-ment
det-ri-men-tal
det-ri-men-tal-ly
de-tri-tus
deuce
deu-te-ri-um
de-val-u-ate
de-val-u-at-ed
de-val-u-at-ing
de-val-u-a-tion
dev-as-tate
dev-as-tat-ed
dev-as-tat-ing

dev-as-ta-tion
de-vel-op
de-vel-op-ment
de-vel-op-er
de-vi-ate
de-vi-at-ed
de-vi-at-ing
de-vi-ant
de-vi-a-tion
de-vice
de-vi-ous
de-vi-ous-ly
de-vise
de-vised
de-vis-ing
de-vis-a-ble
de-vis-al
de-vi-see
de-vi-sor
de-void
de-volve
de-volved
de-volv-ing
dev-o-lu-tion
de-vote
de-vot-ing
de-vot-ed
de-vot-ed-ly
dev-o-tee
de-vo-tion
de-vo-tion-al
de-vour
de-vour-er
de-vour-ing-ly
de-vout
de-vout-ly
de-vout-ness
dew-drop
dew-lap
dewy
dew-i-er
dew-i-est
dew-y-eyed
dex-ter-ous
dex-ter-i-ty
dex-ter-ous-ly
dex-trose
di-a-be-tes
di-a-bet-ic
di-a-bol-ic
di-a-bol-i-cal
di-a-bol-i-cal-ly
di-a-crit-ic

di-a-crit-i-cal
di-a-crit-i-cal-ly
di-a-dem
di-ag-nose
di-ag-nosed
di-ag-nos-ing
di-ag-no-sis
di-ag-no-ses
di-ag-nos-tic
di-ag-nos-ti-cian
di-ag-o-nal
di-ag-o-nal-ly
di-a-gram
di-a-gramed
di-a-gram-ing
di-a-gram-mat-ic
di-a-gram-mat-i-cal
di-al
di-aled
di-al-ing
di-a-lect
di-a-lec-tal
di-a-lec-tic
di-a-lec-ti-cal
di-a-lec-ti-cian
di-a-logue
di-am-e-ter
di-a-met-ric
di-a-met-ric-al
di-a-met-ric-al-ly
dia-mond
dia-per
di-aph-a-nous
di-a-phragm
di-ar-rhea
di-a-ry
di-as-to-le
di-as-tol-ic
di-a-ther-mic
di-a-tom
di-a-ton-ic
dib-ble
dib-bled
dib-bling
di-chot-o-my
di-chot-o-mous
di-cho-tom-ic
dic-tate
dic-ta-tion
dic-ta-tor
dic-ta-to-ri-al
dic-ta-to-ri-al-ly
dic-tion-ary

dic-tum
di-dac-tic
  di-dac-ti-cally
di-er-e-ses
di-e-tary
di-e-tet-ic
  di-e-tet-i-cal
  di-e-tet-i-cal-ly
di-e-tet-ics
di-e-ti-cian
dif-fer-ence
  dif-fer-enced
  dif-fer-en-cing
dif-fer-ent
  dif-fer-ent-ly
dif-fer-en-tial
  dif-fer-en-tial-ly
dif-fer-en-ti-ate
  dif-fer-en-ti-at-ed
dif-fi-cult
  dif-fi-cult-ly
dif-fi-dence
  dif-fi-dent
  dif-fi-dent-ly
dig-ger
dig-gings
dig-it-al
dig-i-tal-is
dig-ni-fied
dig-ni-fy
  dig-ni-fy-ing
dig-ni-tary
  dig-ni-tar-ies
dig-ni-ty
di-gress
  di-gres-sion
  di-gres-sive
di-he-dral
di-lap-i-dat-ed
  di-lap-i-da-tion
dil-a-ta-tion
di-late
  di-lat-ed
  di-lat-ing
  di-lat-a-ble
  di-la-tion
dil-a-to-ry
  dil-a-to-ri-ly
di-lem-ma
dil-et-tan-te
  dil-et-tan-tes
dil-i-gence
  dil-i-gent

dil-i-gent-ly
dil-ly-dal-ly
di-lute
  di-lut-ed
  di-lut-ing
di-men-sion
  di-men-sion-al
di-min-ish
  di-min-ish-a-ble
di-min-u-en-do
  di-min-u-en-dos
dim-i-nu-tion
di-min-u-tive
  di-min-u-tive-ness
dim-ple
  dim-pled
  dim-pling
din-er
di-nette
din-ghy
  din-ghies
din-ner
di-no-saur
di-o-cese
di-oc-e-san
di-o-ram-a
diph-the-ri-a
di-plo-ma
di-plo-ma-cy
  di-plo-ma-cies
dip-lo-mat
  dip-lo-mat-ic
  dip-lo-mat-i-cal-ly
dip-per
dip-so-ma-nia
  dip-so-ma-ni-ac
di-rect
  di-rect-ness
di-rec-tion
  di-rec-tion-al
di-rec-tive
di-rect-ly
di-rec-tor
  di-rec-to-ri-al
  di-rec-tor-ship
di-rec-to-rate
di-rec-to-ry
  di-rec-to-ries
dis-a-buse
  dis-a-bused
  dis-a-bus-ing
dis-ad-van-tage
  dis-ad-van-taged

dis-af-fect
  dis-af-fec-tion
  dis-af-fect-ed
dis-a-gree
  dis-a-gree-ing
dis-a-gree-a-ble
dis-a-gree-ment
dis-al-low
  dis-al-low-ance
dis-ap-pear
  dis-ap-pear-ance
dis-ap-point
  dis-ap-point-ment
dis-ap-pro-ba-tion
dis-ap-prove
  dis-ap-prov-al
dis-arm
dis-ar-ma-ment
dis-ar-range
  dis-ar-ranged
  dis-ar-rang-ing
dis-ar-ray
dis-as-sem-ble
dis-as-ter
  dis-as-trous
  dis-as-trous-ly
dis-a-vow
  dis-a-vow-al
dis-band
  dis-band-ment
dis-be-lieve
  dis-be-lief
  dis-be-liev-er
dis-burse
  dis-bursed
  dis-burs-ing
  dis-burs-er
dis-cern-ing
dis-cern-ment
dis-charge
  dis-charged
  dis-charg-ing
  dis-char-ger
dis-ci-ple
  dis-ci-ple-ship
dis-ci-pline
  dis-ci-plines
  dis-ci-pli-nary
dis-claim-er
dis-close
  dis-closed
  dis-clos-er
  dis-clo-sure

dis-coid
dis-col-or
  dis-col-or-a-tion
dis-com-fit
  dis-com-fi-ture
dis-com-fort
dis-com-mode
  dis-com-mod-ing
dis-com-pose
  dis-com-posed
  dis-com-pos-ing
dis-con-cert
  dis-con-cert-ed
dis-con-nect
  dis-con-nec-tion
dis-con-so-late
dis-con-tent
  dis-con-tent-ed
dis-con-tin-ue
  dis-con-tin-ued
  dis-con-tin-u-ing
dis-con-tin-u-ous
dis-cord
  dis-cord-ance
  dis-cord-ant-ly
dis-count
dis-cour-age
  dis-cour-ag-ing
dis-course
  dis-coursed
  dis-cours-ing
dis-cour-te-ous
  dis-cour-te-sy
dis-cov-er
  dis-cov-er-a-ble
  dis-cov-er-er
dis-cov-er-y
  dis-cov-er-ies
dis-cred-it
  dis-cred-it-a-bly
dis-creet
dis-crep-an-cy
  dis-crep-an-cies
dis-crete
dis-cre-tion
  dis-cre-tion-ary
dis-crim-i-nate
  dis-crim-i-nate-ly
  dis-crim-i-na-to-ry
  dis-crim-i-na-tor
dis-cur-sive
  dis-cur-sive-ly
  dis-cur-sive-ness

dis-cus
  dis-cus-es
dis-cuss
  dis-cuss-i-ble
  dis-cus-sion
dis-dain
  dis-dain-ful
  dis-dain-ful-ly
dis-ease
  dis-eased
dis-em-bark
dis-em-body
  dis-em-bod-ied
  dis-em-bod-y-ing
dis-em-bow-el
  dis-em-bow-eled
  dis-em-bow-el-ing
dis-en-chant
  dis-en-chant-ment
dis-en-cum-ber
dis-en-fran-chise
  dis-en-fran-chised
  dis-en-fran-chis-ing
dis-en-gage
  dis-en-gaged
  dis-en-gag-ing
dis-en-tan-gle
  dis-en-tan-gled
  dis-en-tan-gling
dis-es-tab-lish
dis-fa-vor
dis-fig-ure
  dis-fig-ured
  dis-fig-ur-ing
  dis-fig-ure-ment
dis-gorge
  dis-gorged
  dis-gorg-ing
dis-grace
  dis-graced
  dis-grac-ing
dis-grace-ful
  dis-grace-ful-ly
dis-grun-tle
  dis-grun-tled
  dis-grun-tling
dis-gust
  dis-gust-ed
  dis-gust-ing
dis-ha-bille
dis-har-mo-ny
  dis-har-mo-nies
dis-heart-en

dis-hev-eled
dis-hon-est
  dis-hon-est-ly
  dis-hon-es-ty
  dis-hon-es-ties
dis-hon-or
dis-hon-or-a-ble
  dis-hon-or-a-bly
dis-il-lu-sion
dis-in-cline
  dis-in-clined
dis-in-fect
dis-in-her-it
dis-in-te-grate
dis-in-ter-es-ted
  dis-in-ter-est-ed-ly
dis-junc-tion
dis-loy-al
  dis-loy-al-ty
dis-o-be-di-ence
dis-or-der-ly
dis-o-ri-ent
dis-pos-a-ble
dis-qual-i-fy
dis-qui-et
dis-re-spect
  dis-re-spect-ful
dis-rup-tive
  dis-rupt-er
dis-sat-is-fy
  dis-sat-is-fy-ing
dis-sem-blance
dis-sem-i-nate
  dis-sem-i-nat-ing
  dis-sem-i-na-tor
dis-sent
dis-ser-tate
  dis-ser-ta-ting
  dis-ser-ta-tion
dis-serv-ice
dis-si-dent
dis-sim-i-lar
  dis-sim-i-lar-i-ty
dis-sim-i-late
  dis-sim-i-lat-ing
  dis-sim-i-la-tive
dis-si-pate
  dis-si-pa-tion
dis-so-nance
dis-so-nant
dis-suade
  dis-sua-sion
  dis-sua-sive

dis-tance
dis-taste
  dis-taste-ful-ly
dis-tem-per
dis-til-late
dis-till-ery
dis-tin-guish
dis-tract
  dis-tract-ing
dis-trib-ute
  dis-trib-ut-ed
  dis-tri-bu-tion
  dis-tri-u-tor
dis-u-nite
di-van
di-verge
  di-ver-gence
  di-ver-gent
di-verse
di-ver-sion
div-i-dend
di-vi-sor
di-vulge
  di-vulg-ing
  di-vul-gence
do-a-ble
doc-tor-ate
doc-u-ment
dod-der
dog-ma
dog-mat-ic
  dog-mat-i-cal
dol-drums
dol-or-ous
dol-phin
do-mes-tic
do-mes-ti-cate
do-mes-tic-i-ty
dom-i-cile
  dom-i-cil-ing
dom-i-nance
dom-i-nant
dom-i-neer
do-min-ion
dop-ey
  dop-i-est
  dop-i-ness
dor-mant
dor-mer
dor-mi-to-ry
dos-age
dos-si-er
dou-ble-faced

douche
dow-a-ger
dow-el
down-ward-ly
doz-ing
doz-en
drag-on
dra-per-y
drib-ble
  drib-bled
  drib-bling
  drib-bler
drill-ing
dri-ly
driv-el
  driv-eled
  driv-el-ing
driz-zle
  driz-zling
  driz-zly
drom-e-dar-y
droop
  droop-y
  droop-i-er
  droop-i-est
drop-per
dross
drought
  drought-y
  drought-i-er
  drought-i-est
drowned
drowse
  drowsed
  drows-ing
  drow-si-ness
drudge
drug-gist
dru-id
drum-mer
drunk-ard
drunk-en
  drunk-en-ness
dry-ad
du-al
  du-al-i-ty
du-al-ism
  du-al-ist
  du-al-is-tic
du-bi-ous
  du-bi-e-ty
  du-bi-ous-ly
du-cal

duch-ess
duck-ling
duc-tile
du-el
  du-eled
  du-el-ing
  du-el-ist
duke-dom
dul-cet
dum-found
dunce
dun-ga-ree
dun-geon
dun-nage
du-o-dec-i-mal
du-o-de-num
  du-o-de-na
  du-o-de-nal
du-pli-cate
  du-pli-cat-ing
  du-pli-ca-tor
du-plic-i-ty
du-ra-ble
  du-ra-bil-i-ty
  du-ra-bly
dur-ance
du-ra-tion
du-ti-a-ble
du-ti-ful
  du-ti-ful-ly
  du-ti-ful-ness
dwarf
  dwarf-ish
dwin-dle
  dwin-dled
  dwin-dling
dye-stuff
dy-ing
dy-nam-ic
  dy-nam-i-cal
  dy-nam-i-cal-ly
  dy-na-mism
dy-na-mite
dy-na-mo
dy-nas-ty
  dy-nas-ties
dyne
dys-en-tery
dys-func-tion
dys-pep-sia
dys-pep-tic
  dys-pep-ti-cal
dys-tro-phy

E

ea-ger
  ea-ger-ly
  ea-ger-ness
ea-gle
ea-gle eyed
ea-glet
earl-dom
ear-ly
  ear-li-er
  ear-li-est
ear-mark
ear-muff
earn
  earn-er
ear-nest
  ear-nest-ly
earn-ings
ear-ring
earth-en
earth-ly
  earth-li-er
  earth-li-est
earth-quake
earth-y
ear-wax
ease
  eased
  eas-ing
ea-sel
ease-ment
eas-i-ly
  eas-i-ness
east-er-ly
east-ern
east-ward
eas-y
  eas-i-er
  eas-i-est
eas-y-go-ing
eat
ebb
eb-on-y
  eb-on-ies
e-bul-lience
  e-bul-lient
  e-bul-li-tion
ec-cen-tric
  ec-cen-tri-cal-ly
ec-cen-tric-i-ty
  ec-cen-tric-i-ties
ec-cle-si-as-tic
  ec-cle-si-as-ti-cal
  ec-cle-si-as-ti-cal-ly

ech-e-lon
e-chi-no-derm
ech-o
e-cho-ic
e-clair
ec-lec-tic
  ec-lec-ti-cal-ly
  ec-lec-ti-cism
e-clipse
  e-clipsed
  e-clips-ing
e-clip-tic
e-col-o-gy
  e-c-o-log-ic
  e-c-o-log-i-cal
  e-col-o-gist
e-co-nom-ic
  e-co-nom-i-cal
e-co-nom-ics
e-con-o-mist
e-con-o-mize
  e-con-o-mized
  e-con-o-miz-ing
  e-con-o-miz-er
e-con-o-my
  e-con-o-mies
ec-o-sys-tem
ec-ru
ec-sta-sy
  ec-sta-sies
ec-stat-ic
  ec-stat-i-cal
ec-to-morph
  ec-to-mor-phic
ec-to-plasm
ec-u-men-i-cal
ec-u-men-ic
  ec-u-men-i-cal-ly
  ec-u-men-ism
ec-ze-ma
e-de-ma
  e-de-ma-ta
e-den-tate
edg-y
ed-i-ble
e-dict
ed-i-fice
ed-i-fy
  ed-i-fied
  ed-i-fy-ing
  ed-i-fi-ca-tion
ed-it
e-di-tion

ed-i-tor
  ed-i-tor-ship
ed-i-to-ri-al
  ed-i-to-ri-al-ly
  ed-i-to-ri-al-ize
  ed-i-to-ri-al-lized
ed-u-cate
  ed-u-cat-ed
  ed-u-cat-ing
  ed-u-ca-ble
ed-u-ca-tor
ed-u-ca-tion
  ed-u-ca-tion-al
e-duce
  e-duced
  e-duc-ing
  e-duc-i-ble
  e-duc-tion
eel
ee-rie
  ee-ri-er
  ee-ri-est
  ee-ri-ly
ef-fect
  ef-fec-tive
  ef-fec-tive-ness
  ef-fec-tive-ly
ef-fec-tu-al
  ef-fec-tu-al-i-ty
ef-fec-tu-ate
  ef-fec-tu-at-ed
  ef-fec-tu-at-ing
ef-fem-i-nate
  ef-fem-i-na-cy
  ef-fem-i-na-cies
  ef-fem-i-nate-ly
ef-fete
ef-fi-ca-cious
ef-fi-ca-cy
  ef-fi-ca-cies
ef-fi-cien-cy
  ef-fi-cien-cies
ef-fi-cient
  ef-fi-cient-ly
ef-fi-gy
  ef-fi-gies
ef-flo-resce
ef-flu-ent
  ef-flu-ence
ef-flu-vi-um
  ef-flu-via
  ef-flu-vi-ums
  ef-flu-vi-al

ef-fron-ter-y
ef-fron-ter-ies
ef-ful-gent
ef-ful-gence
ef-fuse
ef-fused
ef-fus-ing
ef-fu-sion
ef-fu-sive
ef-fu-sive-ly
egal-i-tar-i-an
egal-i-tar-i-an-ism
egg-nog
egg-plant
e-go
e-gos
e-go-cen-tric
e-go-ism
e-go-ist
e-go-is-tic
e-go-tism
e-go-tis-tic
e-go-tis-ti-cal
e-gre-gious
e-gre-gious-ly
e-gress
e-gret
ei-der-down
eight
eighth
eight-ball
eight-fold
eight-y
eight-ies
eight-i-eth
ei-ther
e-jac-u-late
e-jac-u-lat-ed
e-jac-u-lat-ing
e-jac-u-la-tion
e-ject
e-jec-tion
e-ject-ment
e-jec-tor
eke
eked
ek-ing
e-lab-o-rate
e-lab-o-rat-ed
e-lab-o-rat-ing
e-lab-o-rate-ly
e-lab-o-ra-tion
e-lapse

e-lapsed
e-laps-ing
e-las-tic
e-las-ti-cal-ly
e-las-tic-i-ty
e-late
e-lat-ed
e-lat-ing
e-la-tion
el-bow
el-bow-room
el-der
eld-er-ship
el-der-ly
eld-er-li-ness
eld-est
e-lect
e-lec-tion
e-lec-tion-eer
e-lec-tive
e-lec-tor
e-lec-tor-ate
e-lec-tric
e-lec-tri-cal
e-lec-tri-cal-ly
e-lec-tri-cian
e-lec-tric-i-ty
e-lec-tri-fy
e-lec-tri-fied
e-lec-tri-fy-ing
e-lec-tri-fi-ca-tion
elec-tro-car-di-o-graph
e-lec-tro-cute
e-lec-tro-cut-ed
e-lec-tro-cut-ing
e-lec-tro-cu-tion
e-lec-trode
e-lec-tro-dy-nam-ics
e-lec-trol-y-sis
e-lec-tro-lyze
e-lec-tro-lyzed
e-lec-tro-lyz-ing
e-lec-tro-lyte
e-lec-tro-lyt-ic
e-lec-tro-mag-net
e-lec-tro-mag-net-ism
e-lec-tro-mag-net-ic
e-lec-tron
e-lec-tron-ic
e-lec-tron-ics
e-lec-tron-i-cal-ly
e-lec-tro-plate
e-lec-tro-plat-ed

e-lec-tro-plat-ing
e-lec-tro-ther-a-py
e-lec-trum
el-ee-mos-y-nar-y
el-e-gant
el-e-gance
el-e-gan-cy
el-e-gant-ly
el-e-ment
el-e-men-tal
el-e-men-tal-ly
el-e-men-ta-ry
el-e-men-ta-ri-ly
el-e-phant
el-e-phan-tine
el-e-vate
el-e-vat-ed
el-e-vat-ing
el-e-va-tion
el-e-va-tor
e-lev-en
e-lev-enth
elf
e-lic-it
el-i-gi-ble
el-i-gi-bil-i-ty
el-i-gi-bly
e-lim-i-nate
e-lim-i-nat-ed
e-lim-i-nat-ing
e-lim-i-na-tion
e-lim-i-na-tor
e-lite
e-lit-ism
e-lit-ist
e-lix-ir
el-lipse
el-lip-sis
el-lip-ses
el-lip-ti-cal
el-lip-tic
el-lip-ti-cal-ly
el-o-cu-tion
el-o-cu-tion-ary
el-o-cu-tion-ist
e-lon-gate
e-lon-gat-ed
e-lon-gat-ing
e-lon-ga-tion
e-lope
el-o-quence
el-o-quent
el-o-quent-ly

else-where
e-lu-ci-date
  e-lu-ci-dat-ed
  e-lu-ci-dat-ing
  e-lu-ci-da-tion
  e-lu-ci-da-tor
e-lude
  e-lud-ed
  e-lud-ing
  e-lu-sion
e-lu-sive
  e-lu-sive-ly
elv-ish
e-ma-ci-ate
  e-ma-ci-at-ed
  e-ma-ci-at-ing
  e-ma-ci-a-tion
em-a-nate
  em-a-nat-ed
  em-a-nat-ing
  em-a-na-tion
e-man-ci-pate
  e-man-ci-pat-ed
  e-man-ci-pat-ing
  e-man-ci-pa-tor
em-balm
  em-balm-er
  em-balm-ment
em-bank-ment
em-bar-go
  em-bar-goes
  em-bar-goed
  em-bar-go-ing
em-bark
  em-bar-ka-tion
  em-bark-ment
em-bar-rass
  em-bar-rass-ing-ly
  em-bar-rass-ment
em-bas-sy
  em-bas-sies
em-bat-tle
  em-bat-tled
  em-bat-tling
  em-bat-tle-ment
em-bed
  em-bed-ded
  em-bed-ding
em-bel-lish
  em-bel-lish-ment
em-ber
em-bez-zle
  em-bez-zled

em-bez-zling
em-bez-zle-ment
em-bez-zler
em-bit-ter
  em-bit-ter-ment
em-blem
  em-blem-at-ic
  em-blem-at-i-cal
em-bod-y
  em-bod-ied
  em-bod-y-ing
  em-bod-i-ment
em-bold-en
em-bo-lism
em-bo-lus
em-bos-om
em-boss
  em-boss-ment
em-bou-chure
em-brace
  em-braced
  em-brac-ing
em-broi-der
  em-broi-dery
  em-broi-der-ies
em-broil
  em-broil-ment
em-bry-o
  em-bry-os
  em-bry-on-ic
em-bry-ol-o-gy
em-cee
  em-ceed
  em-cee-ing
e-mend
em-er-ald
e-merge
  e-merged
  e-merg-ing
  e-mer-gence
  e-mer-gent
e-mer-gen-cy
  e-mer-gen-ies
e-mer-i-tus
em-er-y
e-met-ic
em-i-grant
em-i-grate
  em-i-grat-ed
  em-i-grat-ing
  em-i-gra-tion
em-i-nence
em-i-nent

em-i-ent-ly
em-i-nent do-main
em-is-sary
  em-is-sar-ies
e-mis-sion
  e-mis-sive
e-mit
  e-mit-ted
  e-mit-ting
  e-mit-ter
e-mol-lient
  e-mol-u-ment
e-mote
  e-mot-ed
  e-mot-ing
  e-mo-tive
emo-tion
  emo-tion-al
  emo-ton-al-ly
emo-tion-al-ism
em-pan-el
em-pa-thize
  em-pa-thized
  em-pa-thiz-ing
em-pa-thy
  em-pa-thet-ic
  em-path-ic
em-per-or
em-pha-sis
  em-pha-ses
em-pha-size
  em-pha-sized
  em-pha-siz-ing
em-phat-ic
  em-phat-i-cal-ly
em-phy-se-ma
em-pire
  em-pir-i-cal
  em-pir-i-cal-ly
em-pir-i-cism
  em-pir-i-cist
em-place-ment
em-ploy
  em-ploy-a-ble
  em-ploy-ee
  em-ploy-er
  em-ploy-ment
em-pori-um
  em-po-ri-ums
  em-po-ria
em-pow-er
em-press
emp-ty

emp-ti-er
emp-ti-est
emp-tied
emp-ty-ing
emp-ti-ly
emp-ti-ness
emp-ty--hand-ed
emp-ty--head-ed
e-mu
em-u-late
em-u-lat-ed
em-u-lat-ing
em-u-la-tion
e-mul-si-fy
e-mul-si-fied
e-mul-si-fy-ing
e-mul-si-fi-ca-tion
e-mul-si-fi-er
emul-sion
emul-sive
en-a-ble
en-a-bled
en-a-bling
en-act
e-nam-el
e-nam-eled
e-nam-el-ing
e-nam-el-er
e-nam-el-ware
en-am-or
en-am-ored-ness
en-camp
en-camp-ment
en-cap-su-late
en-cap-su-lat-ed
en-cap-su-lat-ing
en-cap-sule
en-case
en-cased
en-cas-ing
en-ceinte
en-ceph-a-li-tis
en-ceph-a-lit-ic
en-ceph-a-lon
en-ceph-a-la
en-chant
en-chant-er
en-chant-ress
en-chant-ing
en-chant-ing-ly
en-chant-ment
en-chi-la-da
en-cir-cle

en-cir-cled
en-cir-cling
en-cir-cle-ment
en-clave
en-close
en-closed
en-clos-ing
en-clo-sure
en-code
en-cod-ed
en-cod-ing
en-co-mi-ast
en-com-pass
en-com-pass-ment
en-core
en-coun-ter
en-cour-age
en-cour-aged
en-cour-ag-ing
en-cour-ag-ing-ly
en-croach
en-croach-er
en-croach-ment
en-crust
en-crus-ta-tion
en-cum-ber
en-cum-brance
en-cy-clo-pe-di-a
en-cy-clo-pe-dic
en-cy-clo-pe-di-cal
en-cy-clo-pe-di-cal-ly
en-cyst
en-dan-ger
en-dan-ger-ment
en-dear
en-dear-ment
en-dea-vor
en-dem-ic
en-dem-i-cal
en-dem-i-cal-ly
end-ing
end-less
end-less-ly
end-most
en-do-crine
en-do-cri-nol-o-gy
en-do-crin-o-log-ic
en-do-cri-no-log-i-cal
en-do-cri-nol-o-gist
en-dog-e-nous
en-do-sperm
en-dow
en-dow-ment

en-due
en-dued
en-du-ing
en-dur-ance
en-dure
en-dured
en-dur-ing
en-dur-a-ble
en-dur-a-bly
end-ways
en-e-ma
en-e-my
en-e-mies
en-er-get-ic
en-er-get-i-cal
en-er-get-i-cal-ly
en-er-gize
en-er-gized
en-er-giz-ing
en-er-gi-zer
en-er-gy
en-er-gies
en-er-vate
en-er-vat-ed
en-er-vat-ing
en-er-va-tion
en-fee-ble
en-fee-bled
en-fee-bling
en-fee-ble-ment
en-fi-lade
en-fi-lad-ed
en-fi-lad-ing
en-fold
en-fran-chise
en-fran-chised
en-fran-chis-ing
en-fran-chise-ment
en-gage
en-gaged
en-gag-ing
en-gage-ment
en-gen-der
en-gine
en-gi-neer
en-gorge
en-gorged
en-gorg-ing
en-gorge-ment
en-grave
en-graved
en-grav-ing
en-grav-er

en-gross
  en-grossed
  en-gross-er
  en-gross-ing
  en-gross-ing-ly
  en-gross-ment
en-gulf
  en-gulf-ment
en-hance
  en-hanced
  en-hanc-ing
  en-hance-ment
e-nig-ma
  en-ig-mat-ic
  en-ig-mat-i-cal
  en-ig-mat-i-cal-ly
en-join
  en-join-er
  en-join-ment
en-large
  en-larged
  en-larg-ing
  en-large-a-ble
  en-larg-er
en-large-ment
en-light-en
  en-light-en-ment
en-list
  en-list-ed
  en-list-ment
en-liv-en
  en-liv-en-er
en-mesh
en-mi-ty
  en-mi-ties
en-no-ble
  en-no-bled
  en-no-bling
  en-no-ble-ment
  en-no-bler
en-nui
e-nor-mi-ty
  e-nor-mi-ties
e-nor-mous
  e-nor-mous-ly
  e-nor-mous-ness
e-nough
en-plane
  en-planed
  en-plan-ing
en-rage
  en-raged
  en-rag-ing

en-rap-ture
  en-rap-tured
  en-rap-tur-ing
en-rich
  en-rich-er
  en-rich-ment
en-roll
  en-roll-ment
en route
en-sconce
  en-sconced
  en-sconc-ing
en-sem-ble
en-shrine
  en-shrin-ing
en-shroud
en-sign
en-si-lage
  en-si-laged
  en-si-lag-ing
en-slave
  en-slaved
  en-slav-ing
  en-slave-ment
  en-slav-er
en-snare
  en-snared
  en-snar-ing
  en-snare-ment
  en-snar-er
  en-snar-ing-ly
en-sue
  en-sued
  en-su-ing
  en-su-ing-ly
en-sure
  en-sured
  en-sur-ing
  en-sur-er
en-tail
  en-tail-er
  en-tail-ment
en-tan-gle
  en-tan-gled
  en-tan-gling
  en-tan-gle-ment
  en-tan-gler
en-tente
en-ter
  en-ter-a-ble
  en-ter-i-tis
en-tr-prise
  en-ter-pris-ing

  en-ter-pris-ing-ly
en-ter-tain
  en-ter-tain-er
  en-ter-tain-ing
  en-ter-tain-ing-ly
  en-ter-tain-ment
en-thrall
  en-thralled
  en-thrall-ing
  en-thrall-ment
en-throne
  en-throned
  en-thron-ing
  en-throne-ment
en-thuse
  en-thused
  en-thus-ing
en-thu-si-asm
en-thu-si-ast
  en-thu-si-as-tic
  en-thu-si-as-ti-cal-ly
en-tice
  en-ticed
  en-tic-ing
  en-tice-ment
  en-tic-er
  en-tic-ig-ly
en-tire
  en-tire-ly
  en-tire-ness
  en-tire-ty
  en-tire-ties
en-ti-tle
  en-ti-tled
  en-ti-tling
  en-ti-tle-ment
en-ti-ty
  en-ti-ties
en-to-mol-o-gy
  en-to-mol-o-gies
  en-to-mo-log-ic
  en-to-mo-log-i-cal
  en-to-mo-log-i-cal-ly
  en-to-mol-o-gist
en-tou-rage
en-trails
en-train
  en-train-er
en-trance
  en-trance-way
  en-tranced
  en-tranc-ing
  en-trance-ment

en-tranc-ing-ly
en-trant
en-trap
en-trapped
en-trap-ping
en-trap-ment
en-treat
en-treat-ing-ly
en-treat-ment
en-treat-y
en-tree
en-trench
en-trench-ment
en-tre-pre-neur
en-tre-pre-neur-i-al
en-tre-pre-neur-ship
en-tro-py
en-trust
en-trust-ment
en-try
en-tries
en-twine
en-twined
en-twin-ing
e-nu-mer-ate
e-nu-mer-at-ed
e-nu-mer-at-ing
e-nu-mer-a-tion
e-nu-mer-a-tive
e-nu-mer-a-tor
e-nun-ci-ate
e-nun-ci-at-ed
e-nun-ci-at-ing
e-nun-ci-a-tion
e-nun-ci-a-tive
e-nun-ci-a-tor
en-u-re-sis
en-u-ret-ic
en-vel-op
en-vel-oped
en-vel-op-ing
en-vi-a-ble
en-vi-a-ble-ness
en-vi-a-bly
en-vi-ous
en-vi-ous-ly
en-vi-ous-ness
en-vi-ron
en-vi-ron-ment
en-vi-ron-men-tal
en-vi-ron-men-tal-ly
en-vi-rons
en-vis-age

en-vis-aged
en-vis-ag-ing
en-vi-sion
en-voy
en-vy
en-vies
en-vied
en-vy-ing
en-vi-er
en-vy-ing-ly
en-zyme
en-zy-mat-ic
en-zy-mat-i-cal-ly
e-on
ep-au-let
e-phed-rine
e-phem-er-al
e-phem-er-al-ness
e-phem-er-al-ly
ep-ic
ep-i-cal
ep-i-cen-ter
ep-i-cure
epi-cu-re-an
ep-i-dem-ic
ep-i-dem-i-cal-ly
ep-i-der-mis
ep-i-der-mal
ep-i-der-mic
ep-i-glot-tis
ep-i-gram
ep-i-logue
ep-i-log
epis-co-pa-cy
epsi-co-pa-cies
epis-co-pal
epis-co-pa-lian
epis-co-pa-lian-ism
epis-co-pate
ep-i-sode
ep-i-sod-ic
ep-i-sod-i-cal
ep-i-sod-i-cal-ly
e-pis-te-mol-o-gy
e-psi-te-mo-log-i-cal
e-pis-te-mol-o-gist
e-pis-tle
e-pis-to-lar-y
ep-i-taph
ep-i-taph-ic
ep-i-taph-ist
ep-i-thet
ep-i-thet-ic

ep-i-thet-i-cal
e-pit-o-me
epit-o-mize
epit-o-mized
epit-o-miz-ing
ep-och
ep-och-al
ep-ox-y
ep-ox-y res-in
ep-si-lon
eq-ua-ble
eq-ua-bil-i-ty
eq-ua-ble-ness
eq-ua-bly
e-qual
e-qualed
e-qual-ling
e-qual-ly
e-qual-ness
e-qual-i-tar-i-an
e-qual-i-tar-i-an-ism
e-qual-i-ty
e-qual-i-ties
e-qual-ize
e-qual-ized
e-qual-iz-ing
e-qual-i-za-tion
e-qual-iz-er
e-qua-nim-i-ty
e-quate
e-quat-ed
e-quat-ing
e-qua-tion
e-qua-tion-al
e-qua-tion-al-ly
e-qua-tor
e-qua-to-ri-al
e-qua-to-ri-al-ly
e-ques-tri-an
e-ques-tri-enne
e-qui-dis-tance
e-qui-dis-tant
e-qui-dis-tant-ly
e-qui-lat-er-al
e-qui-li-brate
e-qui-li-brat-ed
e-qui-li-brat-ing
e-qui-li-bra-tion
e-qui-l-bra-tor
e-qui-lib-ri-um
e-qui-lib-ri-ums
e-qui-lib-ria
e-quine

e-qui-noc-tial
e-qui-nox
e-quip
  e-quipped
  e-quip-ping
  e-quip-per
eq-ui-page
e-quip-ment
e-qui-poise
eq-ui-ta-ble
  eq-ui-ta-ble-ness
  eq-ui-ta-bly
eq-ui-ty
  eq-ui-ties
e-quiv-a-lance
  e-quiv-a-len-cy
e-quiv-a-lent
  e-quiv-a-lent-ly
e-quiv-o-cal
  e-quiv-o-cal-ly
  e-quiv-o-cal-ness
e-quiv-o-cate
  e-quiv-o-cat-ed
  e-quiv-o-cat-ing
  e-quiv-o-ca-tor
  e-quiv-o-ca-tion
e-ra
e-rad-i-cate
  e-rad-i-cat-ed
  e-rad-i-cat-ing
  e-rad-i-ca-ble
  e-rad-i-ca-tion
  e-rad-i-ca-tive
  e-rad-i-ca-tor
e-rase
  e-rased
  e-ras-ing
  e-ras-a-bil-i-ty
  e-ras-a-ble
e-ras-er
e-ras-ure
e-rect
  e-rect-a-ble
  e-rect-er
  e-rec-tive
  e-rect-ly
  e-rect-ness
e-rec-tile
  e-rec-til-i-ty
e-rec-tion
e-rec-tor
er-go
er-mine

e-rode
  e-rod-ed
  e-rod-ing
e-rog-e-nous
e-ro-sion
e-rot-ic
  e-rot-i-cal-ly
e-rot-i-cism
err
  err-ing-ly
er-rand
er-rant
  er-rant-ly
er-rat-ic
  er-rat-i-cal-ly
er-ra-tum
  er-ra-ta
er-ro-ne-ous
  er-ro-ne-ous-ly
  er-ro-ne-ous-ness
er-ror
  er-ror-less
er-satz
erst-while
er-u-dite
  er-u-dite-ly
  er-u-dite-ness
er-u-di-tion
e-rupt
  e-rup-tion
  e-rup-tive
  e-rup-tive-ly
  e-rup-tive-ness
es-ca-lade
  es-ca-lad-ed
  es-ca-lad-ing
  es-ca-lad-er
es-ca-late
  es-ca-lat-ed
  es-ca-lat-ing
  es-ca-la-tion
es-ca-la-tor
es-cal-lop
es-ca-pade
es-cape
  es-caped
  es-cap-ing
  es-cap-er
es-ca-pee
es-cap-ist
  es-cap-ism
es-carp-ment
es-chew

es-chew-al
es-chew-er
es-cort
es-cri-toire
es-crow
es-cutch-eon
  es-cutch-eoned
e-soph-a-gus
es-o-ter-ic
  es-o-ter-i-cal
  es-o-ter-i-cal-ly
es-pal-ier
es-pe-cial
  es-pe-cial-ly
  es-pe-cial-ness
es-pi-o-nage
es-pla-nade
es-pouse
  es-poused
  es-pous-ing
  es-pous-er
es-pous-al
es-pres-so
es-prit
es-prit de corps
es-py
  es-pied
  es-py-ing
es-quire
  es-quired
  es-quir-ing
es-say
  es-say-er
  es-say-ist
es-sence
es-sen-tial
  es-sen-ti-al-i-ty
  es-sen-tial-ly
  es-sen-tial-ness
es-tab-lish
  es-tab-lish-er
  es-tab-lish-ment
es-tate
es-teem
es-thete
  es-thet-ic
es-ti-ma-ble
  es-ti-ma-ble-ness
  es-ti-ma-bly
es-ti-mate
  es-ti-mat-ed
  es-ti-mat-ing
  es-ti-ma-tive

es-ti-ma-tor
es-ti-ma-tion
es-trange
  es-tranged
  es-trang-ing
  es-trange-ment
  es-tran-ger
es-trus
es-tu-ar-y
  es-tu-ar-ies
  es-tu-ar-i-al
etch
  etch-er
  etch-ing
e-ter-nal
  e-ter-nal-ly
e-ter-ni-ty
e-ter-nize
  e-ter-nized
  e-ter-niz-ing
  e-ter-ni-za-tion
eth-a-nol
e-ther
e-the-re-al
  e-the-re-al-i-ty
  e-the-re-al-ly
  e-the-re-al-ness
e-the-re-al-ize
  e-the-re-al-ized
  e-the-re-al-iz-ing
  e-the-re-al-i-za-tion
eth-ic
  eth-i-cal
  eth-i-cal-ly
  eth-ics
eth-nic
  eth-ni-cal
  eth-ni-cal-ly
eth-nol-o-gy
eth-yl
eti-ol-o-gy
  eti-o-log-ist
  eti-o-log-i-cal
  eti-o-log-i-cal-ly
et-i-quette
e-tude
et-y-mol-o-gy
  et-y-mol-o-gies
  et-y-mo-log-ic
  et-y-mo-log-i-cal
  et-y-mol-o-gist
eu-ca-lyp-tus
  eu-ca-lyp-tus-es

eu-ca-lyp-ti
eu-gen-ic
eu-lo-gise
  eu-lo-gized
  eu-lo-giz-ing
  eu-lo-gis-tic
  eu-lo-gis-ti-cal-ly
eu-nuch
eu-phe-mism
  eu-phe-mist
  eu-phe-mis-tic
  eu-phe-mis-ti-cal
  eu-phe-mis-ti-cal-ly
eu-phe-mize
  eu-phe-mized
  eu-phe-miz-ing
eu-pho-ni-ous
  eu-pho-ni-ous-ly
eu-re-ka
eu-tha-na-sia
e-vac-u-ate
  e-vac-u-at-ed
  e-vac-u-at-ing
  e-vac-u-a-tion
  e-vac-u-a-tive
  e-vac-u-a-tor
e-vac-u-ee
e-vade
  e-vad-ed
  e-vad-ing
  e-vad-a-ble
  e-vad-er
  e-vad-ing-ly
e-val-u-ate
  e-val-u-at-ed
  e-val-u-at-ing
  e-val-u-a-tion
  e-val-u-a-tor
ev-a-nes-cent
  ev-a-nes-cence
  ev-a-nes-cent-ly
e-van-gel
  evan-gel-i-cal
  evan-gel-ic
  evan-gel-i-cal-ism
  evan-gel-i-cal-ly
  evan-gel-i-cal-ness
evan-ge-lism
  evan-ge-lis-tic
  evan-ge-lis-ti-cal-ly
evan-ge-list
evan-ge-lize
  evan-ge-lized

evan-ge-liz-ing
evan-ge-li-za-tion
evan-ge-liz-er
e-va-sion
e-va-sive
  e-va-sive-ly
  e-va-sive-ness
e-ven
  e-ven-ly
  e-ven-ness
e-ven-hand-ed
eve-ning
e-vent
e-vent-ful
  event-ful-ly
  event-ful-ness
e-ven-tu-al
  e-ven-tu-al-ly
  e-ven-tu-al-i-ty
  e-ven-tu-al-i-ties
e-ven-tu-ate
  e-ven-tu-at-ed
  e-ven-tu-at-ing
ev-er
ev-er-green
ev-er-last-ing
  ev-er-last-ing-ly
  ev-er-last-ing-ness
ev-er-more
e-vert
  e-ver-si-ble
  e-ver-sion
eve-ry
eve-ry-body
eve-ry-day
eve-ry-one
eve-ry-thing
eve-ry-where
e-vict
  e-vic-tion
  e-vic-tor
ev-i-dence
  ev-i-denced
  ev-i-denc-ing
ev-i-dent
  ev-i-dent-ly
ev-i-den-tial
  ev-i-den-tial-ly
e-vil
e-vince
  e-vinced
  e-vinc-ing
  e-vin-ci-ble

e-vis-cer-ate
e-vis-cer-at-ed
e-vis-cer-at-ing
e-vis-cer-a-tion
e-voke
e-voked
e-vok-ing
ev-o-ca-tion
ev-o-lu-tion
ev-o-lu-tion-al
ev-o-lu-tion-ary
ev-o-lu-tion-ism
ev-ol-lu-tion-ist
e-volve
e-volved
e-volv-ing
e-volv-a-ble
e-volve-ment
e-volv-er
ew-er
ex-ac-er-bate
ex-ac-er-bat-ed
ex-ac-er-bat-ing
ex-ac-er-ba-tion
ex-act
ex-act-a-ble
ex-ac-tor
ex-act-ing
ex-act-ing-ly
ex-act-ing-ness
ex-act-i-tude
ex-act-ly
ex-ag-ger-ate
ex-ag-ger-at-ed
ex-ag-ger-at-ing
ex-ag-ger-a-tion
ex-ag-ger-a-tor
ex-am
ex-am-i-na-tion
ex-am-ine
ex-am-ined
ex-am-in-ing
ex-am-ple
ex-am-pled
ex-am-pling
ex-as-per-ate
ex-as-per-at-ed
ex-as-per-at-ing
ex-as-per-a-tion
ex-ca-vate
ex-ca-vat-ed
ex-ca-cat-ing
ex-ca-va-tion

ex-ca-va-tor
ex-ceed
ex-ceed-ing
ex-ceed-ing-ly
ex-cel
ex-celled
ex-cel-ling
ex-cel-lence
ex-cel-len-cy
ex-cel-len-cies
ex-cel-lent
ex-cel-lent-ly
ex-cel-si-or
ex-cept
ex-cept-ing
ex-cep-tion
ex-cep-tion-a-ble
ex-cep-tion-al
ex-cerpt
ex-cess
ex-ces-sive
ex-ces-sive-ly
ex-change
ex-changed
ex-chang-ing
ex-change-a-bil-i-ty
ex-change-a-ble
ex-chan-ger
ex-cheq-uer
ex-cise
ex-cised
ex-cis-ing
ex-cis-a-ble
ex-ci-sion
ex-cit-a-ble
ex-cit-a-bil-i-ty
ex-cit-a-bly
ex-ci-ta-tion
ex-cite
ex-cit-ed
ex-cit-ing
ex-cit-ed
ex-cit-ed-ly
ex-cit-ed-ness
ex-cite-ment
ex-cit-ing
ex-cit-ing-ly
ex-claim
ex-cla-ma-tion
ex-clam-a-to-ry
ex-clam-a-to-ri-ly
ex-clude
ex-clu-sion

ex-clu-sive
ex-clu-sive-ly
ex-clu-sive-ness
ex-clu-siv-i-ty
ex-com-mu-ni-cate
ex-co-ri-ate
ex-co-ri-at-ed
ex-co-ri-at-ing
ex-co-ri-a-tion
ex-cre-ment
ex-cre-men-tal
ex-cres-cense
ex-cres-cent
ex-cre-ta
ex-cre-tal
ex-crete
ex-cret-ed
ex-cret-ing
ex-cre-tion
ex-cru-ci-ate
ex-cru-ci-at-ed
ex-cru-ci-at-ing
ex-cru-ci-at-ing-ly
ex-cru-ci-a-tion
ex-cur-sive
ex-cur-sive-ly
ex-cur-sive-ness
ex-cus-a-to-ry
ex-cuse
ex-e-cra-ble
ex-e-cra-ble-ness
ex-e-cra-bly
ex-e-cra-tion
ex-e-cute
ex-e-cut-ed
ex-e-cut-ing
ex-e-cut-a-ble
ex-e-cut-er
ex-e-cu-tion
ex-e-cu-tion-er
ex-ec-u-tive
ex-ec-u-tive-ly
ex-ec-u-tor
ex-ec-u-tor-ship
ex-e-ge-sis
ex-em-pli-fy
ex-em-pli-fied
ex-em-pli-fy-ing
ex-em-pli-fi-a-ble
ex-em-pli-fi-ca-tion
ex-empt
ex-emp-tion
ex-er-cise

ex-er-cised
ex-er-cis-ing
ex-er-cis-er
ex-ert
ex-er-tion
ex-fo-li-ate
ex-fo-li-at-ed
ex-fo-li-at-ing
ex-fo-li-a-tion
ex-hal-la-tion
ex-hale
ex-haled
ex-hal-ing
ex-hal-ant
ex-haust
ex-hib-it
ex-hib-it-a-ble
ex-hib-i-tor
ex-hib-i-to-ry
ex-hi-bi-tion
ex-hi-bi-tion-ism
ex-hi-bi-tion-ist
ex-hi-bi-tion-is-tic
ex-hil-a-rate
ex-hort
ex-hor-ta-tive
ex-hor-ta-to-ry
ex-hort-er
ex-hort-ing-ly
ex-hor-ta-tion
ex-hume
ex-humed
ex-hum-ing
ex-i-gen-cy
ex-i-gen-cies
ex-i-gent
ex-i-gent-ly
ex-ile
ex-iled
ex-ist
ex-ist-ence
ex-ist-ent
ex-is-ten-tial
ex-is-ten-tial-ly
ex-it
ex li-bris
ex-o-dus
ex of-fi-ci-o
ex-og-a-my
ex-og-a-mous
ex-og-e-nous
ex-og-e-nous-ly
ex-on-er-ate

ex-or-bi-tant
ex-or-bi-tance
ex-or-bi-tant-ly
ex-o-tic
ex-ot-i-cal-ly
ex-ot-i-cism
ex-pand
ex-pand-er
ex-panse
ex-pan-si-ble
ex-pan-sion
ex-pan-sion-ism
ex-pan-sion-ist
ex-pan-sive
ex-pan-sive-ly
ex-pan-sive-ness
ex-pa-ti-ate ˙
ex-pa-ti-at-ed
ex-pa-ti-at-ing
ex-pa-ti-a-tion
ex-pa-tri-ate
ex-pa-tri-at-ed
ex-pa-tri-at-ing
ex-pa-tri-a-tion
ex-pect
ex-pect-a-ble
ex-pect-a-bly
ex-pect-ing-ly
ex-pect-an-cy
ex-pect-an-cies
ex-pect-ant
ex-pect-ant-ly
ex-pec-ta-tion
ex-pec-to-rate
ex-pec-to-rat-ed
ex-pec-to-rat-ing
ex-pec-to-ra-tion
ex-pe-dite
ex-pe-dit-ed
ex-pe-dit-ing
ex-pe-dit-er
ex-pe-di-tion
ex-pe-di-tion-ary
ex-pe-di-tious
ex-pe-di-tious-ly
ex-pel
ex-pelled
ex-pel-ling
ex-pend
ex-pend-a-ble
ex-pend-a-bil-i-ty
ex-pend-i-ture
ex-pense

ex-pen-sive
ex-pen-sive-ly
ex-pe-ri-en-tial
ex-pe-ri-en-tial-ly
ex-per-i-ment
ex-per-i-men-ta-tion
ex-per-i-men-tal
ex-per-i-men-tal-ism
ex-per-i-men-tal-ist
ex-per-i-men-tal-ly
ex-pert
ex-pert-ly
ex-pert-ness
ex-per-tise
ex-pi-ra-tion
ex-pir-a-to-ry
ex-pire
ex-pired
ex-pir-ing
ex-plain
ex-plain-a-ble
ex-plain-er
ex-pla-na-tion
ex-plan-a-to-ry
ex-plan-a-to-ri-ly
ex-ple-tive
ex-pli-ca-ble
ex-pli-cate
ex-pli-cat-ed
ex-pli-cat-ing
ex-pli-ca-tion
ex-pli-ca-tive
ex-pli-ca-tor
ex-plic-it
ex-plic-it-ly
ex-plic-it-ness
ex-plode
ex-plod-ed
ex-plod-ing
ex-plod-er
ex-ploit
ex-ploit-a-ble
ex-ploi-ta-tion
ex-ploit-er
ex-ploit-ive
ex-plore
ex-plo-ra-tion
ex-plor-a-to-ry
ex-plor-er
ex-plo-sion
ex-plo-sive
ex-plo-sive-ly
ex-plo-sive-ness

ex-po-nent
  ex-po-nen-tial
  ex-po-nen-tial-ly
ex-port
  ex-port-a-ble
  ex-por-ta-tion
  ex-port-er
ex-pose
  ex-posed
  ex-pos-ing
  ex-pos-er
ex-po-si-tion
  ex-pos-i-tor
  ex-pos-i-to-ry
ex post fac-to
ex-pos-tu-late
ex-po-sure
ex-pound
  ex-pound-er
ex-press
  ex-press-er
  ex-press-i-ble
ex-pres-sion
ex-pres-sive
  ex-pres-sive-ly
  ex-pres-sive-ness
ex-press-ly
ex-press-way
ex-pro-pri-ate
  ex-pro-pri-at-ing
  ex-pro-pri-a-tor
  ex-pro-pri-a-tion
ex-pul-sion
  ex-pul-sive
ex-punge
ex-pur-gate
ex-pur-ga-to-ry
  ex-pur-ga-to-ri-al
ex-qui-site
  ex-qui-site-ly
  ex-qui-site-ness
ex-tant
ex-tem-po-ra-ne-ous
ex-tem-po-rize
  ex-tem-po-rized
  ex-tem-po-riz-ing
  ex-tem-po-ri-za-tion
  ex-tem-po-riz-er
ex-tend
  ex-tend-i-bil-i-ty
  ex-tend-i-ble
ex-tend-ed
  ex-tend-ed-ly

ex-tend-ed-ness
ex-tend-er
ex-ten-si-ble
  ex-ten-si-bil-i-ty
ex-ten-sion
  ex-ten-sion-al
ex-ten-sive
  ex-ten-sive-ly
  ex-ten-sive-ness
ex-tent
ex-ten-u-ate
ex-te-ri-or
  ex-te-ri-or-ly
ex-ter-mi-nate
  ex-ter-mi-nat-ed
  ex-ter-mi-nat-ing
  ex-ter-mi-na-tion
ex-ter-nal
  ex-ter-nal-ly
ex-tinct
ex-tinc-tion
ex-tin-guish
  ex-tin-guish-a-ble
  ex-tin-guish-er
  ex-tin-guish-ment
ex-tir-pate
  ex-tir-pat-ed
  ex-tir-pat-ing
  ex-tir-pa-tion
  ex-tir-pa-tive
ex-tol
  ex-tol-ler
  ex-tol-lingly
  ex-tol-ment
ex-tort
  ex-tor-ter
  ex-tor-tive
ex-tor-tion
ex-tra
ex-tract
  ex-tract-a-ble
  ex-trac-tive
ex-trac-tion
ex-tra-cur-ric-u-lar
ex-tra-dite
ex-tra-ne-ous
  ex-tra-ne-ous-ly
  ex-tra-ne-ous-ness
ex-traor-di-nary
  ex-traor-di-nar-i-ly
ex-trap-o-late
  ex-trap-o-lat-ed
  ex-trap-o-lat-ing

ex-trap-o-la-tion
ex-tra-sen-so-ry
ex-tra-ter-res-tri-al
ex-tra-ter-ri-to-ri-al
ex-trav-a-gance
  ex-trav-a-gan-cy
ex-trav-a-gant
  ex-trav-a-gant-ly
ex-trav-a-gan-za
ex-treme
  ex-treme-ly
  ex-treme-ness
ex-trem-ist
  ex-trem-ism
ex-trem-i-ty
  ex-trem-i-ties
ex-tri-cate
  ex-tri-cat-ed
  ex-tri-cat-ing
  ex-tri-ca-ble
  ex-tri-ca-tion
ex-trin-sic
ex-tro-vert
  ex-tro-ver-sion
ex-trude
ex-u-ber-ance
ex-u-ber-ant
  ex-u-ber-ant-ly
ex-ude
  ex-ud-ed
  ex-ud-ing
  ex-u-da-tion
ex-ult
  ex-ult-ant
  ex-ult-ant-ly
  ex-ul-at-tion
  ex-ult-ing-ly
ex-ur-ban-ite
eye
  eyed
  eye-ing
eye-ball
eye-glass
  eye-glass-es
eye-hole
eye-let
eye-lid
eye-o-pen-er
  eye-o-pen-ing
eye-wit-ness
ey-rie
  ey-ry
  ey-ries

F

fa-ble
  fa-bled
fab-ric
fab-ri-cate
  fab-ri-cated
  fab-ri-cat-ing
  fab-ri-ca-tion
fab-u-lous
  fab-u-lous-ness
fa-cade
  fa-cades
face
  faced
  fac-ing
face card
face--lift
fac-et
fa-ce-tious
  fa-ce-tious-ly
fa-cial
  fa-cial-ly
fac-ile
  fac-ile-ly
  fac-ile-ness
fa-cil-i-tate
fa-cil-i-ty
fac-ing
fac-sim-i-le
fact
fac-tion
  fac-tion-al
  fac-tion-al-ly
fac-ti-tious
  fac-ti-tious-ly
fac-ti-tious-ness
fac-tor
fac-to-ry
  fac-to-ries
fac-to-tum
fac-tu-al
fac-ul-ty
fad
  fad-dish
  fad-dist
fade
  fad-ed
  fad-ing
fa-er-ie
  fa-ery
  fa-er-ies
fag
  faggged
  fag-ging

fag-got
fag-ot
Fahr-en-heit
fail-ing
  fail-ing-ly
fail-safe
fail-ure
faint
  faint-ly
  faint-ness
faint-heart-ed
fair
  fir-ness
fair-ground
fair-ly
fair-mind-ed
fair--trade
fair-y
  fair-ies
fair-y-like
fair-y tale
faith
faith-ful
faith-ful-less
fake
  faked
  fak-ing
  fak-er
fal-con
fal-con-ry
fall
  fall-en
  fall-ing
fal-la-cious
  fal-la-cious-ly
fal-la-cy
fall-guy
fal-li-ble
  fal-li-bly
fail-ing star
fall-out
fal-low
  fal-low-ness
false
  fals-er
  fals-est
false-hood
fal-si-fy
  fal-si-fied
  fal-si-fy-ing
  fal-si-fi-er
fal-si-ty
fal-ter

fal-ter-er
  fal-ter-ing-ly
fame
famed
fa-mil-ial
fa-mil-iar
  fa-mil-iar-ly
fa-mil-i-ar-i-ty
fa-mil-iar-ize
  fa-mil-iar-ized
  fa-mil-iar-iz-ing
fam-ily
  fam-i-lies
fam-ine
fam-ish
fam-ished
fa-mous
  fa-mous-ly
fan
  fan-like
  fan-ner
fa-nat-ic
  fa-nat-i-cal
fa-nat-i-cism
fa-nat-i-cize
  fa-nat-i-cized
fan-ci-er
fan-ci-ul
  fan-ci-ful-ly
fan-cy
  fan-cies
  fan-ci-ly
  fan-ci-ness
fan-cy-work
fan-fare
fang
fanged
fan-light
fan-tas-tic
  fan-tas-ti-cal
fan-ta-sy
  fan-ta-sies
far
  far-ther
  far-thest
far-a-way
farce
  farced
  farc-ing
far-ci-cal
  far-ci-cal-ly
fare
  fared

far-ing
fare-well
far-fetched
far-flung
farm
farm-er
farm-hand
farm-house
farm-ing
farm-yard
far-off
far-reach-ing
  far-reach-ing-ly
far-see-ing
far-sight-ed
  far-sight-ed-ly
far-ther
far-ther-most
far-thest
fas-ci-a
  fas-ci-ae
fas-ci-cle
  fas-ci-cled
fas-ci-nate
  fas-ci-nat-ed
  fas-ci-nat-ing
fas-ci-na-tion
fas-cism
  fas-cist
  fa-scis-tic
fash-ion
fash-ion-ble
fast
fas-ten
  fas-ten-er
  fas-ten-ing
fas-tid-i-ous
  fas-ti-di-ous-ly
fat
  fat-ter
  fat-test
fa-tal
  fa-tal-ly
fa-tal-ism
  fa-tal-ist
fa-tal-i-ty
  fa-tal-i-ties
fate
  fat-ed
  fat-ing
fate-ful
  fate-ful-ly
  fate-ful-ness

fa-ther
fa-ther-hood
  fa-ther-ly
fa-ther-in-law
  fa-thers-in-law
fa-ther-land
fath-om
  fath-om-a-ble
  fath-om-less
fa-tique
  fa-tiqued
  fa-tiq-uing
fat-i-ga-ble
fat-ten
  fat-ten-er
fa-tu-i-ty
  fa-tui-ties
fat-u-ous
  fat-u-ous-ly
fau-cet
fault
fault-find-er
  fault-find-ing
fault-less
fault-less-ly
fault-less-ness
fault-y
  fault-i-er
  fault-i-est
  fault-i-ly
fau-na
  fau-nas
  fau-nae
faux pas
fa-vor
  fa-vor-ing-ly
fa-vor-a-ble
  fa-vor-ably
fa-vored
  fa-vored-ly
  fa-vored-ness
fa-vor-ite
fa-vor-it-ism
fawn
faze
  fazed
  faz-ing
fe-al-ty
fear
fear-ful
  fear-ful-ly
fear-less
  fear-less-ly

fea-si-ble
  fea-si-bil-i-ty
  fea-si-bly
feast
feat
feath-er
  fea-thered
feath-er-bed-ding
fea-ture
  fea-tured
  fea-tur-ing
fea-ture-ness
fe-brile
fe-ces
  fe-cal
feck-less
fe-cund
  fe-cun-di-ty
fe-cun-date
  fe-cun-dat-ed
  fe-cun-da-tion
fed-er-al
fed-er-al-ism
fed-er-li-ist
fed-er-al-ize
  fed-er-al-ized
  fed-er-al-iz-ing
  fed-er-al-i-za-tion
  fed-er-al-ly
fed-er-ate
  fed-er-at-ed
  fed-er-at-ing
fed-er-a-tion
fee
fee-ble
  fee-bler
  fee-blest
  fee-bly
fee-ble-mind-ed
  fee-ble-mind-ed-ness
feed-back
feel
  feel-ing
feel-er
feel-ing
  feel-ing-ly
  feel-ing-ness
feign
  feigned
  feign-ed-ly
  feign-er
  feign-ing-ly
feint

feist-y
feist-i-er
feist-i-est
fe-lic-i-tate
fe-lic-i-tat-ed
fe-lic-i-tat-ing
fe-lic-i-ta-tion
fe-lic-i-tous
fe-lic-i-tous-ly
fe-lic-i-ty
fe-lic-i-ties
fe-line
fe-line-ly
fe-line-i-ty
fell
fel-la-ti-o
fel-low
fel-low-ship
fe-lon
fel-o-ny
fel-o-nies
fe-lo-ni-ous
fe-lo-ni-ous-ly
fe-male
fem-i-nine
fem-i-nine-ly
fem-i-nine-ness
fem-i-nin-i-ty
fem-i-nism
fem-i-nist
fem-i-nis-tic
fem-i-nize
fem-i-nized
fem-i-niz-ing
fe-mur
fe-murs
fem-o-ra
fem-o-ral
fen
fen-ny
fen-ni-er
fen-ni-est
fence
fecned
fenc-ing
fenc-er
fen-der
fe-ral
fer-ment
fer-ment-a-ble
fer-men-ta-tion
fern
fern-er-y

fern-er-ies
fe-ro-cious
fe-ro-cious-ly
fe-ro-ci-ty
fer-ret
fer-ret-er
fer-ro-con-crete
fer-ro-mag-net-ic
fer-ru-gi-nous
fer-rule
fer-ry
fer-ries
fer-ry-boat
fer-ry-man
fer-tile
fer-tile-ly
fer-tile-ness
fer-til-i-ty
fer-ti-li-za-tion
fer-ti-li-za-tion-al
fer-ti-lize
fer-ti-lized
fer-ti-liz-ing
fer-ti-liz-a-ble
fer-ti-liz-er
fer-vent
fer-ven-cy
fer-vid
fer-vid-ly
fer-vid-ness
fer-vor
fes-ter
fes-ti-val
fes-tive
fes-tive-ly
fes-tive-ness
fes-tiv-i-ty
fes-toon
fes-toon-ery
fes-toon-er-ies
fe-tal
fetch
fetch-er
fetch-ing
fetch-ing-ly
fete
fet-id
fet-id-ly
fet-id-ness
fet-ish
fet-ish-ism
fet-ish-ist
fet-ish-is-tic

fet-lock
fet-ter
fet-tle
fe-tus
fe-tus-es
feud
feud-ist
feu-dal
feu-dal-ism
feu-dal-ist
feu-dal-is-tic
feu-dal-i-za-tion
feu-dal-ize
feu-dal-ized
feu-dal-iz-ing
fe-ver
fe-ver blis-ter
fe-ver-ish
fe-ver-ish-ly
fe-ver-ish-ness
fe-ver-ous
fe-ver-ous-ly
few
few-ness
fez-zes
fi-as-co
fi-as-cos
fi-as-coes
fi-at
fib
fi-ber
fi-bered
fi-ber-board
fi-ber-glass
fi-bril
fi-bril-la-tion
fi-broid
fi-brous
fib-u-la
fib-u-las
fib-u-lae
fick-le
fick-le-ness
fic-tion
fic-tion-al
fic-tion-al-ly
fic-ti-tious
fid-dle
fid-dler
fid-dled
fi-del-i-ty
fidg-et
fidg-ety

field-er
field-glass
fiend
  fiend-ish
  fiend-ish-ly
  fiend-ish-ness
fierce
  fierce-ly
  fierce-ness
fier-y
  fier-i-er
  fier-i-est
  fier-i-ly
fier-i-ness
fif-teen
fif-teenth
fifth
fif-ti-eth
fif-ty
  fif-ties
fight
fight-er
fig-ment
fig-u-ra-tion
fig-u-ra-tive
  fig-u-ra-tive-ly
  fid-u-ra-tive-ness
fig-ure
  fig-ured
  fig-ur-ing
  fig-ur-er
fig-ure-head
fig-ur-ine
fil-a-ment
  fil-a-men-ta-ry
  fil-a-ment-ed
  fil-a-men-tous
filch
file
  filed
  fil-ing
fi-let
fi-let mi-gnon
fil-i-al
  fil-i-al-ly
fil-i-bus-ter
fil-i-gree
  fil-i-greed
  fil-i-gree-ing
  fil-lings
fill-er
fil-let
fill-ing

fil-lip
fil-ly
  fil-lies
film-strip
film-y
  film-i-er
  film-i-est
  film-i-ness
fil-ter
filth
  filth-i-ness
  filthy
  filth-i-er
  filth-i-est
fin
  finned
  fin-ning
  fin-less
  fin-like
fi-na-gled
  fi-na-gling
  fi-na-gler
fi-nal
fi-na-le
fi-nal-ist
fi-nal-i-ty
  fi-nal-i-ties
fi-nal-ize
  fi-nal-ized
  fi-nal-iz-ing
  fi-nal-ly
fi-nance
  fi-nanced
  fi-nanc-ing
  fi-nan-cial
  fi-nan-cial-ly
fin-an-cier
finch
find
  found
  find-ing
find-er
fine
  fin-er
  fin-est
  fine-ly
  fine-ness
fin-er-y
  fin-er-ies
fi-nesse
  fi-nessed
  fi-ness-ing
fin-ger

fin-ger-bowl
fin-ger-ing
fin-ger-nail
fin-ger-print
fin-i-al
fin-i-cal
  fin-i-cal-ly
fin-ick-y
  fin-ick-ing
fin-is
  fin-is-es
fin-ish
  fin-ished
  fin-ish-er
fi-nite
  fi-nite-ly
  fi-nite-ness
fire
  fired
  fir-ing
  fir-er
fire-arm
fire-ball
fire-brand
fire-bug
fire-crack-er
fire-fight-er
fire-fly
  fire-flies
fire-man
fire-place
fire-plug
fire-pow-er
fire-proof
fire-side
fire-trap
fire-wa-ter
fire-wood
fire-works
fir-ing-squad
firm
  firm-ly
  firm-ness
fir-ma-ment
first-born
first-hand
first-ling
first-ly
first-rate
first-string
fis-cal
  fis-cal-ly
fish-er

fish-er-man
  fish-er-men
fish-er-y
  fish-er-ies
fish-hook
fish-ing
fish-wife
  fish-wived
fish-y
  fish-i-er
  fish-i-est
fis-sle
fis-sion
fis-sure
  fis-sured
  fis-sur-ing
fist-ic
fist-i-cuff
fit
  fit-ter
  fit-test
  fit-ted
  fit-ting
  fit-ly
  fit-ness
fit-ful
  fit-ful-ly
  fit-ful-ness
fit-ting
  fit-ting-ly
  fit-ting-ness
five-fold
five-and-ten
fix
  fix-a-ble
  fixed
  fix-ed-ly
  fix-er
fix-a-tion
fix-a-tive
fix-ings
fix-i-ty
  fix-i-ties
fix-ture
fiz-zle
  fiz-zled
  fiz-zling
fiz-zy
  fiz-zi-er
  fiz-zi-est
flab-ber-gast
flab-by
  flab-bi-er

flab-bi-est
flab-bi-ly
flab-bi-ness
flac-cid
flag
  flagged
  flag-ging
flag-el-lant
  flag-el-lat-ed
  flag-el-lat-ing
  flag-el-la-tion
fla-gi-tious
flag-on
flag-pole
flag-rank
fla-grant
  fla-grant-ly
flag-ship
flag-stone
flail
flair
flake
  flaked
  flak-ing
flak-y
  flak-i-er
  flak-i-est
  flak-i-ness
flam-boy-ant
  flam-boy-ance
  flam-boy-an-cy
  flam-boy-ant-ly
flame
  flamed
  flam-ing
  flam-ing-ly
flam-ma-ble
flange
flank
  flank-er
flan-nel-ette
flap
  flapped
  flap-ping
  flap-per
flap-jack
flare
  flared
  flar-ing
flare-up
flash-back
flash-light
  flash-i-er

flash-i-est
flash-i-ly
flash-i-ness
flask
flat
  flat-ly
  flat-ted
  flat-ting
  flat-ness
flat-car
flat-foot
flat-foot-ed
  flat-foot-ed-ly
falt-ten
  flat-ten-er
flat-ter
  flat-ter-er
flat-ter-ing-ly
flat-ter-y
  flat-ter-ies
flat-u-lent
  flat-u-lence
  flat-u-len-cy
  flat-u-lent-ly
flat-ware
flaunt
  flaunt-er
  flaunt-ing-ly
  flanty
  flaunt-i-er
  flaunt-i-est
flau-tist
fla-vor
  fla-vored
  fla-vor-less
  fla-vor-ing
  flaw-less
fla-zen
flax-seed
flay-er
flea-bite
  flea-bit-ten
fleck
flec-tion
fledge
  fledged
  fledg-ing
  fledg-ling
flee
  fled
  flee-ing
fleece
  fleeced

fleec-ing
fleec-y
  fleec-i-er
  fleec-i-est
  fleec-i-ness
fleet
  fleet-ly
  fleet-ness
fleet-ing
  fleet-ing-ly
  fleet-ing-ness
flesh-ly
  flesh-li-er
  flesh-li-est
flesh-pots
flesh-y
  flesh-i-ert
  flesh-i-est
  flesh-i-ness
flex-i-ble
  flex-i-bil-i-ty
  flex-i-bly
flex-ion
flex-or
flex-ure
fib-ber-ti-gib-bet
flick-er
  flick-er-ing
fli-er
flight
  flight-less
flight-y
  flight-i-er
  flight-i-est
  flight-i-ly
  flight-i-ness
flim-flam
  flim-flammed
  flim-flam-ming
firm-sy
  firm-si-er
  firm-si-est
  firm-si-ly
  firm-si-ness
flinch
  flinch-er
  flinch-ing-ly
fin-ders
fling
  flung
  fling-ing
flint-y
  flint-i-er

flint-i-est
flint-i-ness
flip
  flipped
  flip-ping
flip-flop
flip-pant
  flip-pan-cy
  flip-pant-ly
flip-per
flirt-er
flir-ta-tion
  flir-ta-tious
flit
  flit-ted
  flit-ting
  flit-ter
float-a-ble
float-a-tion
float-er
float-ing
floc-cu-lent
  floc-cu-lence
flocked
flood-gate
flood-light
  flood-lit
floor-ing
floor-walk-er
floo-zy
  floo-zies
flop
  flopped
  flop-ping
  flop-per
flop-house
flop-py
  flop-pi-er
  flop-pi-est
  flop-pi-ly
flo-ra
  flo-ras
  flo-rae
flo-ral
flo-res-cence
  flo-res-cent
flo-ret
flo-ri-cul-ure
  flo-ri-cul-tur-al
  flo-ri-cul-tur-ist
flor-id
  flo-rid-i-ty
  flor-id-ly

flor-id-ness
flo-rist
floss
  flossy
  floss-i-er
  floss-i-est
flo-ta-tion
flo-til-la
flot-sam
flounce
  flounced
  flounc-ing
floun-der
flour-y
  flour-i-er
  flour-i-est
flour-ish
  flou-rish-ing
flow-er
  flow-ered
  flow-er-ing
flow-ery
  flow-er-i-ness
flub
  flubbed
  flub-bing
fluc-tu-ate
  fluc-tu-at-ed
  fluc-tu-at-ing
  fluc-tu-a-tion
flue
  flu-ent
  flu-ency
  flu-ent-ly
fluff
  fluff-i-ness
  fluff-y
  fluff-i-er
  fluff-i-est
flu-id
  flu-id-ly
  flu-id-ness
fluke
  fluky
  fluk-i-er
  fluk-i-est
flum-mer-y
  flum-mer-ies
flun-ky
  flunk-ies
flu-o-resce
  flu-o-resced
  flu-o-resc-ing

flu-o-res-cence
  flu-o-res-sent
flur-ry
  flur-ries
  flur-ried
  flur-ry-ing
flus-ter
flute
  flut-ed
  flut-ing
  flut-ist
flut-ter
  flut-ter-er
  flut-ter-ing-ly
  flut-tery
  flut-ter-i-er
  flut-ter-i-est
flux-ion
fly-brown
fly-by-night
fly-er
fly-ing
fly-leaf
  fly-leaves
fly-pa-per
fly-speck
fly-wheel
foal
foam
  foam-i-ness
  foam-y
  foam-i-er
  foam-i-est
fob
  fobbed
  fob-bing
fo-cal
  fo-cal-ize
  fo-cal-lized
  fo-cal-iz-ing
fo-cus
  fo-cus-es
  fo-cus-ing
  fo-cus-er
fod-der
foe-tus
  foe-tal
fog
  fogged
  fog-ging
fog-gy
  fog-gi-er
  fog-gi-est

fog-gi-ly
fog-gi-ness
fog-horn
fo-gy
  fo-gies
  fo-gy-ish
foi-ble
fold-er
fol-de-rol
fo-li-a-ceous
fo-li-age
fo-li-ate
  fo-li-at-ed
  fo-li-at-ing
  fol-li-a-tion
fo-li-o
  fo-li-os
  fol-li-oed
  fo-li-o-ing
folk-lore
  folk-lor-ist
flok-sy
  flok-si-er
  flok-si-est
  flok-si-ness
folk-ways
fol-li-cle
  fol-lic-u-lar
fol-low
fol-low-er
fol-low-ing
fol-ly
  fol-lies
fo-ment
  fo-men-ta-tion
  fo-ment-er
fon-dant
fon-dle
  fond-led
  fon-dling
  fon-dler
  fond-ly
  fond-ness
fon-due
food-stuff
fool-er-y
  fool-er-ies
fool-har-dy
  fool-har-di-ness
fool-proof
fools-cap
foot-age
foot-ball

foot-board
foot-can-dle
foot-ed
foot-fall
foot-hill
foot-hold
foot-ing
foot-lights
foot-loose
foot-note
  foot-not-ed
  foot-not-ing
foot-path
foot-print
foot-sore
foot-step
foot-stool
foot-wear
foot-work
foo-zle
  foo-zled
  foo-zling
fop
  fop-pery
  fop-per-ies
  fop-pish
  fop-pish-ly
  fop-pish-ness
for-age
  for-aged
  for-ag-ing
for-ay
for-bear
  for-bore
  for-borned
  for-bear-ing
  for-bear-ance
  for-bear-ing-ly
for-bid
  for-bade
  for-bid-den
  for-bid-ding
force-ful
  force-ful-ly
for-ceps
for-ci-ble
  for-ci-bly
ford-a-ble
  fore-arm
fore-bear
fore-bode
  fore-bod-ed
  fore-bod-ing

fore-bod-er
fore-brain
fore-cast
  fore-cast-ed
  fore-cast-ing
  fore-cast-er
fore-close
  fore-closed
  fore-clos-ing
  fore-clo-sure
fore-fa-ther
fore-fin-ger
fore-foot
  fore-feet
fore-front
fore-gath-er
fore-go
  fore-went
  fore-gone
  fore-go-ing
fore-ground
fore-hand
fore-hand-ed
  fore-hand-ed-ness
fore-head
for-eign
  for-eign-er
  for-eign-ness
fore-leg
fore-lock
fore-man
  fore-men
fore-most
fo-ren-sic
fore-or-dain
fore-quar-ter
fore-run
  fore-ran
  fore-run-ning
fore-run-ner
fore-see
  fore-saw
  fore-seen
  fore-see-ing
  fore-see-a-ble
  fore-se-er
fore-shad-ow
  fore-shad-ow-er
fore-sight
  fore-sight-ed
  fore-sight-ed-ness
fore-skin
for-est

fore-stall
for-est-a-tion
for-es-ter
for-es-try
fore-taste
  fore-tast-ed
  fore-tast-ing
fore-tell
  fore-told
  fore-tell-ing
  fore-tell-er
fore-thought
for-ev-er
for-ev-er-more
fore-warn
fore-word
for-feit
  for-feit-er
for-fei-ture
for-gath-er
forge
  forged
  forg-ing
  forg-er
for-ger-y
  fog-er-ies
for-get
  for-got
  for-got-ten
  for-get-ting
  for-get-ta-ble
  for-get-ter
for-get-ful
  for-get-ful-ly
  for-get-ful-ness
for-give
  for-gave
  for-giv-en
  for-giv-ing
  for-giv-a-ble
  for-give-ness
  for-giv-er
for-go
  for-went
  for-gone
  for-go-ing
  for-go-er
fork-loft
for-lorn
  for-lorn-ly
  for-lorn-ness
for-mal
  for-mal-ly

for-mal-ism
for-mal-i-ty
  for-mal-i-ties
for-mal-ize
  for-mal-ized
  for-mal-iz-ing
  for-mal-i-za-tion
for-mat
for-ma-tion
form-a-tive
for-mer
for-mer-ly
for-mi-da-ble
  for-mi-da-bly
form-less
  form-less-ly
for-mu-la
  for-mu-las
  for-mu-lae
for-mu-lar-y
  for-mu-lar-ies
for-mu-late
  for-mu-lat-ed
  for-mu-lat-ing
  for-mu-la-tion
  for-mu-la-tor
fort
forte
forth-com-ing
forth-right
  forth-right-ness
forth-with
for-ti-fi-ca-tion
for-ti-fy
  for-ti-fied
  for-ti-fy-ing
  for-ti-fi-er
for-tis-si-mo
for-ti-tude
fort-night
for-night-ly
  for-night-lies
for-tress
for-tu-i-tous
  for-tu-i-tous-ly
  for-tu-i-tous-ness
for-tu-nate
  for-tu-nate-ly
for-tune
for-tune-tell-er
  for-tune-tell-ing
for-ty
  for-ties

for-ty-nin-er
fo-rum
  fo-rums
  fo-ra
fos-sil
fos-sil-ize
  fos-sil-ized
  fos-sil-iz-ing
  fos-sil-i-za-tion
fos-ter
  fos-tered
  fos-ter-ing
fought
fou-lard
found
foun-da-tion
  foun-da-tion-al
found-er
found-ling
found-ry
  found-ries
foun-tain
foun-tain-head
four-flush-er
four-square
four-teen
  four-teenth
fourth
  fourth-ly
fowl
  fowl-er
foy-er
fra-cas
  fra-cas-es
frac-tion
  frac-tion-al
frac-tious
  frac-tious-ly
frac-ture
  frac-tured
  frac-tur-ing
frag-ile
  fra-gil-i-ty
frag-ment
  frag-ment-al
  frag-men-ter-i-ness
  frag-men-tary
frag-men-ta-tion
frag-ment-ize
  frag-ment-ized
  frag-ment-iz-ing
fra-grance
  fra-grant

fra-grant-ly
frail
  frail-ty
  frail-ness
frame
  framed
  fram-ing
  fram-er
frame-up
frame-work
franc
fran-chise
  fran-chised
frank-furt-er
frank-in-cense
fran-tic
  fran-ti-cal-ly
fra-ter-nal
  fra-ter-nal-ly
fra-ter-ni-ty
  fra-ter-ni-ties
frat-er-nize
frat-ri-cide
  frat-ri-cid-al
fraud-u-lent
  fraud-u-lence
fraught
fraz-zle
  fraz-zled
  fraz-zling
freak
  freak-ish
freck-le
  freck-led
  freck-li-er
free
  fre-er
  free-ly
free-bie
free-boot-er
free-dom
free-lance
  free-lanced
  free-lanc-ing
free-spoken
  free-spo-ken-ness
free-stone
  free-think-ing
free-way
freeze
  froze
  fro-zen
  freez-ing

freez-er
fre-net-ic
  fre-net-i-cal-ly
fren-zy
  fren-zies
  fren-zied
  fren-zy-ing
fre-quen-cy
  fre-quen-cies
fre-quent
  fre-quent-er
  fre-quent-ly
fresh
  fresh-ly
  fresh-ness
fresh-en
  fresh-en-er
fresh-et
fresh-man
  fresh-men
fret
  fret-ted
fret-work
fri-ary
  fri-ar-ies
fric-as-see
  fric-as-seed
fric-tion
  fric-tion-al
friend
  friend-less
friend-ly
  friend-li-er
  friend-li-est
frieze
fright-ful
  fright-ful-ly
frig-id
  fri-gid-i-ty
  frig-id-ly
  frig-id-ness
frilly
  frill-i-er
  frill-i-est
fringe
  fringed
  fring-ing
frip-pery
  frip-per-ies
frisky
  frisk-i-er
fit-ter
friv-o-lous

fri-vol-i-ty
frizz
  friz-zi-ness
  friz-zi-er
friz-zle
  friz-zled
  friz-zling
frol-ic
  frol-ick-ed
  frol-ick-ing
frol-ic-some
front-age
  fron-tal-ly
fron-tier
frost
  frost-ed
frost-ing
frost-y
  frost-i-er
froth
  frothy
  froth-i-er
  froth-i-est
frou-frou
fro-ward
frown
  frown-ing-ly
frow-zy
  frow-zi-er
fro-zen
  fro-zen-ly
  fro-zen-ness
fruc-ti-fy
  fruc-ti-fied
  fruc-ti-fy-ing
  fruc-ti-fi-ca-tion
fru-gal
  fru-gal-i-ty
  fru-gal-i-ties
  fru-gal-ly
fruit-ful
  fruit-ful-ly
fru-i-tion
  fruit-less-ly
fruity
frump
  frump-ish
  frump-i-est
frus-trate
  frus-trat-ed
  frus-trat-ing
  frus-tra-tion
fry-er

fud-dle
  fud-dled
  fud-dling
fudge
  fudged
  fudg-ing
fu-el
  fu-eled
  fu-el-ing
fu-gi-tive
  fu-gi-tive-ly
ful-crum
  ful-crums
  ful-cra
ful-fill
  ful-filled
  ful-fil-ling
  ful-fil-ment
full
  full-ness
  ful-ly
full-back
ful-mi-nate
  ful-mi-nat-ed
  ful-mi-nat-ing
  ful-mi-na-tion
ful-some
  ful-some-ly
fu-mi-gate
  fu-mi-gat-ed
  fu-mi-gat-ing
func-tion
  func-tion-less
func-tion-al
  func-tion-al-ly
func-tion-ary
  func-tion-ar-ies
fun-da-men-tal
  fun-da-men-tal-ly
fun-da-men-tal-ism
  fun-da-men-tal-ist
fu-ner-al
fu-ner-re-al
fun-gi-cide
  fun-gi-cid-al
  fun-gi-cid-al-ly
fun-gous
fun-gus
  fun-gi
  fun-gus-es
funic-u-lar
funk-y
  funk-i-er

funk-i-est
fun-nel
  fun-neled
  fun-nel-ing
fur
  furred
  fur-ring
fur-bish
fu-ri-ous
  fu-ri-ous-ly
fur-long
fur-lough
fur-nace
fur-nish
fur-nish-ings
fur-ni-ture
for-row
fur-ry
  fur-ri-er
  fur-ri-est
fur-ther
fur-ther-more
fur-ther-most
fur-thest
fur-tive
  fur-tive-ly
fu-ry
  fu-ries
fuse
  fused
  fus-ing
fu-see
fu-se-lage
fu-si-bil-i-ty
fu-si-ble
fu-si-form
fu-si-lade
  fu-si-lad-ed
  fu-si-lad-ing
fu-sion
fussy
  fuss-i-er
  fuss-i-est
  fuss-i-ly
fus-tian
fus-ty
fu-tile
fu-til-i-ty
  fu-til-i-ties
fu-ture
fu-tur-is-tic
fu-tu-ri-ty
fuzz-y

G

gab
  gabbed
  gab-ber
gab-ar-dine
gab-ble
  gab-bled
  gab-bler
gab-by
  gab-bi-er
  gab-bi-est
ga-ble
  ga-bled
  ga-bling
gad
  gad-ded
  gad-ding
gad-a-bout
gad-fly
  gad-flies
gad-get
  gad-get-ry
gaffe
gaf-fer
gag
ga-ga
gai-e-ty
  gai-e-ties
gai-ly
gain-ful
gain-say
  gain-said
  gain-say-ing
gait
ga-la
ga-lac-tic
gal-ax-y
  gal-a-xies
gal-lant
gal-lant-ry
  gal-lant-ries
gal-ler-y
  gal-ler-ies
gal-ley
gal-li-cism
gal-li-mau-fry
  gal-li-mau-fries
gall-ing
gal-li-vant
gal-lon
gal-lop
gal-lows
  gal-lows-es
gall-stone

ga-loot
ga-lore
gal-van-ic
gal-va-nism
gal-va-nize
  gal-va-nized
gal-va-nom-e-ter
gam-bit
gam-ble
  gam-bled
  gam-bling
gam-bol
gam-brel
game
  gam-er
  gam-est
  gamed
  gam-ing
game-keep-er
game-some
game-ster
gam-ete
  ga-met-ic
gam-in
gam-ma
gam-mon
gam-ut
gam-y
  gam-i-er
  gam-i-est
  gam-i-ly
  gam-i-ness
gan-der
gang-land
gan-gling
gan-gli-on
  gan-glia
  gan-gli-ons
gan-gly
  gan-gli-er
  gan-gli-est
gang-plank
gan-grene
  gan-grened
  gan-gren-ing
  gan-gre-nous
gang-ster
gang-way
gant-let
gan-try
  gan-tries
gap
  gapped

gap-ping
gar-bage
gar-ble
  gar-bled
  gar-bling
gar-den
gar-gan-tu-an
gar-gle
  gar-gled
  gar-gling
gar-goyle
gar-ish
gar-land
gar-ment
gar-nish
gar-nish-ee
  gar-nish-ee-ing
gar-nish-ment
gar-ni-ture
gar-ret
gar-ri-son
gar-rote
  gar-rot-ed
  gar-rot-ing
  gar-rot-er
gar-ru-lous
gar-ter
gas-ket
gas-lit
gas-o-line
gas-ser
gas-sy
  gas-si-er
  gas-si-est
gas-tric
gas-ti-tis
gas-tro-in-tes-ti-nal
gas-tron-o-my
  gas-tro-nom-ic
  gas-tro-nom-i-cal
  gas-tro-nom-i-cal-ly
gas-works
gate-crash-er
  gate-crash-ing
gate-house
gate-keep-er
gate-post
gate-way
gath-er
  gath-er-ing
gauche
gau-cho
gaud-y

gaud-i-er
gaud-i-est
gaud-i-ly
gaunt-let
gauze
gauz-i-er
gauz-i-est
gauzy
gay-e-ty
gaze
gazed
gaz-er
gaz-ing
ga-ze-bo
ga-ze-bos
ga-ze-boes
ga-zelle
ga-zette
gaz-et-teer
gear-ing
gear-shift
gear-wheel
gee
geed
gee-ing
gee-zer
gei-sha
gel
gelled
gel-ling
gel-a-tin
gel-lat-i-nous
ge-la-tion
geld
geld-ed
geld-ing
gelt
gel-id
gem
gemmed
gem-ming
gem-ol-o-gy
gem-o-log-i-cal
gem-ol-o-gist
gem-stone
gen-darme
gen-der
gene
ge-ne-al-o-gy
ge-ne-a-log-i-cal
ge-ne-al-o-gist
gen-er-al
gen-er-al-is-si-mo

gen-er-al-is-si-mos
gen-er-al-ist
gen-er-al-i-ty
gen-er-al-i-ties
gen-er-ate
gen-er-at-ed
gen-er-at-ing
gen-er-a-tive
gen-er-a-tive-ly
gen-er-a-tion
gen-er-a-tor
ge-ner-ic
ge-ner-i-cal
ge-ner-i-cal-ly
gen-er-ous
gen-er-os-i-ty
gen-er-os-i-ties
gen-e-sis
ge-net-ic
ge-net-i-cal-ly
ge-net-ics
ge-net-i-cist
gen-ial
ge-ni-al-i-ty
ge-nie
ge-nies
ge-nii
gen-i-tal
gen-i-ta-lia
gen-i-tals
gen-ius
gen-ius-es
gen-o-cide
gen-o-ci-dal
gen-re
gen-teel
gen-tian
gen-tile
gen-til-i-ty
gen-til-i-ties
gen-tle
gen-tler
gen-tlest
gen-tly
gen-tle-folk
gen-tle-man
gen-tle-men
gen-tle-wom-an
gen-tle-wom-en
gen-try
gen-u-flect
gen-u-flec-tion
gen-u-flec-tor

gen-u-ine
ge-nus
gen-e-ra
ge-nus-es
ge-o-cen-tric
ge-o-cen-tri-cal-ly
ge-o-chem-is-try
ge-o-chem-i-cal
ge-o-chem-ist
ge-ode
ge-o-des-ic
ge-o-gra-phy
ge-o-gra-phies
ge-o-gra-pher
ge-o-gra-phic
ge-o-graph-i-cal
ge-o-met-ric
ge-om-e-try
ge-om-e-tries
ge-o-phys-ics
ge-o-phys-i-cal
ge-o-phys-i-cist
ge-o-pol-i-tic
ge-o-pol-i-tics
ge-o-pol-o-tic
ge-o-po-lit-i-cal
ge-o-po-lit-i-cal-ly
ge-o-ther-mal
ger-bil
ger-i-at-ric
ger-i-at-rics
ger-i-a-tri-cian
ger-i-at-rist
ger-mane
ger-mi-cide
ger-mi-cid-al
ger-on-tol-o-gy
ger-on-tol-o-gist
ger-ry-man-der
ger-und
ges-so
ges-tate
ges-tat-ed
ges-tat-ing
ges-ta-tion
ges-tic-u-late
ges-tic-u-lat-ed
ges-tic-u-lat-ing
ges-tic-u-la-tion
ges-tic-u-la-tive
ges-tic-u-la-to-ry
ges-tic-u-la-tor
ges-ture

ges-tured
ges-tur-ing
ges-tur-er
ge-sund-heit
get-a-way
gew-gaw
gey-ser
ghast-ly
ghast-li-er
ghast-li-est
ghast-li-ness
gher-kin
ghet-to
ghe-tos
ghet-toes
ghoul
gi-ant
gib-ber-ish
gib-bon
gibe
gib-er
gib-ing-ly
gib-let
gid-dy
gid-di-er
gid-di-est
gid-di-ly
gid-di-ness
gi-gan-tic
gi-gan-tism
gig-gle
gig-gled
gig-gling
gig-gler
gig-gly
gig-gli-er
gig-gli-est
gig-o-lo
gild-ed
gilt-edged
gim-crack
gim-let
gim-mick
gin-ger
gin-ger-bread
gin-ger-ly
gin-ger-li-ness
gin-ger-snap
gin-ger-y
ging-ham
gird-er
gir-dle
gir-dled

gir-dling
girl-hood
girl-ish
girth
gist
give
gave
giv-en
giv-ing
give-and-take
give-a-way
giz-zard
gla-cial
gla-cier
glad
glad-der
glad-dest
glad-ly
glad-ness
glad-den
glad-i-a-tor
glad-i-a-to-ri-al
glad-i-o-lus
glad-i-o-lus-es
glad-i-o-la
glad-some
glam-or-ize
glam-or-ized
glam-or-iz-ing
glam-or-i-za-tion
glam-or-i-zer
glam-or-ous
glam-or-ous-ly
glam-or-ous-ness
glam-our
glance
glanced
glanc-ing
glan-du-lar
glare
glared
glar-ing
glar-i-ness
glar-y
glar-i-er
glar-i-est
glass-blow-ing
glass-blow-er
glass-ful
glass-ware
glass-y
glass-i-er
glass-i-est

glass-i-ly
glass-i-ness
glau-co-ma
glaze
glazed
glaz-ing
gla-zier
gleam
gleam-ing
gleam-y
glean
glean-er
glean-ing
glee
glee-ful
glee-ful-ly
glee-ful-ness
glen-gar-ry
glib
glib-ber
glib-best
glib-ly
glib-ness
glide
glid-ed
glid-ing
glim-mer
glimpse
glimpsed
glis-san-do
glis-san-di
glis-san-dos
glis-ten
glit-ter
gloam-ing
gloat
gloat-er
gloat-ing
glob
glo-bal
glob-al-ly
globe-trot-ter
globe-trot-ting
glob-u-lar
glob-ule
glock-en-spiel
gloom-y
gloom-i-er
gloom-i-est
gloom-i-ly
gloom-i-ness
glo-ri-fy
glo-ri-fied

glo-ri-fy-ing
glo-ri-fi-ca-tion
glo-ri-fi-er
glo-ri-ous
glo-ri-ous-ly
glo-ri-ou-ness
glo-ry
glo-ries
glo-ried
glo-ry-ing
glos-sa-ry
glos-sa-ries
glossy
gloss-i-er
gloss-i-est
gloss-i-ly
gloss-i-ness
glot-tis
glot-tis-es
glot-ti-des
glove
gloved
glov-ing
glow
glow-er
glow-ing
glow-worm
glu-cose
glue
glued
glu-ing
glum
glum-mer
glum-mest
glut
glut-ted
glut-ting
glu-ten
glu-ti-nous
glut-ton
glut-ton-ous
glut-tony
glyc-er-in
glyc-er-ine
glyc-er-ol
gnarl
gnarled
gnarly
gnarl-i-er
gnarl-i-est
gnash
gnat
gnaw

gnawed
gnaw-ing
gneiss
gnome
gnu
gnus
goad-ed
go-a-head
goal-keep-er
goat-ee
goat-herd
goat-skin
gob-ble
gob-bled
gob-bling
gob-ble-dy-ween
gob-let
gob-lin
go-cart
god-child
god-chil-dren
god-daugh-ter
god-son
god-dess
god-fa-ther
god-head
god-less
god-less-ness
god-like
god-ly
god-li-er
god-li-est
god-li-ness
god-mo-ther
god-par-ent
god-send
go-get-ter
gog-gle
gog-gled
gog-gling
gog-gle-eyed
gog-gles
go-ing
goi-ter
gold-brick
gold-en
gold-smith
go-nad
gon-do-la
gon-do-lier
gon-er
gon-or-rhea
goo-ber

good-by
good-bye
good-for-noth-ing
good-heart-ed
good-ish
good-look-ing
good-ly
good-li-er
good-li-est
good-na-tured
good-ness
good-tem-pered
good-y
good-ies
goof-off
goof-y
goof-i-er
goof-i-est
goof-i-ness
goose-ber-ry
goose-ber-ries
gore
gored
gor-ing
gorge
gorged
gorg-ing
gor-geous
gor-geous-ly
gor-geous-ness
gor-y
gor-i-er
gor-i-est
gos-ling
gos-pel
gos-sa-mer
gos-sa-mery
gos-sa-mer-i-er
gos-sa-mer-i-est
gos-sip
gos-sip-ing
gos-sipy
gouge
gouged
goug-ing
goug-er
gou-lash
gourd
gour-met
gour-mets
gout
gouty
gout-i-er

gout-i-est
gov-ern
gov-ern-a-ble
gov-ern-ess
gov-ern-ment
gov-ern-men-tal
gov-er-nor
gov-er-nor-ship
gow-and
gowned
grab
grabbed
grab-bing
grab-ber
grace
graced
grac-ing
grace-ful
grace-ful-ly
grace-ful-ness
grace-less
gra-cious
gra-da-tion
grade
grad-ed
grad-ing
grad-er
gra-di-ent
grad-u-al
grad-u-al-ly
grad-u-al-ness
grad-u-ate
grad-u-at-ed
grad-u-at-ing
grad-u-ation
graf-fi-to
graf-fi-ti
graft
graft-age
graft-er
graft-ing
gra-ham
grain
grain-y
grain-i-er
grain-i-est
grain-i-ness
gram
gram-mar
gram-mar-i-an
gram-mat-i-cal
gram-mat-i-cal-ly
gra-na-ry

gra-na-ries
grand
grand-ly
grand-child
grand-daugh-ter
gran-dee
gran-deur
grand-fa-ther
gran-dil-o-quence
gran-dil-o-quent
gran-di-ose
gran-di-ose-ly
grand-moth-er
grand-par-ent
grand-son
grand-stand
grange
grang-er
gran-ite
gra-nat-ic
gran-ny
gran-nies
gran-u-lar
gran-u-lar-i-ty
gran-u-late
gran-u-lat-ed
gran-u-lat-ing
gran-u-la-tion
gran-ule
grape-fruit
grape-vine
graph-ic
graph-i-cal
graph-i-cal-ly
graph-ite
graph-ol-o-gy
graph-ol-o-gist
grap-nel
grap-ple
grap-pled
grap-pling
grap-pler
grass
grass-y
grass-i-er
grass-i-est
grass-hop-per
grass-land
grate
grat-ed
grat-ing
grate-ful
grate-ful-iy

grate-ful-ness
grat-i-fy
grat-i-fied
grat-i-fy-ing
gra-tis
grat-i-tude
gra-tu-i-tous
gra-tu-i-ty
gra-tu-i-ties
grave
graved
grav-en
grav-ing
grav-er
grave-ly
grave-ness
grav-el
grav-eled
grav-el-ing
grav-el-ly
grave-stone
grave-yard
grav-i-tate
grav-i-tat-ed
grav-i-tat-ing
grav-i-ta-tion
grav-i-ta-tion-al
grav-i-ty
grav-i-ties
gra-vy
grav-ies
gray
gray-ly
gray-ness
gray-ling
graze
grazed
graz-ing
grease
greas-ed
greas-ing
greas-y
greas-i-er
greas-i-ness
great
great-ly
great-coat
great-heart-ed
greed-y
greed-i-er
greed-i-est
greed-i-ly
greed-i-ness

green-back
green-er-y
  green-er-ies
green-gro-cer
green-horn
green-house
  green-hous-es
green-ing
green-ish
  green-ish-ness
green-sward
greet
  greet-er
greet-ing
gre-gar-i-ous
  gre-gar-i-ous-ly
  gre-gar-i-ous-ness
grem-lin
gren-a-dier
gren-a-dine
grey
  grey-ly
  grey-ness
grid-dle
grid-dle-cake
grid-i-ron
grief
griev-ance
grieve
  grieved
  griev-ing
griev-ous
  griev-ous-ly
grif-fin
  grif-fon
grill
gril-lage
grille
grill-room
grim
  grim-mer
  grim-mest
  grim-ly
grim-ness
grim-ace
  grim-aced
  grim-ac-ing
grime
  grimed
  grim-ing
grim-y
  grim-i-er
  grim-i-est

grim-i-ly
grim-i-ness
grin
  grin-ned
  grin-ning
  grin-ner
grind
  ground
  grind-ing
grind-er
grind-stone
grin-go
  grin-gos
grip
  gripped
  grip-ping
gripe
  griped
  grip-er
grippe
gris-ly
  gris-li-er
  gris-li-est
  gris-li-ness
gris-tle
  gris-tly
  gris-tli-er
  gris-tli-est
grit
  grit-ted
  grit-ting
grit-ty
  grit-ti-er
  grit-ti-est
  grit-ti-ly
  grit-ti-ness
griz-zled
griz-zly
  griz-zli-er
  griz-zli-est
  griz-zlies
groan
  groan-er
gro-cer
gro-cer-y
  gro-cer-ies
grog-gy
  grog-gi-er
groin
grom-met
groom
groove
  grooved

groov-er
groov-y
  groov-i-er
  groov-i-est
grope
  groped
  grop-ing
gros-grain
gross
  gross-es
  gross-ness
gro-tesque
  gro-tesque-ly
  gro-tesque-ness
grot-to
  grot-toes
  grot-tos
grouch
  grouchy
  grouch-i-er
  grouch-i-est
ground-er
ground-less
  ground-less-ly
  ground-less-ness
ground-ling
ground-nut
ground-work
group-ie
grouse
  groused
  grous-ing
  grous-er
grov-el
  grov-eled
  grov-el-er
grow
  grow-ing
  grow-er
growl
  growl-er
grown-up
growth
grub
  grubbed
  grub-bing
  grub-ber
grub-by
  grub-bi-er
  grub-bi-est
grub-stake
  grub-staked
  grub-stak-ing

grudge
  grudged
  grudg-ing
  grudg-ing-ly
gru-el
gru-el-ing
grue-some
  grue-some-ly
gruff
  gruff-ly
  gruff-ness
grum-ble
  grum-bled
  grum-bling
  grum-bler
grump-y
  grump-i-er
  grump-i-ness
grunt
  grunt-er
  grunt-ing
gua-no
  gua-nos
guar-an-tee
  guar-an-teed
  guar-an-tee-ing
guar-an-tor
guar-an-ty
  guar-an-ties
  guar-an-ty-ing
guard-ed
  guard-ed-ly
guard-house
guard-i-an
guards-man
  guards-men
gua-va
gu-ber-na-to-ri-al
gudg-eon
guer-ril-la
  gue-ril-la
guess
  gues-ser
guess-work
guest
guf-faw
guid-ance
guide
  guid-ed
  guid-ing
guide-book
guide-post
gui-don

guid-hall
guile
  guile-ful
  guile-ful-ly
  guile-less
  guile-less-ly
guil-to-tine
  guil-lo-tined
  guil-lo-tin-ing
guilt
  guilt-less
  guilt-less-ly
guilt-y
  guilt-i-er
  guilt-i-ness
guin-ea
guise
gui-tar
  gui-tar-ist
gul-let
gul-li-ble
  gul-li-bil-i-ty
  gul-li-bly
gum
  gummed
  gum-ming
gum-bo
  gum-bos
gum-drop
gum-my
  gum-mi-er
  gum-mi-est
gump-tion
gum-shoe
  gum-shoed
gun
  gunned
  gun-ning
gun-boat
gun-fight
  gun-fight-er
gun-fire
gun-man
  gun-men
gun-ner
  gun-ner-y
gun-ny
  gun-nies
gun-ny-bag
gun-pow-der
gun-stock
gun-wale
gup-py

gup-pies
gur-gle
  gur-gling
gu-ru
gush-er
gush-ing
gush-y
  gush-i-er
  gush-i-est
gus-set
gus-ta-to-ry
  gus-to
gut-ter
gut-tur-al
  gut-tur-al-ly
guz-zle
  guz-zled
  guz-zling
  guz-zler
gym-na-si-um
  gym-na-si-ums
  gym-na-sia
gym-nast
gym-nas-tic
  gym-nas-tics
gy-ne-col-o-gy
  gy-ne-co-log-ic
  gy-ne-co-log-i-cal
  gy-ne-col-o-gist
gyp
  gypped
  gyp-ping
gyp-sum
gyp-sy
  gyp-sies
gy-ral
gy-rate
  gy-rat-ed
  gy-rat-ing
  gy-ra-tion
  gy-ra-tor
  gy-ra-to-ry
gyr-fal-con
gy-roi-dal
gy-rom-e-ter
gy-ro-plane
gy-ro-scope
  gy-ro-scop-ic
gy-rose
gy-rus
gyve
  gyved
  gyv-ing

H

hab-da-lah
ha-be-as cor-pus
hab-er-dash-er
  hab-er-dash-ery
  hab-er-dash-er-ies
ha-bil-i-ment
hab-it
hab-it-a-ble
ha-bi-tant
hab-i-ta-tion
ha-bit-u-al
  ha-bit-u-al-ly
  ha-bit-u-al-ness
ha-bit-u-ate
  ha-bit-u-at-ed
  ha-bit-u-at-ing
  ha-bit-u-a-tion
ha-ci-en-da
  ha-ci-en-das
hack-le
  hack-led
  hack-ling
hack-ney
  hack-neyed
hack-saw
hadn't
had-ron
hae-mo-glo-bin
hae-mo-phil-i-a
haft
ha-gar
hag-gard
  hag-gard-ly
hag-gle
  hag-gled
  hag-gling
  hag-gler
ha-gi-ol-o-gy
  hag-i-ol-o-gies
  hag-i-ol-o-gist
hag-rid-den
haik
hai-ku
hail-fel-low
hail-stone
hail-storm
hair-breadth
hair-brush
hair-cut
hair-do
hair-dress-er
hair-dress-ing
hair-line

hair-pin
hair-split-ter
  hair-split-ting
hair-spring
hair-y
  hair-i-er
  hair-i-est
ha-la-tion
hal-cy-on
hale
  haled
  hal-ing
half-back
half-baked
half-breed
half-caste
half-heart-ed
  half-heart-ed-ly
half hour
half--life
  half-lives
half--mast
half--moon
half note
half step
half-tone
half-track
half-truth
half-way
half--wit
  half--wit-ted
hal-i-but
hal-i-to-sis
hall-mark
hal-lo
hal-low
  hal-lowed
hal-lu-ci-nate
  hal-lu-ci-nat-ed
  hal-lu-ci-nat-ing
hal-lu-ci-na-tion
  hal-lu-ci-na-to-ry
hal-lu-cin-o-gen
  hal-lu-cin-o-gen-ic
hal-lux
hall-way
halo-phile
halt
  halt-ing
  halt-ing-ly
hal-ter
hal-ter-break
halve

halved
halv-ing
halv-ers
halves
hal-yard
ham-burg-er
ham-let
ham-mer
ham-mer-head
ham-mer-less
ham-mock
ham-my
  ham-mi-er
  ham-mi-est
hamp-er
ham-ster
ham-string
  ham-strung
  ham-string-ing
hand-bag
hand-ball
hand-bill
hand-book
hand-cuff
hand-ed
hand-ful
  hand-fuls
hand-i-cap
  hand-i-capped
  hand-i-cap-ping
  hand-i-cap-per
hand-i-craft
hand-i-ly
  handi-ness
hand-i-work
han-ker-chief
han-dle
  han-dled
  han-dling
  han-dler
han-dle-bar
hand-made
hand-maid-en
hand--me--down
hand-out
hand-pick
  hand-picked
hand-rail
hand-shake
hand-some
  hand-som-er
  hand-som-est
  hand-some-ly

hand-some-ness
hand-spike
hand-spring
hand-to-hand
hand--to--mouth
hand-work
hand-writ-ing
handy
  hand-i-er
  hand-i-est
handy-man
  handy-men
hang
  hung
  hanged
  hang-ing
hang-ar
hang-dog
hang-er
hang-er--on
hang-man
  hanf-men
hang-nail
hang-out
hang-o-ver
hang--up
hank-er
han-som
hap-haz-ard
  hap-haz-ard-ly
  hap-haz-ard-ness
hap-less
  hap-less-ly
hap-ly
hap-pen
  hap-pen-ing
  hap-pen-stance
hap-pi-ness
hap-py
  hap-pi-er
  hap-pi-est
  hap-pi-ly
hap-py--go--lucky
hara-kiri
ha-rangue
  ha-rangued
  ha-rangu-ing
ha-rass
  ha-rass-ment
har-bin-ger
har-bor
hard--bit-ten
hard--boiled

hard--core
hard-cov-er
hard-en
  hard-en-er
hard hat
hard-head-ed
hard-heart-ed
har-di-hood
har-di-ness
hard-ly
  har-di-er
  har-di-est
  har-di-ly
hare-brained
hare-lip
har-em
har-le-quin
har-lot
  har-lot-ry
harm-ful
  harm-ful-ly
  harm-ful-ness
harm-less
  harm-less-ly
  harm-less-ness
har-mon-ic
  har-mon-i-cal-ly
har-mon-i-ca
har-mon-ics
har-mo-ni-ous
  har-mo-ni-ous-ly
har-mo-nize
  har-mo-nized
  har-mo-niz-ing
har-mo-ny
  har-mo-nies
har-ness
harp-ist
har-poon
harp-si-chord
har-py
  har-pies
har-que-bus
har-ri-dan
har-row
  har-row-ing
har-ry
  har-ried
  har-ry-ing
harsh
  harsh-ly
  harsh-ness
har-um-scar-um

har-vest
har-ves-ter
has--been
hash-ish
  hash-eesh
hasn't
has-sle
  has-sled
  has-sling
has-sock
has-ten
hasty
  hast-i-er
  hast-i-est
hatch-ery
  hatch-er-ies
hatch-et
hatch-way
hate
  hat-ed
  hat-ing
  hat-er
hate-ful
  hate-ful-ly
  hate-ful-ness
ha-tred
hat-ter
haugh-ty
  haugh-ti-er
  haugh-ti-est
  haugh-ti-ly
  haught-ti-ness
haunch
  haunch-es
haunt-ed
  haunt-ing
hau-teur
ha-ven
have--not
haven't
hav-er-sack
havers
hav-oc
hawk
  hawk-ish
haw-ser
hay-loft
hay-mak-er
hay-mow
hay-seed
hay-stack
hay-wire
haz-ard

haz-ard-ous
haz-ard-ous-ly
haze
hazed
haz-ing
ha-zel
ha-zel-nut
hazy
  ha-zi-er
  ha-zi-est
  ha-zi-ly
  ha-zi-ness
head-ache
head-band
head-dress
head-er
head-first
  head-fore-most
head-gear
head-hunt-er
head-ing
head-land
head-less
head-light
head-line
  head-lined
  head-lin-ing
head-long
head-mas-ter
head-mis-tress
head-most
head--on
head-piece
head-quar-ters
head-set
head-stone
head-strong
head-wait-er
head-wa-ter
head-way
head-wind
heady
  head-i-er
  head-i-est
  head-i-ly
  head-i-ness
heal-er
health-ful
  health-ful-ly
healthy
  health-i-er
  health-i-est
  health-i-ness

heaped
hear
  heared
  hear-ing
  hear-er
hear-ken
hear-say
hearse
heart-ache
heart-break
  heart-break-ing
heart-brok-en
heart-burn
heart-en
heart-felt
hearth-stone
heart-less
  heart-less-ly
  heart-less-ness
heart-rend-ing
heart-sick
heart-strings
heart--to--heart
hearty
  heart-i-er
  heart-i-est
  heart-i-ly
  heart-i-ness
heat-ed
heat-er
heath
hea-then
heave
  heaved
  heav-ing
heav-en
  heav-en-ly
  heav-en-ward
  heav-en-wards
heavy--du-ty
heavy--hand-ed
heavy-weight
heck-le
  heck-led
  heck-ling
  heck-ler
hect-are
hec-tic
  hec-ti-cal-ly
hec-to-gram
hec-to-li-ter
hec-to-me-ter
hedge

hedged
hedg-ing
hedg-er
he-do-nism
he-do-nist
he-do-nis-tic
hee-haw
hefty
heft-i-er
heft-i-est
he-ge-mo-ny
he-ge-mo-nies
heg-e-mon-ic
he-gi-ra
heif-er
height-en
  height-en-er
hei-nous
  hei-nous-ly
heir-ess
heir-loom
heist
he-li-cop-ter
he-li-um
he-lix
  he-li-ces
  he-lix-es
hell--bent
hell-cat
hel-lion
hell-ish
  hell-ish-ly
  hell-ish-ness
hel-lo
  hel-los
helm
  helm-less
hel-met
  hel-met-ed
helms-man
  helms-men
help-er
help-ful
  help-ful-ly
  help-ful-ness
help-ing
help-less
  help-less-ly
help-mate
hel-er--skel-ter
hem
  hemmed
  hem-ming

he--man
he--men
hemi-sphere
hemi-spher-ic
hemi-sper-i-cal
hem-lock
he-mo-glo-bin
he-mo-phil-ia
hem-or-rhage
hem-or-rhag-ing
hem-or-rhag-ic
hem-or-rhoid
hem-or-rhoid-al
hemp-en
hem-stitch
hence-forth
hench-man
hench-men
hench-man-ship
hen-na
hen-peck
hep-a-ti-tis
her-ald
he-ral-dic
her-ald-ry
her-ald-ries
herb-age
her-biv-o-rous
Her-cu-le-an
herd-er
herds-man
herds-men
here-af-ter
he-red-i-tary
he-red-i-tar-i-ly
he-red-i-ty
he-red-i-ties
here-in
here-of
her-e-sy
her-e-sies
her-e-tic
he-ret-i-cal
he-ret-i-cal-ly
here-to
here-to-fore
here-upon
here-with
her-i-ta-ble
her-i-ta-bil-i-ty
her-i-ta-bly
her-i-tage
her-maph-ro-dite

her-maph-ro-dit-ic
her-maph-ro-dit-ism
her-met-ic
her-met-i-cal
her-met-i-cal-ly
her-mit
her-mit-age
her-nia
her-ni-al
her-ni-a-tion
he-ro
he-roes
he-ro-ic
he-ro-ical
he-ro-ical-ly
her-o-in
her-o-ine
her-o-ism
her-on
her-ring-bone
her-ring-boned
her-ring-bon-ing
her-self
hes-i-tant
hes-i-tan-cy
hes-i-tan-cies
hes-i-tant-ly
hes-i-ta-tion
het-ero-dox
het-ero-doxy
het-er-o-ge-neous
het-er-o-ge-ne-ity
het-er-o-ge-neous-ly
het-ero-sex-u-al
het-ero-sex-u-al-i-ty
hew
hewed
hewn
hexa-gon
hex-ag-o-nal
hex-ag-o-nal-ly
hey-day
hey-dey
hi-a-tus
hi-a-tus-es
hi-ba-chi
hi-ber-nate
hi-ber-nat-ed
hi-ber-nat-ing
hi-ber-na-tion
hi-bis-cus
hic-cup
hic-cuped

hic-cup-ing
hid-den
hid-den-ness
hide
hid
hid-den
hid-er
hide-bound
hid-eous
hid-eous-ly
hid-eous-ness
hide-out
hi-er-ar-chy
hi-er-ar-chies
hi-er-ar-chal
hi-er-ar-chic
hi-er-ar-chi-cal
hi-er-ar-chi-cal-ly
hi-ero-glyph
hi-ero-glyph-ic
hi-ero-glyph-i-cal
hi-ero-glyph-i-cal-ly
hi--fi
high-ball
high-born
high-boy
high-brow
high-browed
high-brow-ism
high-er--up
high-fa-lu-tin
high-fa-lu-ting
high--flown
high--grade
high--hand-ed
high--hand-ed-ly
high--hand-ed-ness
high--hat
high-land
high-light
high--mind-ed
high--mind-ed-ly
high--mind-ed-ness
high-ness
high--pressure
high--pressured
high--pressur-ing
high school
high seas
high--spir-it-ed
high--spir-it-ed-ly
high--spir-it-ed-ness
high--strung

high-tail	his-to-ri-an	ho-bo-ism
high--tension	his-tor-ic	hock-er
high--toned	his-tor-i-cal	hock-ey
high-way	his-tor-i-cal-ly	ho-cus-po-cus
high-way-man	his-tor-i-cal-ness	hodge-podge
high-way-men	his-to-ry	hoe
hi-jack	his-to-ries	hoed
hi-jack-er	his-tri-on-ic	hoe-ing
hi-jack-ing	his-tri-on-i-cal	hoe-down
hike	his-tri-on-i-cal-ly	hog
hiked	his-tri-on-ics	hogged
hik-ing	hit	hog-ging
hik-er	hit-ting	hog-gish
hi-lar-i-ous	hit--and--run	hog-gish-ly
hi-lar-i-ous-ly	hitch	hog-gish-ness
hi-lar-i-ous-ness	hitch-er	hogs-head
hi-lar-i-ty	hitch-hike	hog--tie
hill-bil-ly	hitch-hiked	hog--tied
hill-bil-lies	hitch-hik-ing	hog--ty-ing
hill-ock	hitch-hik-er	hog-wash
hill-side	hith-er-to	hoi pol-loi
hill-top	hive	hoist-er
hilly	hived	ho-kum
hill-i-er	hiv-ing	hold-er
hill-i-est	hoary	hold-ing
him-self	hoar-i-er	hold-out
hin-der	hoar-i-est	hold-over
hin-der-er	hoar-i-ness	hold-up
hind-most	hoard	hole
hind-quar-ter	hoard-er	holed
hin-drance	hoard-ing	hol-ing
hind-sight	hoar-frost	holey
hinge	hoarse	hol-i-day
hinged	hoarse-ly	ho-li-ness
hing-ing	hoars-en	Hol-land
hint-er	hoarse-ness	hol-ler
hint-ing-ly	hoax	hol-low
hin-ter-land	hoax-er	hol-low-ly
hipped	hob-ble	hol-low-ness
hip-pie	hob-bled	hol-ly
hip-po	hob-bling	hol-lies
hip-pos	hob-by	hol-ly-hock
hip-po-drome	hob-bies	hol-mi-um
hip-po-pot-a-mus	hob-by-horse	ho-lo-caust
hip-po-pot-a-mus-es	hob-gob-lin	ho-lo-gram
hip-po-pot-a-mi	hob-nail	hol-o-graph
hire-ling	hob-nail-ed	hol-ster
hir-sute	hob-nob	ho-ly
hir-sute-ness	hob-nobbed	ho-li-er
hiss	hob-nob-bing	ho-li-est
hiss-er	ho-bo	ho-lies
his-ta-mine	ho-boes	hom-age
his-ta-min-ic	ho-bos	hom-bre

96

hom-bres
home-com-ing
home-less
home-less-ness
home-ly
home-li-er
home-li-est
home-li-ness
home-made
hom-er
home-sick
home-sick-ness
home-spun
home-stead
home-stead-er
home-ward
home-wards
home-work
homey
hom-i-er
hom-i-est
hom-i-ness
hom-i-cide
hom-i-let-ics
hom-i-ly
hom-i-lies
homing pigeon
hom-i-ny
ho-mo-ge-neous
ho-mo-ge-ne-ity
ho-mo-ge-neous-ness
ho-mog-e-nize
ho-meg-e-nized
ho-mog-e-niz-ing
ho-mo-graph
ho-mol-o-gous
ho-mol-o-gy
ho-mol-o-gies
hom-onym
hom-onym-ic
ho-mo-phone
ho-mo-pho-nic
ho-mo-sex-u-al
ho-mo-sex-u-al-i-ty
hone
honed
hon-ing
hon-est
hon-est-ly
hon-es-ty
hon-es-ties
hon-ey
hon-eys

hon-eyed
hon-ied
hon-ey-ing
hon-ey-bee
hon-ey-comb
hon-ey-moon
hon-ey-moon-er
hon-ey-suck-le
hon-ey-suck-led
hon-ky--tonk
hon-or
hon-or-able
hon-or-ably
hon-o-rar-i-um
hon-o-rar-i-ums
hon-o-rar-ia
hon-or-ary
hon-or-if-ic
hood-ed
hood-lum
hoo-doo
hoo-doo-ism
hood-wink
hood-wink-er
hoo-ey
hoof
hoofs
hooves
hoofed
hooked
hook-er
hook-up
hoo-li-gan
hoo-li-gan-ism
hoop
hooped
hoop-like
hoop-la
hoo-ray
hoose-gow
hoot
hoot-er
hoot-ing-ly
hop
hopped
hop-ping
hop-er
hope-ful
hope-ful-ly
hope-ful-ness
hope-less
hope-less-ly
hope-less-ness

hop-head
hop-per
hop-scotch
horde
hord-ed
hord-ing
ho-ri-zon
hor-i-zon-tal
hor-i-zon-tal-ly
hor-mone
hor-mon-al
horn
horned
horn-like
horny
horn-i-er
horn-i-est
hor-net
horn-swog-gle
horn-swog-gled
horn-swog-gling
hor-rol-o-gy
ho-rol-o-ger
ho-rol-o-gist
horo-scope
hor-ren-dous
hor-ren-dous-ly
hor-ri-ble
hor-ri-bly
hor-rid
hor-rid-ly
hor-rid-ness
hor-ri-fy
hor-ri-fied
hor-ri-fy-ing
hor-ri-fi-ca-tion
hor-ror
horse
hors-es
horsed
hors-ing
horse-back
horse-fly
horse-flies
horse-hair
horse-laugh
horse-men
horse-man-ship
horse-wom-an
horse-wom-en
horse opera
horse-play
horse-pow-er

horse-rad-ish
horse-shoe
  horse-sho-er
horse-whip
  horse-whipped
  horse-whip-ping
hors-ey
  horsy
  hors-i-er
  hors-i-est
  hors-i-ly
  hors-i-ness
hor-ta-to-ry
hor-ti-cul-ture
  hor-ti-cul-tur-al
  hor-ti-cul-tur-ist
ho-san-na
hose
  hos-es
  hosed
  hos-ing
ho-siery
hos-pice
hos-pi-ta-ble
  hos-pi-ta-bly
hos-pi-tal
hos-pi-tal-i-ty
  hos-pi-tal-i-ties
hos-pi-tal-iza-tion
hos-pi-tal-ize
  hos-pi-tal-ized
  hos-pi-tal-iz-ing
hos-tage
hos-tel
  hos-tel-ry
  hos-tel-ries
host-ess
hos-tile
  hos-tile-ly
hos-til-i-ty
  hos-til-i-ties
hos-tler
hot
  hot-ter
  hot-test
  hot-ly
hot-bed
hot--blood-ed
ho-tel
hot-head
  hot-head-ed
  hot-head-ed-ness
hot-house

hot-shot
hound
  hound-er
hour-glass
hour-ly
house
  hous-es
  housed
  hous-ing
house-boat
house-bro-ken
  house-break
  house-broke
  house-break-ing
house-fly
house-hold
house-keep-er
  house-keep-ing
house-maid
house-warm-ing
house-wife
  house-wives
  house-wife-ly
  house-wif-ery
house-work
hous-ing
hov-el
  hov-eled
  hov-el-ing
hov-er
  hov-er-er
  hov-er-ing
how-ev-er
how-it-zer
howl-er
how-so-ev-er
hoy-den
  hoy-den-ish
hob-bub
huck-le-ber-ry
  huck-le-ber-ries
huck-ster
hud-dle
  hud-dled
  hud-dling
  hud-dler
huffy
  huff-i-er
  huff-i-est
  huff-i-ly
  huff-i-ness
hug
  hugged

  hug-ging
  hug-ger
huge
  hug-er
  hug-est
  huge-ly
  huge-ness
hu-la
hulk-ing
hul-la-ba-loo
hum
  hummed
  hum-ming
  hum-mer
hu-mane
  hu-mane-ly
  hu-man-ness
hu-man-ism
  hu-man-ist
  hu-man-ist-ic
hu-man-i-tar-i-an-ism
hu-man-i-ty
  hu-man-i-ties
hu-man-ize
  hu-man-ized
  hu-man-iz-ing
  hu-man-i-za-tion
  hu-man-iz-er
hu-man-kind
hu-man-ly
hum-drum
hu-mer-us
hu-mid
  hu-mid-ly
hu-mid-i-fy
  hu-mid-i-fied
  hu-mid-i-fy-ing
  hu-mid-i-fi-er
hu-mid-i-ty
hum-ming-bird
hum-mock
  hum-mocky
  hum-mock-i-er
  hum-mock-i-est
hu-mor
hu-mor-ist
  hu-mor-is-tic
hu-mor-ous
  hu-mor-ous-ly
  hu-mor-ous-ness
hump-back
hu-mus
hunch-back

hunch-backed
hun-dred
hun-ger
hun-gry
hun-gri-er
hun-gri-est
hun-gri-ly
hur-dle
hur-dled
hur-dling
hur-dler
hur-dy--gur-dy
hur-dy--gur-dies
hurl-er
hurl-y--burl-y
hurl-y--burl-ies
hur-rah
hur-ri-cane
hurt-ful
hurt-ful-ly
hurt-ful-ness
hurt-ing
hur-tle
hur-tled
hur-tling
hurt-less
hus-band-man
hus-band-ry
husk-er
husk-ing
hus-sar
hus-sy
hussies
hus-tings
hus-tle
hus-tled
hus-tling
hus-tler
hutch
hut-ment
huz-zah
huz-za
hy-a-cinth
hy-a-cin-thine
hy-a-line
hy-a-lite
hy-a-loid
hy-a-lo-plasm
hy-brid
hy-brid-ism
hy-brid-i-ty
hy-da-thode
hy-da-tid

hy-dra
hy-dras
hy-dae
hy-dral-azine
hy-dran-gea
hy-drant
hy-dra-ted
hy-dra-ting
hy-dra-tion
hy-dra-tor
hy-drau-lic
hy-drau-li-cal-ly
hy-drau-lics
hy-dro-car-bon
hy-dro-chlo-ric acid
hy-dro-dy-nam-ics
hy-dro-dy-na-mic
hy-dro-elec-tric
hy-dro-gen
hy-drog-e-nous
hy-dro-ly-sis
hy-drom-e-ter
hy-dro-met-ric
hy-dro-met-ri-cal
hy-drom-e-try
hy-dro-pho-bia
hy-dro-plane
hy-dro-plan-er
hy-dro-plan-ing
hy-dro-pon-ics
hy-dro-ther-a-py
hy-dro-ther-a-pist
hy-drous
hy-drox-ide
hy-drox-yl
hy-dro-zo-an
hy-e-na
hy-giene
hy-gien-ic
hy-gien-i-cal-ly
hy-gien-ist
hy-men
hy-me-ne-al
hy-me-ne-al-ly
hym-nal
hy-per-bo-la
hy-per-bo-le
hy-per-bo-lize
hy-per-bo-lized
hy-per-bo-liz-ing
hy-per-bol-ic
hy-per-crit-i-cal
hy-per-crit-i-cal-ly

hy-per-sen-si-tive
hy-per-sen-si-tiv-i-ty
hy-per-sex-u-al
hy-per-sex-u-al-ity
hy-per-ten-sion
hy-per-thy-roid-ism
hy-phen
hy-phen-ate
hy-phen-at-ed
hy-phen-at-ing
hyp-no-sis
hyp-not-ic
hyp-no-tism
hyp-no-tist
hyp-no-tize
hyp-no-tized
hyp-no-tiz-ing
hy-po
hy-po-chon-dria
hy-po-chon-dri-ac
hy-poc-ri-sy
hy-poc-ri-sies
hyp-o-crite
hy-po-der-mic
hy-po-sen-si-tize
hy-po-sen-si-tized
hy-po-sen-si-tiz-ing
hy-po-ten-sion
hy-pot-e-nuse
hy-poth-e-cate
hy-poth-e-cat-ed
hy-poth-e-cat-ing
hy-poth-e-ca-tion
hy-poth-e-ca-tor
hy-poth-e-sis
hy-poth-e-ses
hy-poth-e-size
hy-poth-e-siz-ing
hy-po-thet-i-cal
hy-po-thet-i-cal-ly
hyp-ox-emia
hyp-ox-ia
hyp-sog-ra-phy
hy-son
hys-sop
hys-ter-ec-to-my
hys-ter-ec-to-mies
hys-ter-e-sis
hys-te-ria
hys-ter-ic
hys-ter-i-cal
hys-ter-i-cal-ly
hys-ter-ics

I

iamb
iat-ric
ibid
ibi-dem
ibis
  ibis-es
ice-boat
ice--cream
ice-man
  ice-men
ice--skate
icon
icon-o-clasm
  icon-o-clas-tic
icon-o-clast
ide-al-ize
  ide-al-ized
  ide-al-iz-ing
  ide-al-i-za-tion
ide-al-ly
idem
iden-ti-cal
  iden-ti-cal-ly
iden-ti-fi-a-ble
  iden-ti-fy-ing
  iden-ti-fi-a-bly
iden-ti-fi-ca-tion
iden-ti-fy
  iden-ti-fied
  iden-ti-fy-ing
  iden-ti-fi-er
iden-ti-ty
  iden-ti-ties
ides
id-i-o-cy
  id-i-o-cies
id-i-om
  id-i-o-mat-ic
  id-i-o-mat-i-cal-ly
id-i-o-syn-cra-sy
  id-i-o-syn-cra-sies
  id-i-o-syn-crat-ic
id-i-ot
  id-i-ot-ic
  id-i-ot-i-cal-ly
idle
idol
idol-ize
idyll
  idyl-lic
  idyl-lic-al-ly
ig-ne-ous
ig-nite

ig-ni-tion
ig-no-ble
  ig-no-bil-i-ty
  ig-no-bly
ig-no-ra-mus
ig-no-rant
  ig-no-rance
  ig-no-rant-ly
ig-nore
  ig-nored
  ig-nor-ing
igua-na
ill--ad-vised
  ill--ad-vis-ed-ly
ill--bred
il-le-gal
  il-le-gal-i-ty
  il-le-gal-ly
il-leg-i-ble
  il-leg-i-bil-i-ty
  il-leg-i-bly
il-le-git-i-mate
  il-le-git-i-ma-cy
  il-le-git-i-ma-cies
  il-le-git-i-mate-ly
ill--fat-ed
ill--fa-vored
ill--got-ten
il-lib-er-al
il-lic-it
il-lim-it-able
il-lit-er-a-cy
  il-lit-er-a-cies
il-lit-er-ate
ill-ness
il-log-i-cal
ill-starred
ill-tem-pered
  ill-tem-pered-ly
il-lu-mi-na-tion
il-lu-mine
  il-lu-mined
  il-lu-min-ing
ill-use
il-lu-sion
  il-lu-sive
  il-lu-sive-ly
  il-lu-sive-ness
il-lus-trate
  il-lus-trat-ed
  il-lus-trat-ing
il-lus-tra-tion
  il-lus-tra-tive

  il-lus-tra-tive-ly
  il-lus-tra-tor
il-lus-tri-ous
  il-lus-tri-ous-ly
im-age
  im-aged
im-ag-ing
  im-age-a-ble
  im-ag-er
im-ag-ery
  im-ag-eries
  im-ag-eri-al
imag-in-able
  imag-in-able-ness
  imag-in-ably
imag-i-nary
  imag-i-nar-ies
  imag-i-nar-i-ly
  imag-i-nar-i-ness
imag-i-na-tion
  imag-i-na-tion-al
imag-i-na-tive
  imag-i-na-tive-ly
imag-ine
  imag-ined
  imag-in-ing
im-bal-ance
im-be-cile
  im-be-cil-ic
  im-be-cile-ly
  im-be-cil-i-ty
imbed
  imbed-ded
  im-bed-ding
im-bibe
im-bro-glio
im-brue
  im-brued
  im-bru-ing
im-i-ta-ble
im-i-tate
  im-i-tat-ed
  im-i-tat-ing
  im-i-ta-tor
im-i-ta-tion
  im-i-ta-tive
im-mac-u-late
  im-mac-u-la-cy
  im-mac-u-late-ly
im-ma-te-ri-al
  im-ma-te-ri-al-ness
  im-ma-te-ri-al-i-ty
  im-ma-te-ri-al-ize

im-ma-ture
 im-ma-ture-ly
 im-ma-ture-ness
 im-ma-tu-ri-ty
im-meas-ur-a-ble
 im-meas-ur-a-bly
im-me-di-a-cy
 im-me-di-a-cies
im-me-di-ate
 im-me-di-ate-ly
 im-me-di-ate-ness
im-me-mo-ri-al
 im-me-mo-ri-al-ly
im-mense
 im-mense-ly
 im-mense-ness
 im-men-si-ty
im-merge
 im-merged
im-merse
 im-mersed
 im-mers-ing
 im-mer-sion
im-mi-grant
 im-mi-grat-ed
 im-mi-gra-tion
 im-mi-gra-tor
im-mi-nent
 im-mi-nence
im-mo-bile
 im-mo-bil-i-ty
 im-mo-bi-lize
im-mod-er-ate
 im-mod-er-ate-ly
 im-mod-er-ate-ness
im-mod-est
 im-mod-est-ly
 im-mod-es-ty
im-mo-late
 im-mo-lat-ed
 im-mo-lat-ing
 im-mo-la-tion
 im-mo-la-tor
im-mor-al
 im-mor-al-ist
 im-mo-ral-i-ty
 im-mor-al-ly
im-mor-tal
im-mov-a-ble
 im-mov-a-bli-i-ty
 im-mov-a-bly
im-mune
im-mu-ni-ty

im-mu-ni-ties
im-mu-nize
 im-mu-nized
 im-mu-niz-ing
 im-mu-ni-za-tion
im-mu-nol-o-gy
im-mure
 im-mured
 im-mur-ing
im-mu-ta-ble
 im-mu-ta-bil-i-ty
 im-mu-ta-bly
im-pact
 im-pac-tion
im-pact-ed
im-pair
 im-pair-er
 im-pair-ment
im-pa-la
 im-pal-as
 im-pal-ae
im-pal-pa-ble
 im-pal-pa-bil-i-ty
 im-pal-pa-bly
im-pan-el
 im-pan-eled
 im-pan-el-ing
im-part
im-par-tial
 im-par-ti-al-i-ty
 im-par-tial-ly
im-pass-able
 im-pass-abil-i-ty
 im-pass-able-ness
 im-pass-ably
im-passe
im-pas-si-ble
 im-pas-si-bil-i-ty
 im-pas-si-bly
im-pas-sion
 im-pas-sioned
 im-pas-sioned-ly
im-pas-sive
 im-pas-sive-ly
 im-pas-sive-ness
 im-pas-siv-i-ty
im-pa-tience
im-pa-tient
 im-pa-tient-ly
im-peach
 im-peach-a-ble
 im-peach-ment
im-pec-ca-ble

im-pec-ca-bil-i-ty
 im-pec-ca-bly
im-pe-cu-nious
 im-pe-cu-nious-ly
 im-pe-cu-nious-ness
im-pede
 im-ped-ed
 im-ped-ing
im-ped-i-ment
im-pel
 im-pelled
 im-pel-ling
im-pend
 im-pend-ing
im-pen-e-tra-bil-i-ty
im-pen-e-tra-ble
 im-pen-e-tra-ble-ness
 im-pen-e-tra-bly
im-pen-i-tent
 im-pen-i-tence
 im-pen-i-tent-ly
im-per-cep-ti-ble
 im-per-cep-ti-bil-i-ty
 im-per-cep-tive
 im-per-cep-tive-ness
im-per-fect
 im-per-fect-ly
 im-per-fect-ness
im-per-fec-tion
im-pe-ri-al
 im-pe-ri-al-ly
im-pe-ri-al-ism
 im-pe-ri-al-ist
 im-pe-ri-al-is-tic
 im-pe-ri-al-is-ti-cal-ly
im-per-il
 im-per-iled
 im-per-il-ing
 im-per-il-ment
im-pe-ri-ous
 im-pe-ri-ous-ly
 im-pe-ri-ous-ness
im-per-ish-able
 im-per-ish-abil-i-ty
 im-per-ish-able-ness
 im-per-ish-ably
im-per-ma-nence
im-per-ma-nen-cy
im-per-ma-nent
 im-per-ma-nent-ly
im-per-me-able
 im-per-me-abil-i-ty
 im-per-me-able-ness

im-per-me-ably
im-per-son-al
im-per-son-al-i-ty
im-per-son-al-i-ties
im-per-son-al-ly
im-per-son-ate
im-per-son-at-ed
im-per-son-at-ing
im-per-son-a-tion
im-per-son-ator
im-per-ti-nent
im-per-ti-nence
im-per-ti-nent-ly
im-per-turb-able
im-per-turb-ably
im-per-vi-ous
im-per-vi-ous-ly
im-per-vi-ous-ness
im-pe-ti-go
im-pet-u-os-i-ty
im-pet-u-ous
im-pet-u-ous-ly
im-pet-u-ous-ness
im-pe-tus
im-pe-tus-es
im-pi-ety
im-pi-eties
im-pinge
im-pinged
im-ping-ing
im-pinge-ment
im-ping-er
im-pi-ous
im-pi-ous-ly
im-pi-ous-ness
im-pla-ca-ble
im-pla-ca-bil-i-ty
im-pla-ca-ble-ness
im-pla-ca-bly
im-plant
im-plan-ta-tion
im-plant-er
im-plau-si-ble
im-plau-si-bly
im-plau-si-bil-i-ty
im-ple-ment
im-ple-men-tal
im-ple-men-ta-tion
im-pli-cate
im-pli-cat-ed
im-pli-cat-ing
im-pli-ca-tion
im-plic-it

im-plic-it-ly
im-plic-it-ness
im-plode
im-ploded
im-plod-ing
im-plo-sion
im-plo-sive
im-ply
im-plied
im-ply-ing
im-po-lite
im-po-lite-ly
im-po-lite-ness
im-pol-i-tic
im-pol-i-tic-ly
im-pon-der-a-ble
im-pon-der-a-bil-i-ty
im-pon-der-a-bly
im-pone
im-poned
im-port
im-port-a-ble
im-port-er
im-por-tance
im-por-tant
im-por-tant-ly
im-por-ta-tion
im-por-tu-nate
im-por-tu-nate-ly
im-por-tune
im-por-tuned
im-por-tun-ing
im-pose
im-posed
im-pos-ing
im-pos-ter
im-po-si-tion
im-pos-si-bil-i-ty
im-pos-si-bil-i-ties
im-pos-si-ble
im-pos-si-bly
im-post
im-pos-tor
im-pos-ture
im-po-tence
im-po-ten-cy
im-po-tent
im-po-tent-ly
im-pound
im-pound-age
im-pov-er-ish
im-pov-er-ish-ment
im-prac-ti-ca-ble

im-prac-ti-ca-bil-i-ty
im-prac-ti-ca-ble-ness
im-prac-ti-ca-bly
im-prac-ti-cal
im-pre-cate
im-pre-cat-ed
im-pre-cat-ing
im-pre-ca-tion
im-preg-na-ble
im-preg-na-bil-i-ty
im-preg-na-bly
im-pre-sa-rio
im-pre-sa-ri-os
im-press
im-press-er
im-press-i-ble
im-press-ment
im-pres-sion
im-pres-sion-ist
im-pres-sion-a-ble
im-pres-sion-a-bly
im-pres-sion-ism
im-pres-sion-ist
im-pres-sion-is-tic
im-pres-sive
im-pres-sive-ly
im-pres-sive-ness
im-pri-ma-tur
im-print
im-print-er
im-pris-on
im-pris-on-ment
im-prob-a-bil-i-ty
im-prob-a-ble
im-prob-a-ble-ness
im-prob-a-bly
im-promp-tu
im-prop-er
im-prop-er-ly
im-prop-er-ness
im-pro-pri-ety
im-pro-pri-eties
im-prove-ment
im-prov-i-dence
im-prov-i-dent
im-prov-i-dent-ly
im-pro-vi-sa-tion
im-pro-vi-sa-tion-al
im-pro-vise
im-pro-vised
im-pro-vis-ing
im-pro-vis-er
im-pru-dence

im-pru-dent
im-pru-dent-ly
im-pugn
im-pugn-er
im-pulse
im-pul-sion
im-pul-sive
im-pu-ni-ty
im-pure
im-pure-ly
im-pure-ness
im-pu-ri-ty
im-pu-ri-ties
in-a-bil-i-ty
in-ac-ces-si-ble
in-ac-ces-si-bil-i-ties
in-ac-ces-si-ble-ness
in-ac-ces-si-bly
in-ac-cu-rate
in-ac-cu-rate-ly
in-ac-cu-ra-cy
in-ac-cu-ra-cies
in-ac-tion
in-ac-tive
in-ac-tive-ly
in-ac-tiv-i-ty
in-ad-e-quate
in-ad-e-qua-cies
in-ad-e-qua-cy
in-ad-e-quate-ly
in-ad-mis-si-ble
in-ad-mis-si-bly
in-ad-ver-tence
in-ad-ver-ten-cy
in-ad-ver-tent
in-ad-ver-tent-ly
in-alien-a-ble
in-alien-a-bly
in-am-o-ra-ta
in-am-o-ra-tas
in-an-i-mate
in-ap-pro-pri-ate
in-ap-pro-pri-ate-ly
in-ap-pro-pri-ate-ness
in-apt
in-apt-ti-tude
in-apt-ly
in-apt-ness
in-ar-tic-u-late
in-ar-tic-u-late-ly
in-ar-tic-u-late-ness
in-as-much as
in-at-ten-tion

in-at-ten-tive
in-at-ten-tive-ly
in-au-gu-ral
in-au-gu-rate
in-au-gu-rat-ed
in-au-gu-rat-ing
in-au-gu-ra-tion
in-aus-pi-cious
in-aus-pi-cious-ly
in-board
in-born
in-bred
in-breed
in-breed-ing
in-cal-cu-la-ble
in-cal-cu-la-bly
in-can-des-cent
in-can-des-cence
in-can-des-cent-ly
in-can-ta-tion
in-ca-pa-ble
in-ca-pa-bly
in-ca-pac-i-tate
in-ca-pac-i-tat-ed
in-ca-pac-i-tat-ing
in-ca-pac-i-ty
in-ca-pac-i-ties
in-car-cer-ate
in-car-cer-at-ed
in-car-cer-at-ing
in-car-cer-a-tion
in-car-nate
in-car-nat-ed
in-car-nat-ing
in-car-na-tion
in-cen-di-ary
in-cen-di-aries
in-cense
in-censed
in-ceas-ing
in-cen-tive
in-cep-tion
in-ces-sant
in-ces-sant-ly
in-cho-ate
in-cho-ate-ly
in-cho-ate-ness
in-ci-dence
in-ci-dent
in-ci-den-tal
in-ci-den-tal-ly
in-cin-er-ate
in-cin-er-at-ed

in-cin-er-at-ing
in-cin-er-a-tion
in-cin-er-a-tor
in-cip-i-ent
in-cip-i-ent-ly
in-cise
in-cised
in-cis-ing
in-ci-sion
in-ci-sive
in-ci-sive-ly
in-ci-sive-ness
in-ci-sor
in-cite
in-cit-ed
in-cit-ing
in-cite-ment
in-cit-er
in-clem-en-cy
in-clem-ent
in-clem-ent-ly
in-cli-na-tion
in-cline
in-clined
in-clin-ing
in-clin-er
in-clude
in-clud-ed
in-clud-ing
in-clud-a-ble
in-clu-sion
in-clu-sive
in-clu-sive-ly
in-clu-sive-ness
in-cog-ni-to
in-cog-ni-tos
in-co-her-ence
in-co-her-ent
in-co-her-ent-ly
in-come
in-com-ing
in-com-men-su-ra-ble
in-com-men-su-ra-bly
in-com-men-su-rate
in-com-mo-di-ous
in-com-pa-ra-ble
in-com-pa-ra-bly
in-com-pat-i-bil-i-ty
in-com-pat-i-ble
in-com-pat-i-bly
in-com-pe-tence
in-com-pen-ten-cy
in-com-pe-tent

in-com-pe-tent-ly
in-com-plete
in-com-plete-ly
in-com-plete-ness
in-com-ple-tion
in-com-pre-hen-si-ble
in-com-pre-hen-si-bly
in-com-pre-hen-sion
in-con-ceiv-able
in-con-ceiv-ably
in-con-clu-sive
in-con-clu-sive-ly
in-con-clu-sive-ness
in-con-gru-ity
in-con-gru-ous
in-con-gru-ous-ly
in-con-gru-ous-ness
in-con-gru-i-ties
in-con-se-quen-tial
in-con-se-quen-tial-ly
in-con-sid-er-able
in-con-sid-er-ably
in-con-sid-er-ate
in-con-sid-er-ate-ly
in-con-sid-er-ate-ness
in-con-sis-tent
in-con-sist-ent-ly
in-con-sol-able
in-con-sol-able-ness
in-con-sol-ably
in-con-spic-u-ous
in-con-spic-u-ous-ly
in-con-stant
in-con-stan-cy
in-con-stan-cies
in-con-stant-ly
in-con-test-able
in-con-test-abil-i-ty
in-con-ti-nence
in-con-ti-nen-cy
in-con-ti-nent
in-con-ti-nent-ly
in-con-trol-la-ble
in-con-tro-vert-ible
in-con-ve-nience
in-con-ve-nien-cy
in-con-ve-nient
in-con-ve-nient-ly
in-con-ven-ienc-ing
in-con-vert-ible
in-con-vert-ibly
in-cor-po-rate
in-cor-po-rat-ed

in-cor-po-rat-ing
in-cor-po-ra-tion
in-cor-po-ra-tor
in-cor-po-re-al
in-cor-rect
in-cor-rect-ly
in-cor-ri-gi-ble
in-cor-ri-gi-bil-i-ty
in-cor-ri-gi-ble-ness
in-cor-ri-gi-bly
in-cor-rupt-ible
in-cor-rupt-ibil-i-ty
in-cor-rupt-ible-ness
in-cor-rupt-ibly
in-crease
in-creased
in-creas-ing
in-creas-able
in-creas-ing-ly
in-cred-i-ble
in-cred-i-bil-i-ty
in-cred-i-ble-ness
in-cred-i-bly
in-cre-du-li-ty
in-cred-u-lous
in-cred-u-lous-ness
in-cred-u-lous-ly
in-cre-ment
in-cre-men-tal
in-crim-i-nate
in-crim-i-nat-ed
in-crim-i-nat-ing
in-crim-i-na-tion
in-crim-i-na-tor
in-crim-i-na-to-ry
in-crust
in-crus-ta-tion
in-cu-bate
in-cu-bat-ed
in-cu-bat-ing
in-cu-ba-tion
in-cu-ba-tor
in-cu-bus
in-cu-bus-es
in-cul-cate
in-cul-cat-ed
in-cul-cat-ing
in-cul-ca-tion
in-cul-ca-tor
in-cul-pate
in-cul-pat-ed
in-cul-pat-ing
in-cul-pa-tion

in-cum-ben-cy
in-cum-ben-cies
in-cum-bent
in-cum-bent-ly
in-cur
in-curred
in-cur-ring
in-cur-able
in-cur-a-bil-i-ty
in-cur-a-ble-ness
in-cur-a-bly
in-cur-sion
in-cur-sive
in-debt-ed
in-debt-ed-ness
in-de-cen-cy
in-den-cies
in-de-cent
in-de-cent-ly
in-de-ci-sion
in-de-ci-sive
in-de-ci-sive-ly
in-de-ci-sive-ness
in-deed
in-de-fat-i-ga-ble
in-de-fat-i-ga-bil-i-ty
in-de-fat-i-ga-ble-ness
in-de-fat-i-ga-bly
in-def-i-nite
in-def-i-nite-ly
in-def-i-nite-ness
in-del-i-ble
in-del-i-bil-ity
in-del-i-ble-ness
in-del-i-bly
in-del-i-ca-cy
in-del-i-cate
in-del-i-cate-ness
in-del-i-cate-ly
in-dem-ni-fi-ca-tion
in-dem-ni-fy
in-dem-ni-fied
in-dem-ni-fy-ing
in-dem-ni-fi-er
in-dem-ni-ty
in-dem-ni-ties
in-dent
in-den-ta-tion
in-dent-ed
in-den-ture
in-den-tured
in-den-tur-ing
in-de-pen-dence

in-de-pen-den-cy
in-de-pen-dent
in-de-pen-dent-ly
in-de-scib-able
in-de-scrib-abil-ity
in-de-scrib-able-ness
in-de-scrib-ably
in-de-struc-ti-ble
in-de-struc-ti-bil-i-ty
in-de-struc-ti-ble-ness
in-de-struc-ti-bly
in-det-mi-na-cy
in-de-ter-mi-nate
in-de-ter-mi-nat-ly
in-de-ter-mi-na-tion
in-dex
in-dex-er
in-dex-es
in-di-ces
in-di-cate
in-di-cat-ed
in-di-cat-ing
in-di-ca-tion
in-dic-a-tive
in-dic-a-tive-ly
in-di-ca-tor
in-dic-a-tory
in-dict
in-dict-a-ble
in-dict-er
in-dict-or
in-dict-ment
in-dif-fer-ence
in-dif-fer-ent
in-dif-fer-ent-ist
in-dif-fer-ent-ly
in-dig-e-nous
in-dig-e-nous-ly
in-dig-e-nous-ness
in-di-gent
in-di-gent-ly
in-di-gest-ed
in-di-gest-ible
in-di-gest-ibil-i-ty
in-di-gest-ible-ness
in-di-ges-tion
in-di-ges-tive
in-dig-nant
in-dig-ant-ly
in-dig-na-tion
in-dig-ni-ty
in-dig-ni-ties
in-di-go

in-di-goes
in-di-gos
in-di-rect
in-di-rect-ly
in-di-rect-ness
in-dis-creet
in-dis-creet-ly
in-dis-creet-ness
in-dis-crete
in-dis-cre-tion
in-dis-crim-i-nate
in-dis-crim-i-nate-ly
in-dis-crim-i-nat-ing
in-dis-crim-i-na-tion
in-dis-pens-able
in-dis-pens-able-ness
in-dis-pens-abil-i-ty
in-dis-pens-ably
in-dis-pose
in-dis-posed
in-dis-pos-ing
in-dis-po-si-tion
in-dis-sol-u-ble
in-dis-sol-u-bil-i-ty
in-dis-sol-u-ble-ness
in-dis-sol-u-bly
in-di-um
in-di-vid-u-al
in-di-vid-u-al-ly
in-di-vid-u-al-ism
in-di-vid-u-al-ist
in-di-vid-u-al-is-tic
in-di-vid-u-al-i-ty
in-di-vid-u-al-i-ties
in-di-vid-u-al-ize
in-di-vid-u-al-ized
in-di-vid-u-al-iz-ing
in-doc-tri-nate
in-doc-tri-nat-ed
in-doc-tri-nat-ing
in-doc-tri-na-tion
in-doc-tri-na-tor
in-do-lence
in-do-lent
in-do-lent-ly
in-dom-i-ta-ble
in-dom-i-ta-bil-i-ty
in-dom-ita-ble-ness
in-dom-i-ta-bly
in-door
in-doors
in-du-bi-ta-ble
in-du-bi-ta-bil-i-ty

in-dubi-ta-ble-ness
in-du-bi-tab-ly
in-duce
in-duced
in-duce-ment
in-duc-er
in-duc-i-ble
in-duc-ing
in-duct
in-duct-ee
in-duc-tion
in-duc-tive
in-dulge
in-dulged
in-dulg-ing
in-dul-gence
in-dul-gent
in-dul-gent-ly
in-dus-tri-al
in-dus-tri-al-ly
in-dus-tri-al-ness
in-dus-tri-al-ism
in-dus-tri-al-ize
in-dus-tri-al-ist
in-dus-tri-al-i-za-tion
in-dus-tri-al-ized
in-dus-tri-al-iz-ing
in-dus-tri-ous
in-dus-tri-ous-ly
in-dus-try
in-dus-tries
ine-bri-ate
ine-bri-at-ed
ine-bri-at-ing
ine-bri-a-tion
ine-bri-ety
in-ed-u-ca-ble
in-ef-fa-ble
in-ef-fa-bil-i-ty
in-ef-fa-ble-ness
in-ef-fa-bly
in-ef-fec-tive
in-ef-fec-tive-ly
in-ef-fec-tive-ness
in-ef-fec-tu-al
in-ef-fec-tu-al-i-ty
in-ef-fec-tu-al-ly
in-ef-fec-tu-al-ness
in-ef-fi-cient
in-ef-fi-cien-cy
in-ef-fi-cien-cies
in-ef-ffi-cient-ly
in-el-i-gi-ble

in-el-i-gi-bil-i-ty
in-el-i-gi-bly
in-e-luc-ta-ble
in-ept
in-ept-i-tude
in-ept-ly
in-ept-ness
in-e-qual-i-ty
in-eq-ui-ta-ble
in-eq-ui-ty
in-eq-ui-ties
in-ert
in-ert-ly
in-ert-ness
in-er-tia
in-er-tial
in-es-cap-a-ble
in-es-cap-a-ble
in-es-ti-ma-ble
in-es-ti-ma-bly
in-ev-i-ta-ble
in-ev-i-ta-bil-i-ty
in-ev-i-ta-ble-ness
in-ev-i-ta-ble-ness
in-ev-i-ta-bly
in-ex-haust-i-ble
in-ex-haust-i-bil-i-ty
in-ex-haust-i-ble-ness
in-ex-haust-i-bly
in-ex-o-ra-ble
in-ex-o-ra-bil-i-ty
in-ex-o-ra-ble-ness
in-ex-o-ra-bly
in-ex-pe-ri-ence
in-ex-pe-ri-enced
in-ex-pert
in-ex-per-ly
in-ex-pert-ness
in-ex-pe-ri-ence
in-ex-pe-ri-enced
in-ex-pert
in-ex-pert-ly
in-ex-pert-ness
in-ex-pi-a-ble
in-ex-pi-a-ble-ness
in-ex-pi-a-bly
in-ex-pli-ca-ble
in-ex-pli-ca-bil-i-ty
in-ex-pli-ca-ble-ness
in-ex-pli-ca-bly
in-fal-li-ble
in-fal-i-bil-i-ty
in-fal-li-ble-ness

in-fal-li-bly
in-fa-mous
in-fa-mous-ly
in-fa-mous-ness
in-fa-my
in-fa-mies
in-fan-cy
in-fan-cies
in-fant
in-fant-hood
in-fant-like
in-fan-tile
in-fan-tine
in-fan-til-i-ty
in-fan-try
in-fan-tries
in-fan-try-man
in-fan-try-men
in-fat-u-ate
in-fat-u-at-ed
in-fat-u-at-ing
in-fat-u-at-ed-ly
in-fat-u-a-tion
in-fect
in-fect-ed-ness
in-fect-er
in-fect-or
in-fec-tion
in-fec-tious
in-fec-tious-ly
in-fec-tious-ness
in-fec-tive
in-fer
inferred
in-fer-ring
in-fer-a-ble
in-fer-a-bly
in-fer-ence
in-fer-er
in-fe-ri-or
in-fe-ri-or-i-ty
in-fe-ri-or-ly
in-fer-nal
in-fer-no
in-fer-nos
in-fest
in-fes-ta-tion
in-fest-er
in-fi-del
in-fi-del-i-ty
in-fi-del-i-ties
in-field
in-field-er

in-fight-ing
in-fight-er
in-fil-trate
in-fil-trat-ed
in-fil-trat-ing
in-fil-tra-tion
in-fil-tra-tive
in-fil-tra-tor
in-fi-nite
in-fi-nite-ly
in-fi-nite-ness
in-fin-i-tude
in-fin-i-tes-i-mal
in-fin-i-tes-i-mal-ty
in-fin-i-tive
in-fin-i-tive-ly
in-fin-i-ty
in-fin-i-ties
in-firm
in-firm-lly
in-firm-ness
in-fir-ma-ry
in-fir-ma-ries
in-fir-mi-ty
in-fir-mi-ties
in-flame
in-flamed
in-flam-ing
in-flam-er
in-flam-ma-ble
in-flam-ma-bil-i-ty
in-flam-ma-ble-ness
in-flam-ma-bly
in-flam-ma-tion
in-flam-ma-to-ry
in-flate
in-flat-ed
in-flat-ing
in-flat-a-ble
in-flat-ed-ness
in-fla-tor
in-fla-ter
in-fla-tion
in-fla-tion-ary
in-fla-tion-ism
in-fla-tion-ist
in-flect
in-flec-tion
in-flec-tion-al
in-flec-tion-al-ly
in-flec-tion-less
in-flec-tive
in-flec-tor

106

in-flex-i-ble
in-flex-i-bil-i-ty
in-flex-i-ble-ness
in-flex-i-bly
in-flict
in-flict-a-ble
in-flict-er
in-flict-or
in-flic-tion
in-flic-tive
in-flu-ence
in-flu-enced
in-flu-enc-ing
in-flu-ence-a-ble
in-flu-enc-er
in-flu-en-tial
in-flu-en-tial-ly
in-flu-en-za
in-flu-en-zal
in-flu-en-za-like
in-flux
in-form
in-formed
in-for-mer
in-for-mal
in-for-mal-i-ty
in-for-mal-ly
in-form-ant
in-for-ma-tion
in-for-ma-tion-al
in-for-ma-tive
in-for-ma-tive-ly
in-for-ma-tive-ness
in-for-ma-to-ry
in-frac-tion
in-fran-gi-ble
in-fran-gi-bil-i-ty
in-fran-gi-ble-ness
in-fran-gi-bly
in-fra-red
in-fra-struc-ture
in-fre-quent
in-fre-quen-cy
in-fre-quent-ly
in-fringe
in-fringed
in-fring-ing
in-fringe-ment
in-fring-er
in-fu-ri-ate
in-fu-ri-at-ed
in-fu-ri-at-ing
in-fu-ri-at-ing-ly

in-fu-ri-a-tion
in-fuse
in-fused
in-fus-ing
in-fus-er
in-fus-i-bil-i-ty
in-fus-i-ble
in-fu-sion
in-fu-sive
in-gen-ious
in-gen-ious-ly
in-gen-ious-ness
in-gest
in-ges-tion
in-ges-tive
in-glo-ri-ous
in-glo-ri-ous-ly
in-glo-ri-ous-ness
in-got
in-grain
in-grained
in-grate
in-gra-ti-ate
in-gra-ti-at-ed
in-gra-ti-at-ing
in-gra-ti-a-tion
in-grat-i-tude
in-gre-di-ent
in-group
in-grow-ing
in-grown
in-growth
in-gulf
in-hab-it
in-hab-it-a-ble
in-hab-i-ta-tion
in-hab-it-er
in-hab-it-ed
in-hab-it-ant
in-hal-ant
in-ha-la-tion
in-ha-la-tor
in-hale
in-haled
in-hal-ing
in-hal-er
in-here
in-hered
in-her-ing
in-her-ence
in-her-ent
in-her-ent-ly
in-he-sion

in-her-it
in-her-i-tor
in-her-i-tance
in-hib-it
in-hib-i-tive
in-hib-o-to-ry
in-hib-i-ter
in-hib-it-or
in-hi-bi-tion
in-hos-pi-ta-ble
in-hos-pi-tal-i-ty
in-hu-man
in-hu-man-i-ty
in-hu-mane
in-im-i-cal
in-im-i-ta-ble
in-iq-ui-ty
in-iq-ui-ties
in-iq-ui-tous
in-i-tial
in-i-tialed
in-i-tial-ing
in-i-tial-ly
in-i-ti-ate
in-i-ti-at-ed
in-i-ti-at-ing
in-i-ti-a-tion
in-i-ti-a-tor
in-i-ti-a-tive
in-ject
in-jec-tion
in-jec-tor
in-ju-di-cious
in-junc-tion
in-junc-tive
in-jur
in-jured
in-jur-ing
in-ju-ri-ous
in-ju-ry
in-ju-ries
in-jus-tice
ink-blot
ink-ling
inky
in-law
in-lay
in-laid
in-lay-ing
in-let
in-me-mo-ri-an
in-most
in-nards

in-nate
in-ner
in-ner-most
in-ner-sole
in-ner-vate
  in-ner-vat-ed
  in-ner-vat-ing
  in-ner-va-tion
in-nerve
in-ning
inn-keep-er
in-no-cence
in-no-cent
  in-no-cent-ly
in-noc-u-ous
in-no-vate
  in-no-vat-ed
  in-no-vat-ing
  in-no-va-tion
  in-no-va-tive
  in-no-va-tor
in-nu-en-do
  in-nu-en-dos
  in-nu-en-does
in-nu-mer-a-ble
  in-nu-mer-ous
  in-nu-mer-a-bly
in-ob-serv-ance
  in-ob-serv-ant
  in-ob-serv-ant-ly
in-oc-u-lant
in-oc-u-late
  in-oc-u-lat-ed
  in-oc-u-lat-ing
  in-oc-u-la-tion
  in-oc-u-la-tor
in-oc-u-lum
in-of-fen-sive
in-op-er-a-ble
in-op-er-a-tive
in-op-por-tune
  in-op-por-tun-i-ty
in-or-di-nate
in-pa-tient
in-pour
in-put
in-quest
in-qui-e-tude
in-quire
in-quiry
  in-quir-ies
in-qui-si-tion
in-qui-si-tive

in-quis-i-tor
in-road
in-rush
in-sane
in-san-i-ty
  in-san-i-ties
in-sa-tia-ble
  in-sa-tia-bil-i-ty
  in-sa-tia-bly
in-sa-ti-ate
in-scribe
in-scru-ta-ble
  in-scru-ta-bil-i-ty
  in-scru-ta-bly
in-seam
in-sect
in-sec-ti-cide
  in-sec-ti-cid-al
in-se-cure
  in-se-cu-ri-ty
in-sem-i-nate
  in-sem-i-nat-ed
  in-sem-i-nat-ing
  in-sem-i-na-tion
in-sen-sate
in-sen-si-ble
in-sen-si-tive
  in-sen-si-tiv-i-ty
in-sen-ti-ent
in-sep-a-ra-ble
  in-sep-a-ra-bil-i-ty
  in-sep-a-ra-bly
in-sert
  in-sert-er
in-ser-tion
in-set
  in-set-ting
in-shore
in-side
in-sid-er
in-sid-i-ous
in-sight
  in-sight-ful
in-sig-nia
in-sig-nif-i-cant
  in-sig-nif-i-cance
in-sin-cere
  in-sin-cer-i-ty
  in-sin-cer-i-ties
in-sin-u-ate
  in-sin-u-at-ed
  in-sin-u-at-ing
  in-sin-u-a-tor

in-sin-u-a-tion
in-sip-id
  in-si-pid-i-ty
  in-sip-id-ness
in-sist
  in-sist-ence
  in-sist-ent
in-so-bri-e-ty
in-so-cia-ble
  in-so-cia-bil-i-ty
  in-so-cia-bly
in-so-far
in-sole
in-so-lent
  in-so-lence
in-sol-u-ble
  in-sol-u-bil-i-ty
  in-sol-u-bly
in-solv-a-ble
in-sol-vent
  in-sol-ven-cy
in-som-nia
  in-som-ni-ac
in-so-much
in-spect
in-spec-tion
in-spec-tor
in-spi-ra-tion
  in-spi-ra-tion-al
in-spire
  in-spir-ing
in-spir-it
in-sta-ble
  in-sta-bil-i-ty
in-stall
in-stan-ta-ne-ous
in-stant-ly
in-state
  in-stat-ed
  in-stat-ing
  in-state-ment
in-stead
in-step
in-sti-gate
  in-sti-gat-ed
  in-sti-gat-ing
  in-sti-ga-tion
  in-sti-ga-tor
in-still
in-stinct
in-stinc-tive
  in-stinc-tu-al
  in-stinc-tive-ly

in-sti-tute
in-sti-tut-ed
in-sti-tut-ing
in-sti-tut-er
in-sti-tu-tor
in-sti-tu-tion
in-sti-tu-tion-al
in-sti-tu-tion-al-ism
in-sti-tu-tion-al-ize
in-sti-tu-tion-al-ized
in-struct
in-struc-tion
in-struc-tive
in-struc-tor
in-stru-ment
in-stru-men-tal
in-stru-men-ta-list
in-stru-men-ta-tion
in-sub-or-di-nate
in-sub-or-di-na-tion
in-sub-stan-tial
in-sub-stan-ti-al-i-ty
in-suf-fer-a-ble
in-suf-fer-a-bly
in-suf-fi-cient
in-suf-fi-cien-cy
in-su-lar
in-su-lar-i-ty
in-su-late
in-su-lat-ed
in-su-lat-ing
in-su-la-tion
in-su-la-tor
in-su-lin
in-sult
in-sop-port-a-ble
in-sup-press-i-ble
in-sur-ance
in-sure
in-sured
in-sur-ing
in-sur-er
in-sur-gent
in-sur-gence
in-sur-gen-cy
in-sur-mount-a-ble
in-sur-rec-tion
in-sur-rec-tion-ary
in-sus-cep-ti-ble
in-tact
in-take
in-tan-gi-ble
in-tan-gi-bil-i-ty

in-tan-gi-bly
in-te-ger
in-te-gral
in-te-gral-ly
in-te-grate
in-te-grat-ed
in-te-grat-ing
in-te-gra-tion
in-te-gra-tion-ist
in-teg-ri-ty
in-tel-lect
in-tel-lec-tu-al
in-tel-lec-tu-al-ism
in-tel-li-gence
in-tel-li-gent
in-tel-li-gent-ly
in-tel-li-gent-sia
in-tel-li-gi-ble
in-tel-li-gi-bil-i-ty
in-tel-li-gi-bly
in-tem-per-ance
in-tem-per-ate
in-tend
in-tend-er
in-tend-ed
in-tense
in-tense-ly
in-tense-ness
in-ten-si-fy
in-ten-si-fied
in-ten-si-fy-ing
in-ten-si-fi-ca-tion
in-ten-si-fi-er
in-ten-sion
in-ten-si-ty
in-ten-si-ties
in-ten-sive
in-ten-sive-ly
in-ten-sive-ness
in-tent
in-ten-tion
in-ten-tion-al
in-ten-tion-al-ly
in-ten-tioned
in-ter
in-ter-act
in-ter-ac-tion
in-ter-breed
in-ter-bred
in-ter-cede
in-ter-ced-ed
in-ter-ced-ing
in-ter-ced-er

in-ter-cept
in-ter-cep-ter
in-ter-cep-tor
in-ter-cep-tion
in-ter-cep-tive
in-ter-ces-sion
in-ter-change
in-ter-changed
in-ter-chang-ing
in-ter-chang-a-ble
in-ter-chng-a-bil-i-ty
in-ter-chang-a-bly
in-ter-col-le-gi-ate
in-ter-com
in-ter-com-mun-i-cate
in-ter-con-nect
in-ter-con-nec-tion
in-ter-con-ti-nen-tal
in-ter-course
in-ter-cul-tur-al
in-ter-cur-rent
in-ter-de-part-men-tal
in-ter-de-pend-ent
in-ter-de-pend
in-ter-de-pend-ence
in-ter-de-pend-en-cy
in-ter-dict
in-ter-dic-tion
in-ter-dis-ci-pli-nary
in-ter-est
in-ter-est-ed
in-ter-est-ed-ly
in-ter-est-ing
in-ter-face
in-ter-fa-cial
in-ter-faith
in-ter-fere
in-ter-ga-lac-tic
in-ter-im
in-te-ri-or
in-ter-ject
in-ter-jec-tion
in-ter-jec-to-ry
in-ter-ly-er
in-ter-leaf
in-ter-leaves
in-ter-leave
in-ter-leaved
in-ter-leav-ing
in-ter-line\
in-ter-lined
in-ter-lin-ing
in-ter-link

in-ter-lock
in-ter-lo-cu-tion
  in-ter-loc-u-tor
  in-ter-loc-u-to-ry
in-ter-lop-er
in-ter-lude
in-ter-nar
  in-ter-na-ry
in-ter-mar-ry
  in-ter-mar-ried
  in-ter-mar-ry-ing
  in-ter-mar-riage
in-ter-me-di-ary
  in-ter-me-di-ar-ies
in-ter-me-di-ate
  in-ter-me-di-at-ed
  in-ter-me-di-at-ing
  in-ter-me-di-a-tion
  in-ter-me-di-a-tor
in-ter-mi-na-ble
in-ter-min-gle
  in-ter-min-gledd
  in-ter-min-gling
in-ter-mis-sion
  in-ter-mis-sive
in-ter-mit
in-ter-mix
  in-ter-mix-ture
in-tern
  in-ter-ship
in-ter-nal
  in-ter-nal-ly
in-ter-na-tion-al
  in-ter-na-tion-al-i-ty
  in-ter-na-tion-al-ize
  in-ter-na-tion-al-ized
in-ter-na-tion-al-ism
in-tern-ee
in-tern-ist
in-tern-ment
in-ter-of-fice
in-ter-pen-e-trate
  in-ter-pen-e-tra-tion
in-ter-plan-e-tary
in-ter-play
in-ter-po-late
in-ter-pose
  in-ter-posed
  in-ter-pos-ing
  in-ter-pos-er
  in-ter-po-si-tion
in-ter-pret
  in-ter-pret-a-ble

in-ter-pret-er
in-ter-pre-tive
in-ter-pre-ta-tion
  in-ter-pre-ta-tion-al
  in-ter-pre-ta-tive
in-ter-ro-gate
  in-ter-ro-gat-ed
  in-ter-ro-gat-ing
in-ter-ro-ga-tion
  in-ter-ro-ga-tion
  in-ter-ro-ga-tion-al
in-ter-rog-a-tive
in-ter-ro-ga-tor
in-ter-rupt
  in-ter-rup-tion
  in-ter-rup-tive
in-ter-rupt-er
  in-ter-rupt-or
in-terr-scho-las-tic
in-ter-sect
in-ter-sec-tion
in-ter-space
  in-ter-spaced
  in-ter-spac-ing
in-ter-state
  in-ter-stel-lar
in-ter-tid-al
in-ter-twine
  in-ter-twined
  in-ter-twin-ing
in-ter-ur-ban
in-ter-val
in-ter-vence
in-ter-view
  in-ter-view-er
in-ter-weave
  in-ter-wove
  in-ter-weav-ing
  in-ter-wo-ven
in-tes-tate
in-tes-tine
  in-tes-ti-nal
in-ti-mate
  in-ti-mat-ed
  in-ti-mat-ing
  in-ti-mate-ly
  in-ti-ma-tion
in-tim-i-date
  in-tim-i-dat-ed
  in-tim-i-dat-ing
  in-tim-i-da-tion
  in-tim-i-da-tor
in-ti-tled

  in-ti-ling
in-to
in-tol-er-a-ble
  in-tol-er-a-bly
in-tol-er-ant
  in-tol-er-ance
in-tomb
in-to-mate
  in-to-nat-ed
  in-to-nat-ing
in-to-na-tion
in-tone
  in-toned
  in-ton-ing
  in-ton-er
in-tox-i-cant
in-tox-i-cate
  in-tox-i-cat-ed
  in-tox-i-cat-ing
in-tox-i-ca-tion
in-trac-ta-ble
  in-trac-ta-bil-i-ty
in-tra-mu-ral
  in-tra-mu-ral-ly
in-tran-si-gent
  in-tran-si-gence
in-tran-si-tive
in-tra-state
in-tra-ve-nous
in-trench
in-trep-id
  in-tre-pid-i-ty
in-trique
  in-tri-quing
in-trin-sic
  in-trin-si-cal
  in-trin-si-cal-ly
in-tro-spect
  in-tro-spec-tion
  in-tro-spec-tive
in-tro-ver-sion
  in-tro-ver-sive
in-tro-vert
  in-tro-vert-ed
in-trude
in-trust
in-tu-it
in-tu-i-tion
  in-tu-i-tion-al
in-tu-i-tive
in-un-date
  in-un-dat-ed
  in-un-dat-ing

in-un-da-tion
in-un-da-tor
in-vade
in-val-id
in-va-lid-i-ty
in-va-lid-ism
in-val-u-a-ble
in-var-i-a-ble
in-var-i-a-bil-i-ty
in-var-i-ant
in-var-i-ance
in-va-sion
in-va-sive
in-vec-tive
in-ven-tion
in-ven-tive
in-ven-tive-ness
in-ven-to-ry
in-ven-to-ries
in-ven-to-ried
in-ven-to-ry-ing
in-verse
in-ver-sion
in-vert
in-ver-te-brate
in-vert-ed
in-vest
in-ves-tor
in-ves-ti-gate
in-ves-ti-gat-ed
in-ves-ti-gat-ing
in-ves-ti-ga-tion
in-ves-ti-ga-tor
in-ves-ti-ture
in-vest-ment
in-vet-er-ate
in-vid-i-ous
in-vig-or-ate
in-vig-or-at-ed
in-vig-or-at-ing
in-vig-or-ant
in-vig-or-a-tion
in-vig-or-a-tor
in-vin-ci-ble
in-vin-ci-bil-i-ty
in-vin-ci-bly
in-vi-o-la-ble
in-vi-o-la-bil-i-ty
in-vi-o-la-bly
in-vi-o-late
in-vis-i-ble
in-vis-i-bil-i-ty
in-vis-i-bly

in-vi-ta-tion
in-vi-ta-tion-al
in-vo-ca-tion
in-voice
in-voke
in-voked
in-vok-ing
in-vol-un-tary
in-vol-un-tar-i-ly
in-vo-lute
in-vo-lu-tion
in-volve
in-volved
in-volv-ing
in-volve-ment
in-volv-er
in-vul-ner-a-ble
in-ward
in-wards
in-ward-ly
in-waeve
in-wrought
io-dine
ion
ion-ic
ion-o-sphere
iota
ip-so fac-to
iras-ci-ble
iras-ci-bil-i-ty
iras-ci-bly
irate
ir-i-des-cent
ir-i-des-cence
irid-i-um
iris
irk-some
iron
iron-er
iron-clad
iron-ic
iron-i-cal
iron-smith
iron-ware
iron-work
iron-work-er
iro-ny
iro-nies
ir-rad-i-ca-ble
ir-ra-tion-al
ir-ra-tion-al-i-ty
ir-re-claim-a-ble
ir-rec-on-cil-a-ble

ir-rec-on-cil-a-bil-i-ty
ir-re-cov-er-a-ble
ir-re-duc-i-ble
ir-ref-u-ta-ble
ir-re-gard-less
ir-reg-u-lar
ir-reg-u-lar-i-ty
ir-rel-e-vant
ir-rel-e-vance
ir-rel-e-van-cy
ir-re-li-gion
ir-re-li-gious
ir-re-mis-si-ble
ir-re-mov-a-ble
ir-rep-a-ra-ble
ir-re-plac-a-ble
ir-re-press-i-ble
ir-re-press-i-bil-i-ty
ir-re-press-i-bly
ir-re-proach-a-ble
ir-re-sist-i-ble
ir-re-sist-i-bil-i-ty
ir-res-o-lute
ir-res-o-lu-tion
ir-re-spec-tive
ir-re-spon-si-ble
ir-re-spon-si-bil-i-ty
ir-re-spon-sive
ir-re-triev-a-ble
ir-re-triev-a-bil-i-ty
ir-re-trieev-a-bly
ir-rev-o-ca-ble
ir-rev-o-ca-bil-i-ty
ir-ri-gate
ir-ri-gat-ed
ir-ri-ta-ble
ir-ri-tant
ir-ri-tate
ir-rupt
is-land
isle
iso-bar
iso-gloss
iso-late
iso-lat-ed
iso-met-ric
ison-o-my
iso-ton-ic
is-su-ance
is-sue
item
it-er-ate
ivo-ry

111

J

jab
jabbed
jab-bing
jab-ber
jab-ber-er
jac-a-mar
jac-a-ram-da
jack-al
jack-ass
jack-boot
jack-et
jack-et-ed
jack-ham-mer
jack-knife
jack-kives
jack-knifed
jack-knif-ing
jack--o'--lan-tern
jack-pot
jack rab-bit
jac-o-net
jac-quard
jade
jad-ed
jad-ing
Jaf-fa
jag
jag-ged
jag-ging
jag-uar
jail-bird
jail-break
jail-er
ja-lopy
ja-lop-ies
jal-ou-sie
jam
jammed
jam-ming
jam-mer
jamb
jam-bo-ree
jan-gle
jan-gled
jan-gling
jan-gler
jan-gly
jan-i-tor
jan-i-to-ri-al
jar
jar-ful
jarred
jar-ring

jar-di-niere
jar-red
jar-gon
jar-gon-ize
jas-mine
jas-sid
jaun-dice
jaun-diced
jaun-dic-ing
jaunt
jaun-ty
jaun-ti-er
jaun-ti-est
jaun-ti-ly
jaun-ti-ness
jav-e-lin
jaw-bone
jaw-break-er
jay-gee
jay-walk
jay-walk-er
jazz
jazz-ist
jazz-man
jazzy
jazz-i-er
jazz-i-est
jazz-i-ly
jazz-i-ness
jeal-ous
jeal-ous-ies
jeep
jeer-er
je-hu
jel-li-fy
jel-li-fies
jel-li-fy-ing
jel-ly
jel-lied
jel-lies
jel-ly-ing
jel-ly-like
jel-ly bean
jel-ly-fish
jen-ny
jen-nies
jeop-ar-dy
jeop-ar-dize
jeop-ar-dized
jeop-ar-diz-ing
jerk
jerk-er
jerk-i-ly

jerk-y
jerk-i-er
jerk-i-est
jer-kin
jer-sey
jes-sa-mine
jest-er
jest-ing
Je-sus
jet
jet-ted
jet-ting
jet-lin-er
jet-port
jet-pro-polled
jet-sam
jet-ti-son
jet-ty
jet-ties
jew-el
jew-eled
jew-el-ing
jew-el-er
jew-el-ry
jibe
jibed
jib-ing
jig
jigged
jig-ging
jig-ger
jig-gle
jig-gled
jig-gling
jig-gly
jig-saw
jilt-er
jim-dan-dy
jim-my
jim-mies
jim-mied
jim-my-ing
jin-gle
jin-gled
jin-gling
jinx
jit-ney
jit-neys
jit-ter
jit-ters
jit-tery
jit-ter-bug
jit-ter-bugged

job
  jobbed
  job-bing
job-ber
job-hold-er
jock-ey
  jock-eys
  jock-ey-ing
jock-strap
jo-cose
  jo-cos-i-ty
jo-cund
  jo-cun-di-ty
jodh-pur
jog
  jogged
  jog-ging
  jog-ger
jog-gle
  jog-gled
  jog-gling
join-able
join-er
joint
  joint-ed
  joint-ly
joist
joke
  joked
  jok-ing
  joke-ster
  jok-ing-ly
jok-er
jolt
  jolt-er
  jolt-ing-ly
  jolty
jon-quil
jos-tle
  jos-tled
  jos-tling
  jos-tler
jot
  jott-ed
joule
jour-nal
jour-nal-ism
jour-nal-ist
  jour-na-lis-tic
jour-nal-ize
jour-ney
  jour-ney-man
  jour-ney-men

joust
jo-vi-al
  jo-vi-al-i-ty
jowl
  jowled
  jowy
joy-ful
joy-less
joy-ous
joy-ride
ju-bi-lant
  ju-bi-lance
  ju-bi-lan-cy
ju-bi-lar-i-an
ju-bi-la-tion
  ju-bi-late
  ju-bi-lat-ed
  ju-bi-lat-ing
ju-bi-lee
judge
  judged
  judg-ing
judge-ment
  judge-men-tal
ju-di-ca-ture
ju-di-cial
ju-di-cia-ry
ju-di-cious
Ju-dith
ju-do
jug
  jugged
  jug-gin
  jug-ful
  jug-gler
ju-gate
jug-u-lar
jug-u-lum
ju-gum
juice
  juic-i-er
  juic-i-est
  juic-i-ly
ju-jit-su
juke-box
ju-lep
ju-li-enne
Ju-lius
Ju-ly
jum-ble
  jum-bled
  jum-bling
jum-bo

jum-bos
jump
  jump-ing
  jumpy
jump-er
jump--off
junc-tion
junc-ture
jun-gle
jun-ior
ju-ni-per
junk
  junk-man
  junky
jun-ket
junk-ie
jun-ta
Ju-pi-ter
ju-ris-dic-tion
  ju-ris-dic-tion-al
ju-ris-pru-dence
  ju-ris-pru-den-tial
ju-ris-pru-dent
ju-rist
ju-ris-tic
ju-ror
ju-ry
  ju-ries
  ju-ry-man
just
  just-ly
  just-ness
jus-tice
  jus-tice-less
  jus-tice-like
  jus-ti-fi-ca-tion
jus-ti-fy
  jus-ti-fied
  jus-ti-fy-ing
  jus-ti-fi-a-ble
  jus-tif-i-ca-tory
jut
  jut-ted
  jut-ting
jute
ju-ve-nes-cence
  ju-ve-nes-cent
ju-ve-nile
  ju-ve-nil-i-ty
jux-ta-pose
  jux-ta-posed
  jux-ta-pos-ing
  jux-ta-po-si-tion

113

K

ka-bob
kai-ser
ka-lei-do-scope
  ka-lei-do-scop-ic
ka-mi-ka-ze
kan-ga-roo
ka-olin
  ka-oline
ka-pok
ka-put
ka-ra-te
kar-ma
  kar-mic
ka-ty-did
kay-ak
kay-o
kedge
  kedged
  kedg-ing
keel-haul
keel-son
keen-ly
  keen-ness
keep-ing
keep-sake
keg-ler
kelp
ken-nel
  ken-neled
  ken-nel-ing
ke-no
ker-a-tin
ker-chief
ker-mis
ker-nel
ker-o-sene
kes-trel
ketch-up
ke-tone
ket-tle
ket-tle-drum
key
  keyed
key-board
key-hole
key-note
key-stone
kha-ki
  khak-is
kha-lif
khan
kib-butz
  kib-but-zim

ki-bitz-er
ki-bosh
kick-off
kid
kid-nap
kid-ney
  kid-neys
kill-deer
kill-ing
kill-joy
kiln
kilo
  kil-os
kilo-cy-cle
ki-lo-gram
ki-lo-me-ter
ki-lo-ton
kil-o-watt
kilt
ki-mo-no
kin-der-gar-ten
kin-dle
  kin-dled
  kin-dling
kind-ly
  kind-li-er
  kind-li-est
kin-dred
kin-e-mat-ic
kin-e-scope
ki-net-ic
  ki-net-ics
kin-folk
king-bird
king-dom
king-ly
king-pin
king--size
  king--sized
kink-y
  kink-i-er
  kink-i-est
kins-folk
kins-man
  kins-men
  kins-wom-an
ki-osk
kip-per
kir-mess
kis-met
kiss-a-ble
kiss-er
kitch-en

kitch-en-ette
kite
  kit-ed
  kit-ing
kitsch
kit-ten
kit-ten-ish
  kit-ten-ish-ly
kit-ty
  kit-ties
kit-ty--cor-ner
ki-wi
klatch
  klatsch
klep-to-ma-nia
  klep-to-ma-ni-ac
knack
knap-sack
knave
knav-ery
knav-ish
  knav-ish-ly
knead
knee
  kneed
  knee-ing
knee-cap
knee--deep
kneel
  knelt
  kneel-ing
  kneel-er
knee-pan
knell
knick-knack
knife
  knives
  knifed
  knif-ing
  knife-like
knight
  knight-hood
  knight-ly
knit
  knit-ted
  knit-ting
  knit-ter
knob
  knobbed
  knob-by
  knob-bi-er
  knob-bi-est
knock

knock-a-bout
knock-down
knock-er
knock--knee
  knock--kneed
knock-out
knoll
knot
  knot-ted
  knot-ting
  knot-like
  knot-ty
knot-hole
knout
know
  knew
  known
  know-ing
  know-a-ble
  know-er
know--how
know-ing-ly
knowl-edge
knowl-edge-able
know--noth-ing
knuck-le
  knuck-led
  knuck-ling
ko-ala
ko-bold
ko-el
ko-gas-in
kohl-ra-bi
  kohl-ra-bies
ko-la
ko-lin-sky
  ko-lin-skies
kook
  kooky
  kook-i-er
  kook-i-est
kook-a-bur-ra
ko-peck
ko-ru-na
ko-sher
kou-mis
kow-tow
kro-na
kro-ne
kryp-ton
ku-dos
ku-miss
kum-quat

L

la-bel
  la-beled
  la-bel-ing
  la-bel-er
la-bi-al
  la-bi-al-ly
la-bi-ate
la-bi-o-den-tal
la-bi-um
  la-bia
la-bor
  la-bor-er
lab-o-ra-to-ry
la-bored
la-bo-ri-ous
  la-bo-ri-ous-ly
  la-bo-ri-ous-ness
la-bor-sav-ing
la-bur-num
lab-y-rinth
  lab-y-rin-thine
  lab-y-rin-thi-an
lace
lac-er-ate
  lac-er-at-ed
  lac-er-at-ing
  lac-er-a-tion
lace-wing
la-ches
lach-ry-mal
lach-ry-mose
  lach-ry-mose-ly
lac-ing
lack-a-dai-si-cal
  lack-a-dai-si-cal-ly
lack-ey
lack-lus-ter
la-ci-nia
la-con-ic
  la-con-i-cal-ly
lac-quer
  lac-quer-er
la-crosse
lac-tate
  lac-tat-ed
  lac-tat-ing
  lac-ta-tion
lac-te-al
lac-tic
lac-tose
la-cu-na
  la-cu-nas
  la-cu-nae

lad-der
lad-die
lade
  lad-ed
  lad-en
  lad-ing
la-dle
  la-dled
  la-dling
la-dy
  la-dy-bug
la-dy-fin-ger
la-dy--in--wait-ing
la-dy-like
la-dy-love
lag
  lagged
  lag-ging
la-ger
lag-gard
la-gniappe
la-goon
la-ic
  la-i-cal
  la-i-cal-ly
lair
laird
la-i-ty
  la-i-ties
lake-side
lal-la-tion
la-lop-a-thy
lam
  lammed
  lam-ming
la-ma
la-ma-sery
  la-ma-ser-ies
lam-baste
  lam-bast-ed
  lam-bast-ing
lam-ben-cy
lam-bent
  lam-bent-ly
lam-bre-quin
lamb-skin
lame
la-ment
  lam-en-ta-ble
  lam-en-ta-bly
  lam-en-ta-tion
lam-i-na
  lam-i-nae

lam-i-nas
lam-i-nate
 lam-i-nat-ed
 lam-i-nat-ing
 lam-i-na-tion
lam-poon
lam-prey
 lam-preys
lance
 lanced
 lanc-ing
lance-wood
lan-dau
land-ed
land-ing
land-la-dy
 land-la-dies
land-locked
land-lord
land-lub-ber
land-own-er
 land-own-ing
 land-own-er-ship
land-slide
land-ward
 land-wards
lang syne
lan-gauge
lan-quid
 lan-quid-ly
lan-quish
 lan-quish-ing
 lan-quish-ing-ly
lan-quor
 lan-guor-ous
 lan-guor-ous-ly
lan-o-lin
lan-tern
lan-tha-num
lan-yard
la-pel
lap-ful
 lap-fuls
 laps-ful
lap-i-dary
 lap-i-dar-ies
lap-in
lap-pet
lapse
 lapsed
 laps-ing
lar-board
lar-ce-ny

lar-ce-nies
lar-ce-nous
larch
lar-der
large
 larg-er
 larg-est
large-ly
lar-gess
lar-ghet-to
 lar-ghet-tos
larg-ish
lar-go
 lar-gos
lar-i-at
lar-rup
lar-va
 lar-vae
 lar-val
lar-yn-gi-tis
lar-ynx
 lar-ynx-es
 lar-ynx-ges
 la-ryn-ge-al
las-civ-i-ous
 las-ci-v-i-ous-ly
las-sie
las-si-tude
las-so
 las-sos
 las-soes
 las-so-er
last-ing
 last-ing-ly
last-ly
latch-key
late
 lat-er
 lat-est
 late-ness
late-ly
la-tent
 la-ten-cy
 la-tent-ly
lat-er-al
 lat-er-al-ly
la-tex
 la-tex-es
lathe
lath-er
 lath-er-er
 lath-ery
lath-ing

lat-i-tude
 lat-i-tu-di-nal
lat-i-tu-di-nar-i-an
la-trine
lat-ter
lat-tice
 lat-tied
 lat-tic-ing
lat-tice-work
laud-able
 laud-ably
lau-da-num
lau-da-to-ry
 lau-da-tive
laugh
laugh-ter
launch
 launch-er
laun-der
 laun-der-er
 laun-dress
laun-der-ette
laun-dry
 laun-dries
lau-re-ate
lau-rel
la-va
la-a-liere
lav-a-to-ry
 lav-a-to-ries
lav-en-der
lav-ish
 lav-ish-ly
 la-vish-ness
law-abid-ing
law-break-er
 law-break-ing
law-ful
 law-ful-ly
 law-ful-ness
law-less
 law-less-ly
 law-less-ness
law-mak-er
 law-mak-ing
lawn
law-ren-ci-um
law-suit
law-yer
lax
 lax-i-ty
 lax-ly
 lax-ness

lax-a-tive
lay-er
lay-ette
lay-man
lay-men
lay-off
lay-out
lay-over
laze
  lazed
  laz-ing
la-zy
  la-zi-er
  la-zi-est
  la-zi-ly
la-zy-bones
lea
leach
lead
  lead-ing
lead-en
  lead-en-ly
lead-er
  lead-er-less
  lead-er-ship
leaf-age
leafy
  leaf-i-er
  leaf-i-est
leaque
  leaqued
  leaqu-ing
leak
  leak-age
  leak-i-ness
  leaky
  leak-i-er
  leak-i-est
lean
  lean-ly
  lean-ness
lean-ing
lean--to
  lean--tos
leap
  leaped
  leapt
  leap-ing
  leap-er
leap-frog
learn
  learn-ed
  learnt

learn-ing
  learn-er
learn-ed-ly
learn-ed-ness
lease
  leased
  leas-ing
leash
least-wise
  least-ways
leath-er
  leath-er-neck
leath-ery
leave
  left
  leav-ing
  lev-er
leav-en
leaves
leave-talk-ing
lech-er
  lech-er-ous
  lech-er-ous-ly
  lech-ery
  lech-er-ies
lec-tern
lec-ture
  lec-tured
  lec-tur-ing
  lec-tur-er
ledge
ledg-er
leech
leek
leer-ing-ly
leery
lee-ward
lee-way
left--hand-ed
  left--hand-ed-ly
  left--hand-ed-ness
left-ist
left-over
left--wing
  left--wing-er
leg
  legged
  leg-ging
leg-a-cy
  leg-a-cies
le-gal
  le-gal-ly
le-gal-ist

le-gal-is-tic
le-gal-i-ty
  le-gal-i-ties
le-gal-ize
  le-gal-ized
  le-gal-iz-ing
  le-gal-i-za-tion
leg-ate
leg-a-tee
le-ga-tion
le-ga-to
leg-end
leg-end-ary
leg-er-de-main
leg-gy
  leg-gi-er
  leg-gi-est
leg-horn
leg-i-ble
  leg-i-bil-i-ty
  leg-i-bly
le-gion
  le-gion-ary
  le-gion-ar-ies
  le-gion-naire
leg-is-late
  leg-is-lat-ed
  leg-is-la-tive
  leg-is-la-tor
leg-is-la-tion
leg-is-la-ture
le-git
le-git-i-mate
  le-git-i-mat-ed
  le-git-i-mat-ing
  le-git-i-ma-cy
  le-git-i-mate-ly
le-git-i-mist
le-git-i-mize
  le-git-i-mized
  le-git-i-miz-ing
le-gume
le-gu-mi-nous
lei
  leis
lei-sure
lei-sure-ly
  lei-sure-li-ness
leit-mo-tif
lem-ming
lem-on
lem-on-ade
le-mur

lend
lent
lend-ing
lend-er
length
length-en
length-wise
lengthy
length-i-er
length-i-est
length-i-ly
length-i-ness
le-nient
le-ni-ence
le-ni-en-cy
le-ni-ent-ly
len-i-tive
len-i-ty
lens
len-til
len-to
le-o-nine
leop-ard
leop-ard-ess
le-o-tard
lep-er
lep-i-dop-ter-ous
lep-re-chaun
lep-ro-sy
lep-rous
les-bi-an
les-bi-an-ism
le-sion
les-see
less-en
les-sor
least
let-down
le-thal
le-thal-ly
leth-ar-gy
leth-ar-gies
le-thar-gic
le-thar-gi-cal
let-ter
let-ter-ed
let-ter-head
let-ter-ing
let-ter--per-fect
let-ter-press
let-tuce
let-up
leu-ke-mia

leu-ko-cyte
lev-ee
lev-el
lev-eled
lev-el-ing
lev-el-er
lev-el-ly
lev-el-ness
lev-el-head-ed
lev-el-head-ed-ness
lev-er
lev-er-age
le-vi-a-than
lev-i-tate
lev-i-tat-ed
lev-i-tat-ing
lev-i-ta-tion
lev-i-ty
levy
lev-ies
lev-ied
lev-y-ing
lewd
lewd-ly
lewd-ness
lex-i-cog-ra-phy
lex-i-cog-ra-pher
lex-i-co-graph-ic
lex-i-co-graph-i-cal
lex-i-con
li-a-bil-i-ty
li-a-bil-i-ties
li-a-ble
li-ai-son
li-ar
li-ba-tion
li-bel
li-beled
li-bel-ing
li-bel-er
li-bel-ous
li-bel-ous-ly
lib-er-al
lib-er-al-ly
lib-er-al-ness
lib-er-al-ism
lib-er-al-i-ty
lib-er-al-i-ties
lib-er-al-ize
lib-er-al-ized
lib-er-al-iz-ing
lib-er-al-i-za-tion
lib-er-ate

lib-er-at-ed
lib-er-at-ing
lib-er-a-tion
lib-er-a-tor
lib-er-tar-i-an
lib-er-tine
lib-er-tin-ism
lib-er-ty
lib-er-ties
li-bid-i-nous
li-bid-i-nous-ly
li-bid-i-nous-ness
li-bi-do
li-bid-in-al
li-brar-i-an
li-brary
li-brar-ies
li-bret-to
li-bret-tos
li-bret-ist
li-cense
li-censed
li-cens-ing
li-cen-see
li-cens-er
li-cen-ti-ate
li-cen-tious
li-cen-tious-ly
li-cen-tious-ness
li-chee
li-chen
lic-it
lick-e-ty--split
lick-spit-tle
lic-o-rice
lid-ded
lief
liege
lien
lieu
lieu-ten-an-cy
lieu-ten-ant
life-blood
life-boat
life-guard
life-less
life-less-ly
life-less-ness
life-like
life-line
lif-er
life-sav-er
life--size

118

life--style
life-time
life-work
lift-off
lig-a-ment
lig-a-ture
 lig-tured
 lig-a-tur-ing
light-en
light-er
light-fin-gered
light-foot-ed
 light-foot-ed-ly
light-head-ed
 light-head-ed-ly
 light-head-ed-ness
light-heart-ed
 light-heart-ed-ly
 light-heart-ed-ness
light-house
light-ing
light-ly
light--mind-ed
 light--mind-ed-ly
 light--mind-ed-ness
light-ning
light-weight
light--year
lig-nite
like
 liked
 lik-ing
 lik-a-ble
 lik-a-ble-ness
 lik-a-ble-ness
like-li-hood
like-ly
 like-li-er
 like-li-est
like--mind-ed
lik-en
like-ness
like-wise
lik-ing
li-lac
lilt-ing
lily
 lil-lies
lil-y--liv-ered
li-ma
limb
limb-er
 lim-ber-ness

lim-bo
lime
 limed
 lim-ing
 limy
 lim-i-er
 lim-i-est
 lime-like
lime-light
 lime-light-er
lim-er-ick
lime-stone
lim-it
lim-it-a-ble
lim-i-ta-tive
lim-i-ter
lim-it-less
lim-i-ta-tion
lim-it-ed
 lim-it-ed-ly
 lim-it-ed-ness
lim-ou-sine
limp
 limp-er
 limp-ing-ly
 limp-ly
 limp-ness
lim-pet
lim-pid
 lim-pid-i-ty
 lim-pid-ly
 lim-pid-ness
lin-age
lin-den
line
 lined
 lin-ing
lin-e-age
lin-eal
lin-ea-ment
lin-ear
 lin-ear-ly
line-back-er
 line-back-ing
line-man
 line-men
lin-en
lin-er
line-up
lin-ger
 lin-ger-er
 lin-ger-ing-ly
lin-ge-rie

lin-go
 lin-goes
lin-gua fran-ca
lin-qual
 lin-qual-ly
lin-quist
lin-quis-tic
 lin-quis-tics
 lin-quis-ti-cal
 lin-quis-ti-cal-ly
lin-i-ment
lin-ing
link
 linked
 link-er
link-age
lin-net
li-no-leum
lin-seed
lint
 linty
 lint-i-er
 lint-i-est
lin-tel
li-on
 li-on-ess
 li-on-like
li-on-heart-ed
li-on-ize
 li-on-ized
 li-on-iz-ing
 li-on-i-za-tion
 li-on-iz-er
lip-py
 lip-pi-er
 lip-pi-est
lip-stick
liq-ue-fy
 liq-ue-fied
 liq-ue-fy-ing
 liq-ue-fac-tion
 liq-ue-fi-able
 liq-ue-fi-er
li-queur
liq-uid
 li-quid-i-ty
 li-quid-ness
 li-quid-ly
liq-ui-date
 liq-ui-dat-ed
 liq-ui-dat-ing
 liq-ui-da-tion
 liq-ui-da-tor

liq-uor
lisle
lisp
  lisp-ing-ly
lis-some
  lis-some-ly
  lis-some-ness
list
  list-ed
  list-er
  list-ing
lis-ten
  lis-ten-er
list-less
  list-less-ly
  list-less-ness
lit-a-ny
  lit-a-nies
li-tchi
  li-tchis
li-ter
lit-er-a-cy
lit-er-al
  lit-er-al-i-ty
  lit-er-al-ness
  lit-er-al-ly
lit-er-ary
  lit-er-ar-i-ly
  lit-er-ar-i-ness
lit-er-ate
  lit-er-ate-ly
lit-e-ra-ti
lit-er-a-ture
lithe
  lithe-some
  lithe-ly
  lithe-ness
lith-i-um
lith-o-graph
  lith-o-gra-pher
  lith-o-graph-ic
  lith-o-graph-i-cal-ly
li-thog-ra-phy
lit-i-gate
  lit-i-gat-ed
  lit-i-gat-ing
  lit-i-ga-tion
  lit-i-ga-tor
lit-ter
lit-ter-bug
lit-tle
  lit-tler
  lit-tlest

lit-to-ral
lit-ur-gy
  lit-ur-gies
  lit-ur-gist
  lit-ur-gic
  li-tur-gi-cal
liv-able
  live-able
live-li-hood
live-long
live-ly
  live-li-er
  live-li-est
liv-en
  liv-en-er
liv-er
liv-er-wurst
liv-ery
  liv-er-ies
  liv-er-ied
  liv-er-y-man
  liv-er-y-men
live-stock
liv-id
  li-vid-i-ty
  liv-id-ness
  liv-id-ly
liv-ing
  liv-ing-ly
  liv-ing-ness
liz-ard
lla-ma
lla-no
  lla-mos
loamy
loath
  loath-ness
loathe
  loathed
  loath-ing
  loath-ing-ly
loath-some
  loath-some-ly
  loath-some-ness
lob
  lobbed
  lob-bing
lobe
  lo-bar
  lo-bate
  lobed
lob-ster
lo-cal

lo-cal-ly
lo-cale
lo-cal-i-ty
  lo-cal-i-ties
lo-cal-i-ties
lo-cal-ize
  lo-cal-ized
  lo-cal-iz-ing
  lo-cal-i-za-tion
lo-cate
  lo-cat-ed
  lo-cat-ing
  lo-ca-tor
lo-ca-tion
loch
lock-able
  lock-er
  lock-et
  lock-jaw
  lock-out
  lock-smith
  lock-up
lo-co
lo-co-mo-tion
lo-co-mo-tive
lo-co-weed
lo-cus
  lo-ci
lo-cust
lo-cu-tion
lode-stone
lodge
  lodged
  lodg-ing
  lodg-er
lofty
  loft-i-er
  loft-i-est
  loft-i-ly
lo-gan-ber-ry
  lo-gan-ber-ries
log-a-rithm
  log-a-rith-mic
  log-a-rith-mi-cal
  log-a-rith-mi-cal-ly
log-book
loge
log-ger
log-ger-hed
log-ic
  lo-gi-cian
log-i-cal
  log-i-cal-i-ty

log-i-cal-ly
lo-gis-tic
lo-gis-tics
lo-gis-ti-cal
loin-cloth
loi-ter
loi-ter-er
lol-li-pop
lone-ly
lone-li-er
lone-li-est
lone-li-ly
lon-er
lone-some
lone-some-ly
lone-some-ness
lon-gev-i-ty
long-ing
long-ing-ly
lon-gi-tude
lon-gi-tu-di-nal
lon-gi-tu-di-nal-ly
long-lived
long--play-ing
long-shore-man
long-shore-men
long--suf-fer-ing
long--term
long--wind-ed
long--wind-ed-ly
long-wise
look-out
loose
loos-er
loos-est
loos-en
loot-er
lop
looped
lop-ping
lope
loped
lop-ing
lop-er
lop-sid-ed
lo-qua-cious
lo-qua-cious-ly
lo-quac-i-ty
lo-quac-i-ties
lord-ly
lord-li-er
lord-li-est
lord-ship

lor-gnette
lor-ry
lor-ries
lose
lost
los-ing
los-a-ble
los-er
lot
lo-tion
lot-tery
lot-ter-ies
lot-to
lo-tus
lo-tus-es
loud
loud-ly
loud-ness
loud-mouthed
loud-speak-er
lounge
lounged
loung-ing
loung-er
louse
lice
lou-ver
lou-vered
love
loved
lov-ing
lov-able
love-lorn
lov-er
lov-ing
loving-ly
low-er
low-er-case
low-er-ing
low-er-ing-ly
low-ery
low--key
low--keyed
low-ly
low-li-er
low-li-est
loy-al
loy-al-ist
loy-al-ly
loy-al-ties
loz-enge
lu-au
lub-ber

lub-ber-ly
lu-beak
lu-bri-cate
lu-bri-cat-ed
lu-bri-cat-ing
lu-bri-ca-tion
luck
luck-i-er
luck-i-est
lu-cra-tive
lu-cra-tive-ly
lu-cre
lu-cu-brate
lu-cu-brat-ed
lu-cu-brat-ing
lu-cu-bra-tion
lu-cu-bra-tor
lu-di-crous
lu-di-crous-ly
lug-gage
lug-ger
lug-sail
lu-gu-bri-ous
lu-gu-bri-ous-ly
luke-warm
luke-warm-ly
lull-a-by
lull-a-bies
lum-ba-go
lum-bar
lum-ber
lum-ber-ing-ly
lum-ber-er
lum-ber-ing
lum-ber-jack
lum-ber-man
lum-ber-men
lu-men
lu-mi-nary
lu-mi-nar-ies
lu-mi-nes-cence
lu-mi-nes-cent
lu-mi-nous
lu-mi-nos-i-ty
lu-mi-nous-ly
lum-mox
lumpy
lu-na-cy
lu-na-cies
lu-nar
lu-nate
lu-na-tic
lunch

121

M

lunch-er
lun-cheon
lunge
  lunged
  lung-ing
lu-pine
lurch
lure
  lured
  lur-ing
lu-rid
  lu-rid-ly
lurk
  lurk-er
  lurk-ing-ly
lus-cious
  lus-cious-ly
lust
  lust-ful
  lust-ful-ly
lust-er
lusty
lut-ist
lux-u-ri-ant
  lux-u-ri-ance
  lux-u-ri-an-cy
  lux-u-ri-ant-ly
lux-u-ri-ate
  lux-u-ri-at-ed
  lux-u-ri-at-ing
  lux-u-ri-a-tion
lux-u-ri-ous
  lux-u-ri-ous-ly
lux-u-ry
  lux-u-ries
ly-ce-um
ly-ing
ly-ing--in
lymph
  lym-phoid
lym-phat-ic
lynch
  lynch-er
  lynch-ing
lynx
  lynx-es
  lynx-eyed
lyre
ly-ric
  lyr-i-cal
  lyr-i-cal-ly
ly-ser-gic acid
ly-sine

ma-ca-bre
  ma-ca-bre-ly
mac-ad-am
mac-ad-am-ize
  mac-ad-am ised
  mac-ad-am-iz-ing
  mac-ad-am-i-za-tion
ma-caque
mac-a-ro-ni
ma-caw
mace
  maced
  mac-ing
mac-er-ate
  mac-er-at-ed
  mac-er-at-ing
  mac-er-a-tion
  mac-er-a-tor
ma-chete
mach-i-nate
ma-chine
ma-chin-ery
  ma-chin-er-ies
ma-chin-ist
mack-er-el
mack-i-naw
mack-in-tosh
  mac-in-tosh
mac-ro-cosm
  mac-ro-cos-mic
  mac-ro-cos-mi-cal-ly
ma-cron
mad
  mad-der
  mad-ly
  mad-ness
mad-am
  mes-dames
mad-cap
mad-den
  mad-den-ing
  mad-den-ing-ly
mad-e-moi-selle
  mes-de-moi-selles
made-up
mad-house
mad-man
  mad-men
ma-dras
mad-ri-gal
  mad-ri-gal-ist
mael-strom
mae-stro-so

mag-a-zine
ma-gen-ta
mag-got
  mag-goty
mag-ic
  mag-i-cal
  mag-i-cal-ly
ma-gi-cian
mag-is-te-ri-al
  mag-is-te-ri-al-ly
  mag-is-te-ri-al-ness
mag-is-tra-cy
  mag-is-tra-cies
mag-is-trate
mag-ma
  mag-mas
  mag-ma-ta
  mag-mat-ic
mag-nan-i-mous
  mag-nan-i-mous-ly
  mag-na-nim-i-ty
  mag-na-nim-i-ties
mag-nate
mag-ne-sia
  mag-ne-sian
mag-ne-sium
mag-net
  mag-net-ic
  mag-net-i-cal-ly
mag-net-ism
mag-net-ize
  mag-net-ized
  mag-net-iz-ing
  mag-net-iz-a-ble
  mag-net-i-za-tion
  mag-net-iz-er
mag-ne-to
  mag-ne-tos
mag-ne-tom-e-ter
  mag-ne-to-met-ric
  mag-ne-tom-e-try
mag-nif-i-cent
  mag-nif-i-cence
  mag-nif-i-cent-ly
mag-ni-fy
  mag-ni-fied
  mag-ni-fy-ing
  maf-ni-fi-a-ble
  mag-ni-fi-ca-tion
  mag-ni-fi-er
mag-ni-tude
mag-no-lia
mag-num

mag-uey
ma-ha-ra-jah
ma-ha-ra-ni
ma-hat-ma
  ma-hat-ma-ism
ma-hoe
ma-hog-a-ny
  ma-hog-a-nies
ma-hout
maid-en
mail-a-ble
mail-box
mail-man
  mail-men
maim
  maim-er
main-land
  main-land-er
main-ly
main-mast
main-sail
main-tain
  main-tain-a-ble
main-te-nance
maize
maj-es-ty
  maj-es-ties
  ma-jes-tic
  ma-jes-ti-cal
ma-jol-i-ca
ma-jor
ma-jor-do-mo
  ma-jor-do-mos
ma-jor-i-ty
  ma-jor-i-ties
make
  mak-a-ble
  mak-er
  mak-ing
make-shift
make-up
mal-a-dapt-ed
mal-ad-just-ment
  mal-ad-just-ed
mal-ad-min-is-ter
mal-adroit
  mal-adroit-ly
  mal-adroit-ness
mal-a-dy
  mal-a-dies
mal-aise
mal-a-prop
mal-a-prop-ism

ma-lar-ia
  ma-lar-i-al
  ma-lar-i-an
  ma-lar-i-ous
ma-lar-key
mal-con-tent
male-dict
male-dic-tion
  male-dic-to-ry
male-frac-tion
male-frac-tor
ma-lev-o-lent
  ma-lev-o-lence
  ma-lev-o-lent-ly
mal-fea-sance
  mal-fea-sant
mal-for-ma-tion
  mal-formed
mal-func-tion
mal-ice
  ma-li-cious
  ma-li-cious-ly
ma-lign
  ma-lign-er
  ma-lign-ly
ma-lig-nant
  ma-lig-nan-cy
  ma-lig-nan-cies
  ma-lig-nant-ly
ma-lin-ger
  ma-lin-ger-er
mal-lard
mal-lea-ble
  mal-lea-bil-i-ty
mal-let
ma-low
mal-nour-ished
mal-nu-tri-tion
mal-oc-clu-sion
mal-odor
  mal-odor-ous
  mal-odor-ous-ly
mal-prac-tice
  mal-prac-ti-tion-er
malt
  malty
  malt-i-er
mal-treat
  mal-treat-ment
mam-ma
  ma-ma
mam-mal
  mam-ma-li-an

mam-mam-ries
mam-mon
mam-moth
mam-my
  mam-mies
man
  manned
  man-ning
man-a-cle
  man-a-cled
  man-a-cling
man-age
  man-aged
  man-a-ging
  man-age-a-ble
  man-age-a-bil-i-ty
  man-age-a-bly
man-age-ment
man-ag-er
  man-ag-er-ship
man-a-ge-ri-al
  man-a-ge-ri-al-ly
man-a-tee
man-da-la
man-da-rin
man-date
  man-dat-ed
  man-dat-ing
man-da-to-ry
  man-da-to-ries
  man-da-to-ri-ty
man-di-ble
  man-dib-u-lar
  man-dib-u-lary
  man-dib-u-late
man-do-lin
  man-do-lin-ist
man-drakes
man-drill
man-eat-er
  man-eat-ing
ma-neu-ver
  ma-neu-ver-a-nil-i-ty
  ma-neu-ver-a-ble
  ma-neu-ver-er
man-ga-nese
mange
man-ger
man-gle
  man-gled
  man-gling
man-go
  man-goes

man-gos
man-grove
man-gy
man-gi-er
man-gi-est
man-gi-ly
man-han-dle
man-han-dled
man-han-dling
man-hole
man-hood
man--hour
man-hunt
man-hunt-er
ma-nia
man-ic
ma-ni-ac
ma-ni-a-cal
ma-ni-a-cal-ly
man-ic-de-pres-sive
man-i-cure
man-i-cur-eed
man-i-cur-ing
man-i-cur-ist
man-i-fest
man-i-fest-er
man-i-fest-ly
man-i-fes-ta-tion
man-i-fes-to
man-i-fes-tos
man-i-fes-toes
man-i-fold
man-i-kin
man-a-kin
man-ni-kin
ma-nila
ma-nil-la
ma-nip-u-late
man-kind
man-ly
man-li-er
man-li-est
man--made
man-na
man-ne-quin
man-ner
man-nered
man-ner-ism
man-ner-ly
man-ner-li-ness
man-nish
man--of--war
men--of--war

ma-nom-e-ter
man-or
ma-no-ri-al
man pow-er
man-sard
man-ser-vant
man-sion
man-sized
man-slaugh-ter
man-slay-er
man-til-la
man-tle
man-tled
man-tling
man-trap
man-u-al
man-u-al-ly
man-u-fac-ture
man-u-fac-tured
man-u-fac-tur-ing
man-u-fac-tur-a-ble
man-u-fac-tur-al
man-u-fac-tur-er
ma-nure
manu-script
many
man-y-sid-ed
map
mapped
map-ping
map-per
ma-ple
mar
marred
mar-ring
ma-ra-ca
mar-a-schi-no
mar-a-thon
ma-raud
ma-raud-er
mar-ble
mar-bled
mar-bling
mar-ble-ize
mar-ble-ized
mar-ble-iz-ing
mar-bly
mar-cel
mar-celled
mar-cel-ling
march-er
mar-chio-ness
mare's tail

mar-ga-rine
mar-gin
mar-gi-nal
mar-gi-na-lia
mar-gin-al-i-ty
mar-gin-al-ly
mar-gin-ate
mar-gin-ated
mar-gin-at-ing
mar-gin-a-tion
mar-gue-rite
mar-i-cul-ture
mari-gold
mar-i-jua-na
ma-rim-ba
ma-ri-na
mar-i-nade
mar-i-nad-ed
mar-i-nad-ing
mar-i-na-tion
mar-i-nate
mar-i-nat-ed
mar-i-nat-ing
mar-i-na-tion
ma-rine
mar-i-ner
mar-i-o-nette
mar-i-tal
mar-i-time
mar-jo-ram
marked
mark-ed-ly
mark-er
mar-ket
mar-ket-er
mar-ket-able
mar-ket-abil-i-ty
mar-ket-ing
mar-ket-place
mark-ing
marks-man
marks-men
marks-man-ship
mar-lin
mar-ma-lade
mar-mo-set
mar-mot
ma-roon
mar-quee
mar-quis
mar-quis-es
mar-quess
mar-quise

mar-quis-es
mar-riage
  mar-riage-able
  mar-riage-abil-i-ty
mar-ried
mar-row
  mar-rowy
mar-row-bone
mar-ry
  mar-ried
  mar-ry-ing
mar-shall
  mar-shaled
  mar-shal-ing
marsh-mal-low
marshy
  marsh-i-er
  marsh-i-est
  marsh-i-ness
mar-su-pi-al
mar-tial
mar-tin
mar-ti-ni
  mar-ti-nis
mar-tyr
  mar-tyr-ize
  mar-tyr-ized
  mar-tyr-iz-ing
  mar-tyr-dom
mar-vel
  mar-veled
  mar-vel-ing
mar-vel-ous
  mar-vel-ous-ly
mar-zi-pan
mas-cara
mas-cu-line
  mas-cu-line-ness
  mas-cu-lin-i-ty
mas-cu-lin-ize
  mas-cu-lin-ized
  mas-cu-lin-iz-ing
mash-er
mask
  mask-like
masked
mas-och-ism
  mas-och-ist
  mas-och-is-tic
ma-son
  ma-son-ic
ma-son-ary
  ma-son-ries

masque
mas-quer-ade
  mas-quer-ad-ed
  mas-quer-ad-ing
  mas-quer-ad-er
mas-sa-cre
  mas-sa-cred
  mas-sa-cring
  mas-sa-cre
mas-sage
  mas-saged
  mas-sag-ing
  mas-sag-er
  mas-sag-ist
mas-seur
mas-sause
  mas-seus-es
mas-sive
mass-pro-duce
  mass-pro-duced
  mass-pro-duc-ing
  mass-pro-duc-er
  mass-pro-duc-tion
massy
  masss-i-er
  mass-i-est
  mass-i-ness
mas-tec-to-my
  mas-tec-to-mies
mas-ter
mas-ter-ful
mas-ter-mind
mas-ter-piece
mas-tery
  mas-ter-ies
mast-head
mas-tic
mas-ti-cate
  mas-ti-ca-ted
  mas-ti-ca-ting
  mas-ti-ca-ble
  mas-ti-ca-tion
  mas-ti-ca-tor
mas-tiff
mast-odon
mas-toid
mas-tur-bate
  mas-tur-bat-ed
  mas-tur-bat-ing
  mas-tur-ba-tion
mat
  mat-ted
  mat-ting

mat-a-dor
match-book
match-mak-er
  match-mak-ing
mate
  mat-ed
  mat-ing
  mate-less
ma-te-ri-al
  ma-te-ri-al-ly
ma-te-ri-al-ism
  ma-te-ri-al-ist
  ma-te-ri-al-is-tic
  ma-te-ri-al-is-ti-cal-ly
ma-te-ri-al-ize
  ma-te-ri-al-ized
  ma-te-ri-al-iz-ing
ma-te-ri-el
ma-ter-nal
  ma-ter-nal-ism
  ma-ter-nal-is-tic
  ma-ter-nal-ly
ma-ter-ni-ty
  ma-ter-ni-ties
math-e-mat-i-cal
  math-e-mat-ic
  math-e-mat-i-cal-ly
math-e-ma-ti-cian
math-e-mat-ics
ma-tin
  mat-in-al
mat-i-nee
ma-tri-arch
  ma-tri-ar-chal-ism
  ma-tri-ar-chy
  ma-tri-ar-chies
ma-tri-cide
ma-tric-u-lant
ma-tric-u-late
  ma-tric-u-lat-ed
  ma-tric-u-lat-ing
  ma-tric-u-la-tion
ma-tri-lin-eal
mat-ri-mo-ny
  mat-ri-mo-nies
  mat-ri-mo-ni-al
ma-trix
  ma-tri-ces
  ma-trix-es
ma-tron
ma-tron-ly
mat-ter
mat-ter-of-course

mat-ter--of--fact
  mat-ter--of--fact-ly
  mat-ter--of--fact-ness
mat-ting
mat-tress
mat-u-rate
  mat-u-rat-ed
  mat-u-rat-ing
  mat-u-ra-tion
ma-ture
ma-tur-i-ty
mat-zo
  mat-zoth
  mat-zos
maud-lin
mau-so-le-um
  mau-so-le-ums
  mau-so-lea
mauve
mav-er-ick
mawk-ish
max-im
max-i-mal
  max-i-mal-ly
max-i-mize
  max-i-mized
  max-i-miz-ing
max-i-mum
  max-i-mums
  max-i-ma
may-be
may-flow-er
may-fly
  may-flies
may-hem
may-on-naise
may-or
  may-or-al
may-or-al-ty
  may-or-al-ties
maze
  mazed
  maz-ing
ma-zy
  ma-zi-er
  ma-zi-est
  ma-zi-ly
  ma-zi-ness
mead-ow
mead-ow-lark
mea-ger
  mea-ger-ly
  mea-ger-ness

meal-time
meal-worm
mealy
  meal-i-er
  meal-i-est
  meal-i-ness
meal-y-mouthed
mean
  mean-ing
  mean-ly
  mean-ness
me-an-der
mean-ing-ful
  mean-ing-ful-ly
mean-ing-less
  mean-ing-less-ly
  mean-ing-less-ness
meant
mean-time
mean-while
mea-sles
mea-sly
  mea-sli-er
  mea-sli-est
meas-ur-a-ble
  meas-ur-a-bil-i-ty
  meas-ur-a-bly
meas-ure
  meas-ur-er
mea-sured
mea-sure-ment
meaty
  meat-i-er
  meat-i-est
  meat-i-ness
mec-ca
me-chan-ic
mech-a-nism
mech-a-nis-tic
  mech-a-nis-ti-cal-ly
mech-a-nize
  mech-a-nized
  mech-a-niz-ing
  mech-a-ni-za-tion
  mech-a-niz-er
med-al
  med-aled
  med-al-ing
  me-dal-ic
me-dal-lion
med-dle
  med-dled
  med-dling

  med-dler
med-dle-some
me-dia
me-di-al
me-di-an
  me-di-an-ly
me-di-ate
  me-di-at-ed
  me-di-at-ing
me-di-a-tion
  me-di-a-tive
  me-di-a-to-ry
me-di-a-tor
med-ic
med-i-ca-ble
  med-i-ca-bly
med-i-cal
  med-i-cal-ly
me-di-ca-ment
med-i-cate
  med-i-cat-ed
  med-i-cat-ing
med-i-ca-tion
me-dic-i-nal
  me-dic-i-nal-ly
med-i-cine
  med-i-cined
  med-i-cin-ing
med-i-co
me-di-e-val
  me-di-e-val-ism
me-di-o-cre
me-di-oc-ri-ty
  me-di-oc-ri-ties
med-i-tate
  med-i-tat-ed
  med-i-tat-ing
  med-i-tat-ing-ly
  med-i-ta-tor
med-i-ta-tion
  med-i-ta-tive
Med-i-ter-ra-ne-an
me-di-um
  me-dia
  me-di-ums
med-ley
  med-leys
meet-ing
meet-ing-house
meg-a-city
  meg-a-cit-ies
mega-cy-cle
meg-a-lo-ma-nia

meg-a-lo-ma-ni-ac
meg-a-lo-ma-ni-a-cal
meg-a-lop-o-lis
meg-a-lo-pol-i-tan
mega-phone
mega-phoned
mega-phon-ing
mega-ton
mega-watt
mei-o-sis
mei-ot-ic
mel-a-mine
mel-an-cho-lia
mel-an-cho-li-ac
mel-an-choly
mel-an-chol-ies
mel-an-chol-ic
mel-an-chol-i-cal-ly
mel-an-chol-i-ty
mel-an-chol-i-ness
mel-a-nin
mel-a-no-ma
mel-a-no-mas
mel-a-no-ma-ta
me-lee
me-lio-rate
me-lio-rat-ed
me-lio-rat-ing
me-lio-ra-ble
me-lio-ra-tion
me-lio-ra-tor
mel-lif-lu-ous
mel-lif-lu-nt
mel-lif-lu-ous-ly
mel-low
me-lo-de-on
melo-dra-ma
melo-dra-mat-ic
melo-dra-mat-i-cal-ly
melo-dra-mat-ics
mel-o-dy
mel-o-dies
me-lod-ic
me-lod-i-cal-ly
me-lo-di-ous
me-lo-di-ous-ness
mel-on
melt
melt-ed
melt-ing
melt-a-bil-i-ty
melt-a-ble
melt-er

mem-ber
mem-bered
mem-ber-less
mem-ber-ship
mem-brane
mem-bra-nous
me-men-to
me-men-tos
me-men-toes
memo
mem-oir
mem-o-ra-bil-ia
mem-o-ra-ble
mem-o-ra-bly
mem-o-ran-dum
mem-o-ran-dums
mem-o-ran-da
me-mo-ri-al
me-mo-ri-al-ly
me-mo-ri-al-ize
me-mo-ri-al-ized
me-mo-ri-al-iz-ing
me-mo-ri-al-i-za-tion
me-mo-ri-al-iz-er
me-mo-ri-al-ly
mem-o-rize
mem-o-rized
mem-o-riz-ing
mem-o-riz-a-ble
mem-o-ri-za-tion
mem-o-ry
mem-o-ries
men-ace
men-aced
men-ac-ing
me-nag-er-ie
mend
mend-able
men-da-cious
men-da-cious-ly
men-da-cious-ness
men-dac-i-ty
men-de-le-vi-um
men-di-cant
me-ni-al
me-ni-al-ly
me-nin-ges
men-in-gi-tis
me-nis-cus
me-nis-cus-es
me-nis-ci
men-o-pause
men-o-pau-sal

me-nor-ah
men-sal
men-ses
men-stru-al
men-stru-a-tion
men-stru-ate
men-stru-at-ed
men-stru-at-ing
men-sur-a-ble
men-tal
men-tal-ly
men-tal-i-ty
men-tal-i-ties
men-thol
men-tho-lat-ed
men-tion
men-tion-a-ble
men-tion-er
men-tor
menu
me-ow
mep-ro-bam-ate
mer-can-tile
mer-can-til-ism
mer-can-til-ist
mer-ce-nary
mer-ce-nar-ies
mer-ce-nar-ily
mer-cer-ize
mer-cer-ized
mer-cer-iz-ing
mer-chan-dise
mer-chan-dised
mer-chan-dis-ing
mer-chan-dis-er
mer-chant
mer-chant-man
mer-chant-men
mer-cu-ri-al
mer-cu-ry
mer-cu-ries
mer-cy
mer-cies
mer-ci-ful
mer-ci-ful-ly
mer-ci-less
mere-ly
mer-e-tri-cious
mer-e-tri-cious-ly
mer-e-tri-cious-ness
merge
merged
merg-ing

mer-gence
merg-er
me-rid-i-an
me-rid-i-o-nal
me-ringue
mer-it
  mer-i-ted
  mer-it-ed-ly
  mer-it-less
mer-i-to-ri-ous
mer-maid
  mer-man
  mer-men
mer-ri-ment
mer-ry
  mer-ri-er
  mer-ri-est
  mer-ri-ness
mer-ry--go--round
mer-ry-mak-er
mer-ry-mak-ing
me-sa
mes-cal
mes-dames
mes-de-moi-selles
mesh-work
me-si-al
mes-mer-ism
  mes-mer-ic
  mes-mer-i-cal-ly
  mes-mer-ist
mes-mer-ize
  mes-mer-ized
  mes-mer-iz-ing
  mes-mer-i-za-tion
  mes-mer-iz-er
mes-o-morph
  mes-o-mor-phic
  mes-o-mor-phism
  mes-o-mor-phy
me-son
mes-o-sphere
mes-quite
mess
  mess-i-ly
  mess-i-ness
  messy
  mess-i-er
  mess-i-est
mes-sage
mes-sen-ger
mes-ti-zo
me-tab-o-lism

met-a-bol-ic
  met-a-bol-i-cal
me-tab-o-lize
  me-tab-o-lized
  me-tab-o-liz-ing
met-al
  met-aled
  met-al-ing
met-al-ize
  met-al-ized
  met-al-iz-ing
me-tal-lic
  me-tal-li-cal-ly
met-al-loid
met-al-lur-gy
  met-al-lur-gic
  met-al-lur-gi-cal
  met-al-lur-gi-cal-ly
  met-al-lur-gist
met-al-work
  met-al-work-er
  met-al-work-ing
meta-mor-phism
  meta-mor-phic
meta-mor-phose
  meta-mor-phosed
  meta-mor-phos-ing
meta-mor-pho-sis
  meta-mor-pho-ses
met-a-phor
  met-a-phor-ic
  met-a-phor-i-cal
meta-phys-ic
meta-phys-ics
  meta-phys-i-cal
meta-tar-sus
  meta-tar-si
  meta-tar-sal
meta-zo-an
  meta-zo-al
  meta-zo-ic
mete
  met-ed
  met-ing
me-te-or
me-te-or-ic
me-te-or-ite
  me-te-or-it-ic
me-te-or-oid
me-te-o-rol-o-gy
  me-te-o-ro-log-i-cal
  me-te-o-rol-o-gist
me-ter

met-es-trus
meth-a-done
meth-ane
meth-a-nol
meth-od
me-thodi-cal
  me-thodi-cal-ly
meth-od-ize
  meth-od-ized
  meth-od-iz-ing
  meth-od-iz-er
meth-od-ol-o-gy
  meth-od-ol-o-gies
  meth-od-o-log-i-cal
  meth-od-ol-o-gist
me-tic-u-lous
  me-tic-u-los-i-ty
  me-tic-u-lous-ly
met-ric
met-ri-cal
  met-ri-cal-ly
met-ri-fi-ca-tion
met-ro
met-ro-nome
  met-ro-nom-ic
me-trop-o-lis
met-ro-pol-i-tan
  met-ro-pol-i-tan-ism
met-tle
met-tle-some
mez-za-nine
mez-zo
mi-as-ma
  mi-as-mas
  mi-as-ma-ta
  mi-as-mat-ic
  mi-as-mic
mi-ca
mi-crobe
  mi-cro-bi-al
  mi-cro-bi-an
  mi-cro-bic
mi-cro-bi-ol-o-gy
  mi-cro-bi-o-log-i-cal
  mi-cro-bi-ol-o-gist
mi-cro-copy
  mi-cro-cop-ies
mi-cro-cosm
  mi-cro-cos-mos
  mi-cro-cos-mic
  mi-cro-cos-mi-cal
mi-cro-film
mi-cro-gram

mi-cro-groove
mi-crom-e-ter
mi-crom-e-try
mi-cro-mi-cron
mi-cro-min-ia-ture
mi-cro-mil-li-me-ter
mi-cron
  mi-crons
  mi-cra
mi-cro-or-gan-ism
mi-cro-phone
  mi-cro-phon-ic
mi-cro-pho-to-graph
mi-cro-read-er
mi-cro-scope
  mi-cro-scop-i-cal
  mi-cro-scop-i-cal-ly
mi-cros-co-py
  mi-cros-co-pist
mi-cro-sec-ond
mi-cro-wave
mid-day
mid-dle
  mid-dles
  mid-dling
mid-dle--aged
mid-dle-man
  mid-dle-men
mid-dle-most
mid-dle-weight
mid-dy
  mid-dies
midg-et
mid-land
mid-night
mid-sec-tion
mid-ship
mid-ship-man
  mid-ship-men
midst
mid-sum-mer
mid-term
mid-way
mid-wife
  mid-wives
mid-wife-ry
mid-year
mien
mighty
  might-i-er
  might-i-est
  might-i-ly
  might-i-ness

mi-graine
mi-grant
mi-grate
  mi-grat-ed
  mi-grat-ing
  mi-gra-tion
  mi-gra-tor
  mi-gra-to-ry
mi-la-dy
  mi-la-dies
mild
  mild-ly
  mild-ness
mil-dew
  mil-dewy
mile-age
mil-er
mile-stone
mi-lieu
  mi-lieus
mil-i-tant
  mil-i-tan-cy
  mil-i-tant-ness
mil-i-ta-rism
  mil-i-ta-ris-tic
  mil-i-ta-ris-ti-cal-ly
  mil-i-ta-rize
  mil-i-ta-rized
  mil-i-ta-riz-ing
  mil-i-ta-ri-za-tion
mil-i-tary
  mil-i-tar-i-ly
mi-li-tia
milk
  milk-er
  milky
  milk-i-er
  milk-i-est
milk-maid
milk-man
  milk-men
milk-weed
mill-board
mil-len-ni-um
  mil-len-nia
  mil-len-ni-al
mil-ler
mil-let
mil-li-am-pere
mil-li-bar
mil-li-gram
mil-li-li-ter
mil-li-me-ter

mil-li-mi-cron
mil-li-ner
mil-li-nery
mill-ing
mil-lion
  mil-lionth
mill-lion-aire
mil-li-sec-ond
mill-pond
mill-run
mill-stone
mill-stream
mi-lord
milt
mime
  mimed
  mim-ing
  mim-er
mim-e-o-graph
mim-ic
  mim-icked
  mim-ick-ing
  mim-i-cal
  mim-i-cal
  mim-ick-r
mim-ic-ry
  mim-ic-ries
min-able
  mine-able
min-e-ret
mince
  minced
  minc-ing
  minc-er
  minc-ing-ly
mince-meat
mind-ed
mind-less
  mind-less-ly
  mind-less-ness
min-er
mine-field
min-er-al
min-er-al-ize
  min-er-al-ized
  min-er-al-iz-ing
  min-er-al-i-za-tion
min-er-al-o-gy
  min-er-al-og-ical
  min-er-al-o-gist
min-e-stro-ne
mine-sweep-er
  mine-sweep-ing

min-gle
min-gled
min-gling
min-i-a-ture
min-i-a-tur-ize
min-i-a-tur-ized
min-i-a-tur-iz-ing
min-i-a-tur-i-za-tion
min-im
min-i-mal
min-i-mal-ly
min-i-mize
min-i-mized
min-i-miz-ing
min-i-mi-za-tion
min-i-miz-er
min-i-mum
min-i-mums
min-i-ma
min-ing
min-ion
min-is-ter
min-is-te-ri-al
min-is-trant
min-is-tra-tion
min-is-tries
min-now
mi-nor
mi-nor-i-ty
mi-nor-i-ties
min-strel
mint-age
mint-er
min-u-end
mi-nus
mi-nus-cule
min-ute
min-ut-ed
min-ut-ing
mi-nut-er
mi-nut-est
min-ute-man
min-ute-men
mi-nu-tia
mi-nu-ti-ae
minx
mir-a-cle
mi-rac-u-lous
mi-rage
mire
mired
mir-ing
mir-ror

mirth
mirth-ful
mirth-ful-ly
mirth-ful-ness
mirth-less
mis-ad-ven-tage
mis-ad-vise
mis-ad-vised
mis-ad-vis-ing
mis-al-li-ance
mis-an-thrope
mis-an-tho-pist
mis-an-throp-ic
mis-an-throp-i-cal
mis-an-thro-py
mis-ap-ply
mis-ap-plied
mis-ap-ply-ing
mis-ap-pli-ca-tion
mis-ap-pre-hend
mis-ap-pre-hen-sion
mis-ap-pro-pri-ate
mis-ap-pro-pri-at-ed
mis-ap-pro-pri-at-ing
mis-ap-pro-pri-a-tion
mis-be-have
mis-be-haved
mis-be-hav-ing
mis-be-hav-er
mis-be-ha-vior
mis-cal-cu-late
mis-cal-cu-lat-ed
mis-cal-cu-lat-ing
mis-cal-cu-la-tion
mis-cal-cu-la-tor
mis-call
mis-car-riage
mis-car-ry
mis-car-ried
mis-car-ry-ing
mis-ce-ge-na-tion
mis-ce-ge-net-ic
mis-cel-la-neous
mis-cel-la-ny
mis-cel-la-nies
mis-chance
mis-chief
mis-chie-vous
mis-chie-vous-ly
mis-chie-vous-ness
mis-ci-ble
mis-ci-bil-i-ty
mis-con-ceive

mis-con-ceived
mis-con-ceiv-ing
mis-con-ceiv-er
mis-con-cep-tion
mis-con-duct
mis-con-strue
mis-con-strued
mis-con-stru-ing
mis-con-struc-tion
mis-count
mis-cre-ant
mis-cue
mis-cued
mis-cu-ing
mis-deal
mis-dealt
mis-deal-ing
mis-deed
mis-de-mean-or
mis-di-rect
mis-di-rec-tion
mis-do
mis-did
mis-done
mis-do-ing
mis-em-ploy
mis-em-ploy-ment
mi-ser
mi-ser-li-ness
mi-ser-ly
mis-er-a-ble
mis-er-a-ble-ness
mis-er-a-bly
mis-ery
mis-er-ies
mis-fea-sance
mis-fire
mis-fired
mis-fir-ing
mis-fit
mis-fit-ted
mis-fit-ting
mis-for-tune
mis-giv-ing
mis-gov-ern
mis-gov-ern-ment
mis-guide
mis-guid-ed
mis-guid-ing
mis-guid-ance
mis-han-dle
mis-han-dled
mis-han-dling

130

mis-hap
mish-mash
mis-in-form
  mis-in-form-ant
  mis-in-form-er
  mis-in-for-ma-tion
mis-in-ter-pret
  mis-in-ter-pre-ta-tion
  mis-in-ter-pret-er
mis-judge
  mis-judged
  mis-judg-ing
  mis-judg-ment
mis-lay
  mis-laid
  mis-lay-ing
mis-lead
  mis-led
  mis-lead-ing
  mis-lead-er
mis-man-age
  mis-man-aged
  mis-man-ag-ing
  mis-man-age-ment
mis-match
mis-mate
  mis-mat-ed
  mis-mat-ing
mis-name
  mis-named
  mis-nam-ing
mis-no-mer
mi-sog-a-my
mi-sog-y-ny
  mi-sog-y-nist
  mi-sog-y-nous
mis-place
  mis-placed
  mis-plac-ing
  mis-place-ment
mis-play
mis-print
mis-pri-sion
mis-prize
  mis-prized
  mis-priz-ing
mis-pro-nounce
  mis-pro-nounced
  mis-pro-nouc-ing
  mis-pro-nun-ci-a-tion
mis-quote
  mis-quoted
  mis-quot-ing

mis-quo-ta-tion
mis-read
  mis-read-ing
mis-rep-re-sent
  mis-rep-re-sen-ta-tion
  mis-rep-re-sen-ta-tive
mis-rule
  mis-ruled
  mis-rul-ing
mis-sal
mis-shape
  mis-shaped
  mis-shap-ing
  mis-shap-en
mis-sile
miss-ing
mis-sion
mis-sion-ary
  mis-sion-ar-ies
mis-sive
mis-spell
  mis-spelled
  mis-spel-ling
mis-spend
  mis-spent
  mis-spend-ing
mis-state
  mis-stat-ed
  mis-stat-ing
  mis-state-ment
mis-step
mist
  mist-i-ly
  mist-i-ness
mis-ta-a-ble
mis-take
  mis-took
  mis-tak-en
  mis-tak-ing
  mis-tak-en-ly
  mis-tak-er
mis-tle-toe
mis-tral
mis-treat
  mis-treat-ment
mis-tress
mis-tri-al
mis-trust
  mis-trust-ful
  mis-trust-ful-ly
  mis-trust-ing-ly
misty
  mist-i-er

mist-i-est
mis-un-der-stand
  mis-un-der-stood
  mis-un-der-stand-ing
mis-us-age
mis-use
  mis-used
  mis-us-ing
  mis-us-er
mis-val-ue
  mis-val-ued
  mis-val-u-ing
mi-ter
  mi-tre
mi-ti-cide
  mi-ti-cid-al
mit-i-gate
  mit-i-gat-ed
  mit-i-gat-ing
  mit-i-ga-tion
  mit-i-ga-tive
  mit-i-ga-tor
  mit-i-ga-to-ry
mi-to-sis
mi-tral
mit-ten
mix
  mixed
  mix-ing
mix-er
mix-ture
mix-up
miz-pah
miz-zen
mne-mon-ic
mne-mon-ics
moa
mob
  mobbed
  mob-bing
  mob-bish
mo-bile
  mo-bil-i-ty
mo-bi-lize
  mo-bi-lized
  mo-bi-liz-ing
  mo-bi-li-za-tion
mob-ster
moc-ca-sin
mo-cha
mock
  mock-er
  mock-ing-ly

mock-ery
  mock-er-ies
mock-ing-bird
mock-up
mod-al
  mo-dal-i-ty
  mod-al-ly
mod-el
  mod-cled
  mod-el-ing
  mod-el-er
mod-er-ate
  mod-er-at-ed
  mod-er-at-ing
  mod-er-ate-ly
  mod-er-ate-ness
mod-er-a-tion
mod-er-a-tor
  mod-er-a-tor-ship
mod-ern
mod-ern-ism
  mod-er-ist
  mod-er-ist-ic
mod-ern-ize
  mod-ern-ized
  mod-ern-iz-ing
  mod-ern-iz-er
  mod-ern-i-za-tion
mod-est
  mod-est-ly
  mod-est-ty
  mod-es-ties
mod-i-cum
mod-i-fi-ca-tion
mod-i-fy
  mod-i-fied
  mod-i-fy-ing
  mod-i-fi-a-ble
  mod-i-fi-er
mod-ish
  mod-ish-ly
  mod-ish-ness
mo-diste
mod-u-late
  mod-u-lat-ed
  mod-u-lat-ing
mod-u-la-tion
  mod-u-la-tor
  mod-u-la-to-ry
mod-ule
mod-u-lar
mo-gulmo-hair
moi-ety

  moi-eties
moil
  moil-er
  moil-ing-ly
mois-ten
  moist-en-er
mo-lar
mo-las-ses
mold
  mold-able
  mold-er
mold-board
mold-ing
moldy
  mold-i-er
  mold-i-est
  mold-i-ness
mol-e-cule
mole-hill
mole-skin
mo-lest
  mo-les-ta-tion
  mo-lest-er
mol-li-fy
  mol-li-fied
  mol-li-fy-ing
  mol-i-fi-ca-tion
  mol-li-fi-er
  mol-li-fy-ing-ly
mol-lusk
mol-ly-cod-dle
  mol-ly-cod-dled
  mol-ly-cod-dling
molt
  moult
  molt-er
mol-ten
  mol-ten-ly
mo-lyb-de-num
mo-ment
me-men-tary
  mo-men-tar-i-ly
mo-men-tous
  mo-men-tous-ly
mo-men-tum
mon-arch
  mo-nar-chal
  mo-nar-chal-ly
mo-nar-chi-cal
  mo-nar-chic
  mo-nar-chi-cal-ly
mon-ar-chism
  mon-ar-chist

  mon-ar-chis-tic
mo-nas-tic
mo-nas-ti-cal
  mo-nas-ti-cal-ly
mo-nas-ti-cism
mon-au-ral
  mon-au-ral-ly
mon-e-tary
  mon-e-tar-i-ly
mon-e-tize
  mon-e-tized
  mon-e-tiz-ing
  mon-e-ti-za-tion
mon-ey
mon-ey-chang-er
mon-eyed
  mon-ied
mon-ey--mak-er
  mon-ey--mak-ing
mon-ger
mon-goose
  mon-gooses
mon-grel
mon-i-ker
mo-ni-tion
mon-i-tor
  mon-i-to-ri-al
monk
  monk-ish
  monk-ish-ly
mon-key
  mon-keys
  mon-keyed
  mon-key-ing
mon-key-shine
mon-chro-mat-ic
mon-o-chrome
  mon-o-chro-mic
  mon-o-chro-mi-cal
  mon-o-chro-mi-cal-ly
  mon-o-chrom-ist
mon-o-cle
  mon-o-cled
mon-o-cli-nal
mon-o-cline
  mon-o-cli-nal-ly
  mon-o-cli-nous
mon-o-dist
mon-o-dy
  mon-o-dies
  mo-nod-ic
mo-noe-cious
  mo-noe-cious-ly

132

mo-nog-a-my
  mo-nog-a-mist
  mo-nog-a-mous
mon-o-gram
  mon-o-grammed
  mon-o-gram-ming
  mon-o-gram-mat-ic
mon-o-graph
  mo-nog-ra-pher
  mon-o-graph-ic
mon-o-lith
mon-o-logue
  mon-o-log
  mon-o-logu-ist
  mon-o-log-ist
mon-o-ma-nia
  mon-o-ma-ni-ac
  mon-o-ma-ni-a-cal
mon-o-met-al-lism
  mon-o-me-tal-lic
mo-no-mi-al
mon-nu-cle-o-sis
mon-o-pho-nic
mono-plane
mo-nop-o-lize
  mo-nop-o-lized
  mo-nop-o-liz-ing
  mo-nop-o-li-za-tion
  mo-nop-o-liz-er
mo-nop-o-ly
  mo-nop-o-lies
mono-rail
mon-o-syl-lab-ic
  mon-o-syl-lab-i-cal-ly
mon-o-syl-la-ble
mon-o-the-ism
  mon-o-the-ist
  mon-o-the-is-tic
  mon-o-the-is-ti-cal-ly
mon-o-tone
mo-not-o-nous
  mo-not-o-nous-ly
  mo-not-o-nous-ness
mo-not-o-ny
mone-treme
mono-type
  mon-o-typ-er
  mon-o-typ-ic
mon-o-va-lent
  mon-o-va-lence
  mon-o-va-len-cy
mon-ox-ide
mon-sei-gneur

  mes-sei-gneurs
mon-sieur
mon-soon
mon-ster
mon-stros-i-ty
  mon-stro-i-ties
mon-strous
  mon-strous-i-ties
mon-tage
month-ly
  month-lies
mon-u-ment
mon-u-men-tal
  mon-u-men-tal-ly
mooch
  mooch-er
moon-beam
moon-light
moon-light-er
  moon-light-ing
moon-scape
moon-shine
  moon-shiner
moon-stone
moon-struck
moony
  moon-i-er
  moon-i-est
moor-ing
moot-ness
mop
  mopped
  mop-ping
mop-pet
mo-raine
  mo-rain-al
  mo-rain-ic
mor-al
  mor-al-ly
mo-rale
mor-al-ist
  mor-al-is-tic
mo-ral-i-ty
  mo-ral-i-ties
mor-al-ize
  mor-al-ized
  mor-al-iz-ing
  mor-al-i-za-tion
  mor-al-iz-er
mo-rass
mor-a-to-ri-um
  mor-a-to-ri-ums
  mor-a-to-ria

mo-ray
mor-bid
  mor-bid-ly
  mor-bid-i-ty
  mor-bid-ness
mor-dant
  mor-dan-cy
  mor-dant-ly
more-over
mo-res
mor-ga-nat-ic
  mor-ga-nat-i-cal-ly
morque
mor-i-bund
mo-ri-on
morn-ing
morn-ing glo-ry
  morn-ing glo-ries
mo-roc-co
mo-rose
  mo-rose-ly
mor-pheme
mor-phine
mor-phol-o-gy
  mor-pho-log-ic
  mor-pho-log-i-cal
  mor-phol-o-gist
mor-row
mor-sel
mor-tal
  mor-tal-ly
mor-tal-i-ty
  mor-tal-i-ties
mor-tar
mort-gage
  mort-gaged
  mort-gag-ing
  mort-gag-ee
  mort-gag-er
mor-ti-cian
mor-ti-fy
  mor-ti-fied
  mor-ti-fy-ing
  mor-ti-fi-ca-tion
mor-tise
  mor-tised
  mor-tising
mort-main
mor-tu-ary
  mor-tu-ar-ies
mo-sa-ic
Mo-ses
mo-sey

mo-seyd
mo-sey-ing
mosque
mos-qui-to
  mos-qui-toes
  mos-qui-tos
moss
most-ly
mo-tel
mo-tet
moth-ball
moth-eat-en
moth-er
moth-er-hood
moth-er-in-law
moth-er-ly
mo-tif
mo-tile
  mo-til-i-ty
mo-tion
  mo-tion-less
mo-ti-vate
  mo-ti-vat-ed
  mo-ti-vat-ing
  mo-ti-va-tion
mo-tive
mot-ley
mo-tor
mo-tor-bike
mo-tor-boat
mo-tor-bus
mo-tor-cade
mo-tor-cy-cle
  mo-tor-cy-cling
  mo-tor-cy-clist
mo-tor-ist
mo-tor-ize
  mo-tor-ized
  mo-tor-iz-ing
  mo-tor-i-za-tion
mo-tor-man
  mo-tor-men
mound
mount
  mount-able
  mount-er
moun-tain
moun-tain-eer
moun-tain-ous
moun-te-bank
mount-ing
mourn
  mourn-er

mourn-ful
  mourn-ful-ly
mourn-ing
  mourn-ing-ly
mouse
  moused
  mous-ing
mous-er
mous-tache
mousy
  mous-i-er
  mous-i-est
mouth
  mouthed
  mouth-er
mouth-ful
  mouth-fuls
mouth-piece
mouthy
  mouth-i-er
  mouth-i-est
mou-ton
mov-able
  mov-a-bil-i-ty
  mov-a-bly
move
  moved
  mov-ing
move-ment
mov-ie
mow
mox-ie
mu-ci-lage
  mu-ci-lag-i-nous
muck
  mucky
mu-cous
  mu-cos-i-ty
mu-cus
mu-ez-zin
muf-fin
muf-ti
mug
  mugged
  mug-ging
  mug-ger
mug-gy
  mug-gi-er
  mug-gi-est
mu-lat-to
  mu-lat-toes
mul-ber-ry
  mul-ber-ries

mulch
mu-le-teer
mul-ish
  mul-ish-ly
mul-let
mul-li-gan
mul-li-ga-taw-ny
mul-lion
  mul-lioned
mul-ti-far-i-ous
  mul-ti-far-i-ous-ly
mul-ti-lat-er-al
mul-ti-ple
mul-ti-i-cand
mul-ti-pli-ca-tion
mul-ti-plic-i-ty
mul-ti-pli-er
mul-ti-ply
  mul-ti-plied
  mul-ti-ply-ing
  mul-ti-pli-a-ble
mul-ti-tude
mul-ti-tu-di-nous
  mul-ti-tu-di-nous-ly
mum-ble
mum-mer
mum-mery
mum-mi-fy
  mum-mi-fied
  mum-mi-fy-ing
  mum-mi-fi-ca-tion
mum-my
  mum-mies
  mum-mied
  mum-my-ing
munch
  munch-er
mun-dane
  mun-dane-ly
mu-nic-i-pal
  mu-nic-i-pal-ly
mu-nic-i-pal-i-ty
mu-nif-i-cent
  mu-nif-i-cence
  mu-nif-i-cent-ly
mu-ni-tion
mu-ral
  mu-ral-ist
mur-der
  mur-der-er
  mur-der-ess
mur-der-ous
  mur-der-ous-ly

mu-ri-at-ic ac-id
murky
  murk-i-er
  murk-i-est
  murk-i-ly
mur-mur
mur-rain
mus-cat
  mus-ca-tel
mus-cle
  mus-cled
  mus-cling
mus-cle--bound
mus-cu-lar
  mus-cu-lar-i-ty
  mus-cu-lar-ly
mus-cu-lar dys-tro-phy
mus-cu-la-ture
muse
  mused
  mus-ing
  mus-ing-ly
mu-se-um
mush-room
mu-sic
mu-si-cal
  mu-si-cal-ly
mu-si-cale
mu-si-cian
musk
  musky
  musk-i-er
  misk-i-est
mus-ket
mus-ke-teer
musk-mel-on
musk-rat
mus-lin
muss
  mussy
  muss-i-er
mus-sel
mus-tache
mus-tang
mus-ter
mus-ty
  mus-ti-er
  mus-ti-est
  mus-ti-ly
mu-ta-ble
  mu-ta-bil-i-ty
  mu-ta-bly
mu-tant

mu-ta-tion
mu-tate
mu-tat-ed
mu-tat-ing
mu-ta-tion-al
mute
  mut-ed
mu-ti-late
mu-ti-ny
  mu-ti-nies
  mu-ti-nied
  mu-ti-nous
mut-ter
  mut-ter-er
mut-ton
mu-tu-al
  mu-tu-al-i-ty
  mu-tu-al-ly
muz-zle
my-col-o-gy
  my-col-o-gist
my-na
  my-nah
my-o-pia
  my-op-ic
myr-i-ad
myr-mi-don
myrrh
myr-tle
mys-te-ri-ous
  mys-te-ri-ous-ly
mys-tery
  mys-ter-ies
mys-tic
mys-ti-cal
  mys-ti-cal-ly
mys-ti-cism
mys-ti-fy
  mys-ti-fied
  mys-ti-fy-ing
  mys-ti-fi-ca-tion
mys-tique
myth
  myth-ic
  myth-i-cal
  myth-i-cal-ly
  myth-i-cist
  myth-i-cize
my-thol-o-gy
  my-thol-o-gies
  myth-o-log-ic
  myth-o-log-i-cal
  my-thol-o-gist

N

nab
  nabbed
  nab-bing
na-bob
na-cre
na-cre-ous
na-dir
nag
  nagged
  nag-ging
  nag-ger
nail-er
na-ive
  na-ive-ly
  na-ive-te
na-ked
  na-ked-ly
  na-ked-ness
nam-by-pam-by
name
  named
  nam-ing
  name-less
  name-ly
name-sake
nan-keen
  nan-kin
nan-ny
  nan-nies
nap
  napped
  nap-ping
  nap-per
na-palm
nape
naph-tha
naph-tha-lene
nap-kin
nar-cis-sism
  nar-cism
  nar-cis-sist
nar-co-sis
nar-cot-ic
  nar-co-tize
  nar-co-tized
nar-is
  nar-es
nar-rate
  nar-ra-ted
  nar-ra-ting
  nar-ra-tor
  nar-ra-tion
nar-ra-tive

nar-ra-tive-ly
nar-row
  nar-row-ly
nar-row--mind-ed
nary
na-sal
na-scent
  na-scence
  na-scen-cy
na-stur-tium
nas-ty
  nas-ti-er
  nas-ti-est
na-tal
na-tion
  na-tion-hood
na-tion-al
  na-tion-al-ly
na-tion-al-ism
  na-tion-al-ist
  na-tion-al-is-tic
na-tion-al-i-ty
  na-tion-al-i-ties
na-tion-al-ize
  na-tion-al-ized
  na-tion-al-iz-ing
  na-tion-al-i-za-tion
na-tion-wide
na-tive
  na-tive-ly
na-tiv-i-ty
  na-tiv-i-ties
nat-ty
  nat-ti-er
nat-u-ral
  nat-u-ral-ly
  nat-u-ral-ness
nat-u-ral-ism
nat-u-ral-ist
  nat-u-ral-is-tic
  nat-u-ral-ized
  nat-u-ral-iz-ing
  nat-u-ral-i-za-tion
na-ture
naught
naugh-ty
  naugh-ti-er
  naugh-ti-est
nau-sea
nau-se-ate
  nau-se-at-ed
  nau-se-at-ing
nau-seous

nau-seous-ly
nau-ti-cal
  nau-ti-cal-ly
nau-ti-lus
  nau-ti-lus-es
  nau-ti-li
na-val
na-vel
nav-i-ga-ble
nav-i-gate
  nav-i-gat-ed
  nav-i-gat-ing
nav-i-ga-tion
  nav-i-ga-tion-al
nav-i-ga-tor
na-vy
  na-vies
near
  near-ly
  near-ness
near-by
neat
  neat-ly
  neat-ness
neb-bish
neb-u-la
nec-es-sary
  nec-es-sar-ies
  nec-es-sar-i-ly
  ne-ces-si-tate
  ne-ces-si-ta-ting
ne-ces-si-ty
  ne-ces-si-ties
neck-er-chief
neck-ing
neck-lace
neck-tie
ne-crol-o-gy
  ne-crol-o-gies
nec-ro-man-cy
  nec-ro-man-cer
ne-cro-sis
  ne-crot-ic
nec-tar
  nec-tar-ine
need-ful
  need-ful-ly
  need-ful-ness
nee-dle
  nee-dled
  nee-dling
  nee-dle-like
  nee-dler

nee-dle-point
need-less
  need-less-ly
nee-dle-work
  nee-dle-work-er
needy
  need-i-er
  need-i-est
  need-i-ness
ne'er--do--well
ne-far-i-ous
  ne-far-i-ous-ly
  ne-far-i-ous-ness
ne-gate
  ne-ga-ted
  ne-ta-ting
ne-ga-tion
neg-a-tive
  neg-a-tive-ly
  neg-a-tive-ness
  neg-a-tive-i-ty
  neg-a-tiv-ism
ne-glect
  ne-glec-ter
  ne-glec-tor
  ne-glect-ful-ness
  ne-glect-ful
  ne-glect-ful-ly
neg-li-gee
neg-li-gent
  neg-li-gence
  neg-li-gent-ly
neg-li-gi-ble
  neg-li-gi-bly
  neg-li-gi-bil-i-ty
ne-go-tia-ble
  ne-go-tia-bil-i-ty
ne-go-ti-ate
  ne-go-ti-at-ed
  ne-go-ti-at-ing
  ne-go-ti-a-tion
  ne-go-ti-a-tor
neigh-bor
  neigh-bor-ing
  neigh-bor-ly
  neigh-bor-li-ness
  neigh-bor-hood
nei-ther
nem-e-sis
  nem-e-ses
neo-clas-sic
  neo-clas-si-cism
neo-lith-ic

ne-ol-o-gism
ne-ol-o-gy
ne-on
ne-o-phyte
ne-pen-the
  ne-pen-the-an
neph-ew
ne-phri-tis
  ne-phrit-ic
nep-o-tism
  nep-o-tist
nep-tu-ni-um
nerve
  nerved
  nerv-ing
  nerve-less
nerve--rack-ing
  nerve--wrack-ing
ner-vous
  ner-vous-ly
  ner-vous-ness
nervy
  nerv-i-er
  nerv-i-est
  nerv-i-ness
nes-tle
  nes-tled
  nes-tling
  nes-tler
net
  net-ted
  net-ting
neth-er
  neth-er-most
net-tle
  net-tled
  net-tling
net-work
neu-ral
  neu-ral-ly
  neu-ral-gia
  neu-ral-gic
neu-ras-the-nia
  neu-ra-then-ic
neu-ri-tis
  neu-rit-ic
neu-rol-o-gy
  neu-ro-log-i-cal
  neu-rol-o-gist
neu-ron
  neu-ron-ic
neu-ro-sis
  neu-ro-ses

neu-rot-ic
  neu-rot-i-cal-ly
neu-ter
neu-tral
  neu-tral-i-ty
  neu-tral-ly
neu-tral-ism
  neu-tral-ist
neu-tral-ize
  neu-tral-ized
  neu-tral-iz-ing
neu-tral-i-za-tion
neu-tral-iz-er
neu-tri-no
neu-tron
nev-er
nev-er-more
nev-er-the-less
new
  new-ish
  new-ness
new-born
new-com-er
new-el
new-fan-gled
new-ly
new-ly-wed
news-boy
news-cast
  news-cast-er
news-pa-per
  news-pa-per-man
news-print
news-reel
news-stand
newsy
  news-i-er
  news-i-est
newt
nex-us
ni-a-cin
nib-ble
  nib-bled
  nib-bling
  nib-bler
nib-lick
nice
  nic-er
  nic-est
  nice-ly
  nice-ness
nice-ty
  nice-ties

niche
nick-el
nick-el-ode-on
nick-name
nick-named
  nick-nam-ing
nic-o-tine
  nic-o-tin-ic
niece
nif-ty
  nif-ti-er
  nif-ti-est
nig-gard
  nig-gard-li-ness
  nig-gard-ly
nigh
  nigh-er
  nigh-est
night-cap
night-dress
night-fall
night-gown
night-hawk
night-in-gale
night-ly
night-mare
  night-mar-ish
night-shade
night-shirt
night-time
ni-hil-ism
  ni-hil-ist
  ni-hil-is-tic
nim-ble
  nim-bler
  nim-blest
  nim-ble-ness
  nim-bly
nim-bus
nin-com-poop
nine-pin
nine-teen
  nine-teenth
nine-ty
  nine-ties
  nine-ti-eth
nin-ny
  nin-nines
ninth
nip
  nipped
  nip-ping
  nip-per

nip-ple
nip-py
 nip-pi-er
 nip-pi-est
nir-va-na
nit
 nit-ty
 nit-ti-er
 nit-ti-est
ni-ter
nit-pick
ni-trate
 ni-trat-ed
 ni-trat-ing
 ni-tra-tion
 ni-tra-tor
ni-tric
ni-tro-gen
 ni-trog-e-nous
ni-tro-glyc-er-in
ni-trous ox-ide
nit-ty-grit-ty
nit-wit
no-be-li-um
no-bil-i-ty
 no-bil-i-ties
no-ble
no-body
noc-tur-nal
noc-turne
node
 nod-al
nod-ule
 nod-u-lar
no-el
nog-gin
noise
 noised
 nois-ing
 noise-less
no-mad
 no-mad-ic
 no-mad-i-cal-ly
 no-mad-ism
nom de plume
 noms de plume
no-men-cla-ture
nom-i-nal
 nom-i-nal-ly
nom-i-nee
non-age
nonce
non-cha-lant

non-cha-lance
 non-cha-lant-ly
non-com
 non-com-bat-ant
non-com-mit-tal
 non-com-mit-tal-ly
non-con-duc-tor
 non-con-duc-ing
non-con-form-ist
 non-con-form-i-ty
non-de-script
non-en-ti-ty
 non-en-ti-ties
none-the-less
non-in-ter-ven-tion
non-met-al
 non-me-tal-lic
non-pa-reil
non-par-ti-san
 non-par-ti-san-ship
non-plus
 non-plused
 non-plus-ing
non-prof-it
non-res-i-dent
 non-res-i-dence
 non-res-i-den-cy
 non-res-i-den-cies
non-re-stric-tive
non-sec-tar-i-an
non-sense
 non-sen-si-cal
 non-sen-si-cal-ly
non se-qui-tur
non-stop
non-union
 non-union-ism
 non-union-ist
non-vi-o-lence
 non-vi-o-lent
 non-vi-o-lent-ly
noo-dle
noon
 noon-day
 noon-time
nor-mal
 nor-mal-cy
 nor-mal-i-ty
 nor-mal-ly
nor-mal-ize
 nor-mal-ized
 nor-mal-iz-ing
 nor-mal-i-za-tion

north-east
 north-east-ern
north-east-er
north-er
north-ern
 north-ern-most
 north-ern-er
north-ward
 north-wards
 north-ward-ly
north-west
nose
 nosed
 nos-ing
nose-gay
nos-tal-gia
 nos-tal-gic
nos-tril
nos-trum
no-ta-ble
no-ta-rize
 no-ta-rized
 no-ta-riz-ing
 no-ta-ri-za-tion
no-ta-ry
 no-ta-ries
no-ta-tion
 no-ta-tion-al
notch
 notched
note
 not-ed
not-ed
 not-ed-ly
note-wor-thy
 note-wor-thi-ness
noth-ing
 noth-ing-ness
no-tice
 no-ticed
 no-tic-ing
 no-tice-a-ble
 no-tice-a-bly
no-ti-fy
 no-ti-fied
 no-ti-fy-ing
 no-ti-fi-ca-tion
 no-ti-fi-er
no-tion
no-to-ri-ous
 no-to-ri-ous-ly
 no-to-ri-e-ty
no-trump

nought
nour-ish
  nour-ish-er
  nour-ish-ing
  nour-ish-ment
no-va
  no-vas
nov-el
  nov-el-ist
  nov-el-is-tic
  nov-el-ette
nov-el-ty
  nov-el-ties
no-ve-na
  no-ve-nae
nov-ice
no-vi-tiate
no-where
no-wise
nox-ious
  nox-ious-ly
noz-zle
nu-ance
nub-bin
nu-bile
nu-cle-ar
nu-cle-us
  nu-cle-us-es
  nu-clei
nudge
  nudged
  nudg-ing
  nudg-er
nud-ism
  nud-ist
nug-get
nui-sance
null
  nul-li-ty
  nul-li-ties
nul-li-fy
  nul-li-fied
  nul-li-fy-ing
  nul-li-fi-ca-tion
  nul-li-fi-er
num-ber
  num-ber-er
  num-ber-less
numb-skull
nu-mer-al
  num-er-al-ly
nu-mer-ate
  nu-mer-at-ed

nu-mer-at-ing
nu-mer-a-tion
nu-mer-a-tor
nu-mer-i-cal
  nu-mer-i-cal-ly
nu-mer-ous
  nu-mer-ous-ly
nu-mis-mat-ics
  nu-mis-mat-ic
  nu-mis-mat-i-cal
  nu-mis-ma-tist
num-skull
nun-cio
  nun-ci-os
nun-nery
  nun-ner-ies
nup-tial
  nup-tial-ly
nurse
  nursed
  nurs-ing
  nurs-er
nurse-maid
nurs-ery
  nurs-er-ies
nut
  nut-ted
  nut-ting
nut-crack-er
nut-hatch
nut-meg
nu-tri-ent
  nu-tri-ment
nu-tri-tion
  nu-tri-tion-al
  nu-tri-tion-al-ly
  nu-tri-tion-ist
nu-tri-tious
  nu-tri-tious-ly
nu-tri-tive
  nu-tri-tive-ly
nut-shell
nut-ty
  nut-ti-er
  nut-ti-est
nuz-zle
  nuz-zled
  nuz-zling
ny-lon
nymph
  nym-phal
nym-pho-ma-nia
  nym-pho-ma-ni-ac

O

oaf
  oaf-ish
  oaf-ish-ly
oak-en
oa-kum
oar
  oared
  oars-man
  oars-men
oar-lock
oa-sis
  oa-ses
oat-en
oath
oat-meal
ob-bli-ga-to
  ob-bli-ga-tos
ob-du-rate
  ob-du-ra-cy
  ob-du-rate-ly
obe-di-ence
  obe-di-ent
  obe-di-ent-ly
obei-sance
  obei-sant
obe-lisk
obese
  obese-ness
  obes-i-ty
obey
  obey-er
ob-fus-cate
  ob-fus-ca-ted
  ob-fus-ca-ting
  ob-fus-ca-tion
obit
obit-u-ary
  obit-u-ar-ies
ob-ject
  ob-ject-less
  ob-ject-or
ob-jec-tion
  ob-jec-tion-a-ble
  ob-jec-tion-a-bly
ob-jec-tive
  ob-jec-tive-ly
  ob-jec-tive-ness
  ob-jec-tiv-i-ty
ob-jur-gate
  ob-jur-gat-ed
  ob-jur-gat-ing
  ob-jur-ga-tion
  ob-jur-ga-to-ry

ob-late
  ob-late-ly
  ob-late-ness
ob-li-gate
  ob-li-gat-ed
  ob-li-gat-ing
  ob-li-ga-tion
  ob-lig-a-to-ry
oblige
  obliged
  oblig-ing
  oblig-er
ob-lique
  ob-liqued
  ob-liqu-ing
  ob-lique-ly
oblit-er-ate
  oblit-er-at-ed
  oblit-er-at-ing
  oblit-er-a-tion
  oblit-er-a-tive
obliv-i-on
  obliv-i-ous
  obliv-i-ous-ly
ob-long
ob-lo-quy
  ob-lo-quies
ob-nox-ious
  ob-nox-ious-ly
oboe
obo-ist
ob-scene
  ob-scene-ly
  ob-scen-ity
  ob-scen-i-ties
ob-se-qui-ous
  ob-se-qui-ous-ly
ob-se-quy
  ob-se-quies
ob-serv-able
  ob-serv-ably
ob-ser-vance
ob-ser-vant
  ob-ser-vant-ly
ob-ser-va-tion
  ob-ser-va-tion-al
ob-ser-va-to-ry
  ob-ser-va-to-ries
ob-sess
  ob-ses-sive
  ob-ses-sive-ly
ob-ses-sion
  ob-sid-i-an

ob-so-les-cent
  ob-so-les-cence
  ob-so-les-cent-ly
ob-so-lete
  ob-sta-cle
ob-ste-tri-cian
  ob-stet-rics
  ob-stet-ric
  ob-stet-ri-cal
ob-sti-nate
  ob-sti-na-cy
  ob-sti-na-cies
  ob-sti-nat-ly
ob-strep-er-ous
  ob-strep-er-ous-ly
ob-struct
  ob-struc-tive
  ob-struc-tor
ob-struc-tion
  ob-struc-tion-ism
  ob-struc-tion-ist
ob-tain
  ob-tain-a-ble
  ob-tain-er
  ob-tain-ment
ob-trude
  ob-trud-ed
  ob-trud-ing
  ob-trud-er
  ob-tru-sion
  ob-tru-sive
ob-tuse
  ob-tuse-ly
ob-verse
  ob-verse-ly
ob-vi-ate
  ob-vi-ated
  ob-vi-at-ing
  ob-vi-a-tion
  ob-vi-a-tor
ob-vi-ous
  ob-vi-ous-ly
oc-ca-sion
  oc-ca-sion-al
  oc-ca-sion-al-ly
oc-ci-dent
  oc-ci-den-tal
oc-clude
  oc-clud-ed
  oc-clud-ing
  oc-clu-sive
oc-clu-sion
oc-cult

oc-cult-ism
  oc-cult-ist
oc-cu-pan-cy
  oc-cu-pan-cies
  oc-cu-pant
oc-cu-pa-tion
  oc-cu-pa-tion-al
  oc-cu-pa-tion-al-ly
oc-cu-py
  oc-cu-pied
  oc-cu-py-ing
  oc-cu-pi-er
oc-cur
  oc-curred
  oc-cur-ring
  oc-cur-rence
  oc-cur-rent
ocean
  oce-an-ic
ocean-og-ra-phy
  ocean-og-ra-pher
  ocean-o-graph-ic
oce-lot
ocher
  ocher-ous
  ochery
o'clock
oc-ta-gon
  oc-tag-o-nal
  oc-tag-o-nal-ly
oc-ta-he-dron
  oc-ta-he-drons
  oc-ta-he-dra
  oc-ta-he-dral
oc-tane
oc-tave
oc-ta-vo
oc-tet
oc-to-ge-nar-i-an
  oc-tog-e-nary
oc-to-pus
oc-u-lar
  oc-u-lar-ly
oc-u-list
odd
  odd-ly
  odd-ness
odd-ball
odd-i-ty
  odd-i-ties
od-ic
odi-ous
  odi-ous-ly

odi-um
odom-e-ter
odor
 odored
 odor-less
 odor-ous
 odor-ous-ly
odor-if-er-ous
 odor-if-er-ous-ly
od-ys-sey
oe-di-pal
of-fal
off-beat
off--col-or
of-fend
 of-fend-er
of-fense
 of-fense-less
of-fen-sive
 of-fen-sive-ly
 of-fen-sive-ness
of-fer
of-fer-er
 of-fer-ing
of-fer-to-ry
 of-fer-to-ri-al
 of-fer-to-ries
off-hand
 off-hand-ed-ly
 off-hand-ed-ness
of-fice
of-fice-hold-er
of-fi-cer
of-fi-cial
 of-fi-cial-dom
 of-fi-cial-ism
 of-fi-cial-ly
of-fi-ci-ate
 of-fi-ci-at-ed
 of-fi-ci-at-ing
 of-fi-ci-a-tion
 of-fi-ci-a-tor
of-fi-cious
 of-fi-cious-ly
 of-fi-cious-ness
off-ing
off-set
 off-set-ting
off-shoot
off-shore
off-side
off-spring
off-stage

off--the--cuff
of-ten
of-ten-times
ogle
 ogled
 ogler
 ogling
ogre
 ogre-ish
ohm
 ohm-ic
ohm-age
ohm-me-ter
oil-cloth
oil-er
oil-skin
oily
 oil-i-er
 oil-i-est
 oil-i-ness
oint-ment
okra
old
 old-en
 old-er
 old-est
 old-ish
 old-ness
old--fash-ioned
 old-ster
old--time
 old--tim-er
old--world
ole-ag-i-nous
 ole-ag-i-nous-ly
 ole-ag-i-nous-ness
oleo
 oleo-mar-ga-rine
ol-fac-tion
ol-fac-to-ry
 ol-fac-to-ries
oli-garch
oli-gar-chic
 oli-gar-chi-cal
oli-gar-chy
 oli-gar-chies
oli-gop-oly
ol-ive
om-buds-man
 om-buds-men
om-elet
omen
om-i-nous

om-i-nous-ly
 om-i-nous-ness
omis-sion
omit
 omit-ted
 omit-ting
om-ni-bus
 om-ni-bus-es
om-nip-o-tence
 om-nip-o-tent-ly
om-ni-pres-ence
om-ni-pres-ent
 om-ni-pres-ent-ly
om-ni-science
 om-ni-scient
 om-ni-scient-ly
om-ni-vore
om-niv-o-rous
 om-niv-o-rous-ly
 om-niv-o-rous-ness
onan-ism
 onan-ist
 onan-is-tic
once--over
on-com-ing
oner-ous
 oner-ous-ly
 oner-ous-ness
one-self
one--sid-ed
 one--sid-ed-ly
 one--sid-ed-ness
one-time
one--track
one--way
on-go-ing
on-ion
 on-ion-like
 on-iony
on-ion-skin
on--line
on-look-er
 on-look-ing
on-ly
on-o-mato-poe-ia
 on-o-mato-poe-ic
 on-o-mato-po-et-ic
on-rush
 on-rush-ing
on-set
on-shore
on-slaught
onto-

onus
on-ward
on-yx
oo-dles
ooze
  oozed
  oo-zi-er
  oo-zi-est
  oo-zi-ness
  ooz-ing
  oo-zy
opac-i-ty
  opac-i-ties
opal
opal-es-cence
  opal-es-cent
opaque
  opaque-ly
  opaque-ness
open
  open-er
  open-ly
  open-ness
open--air
open door
open--end
open--eyed
open-hand-ed
  open-hand-ed-ly
open house
open-ing
open--mind-ed
  open--mind-ed-ly
open-mouthed
open ses-a-me
open-work
opera
  op-er-at-ic
  op-er-at-i-cal-ly
op-er-a-ble
  op-er-a-bil-i-ty
  op-er-a-bly
opera glass
opera house
op-er-ate
  op-er-at-ed
  op-er-at-ing
op-er-a-tion
  op-er-a-tive
  op-er-a-tive-ly
op-er-a-tor
op-er-et-ta
oph-thal-mic

oph-thal-mo-log-ic
oph-thal-mol-o-gist
oph-thal-mol-o-gy
opi-ate
opine
  opined
  opin-ing
opin-ion
  opin-ion-at-ed
  opin-ion-at-ed-ly
opi-um
opos-sum
op-po-nent
op-por-tune
  op-por-tune-ly
  op-por-tune-ness
op-por-tun-ism
  op-por-tun-ist
  op-por-tun-is-tic
op-por-tu-ni-ty
  op-por-tu-ni-ties
op-pos-able
  op-pos-a-bil-i-ty
op-pose
  op-posed
  op-pos-er
  op-pos-ing
  op-pos-ing-ly
op-po-site
  op-po-site-ly
op-po-si-tion
  op-po-si-tion-al
op-press
  op-pres-si-ble
  op-pres-sor
op-pres-sion
op-pres-sive
  op-pres-sive-ly
  op-pres-sive-ness
op-pro-bri-ous
  op-pro-bri-ous-ly
op-pro-bri-um
op-tic
  op-ti-cal
  op-ti-cal-ly
op-ti-cian
op-tics
op-ti-mal
op-ti-mism
  op-ti-mist
  op-ti-mis-tic
  op-ti-mis-ti-cal-ly
op-ti-mize

op-ti-mi-za-tion
op-ti-mized
op-ti-miz-ing
op-ti-mum
  op-ti-ma
op-tion
  op-tion-al
  op-tion-al-ly
op-tom-e-trist
op-tom-e-try
  op-to-met-ric
  op-to-met-ri-cal
op-u-lence
op-u-lent
  op-u-lent-ly
opus
  opus-es
or-a-cle
  orac-u-lar
  orac-u-lar-i-ty
  orac-u-lar-ly
oral
  oral-ly
or-ange
or-ange-ade
orang-utan
orate
  orat-ed
  orat-ing
ora-tion
or-a-tor
  or-a-tor-i-cal
  or-a-tor-i-cal-ly
or-a-to-rio
  or-a-to-ri-os
or-a-to-ry
or-bic-u-lar
  or-bic-u-lar-i-ty
  or-bic-u-lar-ly
or-bic-u-late
or-bit
  or-bit-al
  or-bit-er
or-chard
or-ches-tra
  or-ches-tral
  or-ches-tral-ly
or-ches-trate
  or-ches-trat-ed
  or-ches-trat-ing
  or-ches-tra-tion
or-chid
or-dain

or-dain-er
or-dain-ment
or-deal
or-der
  or-dered
  or-der-li-ness
  or-der-ly
or-di-nal
or-di-nance
or-di-nari-ly
or-di-nary
  or-di-nari-ness
or-di-na-tion
ord-nance
or-dure
oreg-a-no
or-gan
or-gan-dy
or-gan-ic
  or-gan-i-cal-ly
or-gan-ism
  or-gan-is-mal
  or-gan-is-mic
or-gan-ist
or-ga-ni-za-tion
  or-gan-i-za-tion-al
or-ga-nize
  or-ga-niz-able
  or-ga-nized
  or-ga-niz-er
  or-ga-niz-ing
  or-ga-niz-a-ble
or-gasm
  or-gas-mic
or-gi-as-tic
  or-gi-as-ti-cal-ly
or-gy
  or-gies
ori-ent
Ori-en-tal
ori-en-tal-ism
  ori-en-tal-ist
  ori-en-tal-ly
ori-en-tate
  ori-en-tat-ed
  ori-en-tat-ing
ori-en-ta-tion
or-i-fice
ori-ga-mi
orig-i-nal
  orig-i-nal-i-ty
  orig-i-nal-ly
orig-i-nate

orig-i-nat-ed
orig-i-nat-ing
orig-i-na-tion
orig-i-na-tive
orig-i-na-tive-ly
orig-i-na-tor
or-i-son
or-na-ment
  or-na-men-tal
  or-na-men-ta-tion
or-nate
  or-nate-ly
  or-nate-ness
or-nery
  or-ner-i-ness
or-ni-thol-o-gy
  or-ni-tho-log-ic
  or-ni-tho-log-i-cal
  or-ni-tho-log-i-cal-ly
  or-ni-thol-o-gist
oro-tund
  oro-tun-di-ty
or-phan
  or-phan-hood
or-phan-age
orth-odon-tics
  orth-odon-tic
  orth-odon-tist
or-tho-dox
  or-tho-dox-ly
  or-tho-dox-ness
or-tho-doxy
  or-tho-dox-ies
or-tho-gen-ic
or-thog-o-nal
  or-thog-o-nal-ly
or-thog-ra-phy
  or-tho-graph-ic
  or-tho-graph-i-cal
  or-tho-graph-i-cal-ly
  or-thog-ra-phies
  or-thog-ra-pher
or-tho-pe-dic
  or-tho-pe-dics
  or-tho-pe-dist
os-cil-late
  os-cil-lat-ed
  os-cil-lat-ing
  os-cil-la-tion
  os-cil-la-tor
  os-cil-la-to-ry
os-cil-lo-scope
os-cu-late

os-cu-lat-ed
os-cu-lat-ing
os-cu-la-tion
os-cu-la-to-ry
os-mi-um
os-mose
  os-mosed
  os-mos-ing
os-mo-sis
  os-mot-ic
  os-mot-i-cal-ly
os-prey
os-si-fy
  os-si-fied
  os-si-fi-er
  os-si-fy-ing
os-ten-si-ble
  os-ten-si-bly
os-ten-sive
  os-ten-sive-ly
os-ten-ta-tion
os-ten-ta-tious
  os-ten-ta-tious-ly
os-te-op-a-thy
  os-teo-path
  os-teo-path-ic
  os-teo-path-i-cal-ly
os-tra-cism
os-tra-cize
  os-tra-cized
  os-tra-ciz-ing
os-trich
oth-er
  oth-er-ness
oth-er-wise
oth-er-world
  oth-er-world-ly
oti-ose
  oti-ose-ly
  oti-os-i-ty
ot-ter
ot-to-man
ought
ounce
our-self
our-selves
oust-er
out-bid
  out-bid-den
  out-bid-ding
  out-bid-der
out-board
out-bound

out-brave
 out-braved
 out-brav-ing
out-break
out-build-ing
out-burst
out-cast
out-come
out-cry
 out-cries
out-dat-ed
out-dis-tance
 out-dis-tanced
 out-dis-tanc-ing
out-do
 out-did
 out-do-ing
 out-done
out-door
out-er
out-er-most
outer space
out-face
 out-faced
 out-fac-ing
out-field
 out-field-er
out-flank
out-fox
out-grow
 out-grew
 out-grow-ing
 out-grown
out-growth
out-guess
out-ing
out-land-ish
 out-land-ish-ly
out-last
out-law
 out-law-ry
out-lay
 out-laid
 out-lay-ing
out-let
out-line
 out-lined
 out-lin-ing
out-live
 out-lived
 out-liv-ing
out-look
out-ly-ing

out-mod-ed
out-num-ber
out--of--date
out-post
out-put
out-rage
 out-raged
 out-rag-ing
out-ra-geous
 out-ra-geous-ly
out-range
 out-ranged
 out-rang-ing
out-rank
out-rig-ger
out-right
out-run
 out-ran
 out-run-ning
out-set
out-shine
 out-shin-ing
 out-shone
out-side
out-sid-er
out-smart
out-spo-ken
 out-spo-ken-ly
out-stand-ing
 out-stand-ing-ly
out-strip
 out-stripped
 out-strip-ping
out-ward
 out-ward-ly
 out-wards
out-weigh
out-wit
 out-wit-ted
 out-wit-ting
ova
oval
 oval-ly
ova-ry
 ovar-i-an
 ova-ries
ovate
ova-tion
ov-en
over
over-act
over-age
over-all

over-awe
 over-awed
 over-aw-ing
over-bear-ing
 over-bear-ing-ly
over-blown
over-board
over-build
 over-build-ing
 over-built
over-cast
over-charge
 over-charged
 over-charg-ing
over-coat
over-come
 over-came
over-con-fi-dence
 over-con-fi-dent
over-do
 over-did
 over-do-ing
 over-done
over-dose
 over-dos-age
over-draft
over-draw
 over-draw-ing
 over-drawn
 over-drew
over-drive
over-due
over-em-pha-sis
 over-em-pha-size
 over-em-pha-sized
 over-em-pha-sizing
over-es-ti-mate
 over-es-ti-mat-ed
 over-es-ti-mat-ing
 over-es-ti-ma-tion
over-flow
 over-flowed
 over-flowing
 over-flown
over-gen-er-ous
over-grow
 over-grew
 over-grow-ing
 over-grown
over-growth
over-hand
 over-hand-ed
over-hang

over-hang-ing
over-hung
over-haul
over-haul-ing
over-head
over-land
over-lap
over-lapped
over-lap-ping
over-lay
over-laid
over-lay-ing
over-look
over-lord
over-ly
over-much
over-night
over-pass
over-play
over-pow-er
over-pow-er-ing
over-reach
over-ride
over-rid-den
over-rid-ing
over-rode
over-rule
over-ruled
over-rul-ing
over-run
over-seas
over-see
over-saw
over-see-ing
over-seen
over-seer
over-shad-ow
over-shoe
over-shoot
over-shoot-ing
over-shot
over-sight
over-sim-pli-fy
over-sim-pli-fi-ca-tion
over-sim-pli-fied
over-sim-pli-fy-ing
over-size
over-sleep
over-sleep-ing
over-slept
over-spread
over-spread-ing
over-stay

over-step
over-stepped
over-step-ping
over-strung
over-stuff
overt
overt-ly
over-tax
over--the--coun-ter
over-time
over-tone
over-ture
over-turn
over-view
over-ween-ing
over-ween-ing-ly
over-weight
over-whelm
over-whelm-ing
over-wrought
ovi-duct
ovip-a-rous
ovip-ar-ous-ly
ovoid
ovoi-dal
ovule
ovu-lar
ovum
ova
owe
owed
ow-ing
owl-ish
own-er
ox-al-ic ac-id
ox-bow
ox-en
ox-ford
ox-i-da-tion
ox-i-da-tive
ox-i-dant
ox-ide
ox-i-dize
ox-i-dized
ox-i-diz-ing
ox-y-a-cet-y-lene
ox-y-gen
ox-y-gen-ate
ox-y-gen-at-ed
ox-y-gen-at-ing
ox-y-gen-a-tion
oys-ter
ozone

P
pab-u-lum
pace
paced
pac-ing
pac-er
pace-mak-er
pa-cif-ic
pa-cif-i-ca-tion
pa-cif-i-ca-tor
pa-cif-i-ca-to-ry
pac-i-fi-er
pac-i-fism
pac-i-fist
pac-i-fy
pac-i-fied
pac-i-fy-ing
pack-age
pack-ag-er
pack-er
pack-et
pack-ing
pad
pad-ded
pad-ding
pad-dle
pad-dock
pad-dy
pad-dies
pad-lock
pae-an
pe-an
pe-gan
pe-gan-ism
pag-eant
pag-ent-ry
pag-i-nate
pag-i-nat-ed
pag-i-nat-ing
pa-go-da
pains-tak-ing
pains-tak-ing-ly
paint-er
pais-ley
pa-ja-mas
pal-ace
pal-at-a-ble
pal-at-a-bil-i-ty
pal-at-a-bly
pal-ate
pa-la-tial
pa-la-tial-ly
pal-a-tiner
pa-lat-i-nate**

pa-lav-er
pale
pa-le-on-tol-o-gy
  pa-le-on-to-log-ic
  pa-le-on-to-log-i-cal
pal-ette
pal-imp-sest
pal-in-drome
pal-ing
pal-i-sade
  pal-i-sad-ed
  pal-i-sad-ing
pal-la-di-um
pall-bear-er
pal-let
pal-li-ate
  pal-li-at-ed
  pal-li-at-ing
  pal-li-a-tion
pal-lid
pal-lor
palm
  pal-ma-ceous
pal-mate
  pal-mate-ly
palm-er
palm-is-try
  palm-ist
pal-o-mi-no
  pal-o-mi-nos
pal-pa-ble
  pal-pa-bil-i-ty
  pal-pa-bly
pal-pate
  pal-pat-ed
  pal-pat-ing
pal-ter
  pal-ter-er
pal-try
  pal-tri-er
  pal-tri-est
pam-pas
  pam-pe-an
pam-per
  pam-per-er
pam-phlet
pan-a-ce-a
  pan-a-ce-an
pa-nache
pan-cake
pan-cre-as
  pan-cre-at-ic
pan-dem-ic

pan-de-mo-ni-um
pan-der
pan-el
  pan-eled
  pan-el-ing
pan-el-ist
pang
pan-ic
  pan-icked
  pan-ick-ing
pan-nier
  pan-ier
pan-ta-loon
pan-the-ism
  pan-the-is-tic
pan-the-on
pan-ther
pan-ties
pan-to-mime
  pan-to-mimed
pan-try
  pan-tries
pant-suit
pant-y-hose
pa-pa
pa-pa-cy
  pa-pa-cies
pa-pal
pa-per
  pa-per-er
  pa-pery
pa-per-back
pa-pil-la
  pa-pil-pae
pa-poose
pap-ri-ka
pa-py-rus
par-a-ble
par-a-digm
  par-a-dig-mat-ic
par-a-dise
  par-a-di-si-a-cal
par-a-dox
  par-a-dox-i-cal
par-af-fin
par-a-gon
par-a-graph
  par-a-graph-er
par-a-keet
par-al-lax
  par-al-al-lac-tic
par-al-lel
  par-al-leled

par-al-lel-ing
par-al-lel-o-gram
pa-ral-y-sis
  pa-ral-y-ses
  par-a-lyt-ic
par-a-lyze
  par-a-lyzed
  par-a-lyz-ing
par-a-me-cium
par-a-med-ic
pa-ram-e-ter
par-a-mount
  par-a-mount-cy
  par-a-mount-ly
par-amour
para-noia
  para-noid
par-a-pet
par-a-pher-nal-ia
para-phrase
  para-phrased
  para-phras-ing
para-ple-gia
  para-ple-gic
para-psy-chol-o-gy
par-a-site
  par-a-sit-ic
para-sol
par-a-sym-pa-thet-ic
para-thi-on
para-troop-er
para-ty-phoid
par-boil
par-cel
  par-celed
  par-cel-ing
parch-ment
par-don
  par-don-a-ble
  par-don-a-bly
pare
  pared
  par-ing
par-e-gor-ic
par-ent
  pa-ren-tal
par-ent-age
pa-ren-the-sis
pa-re-sis
  pa-ret-ic
par-fait
pa-ri-ah
par-i-mu-tu-el

par-ish
  pa-rish-ion-er
par-i-ty
par-ka
par-lance
par-lay
  par-lay-ed
  par-lay-ing
par-ley
  par-leyed
  par-ley-ing
par-lia-ment
par-lia-men-tar-ian
par-lia-men-ta-ry
par-lor
pa-ro-chi-al
par-o-dy
  par-o-dies
  par-o-died
pa-role
  pa-roled
par-ot-id
par-ox-ysm
  par-ox-ys-mal
par-quet
  par-queted
  par-quet-ing
par-quet-ry
par-rot
  par-rot-like
  par-roty
parse
par-si-mo-ny
  par-si-mo-ni-ous
  par-si-mo-ni-ous-ly
pars-ley
pars-nip
par-son-age
par-take
  par-took
  par-tak-en
part-ed
par-the-no-gen-e-sis
par-tial
  par-tial-ly
par-tial-i-ty
  par-tial-i-ties
par-tic-i-pant
par-tic-i-pate
  par-tic-i-pat-ed
  par-tic-i-pat-ing
par-ti-cip-i-al
par-ti-ci-ple

par-ti-cle
par-ti--col-ored
par-tic-u-lar
  par-tic-u-lar-ly
par-tic-u-lar-i-ties
par-tic-u-lar-ize
  par-tic-u-lar-ized
  par-tic-u-lar-iz-ing
par-tic-u-late
part-ing
par-ti-san
  par-ti-san-ship
par-tite
par-ti-tion
par-ti-tive
part-ly
part-ner
  part-ner-ship
par-tridge
  par-tridg-es
part--time
par-tu-ri-ent
par-tu-ri-tion
par-ty
  par-ties
par-ve-nu
pas-chal
pa-sha
pass-able
  pass-ably
pas-sen-ger
pass-er-by
  pass-ers-by
pass-ing
pas-sion
  pas-sion-ies
pas-sion-ate
  pas-sion-ate-ly
pas-sive
pas-ta
paste
  pas-ted
  pas-ting
paste-board
pas-tel
pas-teur-ize
  pas-teur-ized
  pas-teur-iz-ing
  pas-teur-i-za-tion
pas-tille
pas-time
pas-tor
pas-to-ral

pas-to-ral-ly
pas-tor-ate
pas-tra-mi
past-ry
  pas-tries
pas-ture
pas-ty
  past-i-er
  past-i-est
pat-ent
  pa-ten-cy
  pat-ent-ly
pat-en-tee
pat-er-nal
  pat-ter-nal-ly
pa-ter-nal-ism
pa-ter-ni-ty
pa-thet-ic
path-find-er
pa-thol-o-gy
pa-thos
pa-tience
pa-tient
  pa-tient-ly
pat-i-na
pa-tio
  pa-tios
pa-tri-arch
pa-tri-ar-chy
  pa-tri-ar-chies
pa-tri-cian
pat-ri-mo-ny
  pat-ri-mo-nies
pa-tri-ot
  pa-tri-ot-ic
  pa-tri-ot-ism
pa-trol
  pa-trolled
  pa-trol-ling
pa-trol-man
  pa-trol-men
pa-tron
  pa-tron-ess
pa-tron-age
pa-tron-ize
  pa-tron-ized
  pa-tron-iz-ing
  pa-tron-iz-ing-ly
pat-ro-nym-ic
pat-sy
  pat-sies
pat-ter
pat-tern

147

pat-terned
pat-ty
  pat-ties
pau-ci-ty
paunch
pau-per
  pau-per-ism
pause
  paused
  paus-ing
pa-vil-ion
pawn
  pawn-er
pawn-bro-ker
pay-a-ble
pay-off
peace
peace-able
  peace-ably
peace-ful
  peace-ful-ly
peach
pea-cock
peak-ed
pea-nut
pearl
  pear-ly
peas-ant
  peas-ant-ly
peaty
peb-ble
pe-can
pec-ca-dil-lo
  pec-ca-dil-loes
pec-ca-dil-los
peck-er
pec-tin
pec-to-ral
pec-u-late
  pec-u-lat-ed
  pec-u-lat-ing
pe-cu-liar
  pe-cu-liar-ly
  pe-cu-li-ar-i-ty
  pe-cu-li-ar-i-ties
pe-cu-ni-ary
ped-a-go-gue
ped-a-go-gy
ped-al
  ped-aled
  ped-al-ing
ped-dle
ped-es-tal

pe-des-tri-an
  pe-des-tri-an-ism
pe-di-at-ric
  pe-di-at-rics
pe-di-a-tri-cian
  pe-di-at-rist
ped-i-cure
  ped-i-cur-ist
ped-i-gree
  ped-i-greed
ped-i-ment
  ped-i-men-tal
  ped-i-ment-ed
pe-dom-e-ter
peep-hole
peer
peer-less
  peer-less-ly
peeve
  peeved
  peev-ing
pee-vish
  pee-vish-ly
pee-wee
pe-jo-ra-tive
  pe-jo-ra-tive-ly
pe-koe
pel-let
pell--mell
pel-lu-cid
  pel-lu-cid-i-ty
  pel-lu-cid-ly
pelt-er
  pelt-ry
pel-vis
  pel-vis-es
  pel-ves
  pel-vic
pem-mi-can
  pem-i-can
pe-nal
pe-nal-ize
  pe-nal-ized
  pe-nal-iz-ing
pen-al-ty
  pen-al-ties
pen-ance
pen-chant
pen-cil
pend-ant
pend-ent
  pend-en-cy
  pend-ent-ly

pend-ing
pen-du-lous
  pen-du-lous-ly
pen-du-lum
pen-a-tra-ble
  pen-a-tra-bil-i-ty
  pen-a-tra-bly
pen-e-trate
  pen-e-trat-ed
  pen-e-trat-ing
  pen-e-tra-tion
pen-i-cil-lin
pen-in-su-la
  pen-in-su-lar
pe-nis
pen-i-tent
  pen-i-tence
  pen-i-ten-tial
pen-i-ten-tia-ry
  pen-i-ten-tia-ries
pen-knife
  pen-knives
pen-man-ship
pen-nant
pen-non
pen-ny
  pen-nies
pen-ny an-te
pe-nol-o-gy
  pe-no-log-i-cal
  pe-nol-o-gist
pen-sion
pen-sive
  pen-sive-ly
pen-ta-gon
  pen-tag-o-nal
  pen-tag-o-nal-ly
pen-tam-e-ter
pen-tath-lon
pent-up
pe-nult
  pe-nul-ti-ma
  pe-nul-ti-mate
pe-nu-ri-ous
  pe-nu-ri-ous-ly
pen-u-ry
pe-on
  pe-on-age
pe-o-ny
  pe-on-ies
peo-ple
pep
  pepped

pep-ping
pep-per
pep-pery
pep-py
pep-pi-er
pep-pi-est
pep-sin
pep-tic
per-am-bu-late
per-am-bu-la-tor
per an-num
per-cale
per cap-i-ta
per-ceive
per-ceived
per-ceiv-ing
per-ceiv-a-ble
per-cent
per-cent-age
per-cen-tile
per-cep-ti-ble
per-cep-ti-bil-i-ty
per-cep-ti-bly
per-cep-tion
per-cep-tion-al
per-cep-tu-al
per-cep-tu-al-ly
perch
per-co-late
per-co-lat-ed
per-co-lat-ing
per-co-la-tion
per-co-la-tor
per-cus-sion
per-cus-sion-ist
per di-em
per-di-tion
per-e-gri-nate
pe-remp-to-ry
pe-remp-to-ri-ly
pe-ren-ni-al
pe-ren-ni-al-ly
per-fec-tion
per-fec-tion-ist
per-fect-ly
per-fi-dy
per-fid-i-ous
per-fid-i-ous-ly
per-fo-rate
per-fo-rat-ed
per-force
per-form
per-form-a-ble

per-form-er
per-for-mance
per-fume
per-fumed
per-func-to-ry
per-func-to-ri-ly
per-haps
per-i-gee
per-i-ge-al
per-i-ge-an
peri-he-li-on
peri-he-lia
per-il
per-il-ous
per-il-ous-ly
pe-rim-e-ter
per-i-met-ic
per-i-met-ri-cal
pe-ri-od
pe-ri-od-ic
pe-ri-o-dic-i-ty
pe-ri-od-i-cal
pe-ri-od-i-cal-ly
pe-riph-ery
pe-riph-er-ies
pe-riph-er-al
pe-riph-er-al-ly
per-i-phrase
peri-scope
peri-scopic
peri-scop-i-cal
per-ish
per-ish-able
per-ish-abil-i-ty
per-ish-ably
peri-stal-sis
peri-stal-ses
peri-style
peri-to-ne-um
peri-to-ne-ums
peri-to-nea
peri-to-ne-al
peri-to-ni-tis
peri-wig
peri-win-kle
per-jure
per-jured
per-jur-ing
per-jur-er
per-ju-ry
per-ju-ries
perky
perk-i-er

perk-i-est
per-ma-nent
per-me-able
per-me-abil-i-ty
per-me-ably
per-mis-si-ble
per-mis-si-bil-i-ty
per-mis-si-bly
per-mis-sion
per-mis-sive
per-mis-sive-ly
per-mu-ta-tion
per-ni-cious
per-ni-cious-ly
per-ora-tion
per-ox-ide
per-ox-id-ed
per-ox-id-ing
per-pen-dic-u-lar
per-pen-dic-u-lar-i-ty
per-pen-dic-u-lar-ly
per-pe-trate
per-pe-trat-ed
per-pe-trat-ing
per-pe-tra-tion
per-pe-tra-tor
per-pet-u-al
per-pet-u-al-ly
per-pet-u-ate
per-pet-u-at-ed
per-pet-u-at-ing
per-pet-u-a-tion
per-pet-ua-tor
per-pe-tu-ity
per-pe-tu-ities
per-plex
per-plexed
per-plex-ing
per-plex-ing-ly
per-plex-ed-ly
per-plex-i-ty
per-plex-i-ties
per-qui-site
per-se-cute
per-se-cut-ed
per-se-cut-ing
per-se-cu-tive
per-se-cu-tor
per-se-cu-tion
per-se-vere
per-se-vered
per-se-ver-ing
per-sse-ver-ance

per-se-ver-ing-ly
per-si-flage
per-sim-mon
per-sist
per-sist-ence
per-sis-ten-cy
per-sist-ent
per-sist-ent-ly
per-snick-e-ty
per-son
per-son-able
per-son-age
per-son-al-i-ty
per-son-al-i-ties
per-son-al-ize
per-son-al-ized
per-son-al-iz-ing
per-son-al-ly
per-so-na non gra-ta
per-son-ate
per-son-at-ed
per-son-at-ing
per-son-a-tion
per-son-a-tor
per-son-i-fy
per-son-i-fied
per-son-i-fy-ing
per-son-i-fi-ca-tion
per-son-i-fi-er
per-son-nel
per-spec-tive
per-spec-tive-ly
per-spi-ca-cious
per-spi-ca-cious-ly
per-spi-cac-i-ty
per-spi-cu-i-ty
per-spic-u-ous
per-spic-u-ous-ly
per-spi-ra-tion
per-spire
per-spired
per-spiring
per-suade
per-suad-ed
per-suad-ing
per-suad-a-ble
per-suad-er
per-sua-sion
per-sua-sive
per-sua-sive-ly
per-sua-sive-ness
pert
pert-ly

pert-ness
per-tain
per-ti-na-cious
per-ti-na-cious-ly
per-ti-nac-i-ty
per-ti-nent
per-ti-nence
per-ti-nen-cy
per-ti-nent-ly
per-turb
per-turb-a-ble
per-tur-ba-tion
pe-ruke
pe-ruse
pe-rused
pe-rus-ing
pe-rus-al
pe-rus-er
per-vade
per-vad-ed
per-vad-ing
per-vad-er
per-va-sion
per-va-sive
per-va-sive-ly
per-verse
per-verse-ly
per-verse-ness
per-ver-si-ty
per-ver-sion
per-vert
per-vi-ous
per-vi-ous-ness
pes-si-mism
pes-si-mist
pes-si-mist
pes-si-mis-tic
pes-si-mis-ti-cal-ly
pes-ter
pest-hole
pest-i-cide
pes-tif-er-ous
pes-tif-er-ous-ly
per-ti-lence
pes-ti-len-tial
pes-ti-lent
pes-ti-lent-ly
pes-tle
pes-tled
pes-tling
pet-al
pet-aled
pet-cock

pe-ter
pet-i-ole
pe-tite
pe-tite-ness
pet-it four
pe-ti-tion
pe-ti-tion-ary
pe-ti-tion-er
pe-trel
pet-ri-fy
pet-ri-fied
pet-ri-fy-ing
pe-tri-fac-tion
pe-tro-chem-is-try
pe-tro-chem-i-cal
pet-rol
pet-ro-la-tum
pe-trol-leum
pet-ti-coat
pet-tish
pet-tish-ly
pet-tish-ness
pet-ty
pet-u-lant
pet-u-lance
pet-u-lan-cy
pet-u-lant-ly
pe-tu-nia
pew-ter
pey-o-te
pey-o-tes
pha-lanx
pha-lanx-es
pha-lang-es
pal-lus
pal-li
pahl-lus-es
phal-lic
phan-tasm
phan-tas-ma
phan-tas-mal
phan-tas-mic
phan-tas-ma-go-ria
phan-tas-ma-go-ri-al
phan-tas-ma-gor-ic
phan-ta-sy
phan-ta-sies
phan-tom
phar-aoh
phar-ma-ceu-ti-cal
phar-ma-cue-tic
phar-ma-ceu-ti-cal-ly
phar-ma-cue-tics

phar-ma-cist
phar-ma-col-o-gy
  phar-ma-co-log-ic
  phar-ma-co-log-i-ca
  phar-ma-col-o-gist
phar-ma-co-poe-ia
  phar-ma-co-poe-ial
phar-ma-cy
  phar-ma-cies
phar-ynx
  pha-ryn-ges
  pha-ryn-ge-al
  pha-ryn-gal
phase
  phased
  phas-ing
  pha-sic
pheas-ant
phe-no-bar-bi-tal
phe-nol
  phe-nol-ic
phe-nom-e-non
  phe-nom-e-na
  phe-nom-e-nons
  phe-nom-e-nal
  phe-nom-e-nal-ly
phi-al
phi-lan-der
  phi-lan-der-er
phi-lan-thro-py
  phi-lan-thro-pies
  phil-an-throp-ic
  phil-an-throp-i-cal
  phi-lan-thro-pist
phi-late-ly
  phil-a-tel-ic
  phil-a-tel-i-cal
  phi-lat-e-list
phil-har-mon-ic
phil-o-den-dron
  phil-o-den-drons
  phil-o-den-dra
phi-log-o-gy
  phi-lol-o-gist
  phi-lol-o-ger
  phil-o-lo-gi-an
  phil-o-log-i-cal
  phil-o-log-ic
  phil-o-log-i-cal-ly
phi-los-o-pher
phil-o-soph-i-cal
  phil-o-soph-ic
  phil-o-soph-i-cal-ly

phi-los-o-phize
  phi-los-o-phized
  phi-los-o-phiz-ing
  phi-los-o-phiz-er
phi-los-o-phy
  phi-los-o-phies
phil-ter
  phil-tered
  phil-ter-ing
phle-bi-tis
  phle-bit-ic
phle-bot-o-my
  phle-bot-o-mist
phlegm
phleg-mat-ic
  phleg-mat-i-cal
  phleg-mat-i-cal-ly
phlox
pho-bia
  pho-bic
phoe-be
phoe-nix
phone
  phoned
  phon-ing
pho-neme
  pho-ne-mic
pho-net-ic
  pho-net-ics
  pho-net-i-cal
  pho-net-i-cal-ly
phon-ic
phon-ics
pho-no-graph
  pho-no-graph-ic
  pho-no-graph-i-cal-ly
pho-nol-o-gy
  pho-nol-o-gies
  pho-no-log-ic
  pho-no-log-i-cal
  pho-no-log-i-cal-ly
  pho-nol-o-gist
pho-ny
  pho-ni-er
  pho-ni-est
  pho-nies
  pho-ni-ness
phos-phate
phos-pho-res-cence
  phos-pho-resce
  phos-pho-resced
  phos-pho-resc-ing
  phos-pho-res-cent

  phos-pho-res-cent-ly
phos-pho-rus
pho-to
  pho-tos
pho-to-copy
  pho-to-cop-ies
  pho-to-cop-ied
  pho-to-cop-y-ing
pho-to-e-lec-tric
pho-to-en-grav-ing
  pho-to-en-grave
  pho-to-en-graved
  pho-to-en-grav-er
pho-to-flash
pho-to-gen-ic
pho-to-graph
  pho-to-graph-er
pho-tog-ra-phy
  pho-to-graph-ic
  pho-to-graph-i-cal
  pho-to-graph-i-cal-ly
pho-to-gra-vure
pho-to--off-set
pho-to-stat
  pho-to-stat-ed
  pho-to-stat-ing
  pho-to-stat-ic
pho-to-syn-the-sis
phrase
  phrased
  phras-ing
  phras-al
phrase-ol-o-gy
phre-net-ic
phre-nol-o-gy
  phre-nol-o-gist
phy-lac-tery
  phy-lac-ter-ies
phy-log-e-ny
  phy-lo-gen-e-sis
  phy-lo-ge-net-ic
  phy-lo-gen-ic
  phy-log-e-nist
phy-lu
phys-ic
  phys-icked
  phys-ick-ing
phys-i-cal
  phys-i-cal-ly
phy-si-cian
phys-ics
  phys-i-cist
phys-i-og-no-my

phys-i-og-no-mies
phys-i-og-nom-ic
phys-i-og-nom-i-cal
phys-i-og-no-mist
phys-i-og-ra-phy
phys-i-o-graph-ic
phys-i-o-graph-i-cal
phys-i-ol-o-gy
phys-i-o-log-ic
phys-i-o-log-i-cal
phys-i-o-log-i-cal-ly
phys-i-ol-o-gist
phys-i-o-ther-a-py
phy-sique
pi-a-nis-si-mo
pi-an-ist
pi-ano
  pia-nos
pi-ano-forte
pi-az-za
pi-ca
pic-a-dor
pic-a-resque
pic-a-yune
  pic-a-yun-ish
pic-ca-lil-li
pic-co-lo
  pic-co-los
  pic-co-lo-list
pick-ax
picked
pick-er-el
pick-et
  pick-et-er
pick-ing
pick-le
  pick-led
  pick-ling
pick-pock-et
pick-up
picky
  pick-i-er
  pick-i-est
pic-nic
  pic-nicked
  pic-nick-ing
  pic-nick-er
pic-to-ri-al
  pic-to-ri-al-ly
pic-ture
  pic-tured
  pic-tur-ing
pic-tur-esque

pic-tur-esque-ly
pid-dle
  pid-dled
  pid-dling
pid-gin
pie-bald
piece
  piec-er
piece-meal
piece-work
  piece-worker
pied
pier
pierce
  pierc-ed
  pierc-ing
pierc-ing-ly
pi-etism
  pi-etis-tic
  pi-etis-ti-cal
pi-ety
  pi-eties
pif-fle
pig
  pigged
  pig-ging
pi-geon
pe-geon-hole
  pi-geon-holed
  pi-geon-hol-ing
pi-geon--toed
pig-gish
  pig-ish-ly
  pig-gis-ness
pig-head-ed
  pig-head-ed-ly
  pig-head-ed-ness
pig-ment
  pig-men-tary
  pig-men-ta-tion
pig-pen
pig-skin
pig-sty
  pig-sties
pig-tail
pike
  piked
  pik-ing
pik-er
pi-las-ter
pil-chard
pile
  piled

pil-ing
pil-fer
pil-fer-age
pil-fer-er
pil-grim
pil-grim-age
pil-grim-aged
pil-grim-ag-ing
pil-lage
pil-laged
pil-lag-ing
pil-lag-er
pil-lar
pill-box
pil-lion
pil-lo-ry
pil-lo-ries
pil-lo-ry-ing
pil-low
pil-low-case
pi-lot
pi-lot-age
pi-lot-less
pi-lot-house
pi-men-to
pi-men-tos
pim-ple
pim-pled
pim-ply
pin
pinned
pin-ning
pin-afore
pince-nez
pin-cers
pinch
pinch-er
pinch-beck
pin-cush-ion
pin-dling
pine
pine-like
piney
pin-ing
pi-ne-al
pine-ap-ple
pin-feath-er
pin-feath-ered
pin-feath-ery
pin-fold
pin-head
pin-head-ed
pin-hole

pin-ion
pink-eye
pink-ie
pinko
  pink-os
  pink-oes
pin-na
  pin-nas
  pin-nae
  pin-nal
pin-na-cle
  pin-na-cled
  pin-na-cling
pi-nate
  pin-nate-ly
  pin-na-tion
pi-noch-le
  pi-noc-le
pin-point
pin-prick
pin-set-ter
pin-tail
  pin-tailed
pin-tle
pin-to
  pin-tos
pin-up
pin-wheel
pin-worm
pi-o-neer
pi-ous
  pi-ous-ly
  pi-ous-ness
pip
  pipped
  pip-ping
pipe-line
  pipe-lined
  pipe-lin-ing
pip-er
pip-ing
pip-it
pip-pin
pip-squek
pi-quant
  pi-quan-cy
  pi-quant-ly
pique
  piqued
  pi-quing
pi-ra-cy
  pi-ra-cies
pi-ra-nha

pi-rate
  pi-rat-ed
  pi-rat-ing
  pi-rat-i-cal
  pi-rat-i-cal-ly
pi-roque
pir-ou-ette
  pir-ou-et-ted
  pir-ou-et-ting
pi-sci-cul-ture
pis-ta-chio
  pis-ta-chi-os
pis-til
pis-til-late
pis-tol
  pis-toled
  pis-tol-ing
pis-ton
pit
  pit-ted
  pit-ting
pitch--blake
pitch-blend
pitch-er
pitch-fork
pitchy
  pitch-i-er
  pitch-i-est
pit-e-ous
  pit-e-ous-ly
pit-fall
pith
  pith-i-er
  pith-i-est
  pith-i-ly
piti-a-ble
  piti-anle-ness
  piti-a-bly
piti-ful
  piti-ful-ly
  piti-ful-ness
piti-less
  piti-less-ly
pit-man
  pit-men
pit-tance
pi-tu--tar-ies
pity
  pit-ies
  pit-ied
  pit-y-ing
  pit-y-ing-ly
piv-ot

piv-ot-al
  piv-ot-al-ly
pix-i-lat-ed
pixy
  pix-ie
  pix-ies
piz-za
piz-ze-ria
piz-zi-ca-to
place-a-ble
  plac-a-bil-i-ty
  plac-a-bly
plac-ard
pla-cate
  pla-cat-ed
  pla-cat-ing
  pla-ca-tion
  pla-ca-tive
  pla-ca-to-ry
place
  placed
  plac-ing
pla-ce-bo
  pla-ce-bos
  pla-ce-boes
place-ment
pla-cen-ta
  pla-cen-tas
  pla-cen-tae
  pla-cen-tal
plac-er
plac-id
  pla-cid-i-ty
  plac-id-ness
pla-gal
pla-gia-rism
  pla-gia-rized
  pla-gia-riz-ing
  pla-gia-riz-er
pla-gia-ry
  pla-gia-ries
plaque
  plaqued
  pla-quing
  pla-quer
pla-guy
  pla-guey
  pla-gui-ly
plaid
plain
  plain-ly
  plain-ness
plain-song

plain-spo-ken
plain-tiff
plain-tive
  plain-tive-ly
plait
  plait-ing
plan
  planned
  plan-ning
  plan-less
  plan-ner
plane
  planed
  plan-ing
plan-er
plan-et
plan-e-tar-i-um
  plan-e-tar-i-ums
  plan-e-tar-ia
plan-e-tary
plan-e-toid
plan-ish
  plan-ish-er
plank-ing
plank-ton
  plank-ton-ic
plant
  plant-able
  plant-like
plan-tain
plan-ta-tion
plant-er
plaque
plasm
plas-ma
  plas-mic
  plas-mat-ic
plas-ter
  plas-ter-er
  plas-ter-ing
  plas-ter-work
plas-ter-board
plas-tered
plas-tic
  plas-ti-cal-ly
  plas-tic-i-ty
  plas-ti-ciz-er
plat
  plat-ted
  plat-ting
plate
  plat-ed
  plat-ing

plat-er
pla-teau
  pla-teaus
  pla-teaux
plate-ful
  plate-fuls
plate-let
plat-form
plat-i-num
plat-i-tude
  plat-i-tu-di-nal
  plat-i-tu-di-nous
plat-i-tu-di-nize
  plat-i-tu-di-nized
  plat-i-tu-di-niz-ing
pla-ton-ic
  pla-ton-i-cal-ly
pla-toon
plat-ter
platy-pus
  platy-pus-es
  platy-pi
plau-dut
plau-si-ble
  plau-si-bil-i-ty
  plau-si-bly
play-act
  play-act-ing
play-back
play-bill
play-boy
play-er
play-ful
  play-ful-ly
  play-ful-ness
play-go-er
play-ground
play-house
  play-hous-es
play-let
play-mate
play--off
play-pen
play-thing
play-time
play-wright
pla-za
plea
plead
  plead-ed
  plead-ing
  plead-a-ble
  plead-er

pleas-ant
  pleas-ant-ly
  pleas-ant-ness
pleas-ant-ry
  pleas-an-trioes
please
  pleased
  pleas-ing
  pleas-ing-ly
  pleas-ing-ness
plea-sur-a-ble
  plea-sur-able-ness
  plea-sur-ably
pleas-ure
pleat
  pleat-ed
  pleat-er
plebe
ple-be-ian
pleb-i-scite
pledge
  pledged
  pledg-ing
  pledg-ee
  pledg-er
ple-na-ry
pleni-po-ten-tia-ry
  pleni-po-ten-tia-ries
plen-i-tude
plen-te-ous
  plen-te-ous-ly
plen-ti-ful
  plen-ti-ful-ly
plen-ty
pleth-o-ra
  ple-thor-ic
pleu-ra
  pleu-rae
  pleu-ral
pleu-ri-sy
  pleu-rit-ic
plex-us
  plex-us-es
pli-able
  pli-a-bil-i-ty
  pli-a-ble-ness
  pli-a-bly
pli-ant
  pli-an-cy
  pli-ant-ness
  pli-ant-ly
pli-ca-tion
pli-ers

plight
plink
plod
  plod-ded
  plod-ding
  plod-der
plop
  plopped
  plop-ping
plot
  plot-ted
  plot-ting
  plot-ter
plow
  plow-a-ble
  plow-er
  plow-man
plow-share
pluck
  pluck-er
plucky
  pluck-i-er
  pluck-i-est
  pluck-i-ly
  pluck-i-ness
plug
  plugged
  plug-ging
  plug-ger
plum-age
plumb-er
plumb-ing
plume
  plumed
  plum-ing
  plume-like
  plumy
  plum-i-er
  plum-i-est
plum-met
plump
  plump-er
  plump-ly
  plump-ness
plun-der
  plun-der-er
  plun-der-ous
plunge
  plunged
  plung-ing
plung-er
plunk-er
plu-ral

plu-ral-ly
plu-ral-ize
plu-ral-ized
plu-ral-iz-ing
plu-ral-ism
  plu-ral-ist
  plu-ral-is-tic
plu-ral-i-ty
  plu-ral-i-ties
plush
  plush-i-ness
  plushy
  plush-i-er
  plush-i-est
plu-toc-ra-cy
  plu-tac-ra-cies
  plu-ta-crat
  plu-to-cart-ic
plu-to-ni-um
plu-vi-al
ply
  plied
  ply-ing
ply-wood
pneu-mat-ic
  pneu-mat-i-cal-ly
pneu-mat-ics
pneu-mo-nia
pneu-mon-ic
poach
  poach-er
pock-et
pock-et-book
pock-et-ful
pock-et-knife
  pock-et-knives
pock-mark
  pock-marked
pod
  pod-ded
  pod-ding
  pod-like
podgy
  podg-i-er
  podg-i-est
po-di-trist
  po-di-a-try
po-di-um
  po-dia
  po-di-ums
po-esy
  po-esies
po-et

po-et-ess
po-et-ize
  po-et-ized
  po-et-iz-ing
  po-et-iz-er
po-et lau-re-ate
  po-ets lau-re-ate
po-et-ry
po-go
po-grom
poi-gnant
  poi-gnan-cy
  poi-gnant-ly
poin-set-tia
point--blank
point-ed
  point-ed-ly
  point-ed-ness
point-er
poin-til-lism
  poin-til-list
point-less
poise
  poised
  pois-ing
poi-son
  poi-son-er
  poi-son-ing
  poi-son-ous
poi-son--pen
poke
  poked
  pok-ing
pok-er
poky
  pok-i-er
  pok-i-est
  pok-i-ly
  pok-i-ness
po-lar
po-lar-i-ty
  po-lar-i-ties
po-lar-i-za-tion
po-lar-ize
  po-lar-ized
  po-lar-iz-ing
  po-lar-iz-a-ble
  po-lar-iz-er
pole
  poled
  pol-ing
  pole-less
pole-cat

po-lem-ic
po-lem-i-cal
po-lem-i-cal-ly
po-lem-i-cist
po-lem-ics
pole-star
po-lice
po-liced
po-lic-ing
pol-i-cy
pol-i-cies
pol-i-o-my-e-li-tis
pol-ish
pol-ish-er
po-lite
po-lite-ly
po-lite-ness
pol-i-tic
po-lit-i-cal
po-lit-i-cal-ly
pol-i-ti-cian
po-lit-i-cize
po-lit-i-cized
po-lit-i-ciz-ing
pol-i-tick
pol-i-tick-er
pol-i-tics
pol-i-ty
pol-i-ties
pol-ka
pol-kaed
pol-ka-ing
poll
poll-ee
poll-er
pol-len
pol-li-nate
pol-li-nat-ed
pol-li-nat-ing
pol-li-na-tion
pol-li-na-tor
pol-li-wog
poll-ster
pol-lu-tant
pol-lute
pol-lut-ed
pol-lut-ing
pol-lu-ter
pol-lu-tion
po-lo
po-lo-ist
po-lo-naise
po-lo-ni-um

pol-ter-geist
poly-an-dry
poly-an-drous
poly-chro-mat-ic
poly-chrome
poly-es-ter
poly-eth-yl-ene
polyg-a-mist
polyg-a-my
polyg-a-mous
poly-glot
poly-gon
polyg-o-nal
polyg-o-nal-ly
poly-graph
poly-graph-ic
po-lyg-y-ny
po-lyg-y-nous
poly-he-dron
poly-he-drons
poly-he-dra
poly-he-dral
poly-mer
po-ly-mer-ize
po-ly-mer-ized
po-ly-mer-iz-ing
po-lym-er-ism
po-lym-er-i-za-tion
pol-y-mor-phism
pol-y-mor-phic
pol-y-mor-phous
poly-no-mi-al
pol-yp
poly-phon-ic
po-lyph-ony
poly-sty-rene
poly-syl-lab-ic
poly-syl-lab-i-cal-ly
poly-syl-la-ble
poly-tech-nic
poly-the-ism
poly-the-ist
poly-the-is-tic
poly-the-is-ti-cal
poly-un-sat-u-rat-ed
pom-ace
po-made
po-mad-ed
po-mad-ing
pome-gran-ate
pom-mel
pom-meled
pom-mel-ing

pom-pa-dour
pom-pon
pomp-ous
pom-pos-i-ty
pom-pous-ly
pon-cho
pon-der
pon-der-a-ble
pon-der-er
pon-der-ous
pon-der-ous-ly
pon-der-ou-ness
pon-iard
pon-tiff
pon-tif-i-cal
pon-tif-i-cal-ly
pon-tif-i-cate
pon-tif-i-cat-ed
pon-tif-i-cat-ing
pon-toon
po-ny
po-nies
po-nied
po-ny-ing
po-ny-tail
poo-dle
pool-room
poor
poor-ish
poor-ly
pop-corn
pop-ery
pop-ish
pop-eyed
pop-gun
pop-in-jay
pop-lar
pop-lin
pop-per
pop-py
pop-pies
pop-pied
pop-py-cock
pop-u-lace
pop-u-lar
pop-u-lar-ly
pop-u-lar-i-ty
pop-u-lar-ize
pop-u-lar-ized
pop-u-lar-iz-ing
pop-u-lar-i-za-tion
pop-u-lar-iz-er
pop-u-late

pop-u-lat-ed
pop-u-lat-ing
pop-u-la-tion
pop-u-lism
pop-u-list
pop-u-lous
pop-u-lous-ly
por-ce-lain
por-cine
por-cu-pine
pore
pored
por-ing
pork-er
por-nog-ra-phy
por-nog-ra-pher
por-no-graph-ic
por-no-graph-i-cal-ly
po-rous
po-rous-i-ty
po-rous-ly
po-rous-ness
por-poise
por-pios-es
por-ridge
port-a-ble
port-a-bil-i-ty
port-a-bly
por-tage
por-taged
por-tag-ing
por-tal
por-tend
por-tent
por-ten-tous
por-ter
por-ter-house
port-fo-lio
port-fo-lios
port-hole
por-ti-co
por-ti-coes
por-ti-cos
por-tion
por-tion-less
port-ly
port-li-er
port-li-est
por-trait
por-trat-ist
por-trai-ture
por-tray
por-tray-er

por-tray-al
pose
posed
pos-ing
pos-er
po-suer
pos-it
po-si-tion
po-si-tion-al
po-si-tion-er
pos-i-tive
pos-i-tive-ly
pos-i-tive-ness
pos-i-tiv-ism
pos-i-tron
pos-se
pos-sess
pos-ses-sor
pos-sessed
pos-ses-sion
pos-ses-sive
pos-ses-sive-ly
pos-ses-sive-ness
pos-si-bil-i-ty
pos-si-ble
pos-si-bly
pos-sum
post-age
post-box
post-date
post-dat-ed
post-dat-ing
post-er
pos-te-ri-or
pos-te-ri-or-i-ty
pos-ter-i-ty
post-grad-u-ate
post-haste
post-hu-mous
post-hu-mous-ly
post-lude
post-man
post-men
post-mark
post-mas-ter
post-mis-tress
post me-ri-di-em
post-mor-tem
post-na-sal
post-na-tal
post-na-tal-ly
post-paid
post-par-tum

post-pone
post-poned
post-pon-ing
post-pon-a-ble
post-pone-ment
post-pon-er
post-scipt
pos-tu-lant
pos-tu-late
pos-tu-lat-ed
pos-tu-lat-ing
pos-tu-la-tion
pos-tu-la-tor
pos-ture
pos-tured
pos-tur-ing
pos-tur-al
pos-tur-er
post-war
po-sy
po-sies
pot
pot-ted
pot-ting
po-ta-ble
pot-ash
po-tas-si-um
po-ta-to
po-ta-toes
pot-bel-ly
pot-bel-lied
pot-boil-er
po-tent
po-ten-cy
po-tent-ly
po-ten-tate
po-ten-tial
po-ten-ti-al-i-ty
po-ten-tial-ly
pot-hole
po-tion
pot-luck
pot-pour-ri
pot-sherd
pot-tage
pot-ter
pot-tery
pot-ter-ies
pot-ty
pot-ties
pot-ty--chair
pouch
pouched

pouchy
pouch-i-er
pouch-i-est
poul-tice
poul-ticed
poul-tic-ing
poul-try
pounce
pounced
pounc-ing
pound-age
pound--fool-ish
pour
pour-a-ble
pour-er
pout
pov-er-ty
pov-er-ty--strick-en
pow-der
pow-dery
pow-er
pow-er-boat
pow-er-ful
pow-er-ful-ly
pow-er-ful-ness
pow-er-house
pow-er-less
Pow-ha-tan
pow-wow
prac-ti-ca-ble
prac-ti-ca-bil-i-ty
prac-ti-ca-bly
prac-ti-cal
prac-ti-cal-i-ty
prac-ti-cal-ly
prac-tice
prac-ti-tio-ner
prae-di-al
pre-di-al
prag-mat-ic
prag-mat-i-cal
prag-mat-i-cal-ly
prag-ma-tism
prag-ma-tist
prag-ma-tis-tic
prai-rie
praise
praised
prais-ing
prais-er
praise-wor-thy
praise-wor-thi-ly
praise-wor-thi-ness

pra-line
prance
pranced
pranc-ing
pranc-er
prank
prank-ish
prank-ster
prate
prat-ed
prat-ing
prat-er
prat-ing-ly
prat-fall
prat-tle
prat-tled
prat-tling
prat-tler
prat-tling-ly
prawn
prawn-er
pray-er
pray-er-ful
preach
prach-er
preach-ify
preach-ified
preach-ify-ing
preach-ment
preachy
preach-i-er
preach-i-est
pre-ad-o-les-cence
pre-ad-o-les-cent
pre-am-ble
pre-ar-range
pre-ar-ranged
pre-ar-rang-ing
pre-ar-range-ment
pre-as-signed
pre-can-cel
pre-can-celed
pre-can-cel-ing
pre-can-cel-la-tion
pre-car-i-ous
pre-car-i-ous-ly
pre-car-i-ous-ness
pre-cau-tion
pre-cau-tion-ary
pre-cede
pre-ced-ed
pre-ced-ing
prec-e-dence

prec-e-dent
pre-cept
pre-cep-tive
pre-cep-tor
pre-cep-to-ri-al
pre-ces-sion
pre-ces-sion-al
pre-cinct
pre-cious
pre-ci-os-i-ty
pre-cious-ness
prec-i-pice
pre-cip-i-tous
pre-cip-i-tant
pre-cip-i-tant-ly
pre-cip-i-tate
pre-cip-i-tat-ed
pre-cip-i-tat-ing
pre-cip-i-ta-tive
pre-cip-i-ta-tor
pre-cip-i-ta-tion
pre-cip-i-tous
pre-cip-i-tous-ly
pre-cise
pre-cise-ness
pre-ci-sion
pre-ci-sion-ist
pre-clude
pre-clud-ed
pre-clud-ing
pre-clu-sion
pre-clu-sive
pre-co-cious
pre-coc-cious-ly
pre-coc-cious-ness
pre-coc-i-ty
pre-cog-ni-tion
pre-cog-ni-tive
pre-con-ceive
pre-con-ciev-ed
pre-con-ceiv-ing
pre-con-cep-tion
pre-cook
pre-cur-sor
pre-cur-so-ry
pre-date
pred-a-tor
pred-a-to-ry
pred-a-to-ri-ly
pre-dawn
pre-de-ces-sor
pre-des-ti-nate
pre-des-ti-nat-ed

pre-des-ti-nat-ing
pre-des-ti-na-tion
pre-des-tine
pre-des-tined
pre-des-tin-ing
pre-de-ter-mine
pre-de-ter-mined
pre-de-ter-min-ing
pre-de-ter-mi-na-tion
pred-i-ca-ble
pred-i-ca-bil-i-ty
pre-dic-a-ment
pred-i-cate
pred-i-cat-ed
pred-i-cat-ing
pred-i-ca-tion
pred-i-ca-tive
pre-dict
pre-dict-a-ble
pre-dict-a-bly
pre-dict-a-bil-i-ty
pre-dic-tion
pre-dic-tive
pre-di-lec-tion
pre-dis-po-si-tion
pre-dis-pose
pre-dis-posed
pre-dis-pos-ing
pre-dom-i-nant
pre-dom-i-nance
pre-dom-i-nan-cy
pre-dom-i-nate
pre-dom-i-nat-ed
pre-dom-i-nat-ing
pre-dom-i-na-tion
pre-em-i-nent
pre-em-i-nence
pre-empt
pre-emp-tor
pre-emp-tion
pre-emp-tive
preen-er
pre-ex-ist
pre-ex-ist-ence
pre-ex-ist-ent
pre-fab-ri-cate
pre-fab-ri-cat-ed
pre-fab-ri-cat-ing
pre-fab-ri-a-tion
pref-ace
pref-aced
pref-ac-ing
pref-a-to-ry

pre-fer
pre-ferred
pre-fer-ring
pre-fer-rer
pref-er-a-ble
pre-fer-a-bil-i-ty
pref-er-a-bly
pref-er-ence
pref-er-en-tial
pref-er-en-tial-ly
pre-fer-ment
pre-fix
pre-flight
pre-form
preg-n-able
preg-na-bil-i-ty
preg-nan-cy
preg-nan-cies
preg-nant
pre-heat
pre-hen-sile
pre-hen-sil-i-ty
pre-his-tor-ic
prej-u-dice
prej-u-diced
prej-u-dic-ing
prej-u-di-cial
prej-u-di-cial-ly
prel-ate
prel-ate-ship
prel-a-ture
pre-lim-i-nar-y
pre-lim-i-nar-ies
pre-lim-i-nar-i-ly
prel-ude
prel-uded
prel-ud-ing
pre-ma-ture
pre-na-tu-ri-ty
pre-med-i-cal
pre-med-i-tate
pre-med-i-tat-ed
pre-med-i-ta-tion
pre-men-stru-al
pre-mier
pre-mier-ship
pre-miere
prem-ise
prem-ised
prem-is-ing
pre-mi-um
pre-mo-ni-tion
pre-mon-i-to-ry

pre-mon-i-to-ri-ly
pre-na-tal
pre-na-tal-ly
pre-oc-cu-pa-tion
pre-oc-cu-py
pre-oc-cu-pied
pre-oc-cu-py-ing
prep-a-ra-tion
pre-par-a-to-ry
pre-par-a-to-ri-ly
pre-plan
pre-planned
pre-plan-ning
pre-pon-der-ant
pre-pon-der-ance
pre-pon-der-an-cy
pre-pon-der-ant-ly
pre-pon-der-ate
pre-pon-der-at-ed
pre-pon-der-at-ing
pre-pon-der-at-ing-ly
pre-pon-der-a-tion
prep-o-si-tion
prep-o-si-tion-al
pre-pos-sess
pre-pos-sess-ing
pre-pos-sess-ing-ly
pre-pos-ter-ous
pre-puce
pre-pu-tial
pre-re-cord
pre-re-ui-site
pre-rog-a-tive
pres-age
pres-aged
pres-ag-ing
pres-ag-er
pres-by-ter-y
pres-by-ter-ies
pre-school
pre-script
pre-scrip-tion
pre-scrip-tive
pre-sea-son
pres-ence
pre-sent
pre-sent-er
pres-ent
pre-sent-a-ble
pre-sent-a-bil-i-ty
pre-sent-a-ble-ness
pre-sent-a-bly
pres-en-ta-tion

159

pres-ent-day
pres-ent-ly
pre-serv-a-tive
per-serve
  pre-served
  pre-serv-ing
  pre-serv-a-ble
  pres-er-va-tion
  pre-serv-er
pre-side
  pre-sid-ed
  pre-sid-ing
  pre-sid-er
pres-i-den-cy
  pres-i-den-cies
pres-i-dent
  pres-i-den-tial
press-board
press-ing
pres-sure
  pres-sured
  pres-sur-ing
press-work
pres-ti-dig-i-ta-tion
  pres-ti-dig-i-ta-tor
pres-tige
pres-tig-ious
pres-to
pe-sum-a-ble
  pre-sum-a-bly
pre-sumption
pre-sump-tive
pre-sum-tu-ous
pre-sup-pose
  pre-sup-posed
  pre-sup-pos-ing
  pre-sup-po-si-tion
pre-tend
  pre-tend-ed
pre-tend-er
pre-tense
pre-ten-sion
pre-ten-tious
  pre-ten-tious-ness
pre-test
pre-text
pret-ti-fy
  pret-ti-fied
  pret-ti-fy-ing
  pret-ti-fi-ca-tion
pret-zel
pre-vail
  pre-vail-ing

prev-a-lent
  prev-a-lence
pre-vent
  pre-vent-a-ble
  pre-vent-a-bil-i-ty
  pre-vent-er
pre-ven-tion
pre-view
pre-vi-ous
pre-war
prey
  prey-er
price-less
prick-er
prick-le
prick-ly
  prick-li-er
  prick-li-est
  prick-li-ness
pride
  prid-ed
  prid-ing
pride-ful
pri-er
priest
  priest-ess
  priest-hood
pri-ma-cy
  pri-ma-cies
pri-ma don-na
  pri-ma don-nas
pri-mal
pri-ma-ri-ly
pri-ma-ry
  pri-mar-ies
pri-mate
prime
  primed
  prim-ing
prime me-rid-i-an
prim-er
pr-me-val
prim-i-tive
pri-mo-gen-i-tor
pri-mo-gen-i-ture
pri-mor-di-al
  pri-mor-di-al-ly
primp
prim-rose
prince-ly
  prince-li-er
  prince-li-est
prin-cess

prin-ci-pal
  prin-ci-pal-ly
prin-ci-pal-i-ty
  prin-ci-pal-i-ties
prin-ci-ple
  prin-ci-pled
print-a-ble
print-ing
print-out
pri-or
  pri-or-ate
pri-or-ess
pri-or-i-ty
  pri-or-i-ties
pri-or-y
  pri-or-ies
prism
  pris-mat-ic
  pris-mat-i-cal-ly
pris-on
pris-on-er
pris-tine
pri-va-cy
pri-vate
pri-va-tion
priv-et
priv-i-ledge
  priv-i-ledged
  priv-i-leg-ing
prize
  prized
prize-fight
prob-a-bil-i-ty
  prob-a-bil-i-ties
prob-a-ble
  prob-a-bly
pro-bate
  pro-bat-ed
  pro-bat-ing
pro-ba-tion
  pro-ba-tion-al
  pro-ba-tion-ary
pro-na-tion-er
pro-ba-tive
probe
  probed
  prob-ing
  prob-er
prob-lem
prob-lem-at-ic
  pro-lem-at-i-cal
pro-bos-cis
  pro-bos-cis-es

pro-bos-ci-des
pro-ce-dure
pro-ce-dur-al
pro-ce-dur-al-ly
pro-ceed
pro-ceed-ing
pro-ceeds
pro-ces-sion
pro-ces-sion-al
pro-claim
pro-claim-er
proc-la-ma-tion
pro-cliv-i-ty
pro-cliv-i-ties
pro-cre-ate
pro-cre-at-ed
pro-cre-at-ing
pro-cre-a-tion
proc-tor
proc-to-ri-al
proc-u-ra-tor
proc-u-ra-to-ri-al
proc-u-ra-tor-ship
pro-cure
pro-cured
pro-cur-ing
pro-cure-ment
prod-i-gal
prod-i-gal-i-ty
prod-i-gal-ly
pro-di-gious
pro-di-gious-ness
prod-i-gy
prod-i-gies
pro-duce
pro-duced
pro-duc-ing
pro-duc-er
prod-uct
pro-duc-tion
pro-duc-tive
pro-duc-tive-ness
pro-duc-tiv-i-ty
pro-fane
pro-faned
pro-fan-i-ty
pro-fess
pro-fessed
pro-fess-ed-ly
pro-fes-sion
pro-fes-sion-al
pro-fes-sion-al-ism
pro-fes-sion-al-ize

pro-fes-sion-al-ized
pro-fes-sion-al-iz-ing
pro-fes-sor
pro-fes-so-ri-al
pro-fes-sor-ship
prof-fer
prof-fer-er
pro-fi-cien-cy
pro-fi-cient
pro-file
pro-filed
pro-fil-ing
prof-it
prof-it-less
prof-it-able
prof-it-a-bil-i-ty
prof-it-ably
prof-i-teer
prof-li-gate
prof-li-ga-cy
pro-found
pro-fun-di-ty
pro-fun-di-ties
pro-fuse
pro-fu-sion
pro-gen-i-tor
prog-e-ny
prog-e-nies
pro-ges-ter-one
prog-no-sis
prog-no-ses
prog-nos-tic
pro-gram
prog-ress
pro-gres-sion
pro-gres-sive
pro-gres-siv-ism
pro-hib-it
pro-hi-bi-tion
pro-hi-bi-tion-ist
pro-hib-i-tive
pro-ject
pro-jec-tile
pro-jec-tion
pro-jec-tion-ist
pro-jec-tive
pro-jec-tive-ly
pro-jec-tiv-i-ty
pro-jec-tor
pro-le-tar-i-at
pro-le-tar-i-an
pro-lif-er-ate
pro-lif-er-at-ed

pro-lif-ic
pro-lif-i-ca-cy
pro-lix
pro-lix-i-ty
pro-logue
pro-logued
pro-logu-ing
pro-long
pro-lon-ga-tion
pro-long-er
prom-i-nence
prom-i-nent
prom-i-nent-ly
pro-mis-cu-ity
pro-mis-cu-i-ties
pro-mis-cu-ous
pro-mis-cu-ous-ly
prom-ise
prom-ised
prom-is-ing
prom-is-so-ry
prom-on-to-ry
prom-on-to-ries
pro-mot-er
pro-mo-tion
pro-mo-tive
pro-mul-gate
pro-mul-gat-ed
pro-mul-ga-tion
prone
prong
pro-noun
pro-nounce
pro-nounced
pro-nounce-ment
pron-to
pro-nun-ci-a-tion
proof
proof-read
prop
pro-pa-gan-da
pro-pa-gate
pro-pa-ga-tion
pro-pa-ga-tion-al
pro-pane
pro-pel
pro-pelled
pro-pel-ling
pro-pel-lant
pro-pel-ler
pro-pen-si-ty
pro-pen-si-ties
prop-er

161

proph-e-cy
proph-e-cies
proph-e-sy
proph-e-sied
proph-e-sy-ing
proph-et
pro-phet-ic
pro-phet-i-cal-ly
pro-phy-lax-is
pro-pin-qui-ty
pro-pi-ti-ate
pro-pi-ti-at-ed
pro-pi-ti-a-tion
pro-pi-tious
pro-pi-tious-ly
pro-po-nent
pro-por-tion
pro-por-tion-a-ble
pro-por-tion-a-bly
pro-por-tion-al
pro-por-tion-al-i-ty
pro-por-tion-ate
pro-por-tion-at-ed
pro-por-tion-at-ing
pro-pos-al
pro-pose
pro-posed
prop-o-si-tion
prop-o-si-tion-al
pro-pound
pro-pound-er
pro-pri-e-tary
pro-pri-e-tar-ies
pro-pri-etor
pro-pri-e-tor-ship
pro-pri-ety
pro-pul-sion
pro-pul-sive
pro-rate
pro-rat-ed
pro-sa-ic
pro-sa-i-cal-ly
pro-scrip-tion
pro-srip-tive
prose
pros-e-cute
pros-e-cute-a-ble
pros-e-cu-tion
pros-e-cu-tor
pros-pect
pros-pec-tor
pro-spec-tive
pro-spec-tus

pros-per-i-ty
pros-per-ous
pros-tate
pros-the-sis
pros-the-ses
pros-thet-ic
pros-thet-ics
pros-the-tis
prosth-odon-tics
prosth-odon-tist
pros-ti-tute
pros-trate
pros-trat-ing
pros-tra-tor
pros-tra-tive
pro-tag-o-nist
pro-te-an
pro-tect
pro-tect-ing
pro-tec-tive
pro-tec-tor
pro-tec-tion
pro-tec-tion-ism
pro-tec-tion-ist
pro-tec-tor-ate
pro-tein
pro-test
prot-es-ta-tion
pro-tist
pro-tis-tan
pro-to-col
pro-ton
pro-to-plasm
pro-to-plas-mic
pro-to-type
pro-to-typ-i-cal
pro-to-typ-ic
pro-to-typ-i-cal-ly
pro-to-zo-an
pro-to-zo-ic
pro-tract
pro-trac-tion
pro-trac-tive
pro-trac-tile
pro-trac-tor
pro-trude
pro-trud-ed
pro-trud-ing
pro-tru-sion
pro-tru-sive
pro-tu-ber-ance
pro-tu-ber-ant
proud

proud-ly
prov-erb
pro-ver-bi-al
pro-ver-bi-al-ly
prov-i-dence
prov-i-den-tial
prov-i-dent
prov-ince
pro-vin-cial
pro-vin-cial-ism
pro-vi-sion
pro-vi-sion-er
pro-vi-sion-al
pro-vi-sion-ary
prov-o-ca-tion
pro-voc-a-tive
pro-voc-a-tive-ly
pro-voc-a-tive-ness
pro-vost
prow-ess
prowl
prowl-er
prox-i-mal
prox-i-mate
prox-i-mate-ly
prox-im-i-ty
proxy
prox-ies
prude
pru-dence
pru-dent
pru-den-tial
prud-ish
prune
pruned
prun-ing
psalm-book
psalm-ist
pseu-do
pseud-onym
pseud-on-y-mous
pseu-do-preg-nan-cy
pseu-do-preg-nant
pseu-do-sci-ence
pseu-do-sci-en-tif-ic
pshaw
psil-o-cy-bin
pso-ri-a-sis
pso-ri-at-ic
psych
psyched
psych-ing
psy-che-del-ic

psy-chi-a-trist
psy-chi-a-try
  psy-chi-at-ric
  psy-chi-at-ri-cal-ly
psy-chic
  psy-chi-cal
  psy-chi-cal-ly
psy-cho
psy-cho-anal-y-sis
  psy-cho-an-a-lyt-ic
  psy-cho-an-a-lyt-i-cal
psy-cho-bi-ol-o-gy
  psy-cho-bi-o-log-ic
  psy-cho-bi-o-log-i-cal
psy-cho-dra-ma
psy-cho-dy-nam-ic
  psy-cho-dy-nam-ics
psy-cho-gen-e-sis
  psy-cho-ge-net-ic
psy-cho-gen-ic
  psy-cho-gen-i-cal-ly
psy-cho-log-i-cal
  psy-cho-log-ic
  psy-cho-log-i-cal-ly
psy-chol-o-gist
psy-chol-o-gy
psy-cho-mo-tor
psy-cho-neu-ro-sis
  psy-cho-neu-rot-ic
psy-cho-path
psy-cho-pa-thol-o-gy
  psy-cho-path-o-log-ic
psy-chop-a-thy
  psy-cho-path-ic
  psy-cho-path-i-cal-ly
psy-cho-ther-a-py
  psy-cho-ther-a-pist
pto-maine
pu-ber-ty
pu-bes-cence
  pu-bes-cen-cy
  pu-bes-cent
pu-bic
pub-lic
  pub-lic-ly
pub-li-ca-tion
pub-li-cist
pub-li-ci-ty
pub-li-cize
  pub-li-cized
  pub-li-ciz-ing
pub-lish
  pub-lish-a-ble

pub-lish-er
puce
puck-er
pud-ding
pud-dle
  pud-dled
  pud-dling
pueb-lo
  pueb-los
pu-er-ile
  pu-er-il-i-ty
puff
  puffy
puff-er
pu-gi-lism
  pu-gi-list
  pu-gi-lis-tic
pug-na-cious
  pug-nac-i-ty
pulke
  puked
  puk-ing
pull-back
pul-let
pul-ley
pul-mo-nary
pulp
pul-pit
pulp-wood
pul-sate
  pul-sat-ed
  pul-sat-ing
pul-sa-tion
pul-sa-tor
  pul-sa-to-ry
pulse
  pulsed
  puls-ing
pul-ver-ize
pu-ma
  pu-mas
pum-ice
  pu-mi-ceous
pum-mel
pum-per-nick-el
pump-kin
pun
  punned
  pun-ning
punch
  punch-er
punc-tu-al
punc-tu-ate

punc-tu-at-ed
punc-tu-at-ing
punc-tu-a-tor
punc-tu-a-tion
punc-ture
  punc-tured
  punc-tur-ing
pun-dit
pun-gent
  pun-gen-cy
  pun-gent-ly
pun-ish
  pun-ish-able
pun-ish-ment
pu-ni-tive
pun-ster
punt-er
pu-ny
  pu-ni-er
  pu-ni-est
pup
  pupped
  pup-ping
pu-pil
pep-pet-ry
  pup-pet-ries
pure
  pure-ly
pur-ga-tive
pur-ga-to-ry
  pur-ga-to-ries
  pur-ga-to-ri-al
purge
  purged
pu-ri-fy
pur-ism
  pur-ist
  pu-ris-tic
pu-ri-ty
purl
pur-loin
  pur-loin-er
pur-port
  pur-port-ed
  pur-port-ed-ly
pur-pose
  pur-posed
  pur-pos-ing
pur-pose-ly
pur-pos-ive
purse
  pursed
  purs-ing

Q

purs-er
pur-su-ant
pur-sue
 pur-sued
 pur-su-ing
pur-suit
pur-sy
pu-ru-lent
 pu-ru-lence
 pu-ru-len-cy
pur-vey
 pur-vey-or
pur-vey-ance
pur-view
pushy
pu-sil-lan-i-mous
 pu-sil-la-nim-i-ty
 pu-sal-lan-i-mous-ly
pus-sy
pussy-foot
pussy-wil-low
pus-tule
 pus-tu-lar
 pus-tu-late
pu-ta-tive
 pu-ta-tive-ly
put--on
pu-tre-fac-tion
pu-tre-fy
 pu-tre-fied
 pu-tre-fy-ing
pu-trid
 pu-trid-i-try
putt
 putt-ed
 putt-ing
putt-er
 put-ter-er
put--up
puz-zle
puz-zle-ment
py-lon
pyr-a-mid
 py-ra-mi-dal
pyre
py-ric
py-ro-ma-nia
 py-ro-ma-ni-ac
 py-ro-ma-ni-a-cal
py-ro-tech-nics
 py-ro-tech-nic
 py-ro-tech-ni-cal
py-thon

quack-ery
 quack-er-ies
quad-ran-gle
 quad-ran-gu-lar
quad-rant
 quad-ran-tal
quad-ra-phon-ic
quad-rate
 quad-rat-ed
 quad-rat-ing
qua-drat-ic
 qua-drat-i-cal-ly
qua-drat-ics
quad-ra-ture
quad-ri-lat-er-al
qua-drille
qua-dril-lion
 qua-dril-lionth
qua-droon
quad-ru-ped
 quad-ru-pe-dal
qua-dru-ple
 qua-dru-pled
 qua-dru-pling
qua-dru-plet
qua-dru-pli-cate
 qua-dru-pli-cat-ed
 qua-dru-pli-cat-ing
quaff
 quaff-er
quag-mire
 quag-mired
 quag-miry
quail
quaint
quake
qual-i-fi-ca-tion
qual-i-fied
 qual-i-fied-ly
qual-i-fy
 qual-i-fy-ing
 qual-i-fi-a-ble
 qual-i-fier
qual-i-ta-tive
qual-i-ty
 qual-i-ties
qualm
 qualm-ish
quan-da-ry
 quan-dar-ies
quan-ti-fy
 quan-ti-fy-ing
 quan-ti-fi-ca-tion

quan-ti-ta-tive
quan-ti-ty
 quan-ti-ties
quan-tum
 quan-ta
quar-an-tine
 quar-an-tin-able
quar-rel
 quar-reled
 quar-rel-ing
 quar-rel-er
quar-rel-some
quar-ri-er
quar-ry
 quar-ries
 quar-ried
 quar-ry-ing
quart
quar-ter
quar-ter-back
quar-ter-ing
quar-ter-ly
 quar-ter-lies
quar-ter-mas-ter
quar-tet
quartz
quash
qua-si
qua-ter-na-ry
qua-train
qua-ver
 quav-er-ing-ly
 qua-very
quay
quea-sy
 quea-si-er
 quea-si-est
 quea-si-ly
queen
quell
 quell-er
quench
 quench-able
 quench-er
que-ry
 que-ries
 que-ried
quest
ques-tion
 ques-tion-er
ques-tion-able
 ques-tion-ably
ques-tion-naire

queue
  queued
  queu-ing
quib-ble
quick
quick-en
  quick-en-er
quick--freeze
quick--wit-ted
  quick--wit-ted-ly
qui-es-cent
  qui-es-cence
qui-et
  qui-et-ly
  qui-et-ter
qui-e-tude
quill
quilt
  quilt-ing
quince
quin-til-lion
quin-tu-ple
  quin-tu-pled
  quin-tu-pling
quin-tu-plet
quip
  quipped
  quip-ping
quirk
  quirky
quis-ling
quit
  quit-ed
  quit-ing
quit-claim
quite
quit-er
quiv-er
quix-ot-ic
quiz
quiz-zi-cal
  quiz-zi-cal-ly
quoin
quoit
quon-dam
quo-rum
quo-ta
quot-able
  quot-a-bil-i-ty
quo-ta-tion
quote
quo-tid-i-an
quo-tient

R

rab-bet
  rab-bet-ted
  rab-bet-ting
rab-bi
  rab-bis
ra-bin-ate
rab-bin-i-cal
  rab-bin-i-al-ly
rab-bit
rab-ble
  rab-bled
  rab-bling
ra-bid
  ra-bid-ly
ra-bies
rac-coon
race-horse
ra-ceme
rac-er
ra-ce-ric
ra-ce-ri-za-tion
race-track
ra-chis
  ra-chis-es
  rach-i-des
ra-cial
  ra-cial-ism
  ra-cial-ly
rac-ism
  ra-cial-ism
  rac-ist
rack-et
rack-e-teer
ra-con-teur
racy
  rac-i-ly
ra-dar
ra-di-al
  ra-di-al-ly
ra-di-ance
  ra-di-an-cy
ra-di-ant
ra-di-ate
  ra-di-at-ed
  ra-di-at-ing
  ra-di-a-tion
  ra-di-a-tor
rad-i-cal
  rad-i-cal-ly
  rad-i-cal-ism
ra-dio
ra-dio-ac-tive
  ra-dio-ac-tive-i-ty

ra-dio-gram
ra-dio-graph
  ra-diog-ra-phy
ra-di-ol-o-gy
  ra-di-ol-o-gist
rad-ish
ra-di-um
ra-di-us
  ra-dii
  ra-di-us-es
ra-don
raf-fia
raf-fi-nose
raff-ish
raf-fle
  raf-fled
  raf-fling
raft
raft-er
rag
  rag-ged
rag-gle
rail-ing
rail-lery
  rail-ler-ies
rail-road
  rail-road-er
  rail-road-ing
rail-way
rai-ment
rain-bow
rain-fall
rainy
raise
  raised
rai-sin
rake
  raked
  rak-ing
rake--off
rak-ish
  rak-ish-ly
ral-li-form
ral-ly
  ral-lied
ram
  rammed
ram-ble
  ram-bled
  ram-bling
ram-bler
ram-bunc-tious
ram-bu-tan

165

ram-i-fi-ca-tion
ram-i-fy
  ram-i-fied
  ram-i-fy-ing
ram-page
  ram-paged
  ram-pag-ing
ram-pan-cy
ram-pant
  ram-pant-ly
ram-part
ram-rod
ram-shack-le
ranch-er
ran-cid
  ran-cid-i-ty
ran-cor
  ran-cor-ous
ran-dom
  ran-dom-ly
range
  ranged
  rang-ing
rang-er
rangy
  rang-i-er
  rang-i-est
ran-sack
rant-er
ran-u-la
rape
  rap-ist
ra-phe
raph-ide
rap-id
ra-pi-er
rap-ine
rap-pel
rap-proche-ment
rap-scal-lion
rap-to-ri-al
rap-ture
  rap-tur-ous
rare
  rar-er
  rar-est
rare-bit
rar-efy
  rar-efied
  rar-efy-ing
rare-ly
rar-i-ty
  rar-i-ties

rash
ra-so-ri-al
rasp
rasp-ber-ry
rat-able
ratch-et
rate
  rat-ed
  rat-ing
rath-er
rat-icide
rat-i-fy
  rat-i-fi-ca-tion
ra-tio
  ra-tios
ra-ti-o-ci-na-tion
ra-tion
ra-tio-nal
  ra-tio-nal-i-ty
  ra-tio-nal-ly
ra-tion-able
ra-tio-nal-ism
ra-tio-nal-ize
  ra-tio-nal-iz-ing
  ra-tio-nal-i-za-tion
rat-line
rat-tan
rat-tle
  rat-tled
  rat-tling
rat-tle-snake
rat-ty
  rat-ti-er
  rat-ti-est
rau-cous
  rau-cous-ly
rav-age
  rav-aged
rave
rav-el
ra-ven
rav-en-ous
  rav-en-ous-ly
ra-vine
rav-i-o-li
rav-ish
  rav-ish-ment
rav-ish-ing
raw
raw-hide
ray-on
raze
  razed

  raz-ing
ra-zor
raz-zle--daz-zle
re-act
  re-ac-tive
re-ac-tion
re-ac-tion-ary
  re-ac-tion-ar-ies
re-ac-ti-vate
  re-ac-ti-vat-ed
  re-ac-ti-vat-ing
re-ac-tor
read-able
read-er
read-ing
re-ad-just
  re-ad-just-ment
ready--made
re-agent
re-al
re-al-ism
  re-al-ist
  re-al-is-tic
  re-al-is-ti-cal-ly
re-al-ly
realm
Re-al-tor
re-al-ty
ream-er
re-an-i-mate
  re-an-i-mat-ed
  re-an-i-mat-ing
  re-an-i-ma-tion
reap-er
re-ap-pear
  re-ap-pear-ance
re-ap-por-tion
  re-ap-por-tion-ment
rear ad-mir-ral
re-arm
  re-ar-ma-ment
re-ar-range
  re-ar-ranged
  re-ar-rang-ing
  re-ar-range-ment
rear-ward
rea-son
  rea-son-er
rea-son-able
  rea-son-abil-i-ty
  rea-son-able-ness
  rea-son-ably
rea-son-ing

re-as-sem-ble
  re-as-sem-bled
  re-as-sem-bling
  re-as-sem-bly
re-as-sume
  re-as-sump-tion
re-as-sure
  re-as-sured
  re-as-sur-ing
  re-as-sur-ance
  re-as-sur-ing-ly
re-bate
  re-bat-ed
  re-bat-ing
  re-bat-er
reb-el
re-bel
  re-belled
  re-bel-ling
re-bel-lion
re-bel-lious
  re-bel-lious-ly
re-birth
re-born
re-bound
re-buff
re-build
  re-built
  re-build-ing
re-buke
re-bus
  re-bus-es
re-but
re-but-tal
re-cal-ci-trant
  re-cal-ci-trance
  re-cal-ci-tran-cy
re-call
re-cant
  re-can-ta-tion
re-ca-pit-u-late
re-cap-ture
  re-cap-tured
re-cede
  re-ced-ed
  re-ced-ing
re-ceipt
re-ceiv-able
re-ceive
  re-ceiv-ed
  re-ceiv-ing
re-ceiv-er
re-ceiv-er-ship

re-cent
  re-cent-ly
  re-cen-cy
re-cep-ta-cle
re-cep-tion
  re-cep-tion-ist
re-cep-tive
re-cess
re-ces-sion
  re-ces-sion-ary
re-ces-sion-al
re-ces-sive
re-charge
  re-charg-ed
  re-charg-ing
rec-i-pe
re-cip-i-ent
  re-cip-i-ence
  re-cip-i-en-cy
re-cip-ro-cal
  re-cip-ro-cal-ly
re-cip-ro-cate
rec-i-proc-i-ty
rec-it-al
rec-i-ta-tion
rec-i-ta-tive
re-cite
  re-cited
  re-cit-ing
reck-less
  reck-less-ly
reck-on
re-claim
rec-la-ma-tion
re-cline
  re-clined
rec-luse
rec-og-ni-tion
re-cog-ni-zance
rec-og-nize
  rec-og-nized
  rec-og-niz-ing
  rec-og-niz-a-ble
re-coil
  re-coil-less
re-col-lect
re-col-lect
  re-col-lec-tion
rec-om-mend
  rec-om-mend-able
  rec-om-mend-er
rec-om-men-da-tion
rec-om-pense

rec-om-pensed
rec-om-pens-ing
rec-on-cile
  rec-on-ciled
rec-con-dite
re-con-di-tion
re-con-firm
re-con-nais-sance
re-con-noi-ter
  re-con-noi-tered
  re-con-noi-ter-ing
re-con-sid-er
  re-con-sid-er-a-tion
re-con-struct
re-con-struc-tion
re-cord
re-cord-er
re-count
re-coup
re-course
re-cov-er
re-cov-ery
  re-cov-er-ies
rec-re-ant
re-cre-ate
  re-cre-at-ed
  re-cre-at-ing
  re-cre-a-tion
rec-re-ation
  rec-re-ation-al
re-crim-i-nate
  re-crim-i-nat-ed
  re-crim-i-nat-ing
re-cruit
  re-cruit-er
  re-cruit-ment
rec-tal
rect-an-gle
rect-an-gu-lar
rec-ti-fi-er
rec-ti-fy
  rec-ti-fied
  rec-ti-fy-ing
  rec-ti-fi-ca-tion
rec-ti-lin-ear
rec-ti-tude
rec-tor
rec-to-ry
  rec-to-ries
rec-tum
  rec-tums
rec-ta
re-cum-bent

re-cum-ben-cy
re-cum-bent-ly
re-cu-per-ate
re-cur
  re-cur-ring
  re-cur-rence
re-cur-rent
red-bird
red--blood-ed
re-dec-o-rate
  re-dec-o-rat-ed
  re-dec-o-ra-tion
re-ded-i-cate
  re-ded-i-cat-ed
  re-ded-i-ca-tion
re-deem
  re-deem-able
re-deem-er
re-demp-tion
  re-demp-tive
red--hand-ed
red--hot
re-di-rect
  re-di-rec-tion
red--let-ter
red--neck
re-do
red-o-lence
red-o-len-cy
red-o-lent
re-dou-ble
  re-dou-bled
  re-dou-bling
re-doubt-able
  re-doubt-ably
re-dound
re-dress
red-start
re-duce
re-duc-tion
re-dun-dance
re-dun-dant
re-du-pli-cate
  re-du-pli-cat-ed
  re-du-pli-ca-tion
red-wood
re-echo
  re-ech-oed
reedy
  reed-i-er
reef-er
re-elect
  re-elec-tion

re-em-pha-sie
  re-em-pha-sized
  re-em-pha-siz-ing
re-en-force
  re-en-forced
  re-en-forc-ing
  re-en-force-ment
re-en-list
  re-en-list-ment
re-en-ter
  re-en-trance
re-en-try
  re-en-tries
re-es-tab-lish
  re-es-tab-lish-ment
re-ex-am-ine
  re-ex-am-i-na-tion
re-fec-to-ry
  re-fec-to-ries
re-fer
  re-fer-ral
ref-er-ee
ref-er-ence
  ref-er-enced
  ref-er-enc-ing
ref-er-en-dum
  ref-er-en-dums
  ref-er-en-da
ref-er-ent
re-fill
  re-fill-able
re-fine
  re-fined
  re-fin-ing
re-fine-ment
re-fin-ery
  re-fin-er-ies
re-fin-ish
re-fit
  re-fit-ted
  re-fit-ting
re-flect
re-flec-tion
re-flec-tive
  re-flec-tive-ly
  re-flec-tive-ness
re-flec-tor
re-flex
re-flex-ive
re-for-est
  re-for-est-a-tion
re-form
re-form-a-tory

re-fract
  re-frac-tive
re-frac-tion
re-frac-to-ry
  re-frac-to-ri-ly
re-frain
re-fresh
  re-fresh-ing
re-fresh-ment
re-frig-er-ant
  re-frig-er-ate
  re-frig-er-at-ed
re-frig-er-a-tor
re-fu-el
ref-uge
ref-u-gee
re-ful-gence
re-ful-gent
re-fund
re-fur-bish
re-fus-al
re-fuse
  re-fused
  re-fus-ing
ref-use
re-fute
re-gain
re-gal
  re-gal-ly
re-gale
  re-galed
  re-gal-ing
re-ga-lia
re-gard
re-gard-ful
re-gard-ing
re-gard-less
  re-gard-less-ly
re-gat-ta
re-gen-cy
  re-gen-cies
re-gen-er-ate
  re-gen-er-at-ed
  re-gen-er-at-ing
  re-gen-er-a-vy
  re-gen-er-a-tion
  re-gen-er-a-tive
re-gent
re-grime
reg-i-men
reg-i-ment
  reg-i-men-tal
  reg-i-men-ta-tion

re-gion
re-gion-al
  re-gion-al-ly
reg-is-ter
  reg-is-tered
  reg-is-trant
reg-is-trar
reg-is-tra-tion
reg-is-try
  reg-is-tries
re-gress
  re-gres-sion
  re-gres-sor
re-gret
  re-gret-ted
  re-gret-ting
  re-gret-ta-ble
  re-gret-ta-bly
  re-gret-er
  re-gret-ful
  re-gret-ful-ly
reg-u-lar
  reg-u-lar-i-ty
reg-u-late
  reg-u-lat-ed
  reg-u-lat-ing
  reg-u-la-tive
  reg-u-la-tor
  reg-u-la-to-ry
reg-u-la-tion
re-gur-gi-tate
  re-gur-gi-tat-ed
  re-gur-gi-tat-ing
  re-gur-gi-ta-tion
re-ha-bil-i-tate
  re-ha-bil-i-tat-ed
  re-ha-bil-i-tat-ing
  re-ha-bil-i-ta-tion
  re-ha-bil-i-ta-tive
re-hash
re-hears-al
re-hearse
  re-hearsed
  re-hears-ing
  re-hears-er
reign
re-im-burse
  re-im-bursed
  re-im-burs-ing
  re-im-burse-meny
rein
re-in-car-na-tion
rein-deer

re-in-force
  re-in-forced
  re-in-forc-ing
re-in-force-ment
re-in-state
  re-in-stat-ed
  re-in-stat-ing
  re-in-state-ment
re-it-er-ate
  re-it-er-at-ed
  re-it-er-at-ing
  re-it-er-a-tion
re-ject
  re-jec-tion
re-joice
  re-joiced
  re-joic-ing
  re-joic-er
  re-joic-ing-ly
re-join
re-join-der
re-ju-ve-nate
  re-ju-ve-nat-ed
  re-ju-ve-nat-ing
  re-ju-ve-na-tion
  re-ju-ve-na-tor
re-kin-dle
  re-kin-dled
  re-kin-dling
re-lapse
  re-lapsed
  re-laps-ing
  re-laps-er
re-late
  re-lat-ed
  re-lat-ing
  re-lat-er
  re-lat-or
re-la-tion
  re-la-tion-al
re-la-tion-ship
rel-a-tive
  rel-a-tive-ly
rel-a-tiv-ism
  rel-a-tiv-ist
rel-a-tiv-is-tic
rel-a-tiv-i-ty
rel-a-tiv-ize
re-la-tor
re-lax
  re-lax-er
re-lax-ation
re-lay

re-laid
re-lay-ing
re-lay
  re-layed
  re-lay-ing
re-lease
  re-leas-ed
  re-leas-ing
  re-leas-a-ble
  re-leas-er
rel-e-gate
  rel-e-gat-ed
  rel-e-ga-tion
re-lent
re-lent-less
rel-e-vant
  rel-e-vance
  rel-e-van-cy
  rel-e-vant-ly
re-li-able
  re-li-abil-i-ty
  re-li-able-ness
  re-li-ably
re-li-ance
  re-li-ant
rel-ic
re-lief
re-leive
  re-liev-ed
  re-liev-ing
  re-liev-able
  re-liev-er
re-li-gion
re-li-gi-os-i-ty
re-li-gious
re-lin-quish
rel-ish
re-live
  re-lived
  re-liv-ing
re-lo-cate
  re-lo-ct-ed
  re-lo-cat-ing
  re-lo-ca-tion
re-luc-tance
  re-luc-tant
re-ly
  re-lied
  re-ly-ing
re-main
re-main-der
re-mand
re-mark

re-mark-able
  re-mark-able-ness
  re-mark-ably
re-me-di-a-ble
re-me-di-al
rem-e-dy
  rem-e-dies
  rem-e-died
  rem-e-dy-ing
re-mem-ber
re-mem-brance
re-mind
  re-mind-er
re-mind-ful
rem-i-nisce
  rem-i-nisced
  rem-i-nisc-ing
rem-i-nis-cence
rem-i-nis-cent
re-miss
re-mis-sion
re-mit
  re-mit-ted
  re-mit-ting
re-mit-tance
rem-nant
re-mod-el
re-mon-strance
re-mon-strate
  re-mon-strat-ed
  re-mon-strat-ing
re-morse
  re-morse-ful
  re-morse-ful-ly
  re-morse-less
re-mote
  re-mot-er
  re-mot-est
re-mount
re-mov-able
re-mov-al
re-move
  re-moved
  re-mov-ing
re-mu-ner-ate
  re-mu-ner-at-ed
  re-mu-ner-at-ing
  re-mu-ner-a-tion
re-nais-sance
re-na-scence
  re-na-scent
rend
rend-er

ren-dez-vous
  ren-dez-voused
  ren-dez-vous-ing
ren-di-tion
ren-e-gade
re-nege
  re-neged
  re-neg-ing
re-new
re-new-al
ren-net
re-nounce
  re-nounced
  re-nounc-ing
ren-o-vate
  ren-o-vat-ed
  ren-o-vat-ing
  ren-o-va-tion
re-nown
  re-nowned
rent-al
re-nun-ci-a-tion
re-or-ga-ni-za-tion
re-or-ga-nize
  re-or-ga-niz-ed
  re-or-gan-iz-ing
re-pair
re-pair-man
  re-pair-men
rep-a-ra-ble
rep-a-ra-tion
rep-ar-tee
re-pa-tri-ate
  re-pa-tri-at-ed
re-pay
  re-paid
  re-pay-ing
  re-pay-ment
re-peal
re-peat
  re-peat-able
  re-peat-ed
  re-peat-er
re-pel
  re-pelled
  re-pel-ling
re-pel-lent
re-pent
  re-pent-ance
  re-pen-tant
re-per-cus-sion
rep-er-toire
rep-er-to-ry

rep-er-to-ries
rep-e-ti-tion
  rep-e-ti-tious
re-pet-i-tive
re-place
  re-placed
  re-plac-ing
  re-plac-able
re-place-ment
re-plen-ish
re-plete
  re-ple-tion
rep-li-ca
re-ply
  re-plied
  re-ply-ing
  re-plies
re-port
re-port-ed-ly
re-port-er
  rep-or-to-ri-al
re-pose
  re-posed
  re-pos-ing
  re-pose-ful
re-pos-i-to-ry
  re-pos-i-tor-ies
re-pos-sess
  re-pos-ses-sion
rep-re-hend
rep-re-hen-si-ble
rep-re-sent
rep-re-sen-ta-tion
rep-re-sen-ta-tive
re-press
  re-pres-sion
re-prieve
  re-prieved
  re-priev-ing
rep-ri-mand
re-print
re-pris-al
re-proach
re-proach-ful
rep-ro-bate
rep-ro-ba-tion
re-pro-duce
  re-pro-duced
  re-pro-duc-ing
re-pro-duc-tion
re-pro-duc-tive
re-proof
re-prove

re-proved
re-prov-ing
rep-tile
rep-til-ian
re-pub-lic
re-pub-li-can
re-pub-li-can-ism
re-pu-di-ate
re-pu-di-at-ed
re-pu-di-at-ing
re-pu-di-a-tion
re-pu-di-a-tion-ist
re-pugn
re-pug-nan-cy
re-pug-nant
re-pulse
re-pulsed
re-puls-ing
re-pul-sion
re-pul-sive
rep-u-ta-ble
rep-u-ta-bly
rep-u-ta-bil-i-ty
rep-u-ta-tion
re-pute
re-put-ed
re-put-ing
re-put-ed-ly
re-quest
re-qui-em
re-quire
re-quired
re-quir-ing
re-quire-ment
req-ui-site
re-quit-al
re-quite
re-quit-ed
re-quit-ing
re-run
re-run-ning
re-sale
re-scind
res-cue
res-cued
res-cu-ing
res-cu-er
re-search
re-search-er
re-sem-blance
re-sem-ble
re-sem-bled
re-sem-bling

re-sent
re-sent-ful
re-sent-ment
re-ser-va-tion
re-serve
re-served
re-serv-ing
re-serv-ist
res-er-voir
re-set
re-set-ting
re-side
re-sid-ed
re-sid-ing
res-i-dence
res-i-den-cy
res-i-den-cies
res-i-dent
res-i-den-tial
re-sid-u-al
res-i-due
re-sign
res-ig-na-tion
re-signed
re-sil-ient
re-sil-ience
re-sil-ien-cy
res-in
res-in-ous
re-sist
re-sist-er
re-sist-ible
re-sist-ance
re-sis-tant
re-sist-less
re-sis-tor
res-o-lute
res-o-lu-tion
re-solve
re-solved
re-solv-ing
res-o-nance
res-o-nant
res-o-nate
res-o-nat-ed
res-o-nat-ing
res-o-na-tor
re-sort
re-sound
re-sound-ing
re-source
re-source-ful
re-spect

re-spect-ful
re-spect-ful-ly
re-spect-able
re-spect-a-bil-i-ty
re-spect-ing
re-spec-tive
re-spec-tive-ly
res-pi-ra-tion
res-pi-ra-to-ry
res-pi-ra-tor
re-spire
re-spired
re-spir-ing
re-spite
re-splend-ant
re-splend-ence
re-spond
re-spon-dent
re-sponse
re-spon-si-bil-i-ty
re-spon-si-bil-i-ties
re-spon-si-ble
re-spon-sive
res-tau-rant
rest-ful
res-ti-tu-tion
res-tive
rest-less
res-to-ra-tion
re-stor-a-tive
re-store
re-stored
re-stor-ing
re-strain
re-straint
re-strict
re-strict-ed
re-strict-ed-ly
re-stric-tion
re-stric-tive
re-sult
re-sul-tant
re-sume
re-sumed
re-sum-ing
re-sump-tion
re-sur-gence
re-sur-gent
res-ur-rect
res-ur-rec-tion
re-sus-ci-tate
re-sus-ci-tat-ed
re-sus-ci-tat-ing

re-sus-ci-ta-tion
re-sus-ci-ta-tor
re-tail
  re-tail-er
re-tain
re-tainer
re-take
  re-took
  re-tak-en
  re-tak-ing
re-tal-i-ate
  re-tal-i-at-ed
  re-tal-i-at-ing
  re-tal-i-a-tion
re-tard
  re-tard-ant
re-tar-da-tion
re-tard-ed
re-ten-tion
re-ten-tive
ret-i-cence
ret-i-cent
ret-i-nue
re-tire
  re-tired
  re-tir-ing
re-tire-ment
re-tool
re-tort
re-touch
re-trace
  re-traced
  re-trac-ing
re-tract
  re-trac-tion
  re-trac-tor
re-trac-tile
re-tread
re-treat
re-trench
  re-trench-ment
re-tri-al
ret-ri-bu-tion
re-trieve
  re-trieved
  re-triev-ing
re-triev-er
ret-ro-ac-tive
ret-ro-grade
  ret-ro-grad-ed
  ret-ro-grad-ing
ret-ro-gress
  ret-ro-gees-sion

ret-ro-ges-sive
ret-ro--rock-et
ret-ro-spect
  ret-ro-spec-tion
  ret-ro-spec-tive
re-turn
re-turn-able
re-turn-ee
re-union
re-unite
  re-unit-ed
  re-unit-ing
rev
  rev-ved
  rev-ving
re-vamp
re-veal
rev-eil-le
rev-el
  rev-el-er
rev-e-la-tion
rev-el-ry
  rev-el-ries
re-venge
  re-venged
  re-veng-ing
re-venge-ful
rev-e-nue
rev-e-nu-er
re-ver-ber-ate
  re-ver-ber-at-ed
  re-ver-ber-at-ing
  re-ver-ber-a-tion
re-vere
  re-vered
  re-ver-ing
rev-er-ence
  rev-er-enced
  rev-er-enc-ing
rev-er-end
rev-er-ent
rev-er-en-tial
rev-er-ie
re-ver-sal
re-verse
  re-versed
  re-vers-ing
re-vers-i-ble
re-ver-sion
re-vert
re-view
re-view-er
re-vile

re-viled
re-vil-ing
re-vise
  re-vised
  re-vis-ing
re-vi-sion
re-vi-sion-ist
  re-vi-sion-ism
re-viv-al
re-viv-al-ist
re-vive
  re-vived
  re-viv-ing
rev-o-ca-ble
rev-o-ca-tion
re-voke
  re-voked
  re-vok-ing
re-volt
rev-o-lu-tion
  rev-o-lu-tion-ary
  rev-o-lu-tion-ar-ies
rev-o-lu-tion-ist
rev-o-lu-tion-ize
  rev-o-lu-tion-ized
  rev-o-lu-tion-iz-ing
re-volve
  re-volved
  re-volv-ing
re-volv-er
re-vue
re-vul-sion
re-write
  re-wrote
  re-writ-ten
  re-writ-ting
rhap-sod-ic
  rhap-sod-i-cal
  rhap-sod-i-cal-ly
rhap-so-dize
  rhap-so-dized
  rhap-so-diz-ing
rhap-so-dy
  rhap-so-dies
  rhap-so-dist
rhea
rhe-ni-um
rheo-stat
rhe-tor
rhet-o-ric
rhe-tor-i-cal
rhet-o-ri-cian
rheum

rheu-mat-ic
  rheu-mat-i-cal-ly
rheu-ma-tism
rhine-stone
rhi-no
rhi-noc-er-os
  rhi-noc-er-os-es
rhi-zome
rho-di-um
rho-do-den-dron
rhom-bic
rhom-boid
  rhom-boi-dal
rhom-bus
  rhom-bus-es
  rhom-bi
rhu-barb
rhyme
  rhymed
  rhym-ing
rhyme-ster
rhythm
  rhyth-mic
  rhyth-mi-cal
  rhyth-mi-cal-ly
rib
  ribbed
  rib-bing
rib-ald
  rib-ald-ry
  rib-ald-ries
rib-bon
ri-bo-fla-vin
rib-bo-nu-cle-ase
rice
  riced
  ric-ing
rich-es
rich-less
rick-ets
rick-ety
  rick-et-i-er
  rick-et-i-est
rick-shaw
ric-o-chet
rid
  rid-ded
  rid-ding
rid-dance
rid-dle
  rid-dled
  rid-dling
ride

rid-den
rid-ding
ride-er
ridge
  ridged
  ridg-ing
ridge-pole
rid-i-cule
  rid-i-culed
  rid-i-cul-ing
ri-dic-u-lous
rif-fle
  rif-fled
  rif-fling
riff-raff
rig
  rigged
  rig-ging
rig-ger
righ-teous
right-ful
right-hand
right--hand-ed
right-ism
rig-id
  ri-gid-i-ty
rig-ma-role
rig-or
rig-or-ous
rile
  riled
  ril-ing
rim
rime
ring-er
ring-lead-er
ring-let
ring-mas-ter
ring-worm
rinse
  rinsed
  rins-ing
ri-ot-ous
rip
  ripped
  rip-ping
  rip-per
ri-par-i-an
rip-en
rip--off
rip-ple
  rip-pled
  rip-pling

rip-saw
rip-tide
rise
  rose
  ris-en
  ris-ing
ris-er
ris-i-ble
  ris-i-bil-i-ty
rit-u-al
rit-u-al-ism
  rit-u-al-ist
  rit-u-al-is-tic
  rit-u-al-is-ti-cal-ly
ritzy
  ritz-i-er
  ritz-i-est
ri-val
ri-val-ry
  ri-val-ries
riv-er
riv-er-side
riv-et
  riv-et-er
riv-i-era
riv-u-let
roach
road-ster
road-way
roast-er
rob
  robbed
  rob-bing
  rob-ber
rob-bery
  rob-ber-ies
robe
  robed
  rob-ing
rob-in
ro-bot
ro-bust
rock-er
rock-et
rock-et-ry
rocky
  rock-i-er
  rock-i-est
ro-co-co
ro-dent
ro-deo
  ro-de-os
roe-buck

roent-gen
rog-er
roque
  ro-guish
  ro-guish-ly
roqu-ery
  roqu-er-ies
roist-er
roll-er
roll-er bear-ing
roll-er coast-er
roll-er skate
rol-lick
  rol-lick-ing
roll-ing pin
ro-ly--po-ly
  ro-ly--po-lies
ro-maine
ro-mance
  ro-manced
  ro-manc-ing
ro-man-tic
ro-man-ti-cism
ro-man-ti-cize
  ro-man-ti-ciz-ing
romp-er
roof-ing
rook-ery
  rook-er-ies
rook-ie
room-er
room-ful
room-mate
roomy
  room-i-er
  room-i-est
  room-i-ly
  room-i-ness
roos-ter
root-stock
rope
  roped
  rop-ing
ropy
  rop-i-er
  rop-i-est
ro-sa-ry
  ro-sa-ries
ro-se-ate
rose-bud
rose--col-ored
rose-mary
  rose-mar-ies

ro-sette
ros-in
ros-ter
ros-trum
  ros-tra
  ros-trums
ro-ta-ry
  ro-tar-ies
ro-tate
  ro-tat-ed
  ro-tat-ing
ro-ta-tion
ro-tis-ser-ie
ro-tor
rot-ten
ro-tund
  ro-tun-di-ty
  ro-tun-di-ties
ro-tun-da
rouge
  rouged
  roug-ing
rough-age
rough--and--tumble
rough-en
rough-house
rough-neck
rough-shod
rou-lette
round-er
round-ish
round-up
rouse
  roused
  rous-ing
  rous-er
roust
roust-a-bout
rout
route
  rout-ed
  rout-ing
rout-er
rou-tine
rou-tin-ize
  rou-tin-ized
  rou-tin-iz-ing
row-boat
row-dy
  row-dies
  row-di-er
  row-di-est
roy-al-ist

roy-al-ty
  roy-al-ties
rub-ber
  rub-bery
rub-ber-ize
  rub-ber-ized
  rub-ber-iz-ing
rub-ber-neck
rub-bish
  rub-bish-ly
rub-ble
  rub-bly
  rub-bli-er
  rub-bli-est
rub-down
ru-bel-la
ru-be-o-la
ru-bi-cund
ru-bid-i-um
ru-bric
ru-by
  ru-bies
ruck-sack
ruck-us
rud-der
rud-dy
  rud-di-er
  rud-di-est
  rud-di-ly
rude
ru-di-ment
  ru-di-ment-al
  ru-di-men-ta-ry
rue-ful
  rue-ful-ly
ruff
  ruffed
ruf-fi-an
ruf-fle
  ruf-fled
  ruf-fling
rug-ged
  rug-ged-ly
  rug-ged-ness
ru-in
ru-in-ation
ru-in-ous
rule
  ruled
  rul-ing
rul-er
rum-ba
  rum-baed

rum-ba-ing
ru-mi-nant
rum-mage
rum-maged
rum-mag-ing
rum-mag-er
rum-my
rum-mies
ru-mor
ru-mor-mon-ger
rum-ple
rum-pled
rum-pling
rum-pus
run
run-ning
run-about
run-around
run-away
run-ner
run-ner--up
run-ny
run-ni-er
run-ni-est
run-off
run--on
run--through
run-way
rup-ture
rup-tured
rup-tur-ing
ru-ral
rus-tic
rus-ti-cate
rus-ti-cat-ed
rus-ti-cat-ing
rus-ti-ca-tion
rus-tle
rus-tled
rus-tling
rus-tler
rust-proof
rus-ty
rust-i-er
rust-i-est
rut
rut-ted
rut-ting
ru-ta-ba-ga
ru-the-ni-um
ruth-less
ruth-less-ly
rut-ty

S

sa-ber
sa-ber-toothed ti-ger
sa-ble
sab-o-tage
sab-o-taged
sab-o-tag-ing
sab-o-teur
sa-bra
sac-cha-rin
sac-er-do-tal
sa-chet
sack-cloth
sack-ful
sack-fuls
sack-ing
sac-ra-ment
sac-ra-men-tal
sa-cred
sa-cred-ly
sa-cred-ness
sac-ri-fice
sac-ri-ficed
sac-ri-fic-ing
sac-ri-fic-er
sac-ri-fi-cial
sac-ri-lege
sac-ri-le-gious
sc-ro-il-li-ac
sac-ro-sanct
sac-ro-sanc-i-ty
sac-rum
sac-rums
sac-ra
sa-cral
sad-den
sad-dle
sad-dled
sad-dling
sad-dle-backed
sad-dle-bag
sad-ism
sad-ist
sa-dis-tic
sad-o-mas-o-chism
sad-o-mas-o-chist
sa-fa-ri
sa-fa-ris
safe
saf-er
saf-est
safe--con-duct
safe-crack-er
safe-crack-ing

safe--de-pos-it
safe-guard
safe-keep-ing
safe-ty
safe-ties
safe-ty match
safe-ty pin
safe-ty valve
safe-ty zone
saf-flow-er
sag
sagged
sag-ging
sa-ga
sa-ga-cious
sa-gac-i-ty
sage
sag-er
sag-est
sage-brush
sail-er
sail-fish
sail-ing
sail-or
saint
saint-hood
saint-ed
saint-ly
saint-li-er
saint-li-est
sa-ke
sal-a-ble
sal-a-ble
sal-a-bil-i-ty
sal-a-bly
sa-la-cious
sal-ad
sal-a-man-der
sa-la-mi
sal-a-ry
sal-a-ries
sales-man
sales-men
sales-man-ship
sales-per-son
sales-peo-ple
sales-room
sa-li-ent
sa-li-ence
sa-li-en-cy
sa-li-ent-ly
sa-line
sa-lin-i-ty

sa-li-va
 sal-i-vary
sal-low
 sal-low-ish
salm-on
sa-lon
sa-loon
salt-cel-lar
sal-tine
salt-shak-er
salt-wa-ter
salt-wort
salt-y
 salt-i-er
 salt-i-est
 salt-i-ness
sa-lu-bri-ous
sal-u-tar-y
sal-u-ta-tion
sa-lu-ta-to-ry
 sa-lu-ta-to-ries
sa-lute
 sa-luted
 sa-lut-ing
 sa-lut-er
sal-va-tion
salve
 salved
 salv-ing
 salv-or
sam-ba
 sam-baed
 sam-ba-ing
same-ness
sam-o-var
sam-ple
 sam-pled
 sam-pling
sam-pler
san-a-to-ri-um
sanc-ti-fy
 sanc-ti-fied
 sanc-ti-fy-ing
 sanc-ti-fi-ca-tion
 sanc-ti-fi-er
sanc-ti-mo-ny
 sanc-ti-mo-ni-ous
sanc-tion
 sanc-tion-a-ble
 sanc-tion-er
sanc-ti-ty
 sanc-ti-ties
sanc-tu-ary

sanc-tu-ar-ies
sanc-tum
 sanc-ta
san-dal
san-dal-wood
sand-bag
 sand-bagged
sand-bank
sand-blast
sand-box
sand-cast
 sand-cast-ed
 sand-cast-ing
sand-lot
sand-man
 sand-men
sand-pa-per
sand-pi-per
sand-stone
sand-wich
sane
 san-er
 san-est
 sane-ly
sang-froid
san-gui-nary
san-quine
 san-quine-ly
san-i-tar-i-um
 san-i-tar-i-ums
 san-i-tar-ia
san-i-tary
 san-i-tar-i-ly
san-i-ta-tion
san-i-tize
 san-i-tized
 san-i-tiz-ing
san-i-ty
sap
 sapped
 sap-ping
sap-head
 sap-head-ed
sa-pi-ent
 sa-pi-ence
 sa-pi-en-cy
sap-less
sap-ling
sa-pon-i-fy
 sa-pon-i-fied
 sa-pon-i-fy-ing
sap-per
sap-phire

sap-phism
sap-py
 sap-pi-er
 sap-pi-est
sap-suck-er
sap-wood
sa-ran
sar-casm
 sar-cas-tic
 sar-cas-ti-cal-ly
sar-co-ma
 sar-co-mas
 sar-co-ma-ta
sar-coph-a-gus
 sar-coph-a-gus-es
sar-dine
sar-don-ic
 sar-don-i-cal-ly
sar-gas-sum
sa-ri
 sa-ris
sa-rong
sar-sa-pa-ril-la
sar-to-ri-al
sa-shay
sas-sa-fras
sas-sy
 sas-si-er
 sas-si-est
sa-tan-ic
 sa-tan-i-cal
sa-tan-ism
 sa-tan-ist
satch-el
sate
 sat-ed
 sat-ing
sa-teen
sat-el-lite
sa-ti-a-ble
 sa-ti-a-bly
 sa-ti-a-bil-i-ty
sa-ti-ate
 sa-ti-at-ed
 sa-ti-at-ing
 sa-ti-a-tion
sa-ti-e-ty
sat-in
 sat-iny
sat-ire
sa-tir-i-cal
 sa-tir-i-cal-ly
sat-i-rist

sat-i-rize
  sat-i-rized
  sat-i-riz-ing
  sat-i-riz-er
sat-is-fac-tion
sat-is-fac-to-ry
  sat-is-fa-to-ri-ly
sat-is-fy
  sat-is-fied
  sat-is-fy-ing
  sat-is-fi-a-ble
  sat-is-fi-er
  sat-is-fy-ing-ly
sat-u-rate
  sat-u-rat-ed
  sat-u-rat-ing
  sat-u-ra-tion
sat-ur-na-li-a
sat-ur-nine
sa-tyr
  sa-tyr-ic
sauce
  sauced
  sauc-ing
sau-cer
sau-cy
sau-er-bra-ten
sau-er-kraut
sau-na
saun-ter
  saun-ter-er
sau-sage
  sau-sage-like
sav-age
  sav-age-ry
  sav-age-ries
sa-van-na
sa-vant
save
  saved
  sav-ing
  sav-er
sav-ior
sa-voir-faire
sa-vor
  sa-vor-er
sa-vory
  sa-vor-i-er
  sa-vor-i-est
sav-vy
saw-buck
saw-dust
sawed--off

saw-horse
saw-mill
saw-toothed
saw-yer
sax-o-phone
  sax-o-phon-ist
say
  said
  say-ing
  say-a-ble
  say-er
  say-s-o
scab
  scabbed
  scab-bing
scab-bard
sca-bies
scaf-fold
sac-fold-ing
sca-lar
scal-a-wag
scald
  scald-ing
scale
  scaled
  scal-ing
  scale-less
scamp
  scamp-er
scan
scan-dal
scan-dal-ize
  scan-dal-ized
  scan-dal-iz-ing
scan-dal-mon-ger
scan-dal-ous
scan-sion
scant
  scant-ness
scan-ties
scanty
  scant-i-er
  scant-i-est
scape-goat
scape-grace
scap-u-la
  scap-u-las
scap-u-lae
scar
  scarred
  scar-ring
scarce
  scar-ci-ty

scare-crow
scare-mon-ger
scarf
  scarfs
scarf-skin
scar-i-fy
  scar-i-fied
  scar-i-fy-ing
scar-let
scarp
scary
  scar-i-er
  scar-i-est
scat
  scat-ted
  scat-ting
scathe
scat-o-log-i-cal
scat-ter
  scat-ter-a-ble
  scat-ter-er
scav-enge
  scav-enged
  scav-eng-ing
scav-en-ger
sce-nar-i-o
  sce-nar-i-os
sce-nar-ist
scen-ery
  scen-er-ies
sce-nic
  sce-ni-cal
scent
  scent-ed
scep-ter
  scep-tered
  scep-ter-ing
sched-ule
  sched-ul-ed
  sched-ul-ing
sche-ma-tize
  sche-ma-tized
  sche-ma-tiz-ing
scheme
  schem-er
  schem-ing
scher-zo
  scher-zos
  scher-zi
schism
schis-mat-ic
  schis-mat-i-cal
schist

schizo
schiz-os
schiz-oid
schiz-o-phre-ni-a
schiz-o-phren-ic
schle-miel
schmaltz
schmaltzy
schmo
schnapps
schnau-zer
schnit-zel
schnook
schnor-kel
schnoz-zle
schol-ar
schol-ar-ly
schol-ar-li-ness
schol-ar-ship
scho-las-tic
scho-las-ti-cal
scho-las-ti-cism
school board
school bus
school-child
school-chil-dern
school-ing
school-mas-ter
school-teach-er
school-teach-ing
school-work
schoon-er
schuss
schwa
sci-at-ic
sci-ence
sci-en-tif-ic
sci-en-tif-i-cal-ly
sci-en-tist
scim-i-tar
scin-tig-ra-phy
scin-til-la
scin-til-lant
scin-til-late
scin-til-lat-ed
scin-til-lat-ing
scin-til-la-tion
sci-on
scis-sor
scle-ra
scle-rot-i-ca
scle-ro-sis
scle-ro-ses

scle-rot-ic
scle-rous
scoff
scoff-er
scoff-ing-ly
scold
scold-er
scold-ing
scol-lop
sconce
scone
scoop
scoot-er
scope
scorch
scorched
scorch-ing
scorch-er
score
scored
scor-ing
score-less
scor-er
score-board
score-keep-er
scorn
scorn-er
scorn-ful
scot-free
scot-tie
scoun-drel
scoun-drel-ly
scour
scour-er
scourge
scourged
scourg-ing
scourg-er
scour-ing
scout-ing
scout-mas-ter
scowl
scowl-er
srab-ble
scrab-bled
scrab-bling
scrab-bler
scrag
scragged
scrag-ging
scrag-gly
scrag-gli-er
scrag-gli-est

scrag-gy
scrag-gi-er
scrag-gi-est
scram
scrammed
scram-ming
scram-ble
scram-bled
scram-bling
scram-bler
scrap
scrapped
scrap-ping
scrap-book
scrape
scrap-per
scrap-py
scrap-pi-er
scrap-pi-est
scrap-pi-ly
scratch
scratch-a-ble
scratch-er
scratch-y
scratch-i-er
scratch-i-est
scratch-i-ly
scratch-i-ness
scrawl
scrawn-y
scrawn-i-er
scrawn-i-est
screamer
scream-ing-ly
screech
screech-er
screen
scrren-a-ble
screen-er
screen-play
screw
screw-driv-er
screw-y
screw-i-er
screw-i-est
scrib-ble
scrib-bled
scrib-bling
scrib-bler
scribe
scribed
scrib-ing
scrib-al

scrim
scrim-mage
scrim-mag-ing
scrimp-y
scrimp-i-er
scrimp-i-est
script
scrip-tur-al
scrip-ture
script-writ-er
scroll-work
scrooge
scro-tum
scro-ta
scrounge
scroung-er
scrub
scrubbed
scrub-bing
scrub-ber
scrub-by
scrub-bi-er
scrub-bi-est
scrub-wom-an
scrub-wom-en
scruffy
scruff-i-er
scruff-i-est
scrump-tious
scru-ple
scru-bled
scru-bling
scru-pu-lous
scru-pu-los-i-ty
scru-pu-lous-ly
scru-ta-ble
scru-ti-nize
scru-ti-nized
scru-ti-ny
scru-ti-nies
scu-ba
scud
scud-ded
scud-ding
scuf-fle
scuf-fled
scuf-fling
scul-ler-y
scul-ler-ies
sculp-tor
sculp-ture
sculp-tur-ed
sculp-tur-ing

sculp-tur-al
scum
scummed
scum-ming
scur-ri-lous
scur-ril-i-ty
scur-ril-i-ties
scur-ry
scur-ri-ed
scur-ry-ing
scur-vy
scut-tle
scut-tled
scut-tling
scut-tle-butt
scythe
scythed
scyth-ing
sea-bed
sea-coast
sea-drome
sea-far-ing
sea-far-er
sea-food
sea gull
sea horse
seal
seal-er
sea-lam-prey
sea legs
sea lev-el
seal-ing wax
sea li-on
seal-skin
seam
seam-er
sea-maid
sea-man
sea-men
sea-man-ship
seam-stree
seam-y
seam-i-er
seam-i-est
sea ot-ter
sea-plane
sea-port
search
search-a-ble
search-er
search-ing
search-light
search war-rant

sea-scape
sea ser-pent
sea-shell
sea-shore
sea-sick
sea-sick-ness
sea-side
sea-son
sea-son-er
sea-son-a-ble
sea-son-al
sea-son-al-ly
sea-son-ing
seat-ing
sea ur-chin
sea-ward
sea-weed
sea-wor-thy
sea-wor-thi-ness
se-ba-ceous
se-cant
se-cede
se-ced-ed
se-ced-ing
se-ced-er
se-ces-sion
se-ces-sion-ist
se-clude
se-clud-ed
se-clud-ing
se-clu-sion
se-clu-sive
sec-ond
sec-ond-ar-y
sec-ond-ar-i-ly
sec-ond--best
sec-ond--class
sec-ond-quess
sec-ond-hand
sec-ond-rate
sec-ond--sto-ry man
se-cre-cy
se-cre-cies
se-cret
sec-re-tar-i-at
sec-re-tary
sec-re-tar-ies
sec-re-tar-i-al
se-crete
se-cret-ed
se-cret-ing
se-cre-tion
se-cre-tive

se-cre-to-ry
  se-cre-to-ries
sec-tar-i-an
  sec-tar-i-an-ism
sec-tion
sec-tion-al
sec-tor
  sec-to-ri-al
sec-u-lar
sec-u-lar-ism
sec-u-lar-ize
  sec-u-lar-ized
  sec-u-lar-iz-ing
se-cure
  se-cured
  se-cur-ing
se-cu-ri-ty
  se-cu-ri-ties
se-dan
se-date
  se-dat-ed
  se-dat-ing
  se-da-tion
sed-a-tive
sed-en-tary
  sed-en-tar-i-ness
sedge
sed-i-ment
  sed-i-men-tal
  sed-i-men-ta-ry
  sed-i-men-ta-tion
se-di-tion
  se-di-tion-ary
se-di-tious
se-duce
  se-duced
  se-duc-ing
  se-duc-er
se-duc-tive
  se-duc-tive-ness
sed-u-lous
  se-du-li-ty
  sed-u-lous-ness
seed-bed
seed-case
seed-ing
seed-pod
seedy
  seed-i-er
  seed-i-est
see-ing
seek
  sought

seek-ing
seem-ing
  seem-ing-ness
seem-ly
seep
  seepy
  seep-i-er
  seep-i-est
seep-age
se-er
  seer-ess
seer-suck-er
see-saw
seethe
  seethed
  seeth-ing
seg-ment
  seg-men-tal
  seg-men-tary
  seg-men-ta-tion
seg-re-gate
  seg-re-gat-ed
  seg-re-gat-ing
  seg-re-ga-tion
  seg-re-ga-tion-sit
sei-gneur
seine
  seined
  sein-ing
seis-mic
  seis-mal
  seis-mi-cal
  seis-mi-cal-ly
seis-mo-graph
  seis-mog-ra-pher
  seis-mo-graph-ic
  seis-mog-ra-phy
seis-mol-o-gy
  seis-mo-log-ic
  seis-mo-log-i-cal
  seis-mol-o-gist
seize
  seized
  seiz-ing
  seiz-er
sei-zure
sel-dom
se-lect
  se-lect-ed
  se-lec-tor
se-lec-tion
se-lec-tive
se-lec-tiv-i-ty

se-le-ni-um
self-a-base-ment
self-ab-ne-ga-tion
self-a-buse
self--ad-dressed
self-ag-gran-dize-ment
  self-ag-gran-diz-ing
self--as-sur-ance
  self--as-sured
self--cen-tered
  self--cen-tered-ness
self--col-lect-ed
self--com-mand
self--com-posed
self--con-fessed
self--con-fi-dence
  self--con-fi-dent
self--con-scious
  self--con-scious-ness
self--con-tained
self--con-trol
  self--con-trolled
self--cor-rect-ing
self--crit-i-cal
self--crit-i-cism
self--de-cep-tion
  self--de-cep-tive
self--de-fense
self--de-ni-al
  self--de-ny-ing
self--de-ter-mi-na-tion
  self--de-ter-min-ing
self--dis-ci-pline
  self--dis-ci-plined
self--ed-u-cate-ed
  self--ed-u-ca-tion
self--ef-fac-ing
self--em-ployed
  self--em-ploy-ment
self--es-teem
self--ev-i-dent
  self--ev-i-dence
self--ex-plan-a-to-ry
self--ex-pres-sion
  self--ex-pres-sive
self--ful-fill-ing
self--ful-fill-ment
self--gov-ern-ment
  self--gov-erned
  self--gov-ern-ing
self--help
self--im-age
self--im-por-tance

self--im-por-tant
self--im-posed
self--im-prove-ment
self--in-duced
self--in-dul-gence
self--in-dul-gent
self--in-flict-ed
self--in-ter-est
self--in-ter-est-ed
self-ish
self-ish-ness
self--kow-ledge
self-less
self-less-ness
self--love
self--lov-ing
self--made
self--per-pet-u-at-ing
self-per-pet-u-a-tion
self--pity
self--pit-y-ing
self--pol-li-na-tion
self--pos-sessed
self--pos-sess-ed-ly
self--pos-ses-sion
self--pres-er-va-tion
self--pro-pelled
self--pro-pel-ling
self--re-al-i-za-tion
self--re-li-ance
self--re-li-ant
self--re-spect
self--re-spect-ing
self--re-straint
self--re-strain-ing
self--right-eous
self--right-eous-ness
self--sac-ri-fice
self--sac-ri-fic-ing
self--same
self--sat-is-fied
self--sat-is-fac-tion
self--sat-is-fy-ing
self--ser-vice
self--serv-ing
self--start-er
self--start-ing
self--styled
self--suf-fi-cient
self--suf-fic-ing
self--suf-fi-cien-cy
self--sup-port
self--sup-port-ing

self--taught
self--will
self--willed
sell
sell-ing
sell-er
sell-out
sel-vage
sel-vaged
se-man-tics
se-man-tic
se-man-ti-cal
se-man-ti-cal-ly
sem-a-phore
sem-a-phor-ed
sem-a-phor-ing
sem-blance
se-men
se-mes-ter
sem-i-an-nu-al
sem-i-an-nu-al-ly
sem-i-ar-id
sem-i-au-to-mat-ic
sem-i-cir-cle
sem-i-cir-cu-lar
sem-i-clas-si-cal
sem-i-clas-sic
sem-i-co-lon
sem-i-con-duc-tor
sem-i-con-duct-ing
sem-i-con-scious
sem-i-con-sious-ness
sem-i-de-tached
sem-i-fi-nal
sem-i-fi-nal-ist
sem-i-flu-id
sem-i-for-mal
sem-i-gloss
sem-i-liq-uid
sem-i-month-ly
sem-i-nal
sem-i-nal-ly
sem-i-nar-y
sem-i-nar-ies
sem-i-nar-ian
sem-i-of-fi-cial
sem-i-of-fi-cial-ly
sem-i-per-ma-nent
sem-i-per-me-a-ble
sem-i-pre-cious
sem-i-pri-vate
sem-i-pro-fes-sion-al
sem-i-pro

sem-i-pub-lic
sem-i-skilled
sem-i-sol-id
sem-i-trail-er
sem-i-trop-ic
sem-i-trop-i-cal
sem-i-trop-ics
sem-i-vow-el
sem-i-week-ly
sem-i-week-lies
sem-i-year-ly
sen-a-ry
sen-ate
sen-a-tor
sen-a-tor-ship
sen-a-to-ri-al
sen-a-to-ri-al-ly
send--off
se-nile
se-nil-i-ty
sen-ior
sen-ior-i-ty
sen-na
sen-sate
san-sa-tion
sen-sa-tion-al
sen-sa-tion-al-ly
sen-sa-tion-al-ism
sense
sensed
sens-ing
sense-less
sense-less-ness
sen-si-bil-i-ty
sen-si-ble-ness
sen-si-ble
sen-si-ble-ness
sen-si-bly
sen-si-tive
sen-si-tiv-i-ty
sen-si-tiv-i-ties
sen-si-tize
sen-si-tized
sen-si-tiz-ing
sen-si-ti-za-tion
sen-si-tizer
sen-sor
sen-so-ry
sen-so-ri-al
sen-su-al
sen-su-al-i-ty
sen-su-al-ly
sen-su-al-ism

181

sen-su-al-ist
sen-su-al-ize
sen-su-al-ized
sen-su-al-iz-ing
sen-su-al-i-za-tion
sen-su-ous
sen-tence
sen-tenced
sen-tenc-ing
sen-tient
sen-ti-ment
sen-ti-men-tal
sen-ti-men-tal-ly
sen-ti-men-til-i-ty
sen-ti-men-tal-i-ties
sen-ti-men-tal-ist
sen-ti-men-tal-ize
sen-ti-men-tal-ized
sen-ti-men-tal-iz-ing
sen-ti-nel
sen-ti-neled
sen-ti-nel-ing
sen-try
sen-tries
se-pal
se-paled
se-palled
sep-a-ra-ble
sep-a-ra-bil-i-ty
sep-e-ra-bly
sep-a-rate
sep-a-rat-ed
sep-a-rat-ing
sep-a-ra-tion
sep-a-ra-tist
sep-a-ra-tism
sep-a-ra-tive
sep-a-ra-tor
se-pi-a
sep-sis
sep-ses
sep-ten-ni-al
sep-tet
sep-tic
sep-ti-cal-ly
sep-tic-i-ty
sep-tu-a-ge-nar-i-an
sep-tum
sep-ta
sep-tu-ple
sep-tu-pled
sep-tu-pling
sep-ul-cher

sep-u-chered
sep-u-cher-ing
se-pul-chral
se-quel
se-quence
se-quent
se-quen-tial
se-quen-tial-ly
se-ques-ter
se-ques-tered
se-ques-tra-ble
se-ques-tra-tion
se-quin
se-quined
se-quoi-a
se-ra-pe
ser-aph
ser-aphs
ser-a-phim
se-raph-ic
ser-e-nade
ser-e-nad-ed
ser-e-nad-ing
ser-e-nad-er
ser-en-dip-i-ty
ser-en-dip-i-tous
se-rene
se-rene-ness
se-ren-i-ty
se-ren-i-ties
serf
serge
ser-geant
ser-geant at arms
ser-geant ma-jor
se-ri-al
se-ri-al-ly
se-ri-al-ist
se-ri-al-i-za-tion
se-ri-al-ize
se-ri-al-ized
se-ri-al-iz-ing
se-ries
se-ri-ous
se-ri-ous-ly
se-ri-ous-ness
se-ri-ous--mind-ed
se-ri-us--mind-ed-ly
ser-mon
ser-mon-ize
ser-mon-ized
ser-mon-iz-ing
se-rol-o-gy

se-ro-log-ic
se-ro-log-i-cal
se-rol-o-gist
se-rous
ser-pent
ser-pen-tine
ser-rate
ser-rat-ing
ser-ra-tion
se-rum
se-rums
se-ra
serv-ant
serve
served
serv-ing
serv-er
serv-ice
serv-iced
serv-ic-ing
serv-ice-a-ble
serv-ice-a-bil-i-ty
serv-ice-a-ble-ness
serv-ice-a-bly
serv-ice-man
ser-vile
ser-vil-i-ty
ser-vile-ness
ser-vi-tude
ser-vo-mech-an-ism
ses-a-me
ses-qui-cen-ten-ni-al
ses-sion
set-back
set-in
set-off
set-ter
set-ting
set-tle
set-tled
set-tling
set-tle-ment
set-tler
set-to
set-up
sev-en
sev-enth
sev-en-teen
sev-en-teenth
sev-en-ty
sev-en-ti-eth
sev-er
sev-er-a-bil-i-ty

sev-er-a-ble
sev-er-al
sev-er-al-ly
sev-er-al-fold
sev-er-ance
se-vere
se-ver-er
se-ver-est
se-vere-ness
se-ver-i-ty
se-ver-i-ties
sew
sew-age
sew-ing
sew-ing ma-chine
sex-less
sex-ol-o-gy
sex-o-log-i-cal
sex-ol-o-gist
sex-tant
sex-tet
sex-ton
sex-tu-ple
sex-tu-pled
sex-tu-pling
sex-tu-plet
sex-u-al
sex-u-al-ly
sex-u-al-i-ty
sex-y
sex-i-er
sex-i-est
shab-by
shab-bi-er
shab-bi-est
shab-bi-ly
shack-le
shack-led
shack-ling
shack-ler
shade
shad-ed
shad-ing
shade-less
shad-ow
shad-ow-box
shad-owy
shad-y
shad-i-er
shad-i-est
shad-i-ly
shaft-ing
shag

shagged
shag-ging
shag-gi-ly
shake
shak-en
shak-ing
shake-down
shak-er
shake-up
shak-y
shak-i-er
shak-i-est
shak-i-ly
shal-lot
shal-low
shal-low-ness
sham
shammed
sham-ming
sha-man
sha-man-ism
sha-man-ist
sham-bles
shame
shamed
sham-ing
shame-faced
shame-fac-ed-ly
shame-ful
shame-ful-ly
shame-ful-ness
sham-mer
sham-my
sham-poo
sham-pooed
sham-poo-ing
sham-poo-er
sham-rock
shan-tey
shan-ties
shan-ty-town
shape
shaped
shap-ing
shap-a-ble
shap-er
shape-less
shape-ly
shape-li-ier
shape-li-est
share
shared
shar-ing

shar-er
share-crop-per
share-crop
share-cropped
share-crop-ping
share-hold-er
shark-skin
sharp-en
sharp-en-er
sharp-er
sharp-eyed
sharp-ie
sharp-shoot-er
sharp-shoot-ing
sharp-tongued
sharp-wit-ted
sharp-wit-ted-ly
sharp-wit-ted-ness
shat-ter
shat-ter-proof
shave
shaved
shav-ing
shav-er
shawl
sheaf
sheaves
shear
sheared
shear-ing
shear-er
sheath
sheath-less
sheathe
sheathed
sheath-ing
sheath-er
shed
shed-ding
sheen
sheeny
sheen-i-er
sheep-dog
sheep-herd-er
sheep-herd-ing
sheep-ish
sheep-skin
sheer
sheer-ly
sheet-ing
sheik
shelf
shelves

shell
  shelled
shel-lac
  shel-lacked
  shel-lack-ing
shell-fire
shell-fish
shell shock
shel-ter
  shel-ter-er
shelve
  shelved
  shelv-ing
she-nan-i-gan
shep-herd
  shep-herd-ess
sher-bet
sher-iff
sher-ry
  sher-ries
shib-bo-leth
shield
  shield-er
shift
  shift-er
shift-less
shift-y
  shift-i-er
  shift-i-est
  shift-i-ly
shil-ly--shal-ly
  shil-ly-shal-lied
  shil-ly-shal-ly-ing
shim-mer
  shim-mery
  shim-mer-i-er
  shim-mer-i-est
shim-my
  shim-mies
  shim-mied
  shim-my-ing
shin
  shinned
  shin-ning
shin-bone
shin-dig
shine
  shined
  shone
  shin-ing
shin-er
shin-gle
  shin-gled

shin-gling
shin-gler
shin-gles
shin-ing
  shin-ing-ly
shin-ny
  shin-nied
  shin-ny-ing
shin-y
  shin-i-er
  shin-i-est
ship
  shipped
  ship-ping
  ship-a-ble
ship-board
ship-build-er
  ship-build-ing
ship-mate
ship-ment
ship-per
ship-yard
shirk
  shirker
shirt-tail
shirt-waist
shish ke-bab
shiv-er
  shiv-ery
  shiv-er-i-er
  shiv-er-i-est
shoal
shock-er
shock-ing
shod-dy
  shod-di-er
  shod-di-ly
  shod-di-ness
shoe-horn
shoe-lace
shoe-mak-er
sho-er
shoe-string
shoo--in
shoot
  shot
  shoot-ing
  shoot-er
shop
  shopped
  shop-ping
shop-keep-er
shop-lift-er

shop-lift-ing
shop-per
shop-talk
shop-worn
shore
  shore-line
short
  short-ly
  short-ness
short-age
short--change
  short--changed
  short--ch ang-ing
short-com-ing
short-cut
  short-cut-ting
short-en
  short-en-er
short-en-ing
short-hand
short--hand-ed
short--lived
short--sight-ed
  short--sight-ed-ly
  short--sight-ed-ness
short--tem-pered
short--term
short-wave
short--wind-ed
shot-gun
  shot-gunned
  shot-gun-ning
shoul-der
shoul-der blade
shout-er
shout-ing
shove
  shoved
  shov-ing
  shov-er
shov-el
  shov-eled
  shov-el-ing
shov-el-ful
show
  showed
  shown
  show-ing
show-bill
show-boat
  show-case
  show-cased
  show-cas-ing

show-down
show-er
show-ery
show-man
show-men
show-man-ship
show-off
show-piece
show-place
show-room
show-y
show-i-er
show-i-est
show-i-ly
shrap-nel
shred
shred-ded
shred-ding
shred-der
shrew
shrewd
shrewd-ly
shrewd-ness
shrew-ish
shriek
shrill
shirl-ly
shrimp
shrine
shrined
shrin-ing
shrink
shrunk-ed
shrink-a-ble
shrink-er
shrink-age
shriv-el
shriv-eled
shriv-el-ing
shroud
shrub-bery
shrub-ber-ies
shrub-by
shrub-bi-er
shrub-bi-est
shrug
shrugged
shrug-ging
shuck-er
shud-der
shud-dery
suf-fle
shuf-fled

shuf-fling
shuf-fler
shuf-fle-board
shun
shunned
shun-ning
shun-ner
shunt
shunt-er
shut-down
shut-eye
shut-in
shut-off
shut-out
shut-ter
shut-tle
shut-tled
' shut-tling
shut-tle-like
shy
shi-er
shy-est
shy-ness
shy-ster
sib-i-lant
sib-i-lance
sib-ling
sick
sicked
sick-ing
sick-bed
sick-en
sick-en-ing
sick-ish
sick-le
sick-ly
sick-li-er
sick-li-est
sick-ness
sick-room
side-arm
side-board
sid-ed
side-kick
side-line
side-lined
side-lin-ing
side--long
side-show
side-split-ting
side-step
side-step-ped
side-step-ping

side-swipe
side-swiped
side-swip-ing
side-track
side-ways
sid-ing
si-dle
si-dled
si-dling
siege
si-en-na
si-er-ra
si-es-ta
sieve
sieved
siev-ing
sift-er
sift-ings
sigh-er
sight-ed
sight-less
sight-ly
sight-read
sight-read-ing
sight-see-ing
sight-see-er
sig-nal
sig-naled
sig-nal-ing
sig-nal-er
sig-nal-man
sig-nal-men
sig-na-to-ry
sig-na-to-ries
sig-na-ture
sign-board
sig-net
sig-nif-i-cance
sig-nif-i-cant
sig-ni-fi-ca-tion
sig-ni-fy
sig-ni-fied
sig-ni-fy-ing
sig-ni-fi-a-ble
sig-ni-fi-er
sign-post
si-lage
si-lence
si-lenced
si-lenc-ing
si-lenc-er
si-lent
si-lent part-ner

sil-hou-ette
  sil-hou-et-ted
  sil-hou-et-ting
sil-ic-a
sil-i-con
sil-i-cone
silk-en
silk-like
silk-weed
silk-worm
silk-y
  silk-i-er
  silk-i-est
  silk-i-ly
sil-ly
  sil-li-er
  sil-li-est
  sil-li-ness
si-lo
  si-los
  si-loed
  si-lo-ing
silt
  sil-ta-tion
  silt-y
  silt-i-er
  silt-i-est
sil-ver
sil-ver-fish
sil-ver-fox
sil-ver-ware
sil-ver-y
sim-i-an
sim-i-lar
  sim-i-lar-i-ty
  sim-i-lar-i-ties
sim-i-le
si-mil-i-tude
sim-mer
si-mon-ize
  si-mon-ized
  si-mon-iz-ing
sim-pa-ti-co
sim-per
  sim-per-er
  sim-per-ing-ly
sim-ple
  sim-pler
  sim-plest
  sim-ple-ness
sim-ple--mind-ed
sim-ple sen-tence
sim-ple-ton

sim-plex
sim-plic-i-ty
  sim-plic-i-ties
sim-pli-fy
  sim-pli-fied
  sim-pli-fy-ing
  sim-pli-fi-ca-tion
  sim-pli-fi-er
sim-plism
  sim-plis-tic
  sim-plis-ti-cal-ly
sim-ply
sim-u-late
  sim-u-lat-ed
  sim-u-lat-ing
  sim-u-la-tion
  sim-u-la-tive
  sim-u-la-tor
si-mul-cast
  si-mul-cast-ing
si-mul-ta-ne-ous
  si-mul-ta-ne-ous-ly
  si-mul-ta-ne-i-ty
sin
  sinned
  sin-ning
sin-cere
  sin-cer-i-ty
si-ne-cure
si-ne qua non
sin-ew
sin-ew-y
sin-ful
  sin-ful-ly
  sin-ful-ness
sing
  sing-ing
  sing-a-ble
singe
  singed
  singe-ing
sing-er
sin-gle
  sin-gled
  sin-gling
  sin-gle-ness
sin-gle-brest-ed
sin-gle--hand-ed
  sin-gle-hand-ed-ly
sin-gle--mind-ed
  sin-gle--mind-ed-ly
sin-gle--space
  sin-gle--spaced

sin-gle--spac-ing
sin-gle-ton
sin-gle--track
sin-gly
sing-song
sin-gu-lar
sin-gu-lar-i-ty
  sin-gu-lar-i-ties
sin-is-ter
  sin-is-ter-ness
sink-a-ble
sink-er
sink-hole
sin-less
sin-ner
sin-u-ate
  sin-u-at-ed
  sin-u-at-ing
sin-u-ous
  sin-u-os-i-ty
  sin-u-ous-ness
si-nus
si-nus-i-tis
sip
  sipped
  sip-ping
  sip-per
si-phon
sire
  sired
  sir-ing
si-ren
sir-loin
sis-sy
  sis-sies
  sis-si-fied
  sis-sy-ish
sis-ter
  sis-ter-li-ness
  sis-ter-ly
sis-ter-in-law
  sis-ters-in-law
si-tar
sit-in
sit-ter
sit-ting
sit-u-ate
  sit-u-at-ed
  sit-u-at-ing
sit-u-a-tion
six--pack
six--shoot-er
six-teen

six-teenth
sixth
six-ty
six-ti-eth
siz-a-ble
siz-a-ble-ness
siz-a-bly
size
sized
siz-ing
siz-zle
siz-zled
siz-zling
siz-zler
skate
skat-ed
skat-ing
skat-er
ske-dad-dle
ske-dad-dled
ske-dad-dling
skein
skel-e-ton
skel-e-tal
skep-tic
skep-ti-cal
skep-ti-cism
sketch
sketch-er
sketch-book
sketch-y
sketch-i-er
sketch-i-est
sketch-i-ly
skew-er
skew-ness
ski
skied
ski-ing
ski-er
skid
skid-ded
skid-ding
skid-der
skilled
skil-let
skill-ful
skill-ful-ly
skill-ful-ness
skim
skimmed
skim-ming
skim-mer

skimp
skimp-i-ly
skimp-y
skimp-i-er
skimp-i-est
skin
skinned
skin-ning
skin--deep
skin dive
skin div-ing
skin div-er
skin-flint
skin-less
skin-ner
skin-ny
skin-ni-er
skin-ni-est
skin-tight
skip-per
skir-mish
skir-mish-er
skirt-er
skirt-ing
skit-ter
skit-tish
skiv-vy
skiv-vies
skoal
skul-dug-ger-y
skulk-er
skull-cap
skunk
sky
skies
skied
sky-ing
sky-blue
sky-cap
sky-div-ing
sky-rock-et
sky-svap-er
sky-ward
sky-way
sky-writ-ing
sky-writ-er
slab
slabbed
slab-bing
slack
slack-ness
slack-en
slack-er

slack-jawed
slake
slaked
slak-ing
sla-lom
slam
slammeed
slam-ming
slam-bang
slan-der
slan-der-er
slan-der-ous
slang
slang-i-er
slang-i-est
slant
slant-ways
slant-wise
slap
slapp-ed
slap-ping
slap-per
slap-dash
slap-hap-py
slap-hap-pi-er
slap-hap-pi-est
slap-stick
slash-er
slash-ing
slat
slat-ted
slat-ting
slate
slat-ed
slat-ing
slath-er
slat-tern
slat-tern-ly
slaugh-ter
slaugh-ter-er
slaugh-ter-house
slave
slaved
slav-ing
slav-er
slav-er-y
slav-ish
sla-vish-ly
slay
slain
slay-ing
slay-er
slea-zy

slea-zi-er
slea-zi-est
sled
sled-ded
sled-ding
sled-der
sledge
sledged
sledg-ing
sleek
sleek-er
sleek-ness
sleep-er
sleep-less
sleep-less-ness
sleep-walk
sleep-walk-er
sleep-walk-ing
sleep-y
sleep-i-er
sleep-i-est
sleep-i-ly
sleep-y-head
sleet
sleet-y
sleet-i-ness
sleeve
sleeved
sleev-ing
sleeve-less
sleigh
sleigh-er
sleight
slen-der
slen-der-ness
slen-der-ize
slen-der-ized
slen-der-iz-ing
sleuth
slice
sliced
slic-ing
slic-er
slick-er
slick-ness
slide
slid
slid-ing
slid-er
slight
slight-er
slight-ing
slim

slim-mer
slim-mest
slimmed
slim-ming
slim-ness
slime
slimed
slim-ing
slimy
slim-i-er
slim-i-est
slim-i-ly
sling-er
sling-shoot
slink-y
slink-i-er
slink-i-est
slip
slipped
slip-ping
slip-cov-er
slip-knot
slip--on
slip-o-ver
slip-page
slip-per
slip-per-y
slip-per-i-er
slip-per-i-est
slip-py
slip-shod
slip-stick
slip-up
slit
slit-ting
slit-ter
slith-er
slith-ery
sliv-er
sliv-er-er
sliv-er-like
slob-ber
slob-ber-er
slob-ber-ing-ly
sloe--eyed
slo-gan
slo-gan-eer
slop
slopped
slop-ping
slope
sloped
slop-ing

slop-er
slop-py
slop-pi-er
slop-pi-est
slo-pi-ly
slop-pi-ness
slosh-y
slosh-i-er
slosh-i-est
slot
slot-ted
slot-ting
sloth
sloth-ful
sloth-ful-ly
slouch
slouch-er
slouch-i-ly
slouch-i-ness
slouch-y
slouch-i-er
slouch-i-est
slough
slough-y
slough-i-er
slough-i-est
slov-en
slov-en-ly
slov-en-li-ness
slow-down
slow--mo-tion
slow-poke
slow--wit-ted
sludge
slug-y
sludg-i-er
sludg-i-est
slug
slugged
slug-ging
slug-ger
slug-gard
slug-gard-li-ness
slug-gish
slug-gish-ness
sluice
sluiced
sluic-ing
slum
slummed
slum-ming
slum-ber
slum-ber-er

slum-ber-ous
slur
  slurred
  slur-ring
slush
  slush-i-ness
  slush-y
  slush-i-er
  slush-i-est
slut
  slut-tish
sly
smack
smack-ing
small--mind-ed
  small--mind-ed-ness
small-pox
small--time
  small--tim-er
smart
  smart-ness
smart al-eck
  smart-al-eck-y
smart-en
smash
smash-ing
smash--up
smat-ter
  smat-ter-er
  smat-ter-ing
smear
  smear-er
smear-y
  smear-i-er
  smear-i-est
smell
  smelled
  smel-ling
  smell-er
  smell-y
  smell-i-er
  smell-i-est
smelt
smelt-er
  smelt-ery
smid-gen
snile
  smil-er
  smil-ing-ly
smirch
smirk
  smirk-er
  smirk-ing-ly

smite
  smote
  smit-ten
  smit-ting
  smit-er
smith-er-eens
smit-ten
smock-ing
smog-gy
  smog-gi-er
  smog-gi-est
smoke
  smoked
  smok-ing
  smoke-less
smoke-house
smok-er
  smoke-stack
  smok-ing jack-et
smok-y
  smok-i-er
  smok-i-est
  smok-i-ly
smol-der
smooth
  smooth-er
  smooth-ness
smooth-en
smooth-ie
smoth-er
  smoth-er-y
  smoth-er-i-er
  smoth-er-i-est
smudge
  smudged
  smudg-ing
  smudg-i-ly
smug
  smug-ger
  smug-gest
  smug-ly
  smug-ness
smug-gle
  smug-gled
  smug-gling
  smug-gler
smut
  smut-ted
  smut-ting
smut-ty
  smut-ti-er
  smut-ti-est
  smut-ti-ly

sna-fu
  sna-fued
  sna-fu-ing
snag
  snagged
  snag-ging
  snag-gy
snag-gle-tooth
  snag-gle-teeth
  snag-gle-toothed
snail
  snail-like
  snail-paced
snake
  snake-bite
  snake-skin
snak-y
  snak-i-er
  snak-i-est
snap
  snapped
  snap-ping
snap-back
snap-drag-on
snap-per
snap-pish
  snap-pish-ness
snap-py
  snap-pi-er
  snap-pi-est
  snap-pi-ly
snap-shot
snare
  snared
  snar-ing
  snar-er
snarl
  snarl-er
  snarl-y
  snarl-i-er
  snarl-i-est
snatch
  snatch-i-er
  snatch-i-est
  snatch-i-ly
snaz-zy
  snaz-zi-er
  snaz-zi-est
sneak-er
sneak-ing
sneak-y
  sneak-i-er
  sneak-i-est

sneak-i-ly
sneer
sneer-er
sneer-ing-ly
sneeze
sneezed
sneez-ing
sneez-er
sneez-y
sneez-i-er
sneez-i-est
snick-er
snif-fle
snif-fled
snif-fling
snif-fler
snif-fy
snif-fi-er
snif-fi-est
snif-fi-ly
snif-ter
snip
snipped
snip-ping
snip-per
snipe
sniped
snip-ing
snip-er
snip-py
snip-pi-er
snip-pi-est
snip-pi-ly
snitch-er
sniv-el
sniv-eled
sniv-el-ing
sniv-el-er
snob
snob-ber-y
snob-bish
snob-bish-ness
snoop
snoop-y
snoop-i-er
snoop-i-est
snoop-er
snoot-y
snoot-i-er
snoot-i-est
snoot-i-ly
snoot-i-ness
snooze

snoozed
snooz-ing
snooz-er
snore
snored
snor-ing
snor-er
snor-kel
snort
snort-er
snot-ty
snot-ti-er
snot-ti-est
snout
snout-ed
snout-y
snout-i-er
snout-i-est
snow-ball
snow-blow-er
snow-bound
snow-cap
snow-drift
snow-fall
snow-flake
snow-man
snow-men
snow-mo-bile
snow-plow
snow-shoe
snow-shoed
snow-shoe-ing
snow-suit
snow--white
snow-y
snow-i-er
snow-i-est
snub
snubbed
snub-bing
snub-ber
snub-by
snub-bi-er
snub-bi-est
snub-bi-ness
snub--nosed
snuf-fle
snuff-y
snuff-i-er
snuff-i-est
snug
snug-gle
snug-gled

snug-gling
soak
soak-age
soak-er
soak-ing-ly
so--and--so
soap-box
soap-suds
soap-y
soap-i-er
soap-i-est
soap-i-ly
soap-i-ness
soar-er
sob
sobbed
sob-bing
sob-ber
so-ber
so-ber-ing-ly
so-ber-ness
so-bri-e-ty
so-bri-quet
so--called
soc-cer
so-cia-ble
so-cia-bil-i-ty
so-cia-bly
so-cial
so-ci-al-i-ty
so-cial-ly
so-cial-ism
so-cial-ist
so-cial-is-tic
so-cial-is-ti-cal-ly
so-cial-ite
so-cial-ize
so-cial-ized
so-cial-iz-ing
so-cial-i-za-tion
so-cial-iz-er
so-ci-e-ty
so-ci-e-ties
so-ci-e-tal
so-ci-o-ec-o-nom-ic
so-ci-ol-o-gy
so-ci-o-log-i-cal
so-ci-ol-o-gist
so-ci-o-po-lit-i-cal
sock-et
sod
sod-ded
sod-ding

so-da
so-dal-i-ty
  so-dal-i-ties
sod-den
  sod-den-ness
so-di-um
sod-om-y
so-ev-er
so-fa
soft
  soft-ness
soft-ball
soft--boiled
sof-ten
  sof-ten-er
soft--head-ed
soft--heart-ed
  soft--heart-ed-ness
soft ped-al
  soft-ped-aled
  soft-ped-al-ing
soft--shell
soft--shoe
soft--spok-en
soft-ware
soft-wood
soft-y
  sof-ties
sog-gy
  sog-gi-er
  sog-gi-est
  sog-gi-ly
  sog-gi-ness
so-journ
  so-journ-er
sol-ace
  sol-aced
  sol-ac-ing
  sol-ac-er
so-lar
so-lar-i-um
  so-lar-i-ums
  so-lar-ia
so-lar-ize
  so-lar-ized
  so-lar-iz-ing
  so-lar-i-za-tion
sol-der
  sol-der-er
sol-dier
sol-dier-y
sol-e-cism
sole-ly

sol-emn
  sol-emn-ly
  sol-emn-less
so-lem-ni-ty
  so-lem-ni-ties
sol-em-nize
  sol-em-nized
  sol-em-niz-ing
  sol-em-ni-za-tion
sole-ness
so-lic-it
  so-lic-i-ta-tion
so-lic-i-tor
so-lic-i-tous
  so-lic-i-tous-ness
so-lic-i-tude
sol-id
  so-lid-i-ty
  sol-id-ness
sol-i-dar-i-ty
  sol-i-dar-i-ties
so-lid-i-fy
  so-lid-i-fied
  so-lid-i-fy-ing
  so-lid-i-fi-ca-tion
so-lil-o-quize
  so-lil-o-quized
  so-lil-o-quiz-ing
  so-lil-o-quist
so-lil-o-quy
  so-lil-o-quies
sol-i-taire
sol-i-tar-y
  sol-i-tar-ies
  sol-i-tar-i-ly
  sol-i-tar-i-ness
sol-i-tude
so-lo
  so-loed
  so-lo-ing
  so-lo-ist
sol-stice
sol-u-ble
  sol-u-bil-i-ty
  sol-u-bly
sol-ute
so-lu-tion
solve
  solved
  solv-ing
  solv-a-ble
  solv-a-bil-i-ty
  solv-er

sol-vent
  sol-ven-cy
so-mat-ic
so-ma-to-type
som-ber
  som-ber-ly
  som-ber-ness
som-bre-ro
  som-bre-ros
some-bod-y
  some-bod-ies
some-day
some-how
some-place
som-er-sault
some-thing
some-time
some-times
some-way
some-what
some-where
sosm-nam-bu-late
som-no-lent
  som-no-lence
  som-no-len-cy
so-nar
so-na-ta
song-bird
song-fest
song-ster
  song-stress
song-writ-er
son-ic
son--in--law
  sons--in--law
son-net
son-ny
  son-nies
so-no-rous
  so-nor-i-ty
  so-no-rous-ness
soon-er
soothe
  soothed
  sooth-ing
  sooth-er
sooth-say-er
  sooth-say-ing
soot-y
  soot-i-er
  soot-i-est
  soot-i-ly
sop

sopped
sop-ping
soph-ist
soph-ism
so-phis-tic
so-phis-ti-cal
so-phis-ti-cate
so-phis-ti-cat-ed
so-phis-ti-cat-ing
so-phis-ti-ca-tion
so-phis-ti-ca-tor
soph-ist-ry
soph-ist-ries
soph-o-more
soph-o-mor-ic
soph-o-mor-i-cal
soph-o-mor-i-cal-ly
sop-o-rif-ic
sop-py
sop-pi-er
sop-pi-est
so-pran-o
so-pran-os
sor-cer-er
sor-cer-ess
sor-cer-y
sor-cer-ies
sor-cer-ous
sor-did
sor-did-ness
sore
sor-er
sor-est
sore-ly
sore-ness
sore-head
sore-head-ed
sor-ghum
so-ror-i-ty
so-ror-i-ties
sor-rel
sor-row
sor-row-er
sor-row-ful
sor-ry
sor-ri-er
sor-ri-est
sor-ri-ly
sort-a-ble
sort-er
sor-tie
so--so
sot

sot-ted
sot-tish
sot-tish-ness
sot-vo vo-ce
sought
soul-ful
soul-ful-ly
soul-ful-ness
soul-less
soul-searching
sound
sound-a-ble
sound-ly
sound-ness
sound-box
sound-er
sound-ing
sound-less
sound-less-ly
sound-proof
soup-y
soup-i-er
soup-i-est
sour
sour-ish
sour-ness
sour-ball
source
souse
soused
sous-ing
south-bound
south-east
south-east-er
south-east-er-ly
south-east-ern
south-east-ward
south-east-ward-ly
south-er
south-er-ly
south-ern
south-ern-most
south-ern-er
south-paw
south-ward
south-ward-ly
south-west
south-west-er
south-west-ern
south-west-ern-er
south-west-ward
south-west-ward-ly
sou-ve-nir

sov-er-eign
sov-er-eign-ty
sov-er-eign-ties
so-vi-et
sow-er
soy-bean
space
spaced
spac-ing
space-less
spac-er
space-craft
space-man
space-men
space-ship
space-walk
spa-cious
spa-cious-ness
spade
spad-ed
spad-ing
spade-ful
spad-er
spade-work
spa-ghet-ti
span
spanned
span-ning
span-gle
span-gled
span-gling
span-iel
spank-er
spank-ing
spar
sparred
spar-ring
spare
spared
spar-ing
spar-er
spar-est
spar-a-ble
spare-ness
spare-rib
spar-ing
spar-ing-ness
spark-er
spar-kle
spar-kled
spar-kling
spar-kler
spar-row

spar-row-grass
sparse
  spars-er
  spars-est
spasm
spas-mod-ic
  spas-mod-i-cal
  spas-mod-i-cal-ly
spas-tic
  spas-ti-cal-ly
spat
  spat-ted
  spat-ting
spa-tial
  spa-cial
  spa-ti-al-i-ty
  spa-tial-ly
spat-ter
spat-u-la
spawn
speak
  spok-en
  speak-ing
  speak-a-ble
speak-eas-y
  speak-eas-ies
speak-er
  speak-er-ship
spear-er
spear-head
spear-mint
spe-cial
  spe-cial-ly
spe-cial-ist
spe-cial-ize
  spe-cial-ized
  spe-cial-iz-ing
  spe-cial-i-za-tion
spe-cial-ty
  spe-cial-ties
spe-cie
spe-cies
spec-i-fia-ble
spe-cif-ic
  spe-cif-i-cal-ly
  spec-i-fic-i-ty
spec-i-fi-ca-tion
spec-i-fy
  spec-i-fied
  spec-i-fy-ing
  spec-i-fi-er
spec-i-men
spe-cious

spe-ci-os-i-ty
spe-ci-os-i-ties
spe-cious-ness
speck-le
  speck-led
  speck-ling
spec-ta-cle
  spec-ta-cled
spec-tac-u-lar
  spec-tac-u-lar-ly
spec-ta-tor
spec-ter
spec-tral
spce-tro-scope
  spec-tro-scop-ic
  spec-tro-scop-i-cal
  spec-tros-co-py
spec-trum
  spec-tra
  spec-trums
spec-u-late
  spec-u-lat-ed
  spec-u-lat-ing
  spec-u-la-tion
  spec-u-la-tive
  spec-u-la-tor
speech-i-fy
  speech-i-fie
  speech-i-fy-ing
speech-less
  speech-less-ness
speed
  speed-ed
  speed-ing
  speed-er
  speed-ster
speed-boat
  speed-boat-ing
speed-om-e-ter
speed--up
speed-way
speed-y
  speed-i-er
  speed-i-est
  speed-i-ly
  speed-i-ness
spe-le-ol-o-gy
  spe-le-ol-o-gist
spell
  spelled
  spell-ing
spell-bind
  spell-bouns

spell-bind-ing
spell-bind-er
spell-er
spe-lun-ker
spend
  spent
  spend-ing
  spend-a-ble
  spend-er
spend-thrift
sper-ma-cet-i
sper-mat-ic
sper-ma-to-zo-on
  sper-ma-to-zo-a
  sper-ma-tozo-ic
spew-er
sphag-num
sphere
  sphered
  spher-ing
  spher-ic
  sphe-ric-i-ty
sphe-roid
  sphe-roi-dal
sphinc-ter
  sphin-ter-al
  sphin-ter-ic
sphinx
  sphinxes
  sphin-ges
spice
  spiced
  spic-ing
spi-cule
  spic-u-lar
  spic-u-late
spic-y
  spic-i-er
  spic-i-esst
  spic-i-ly
spi-der
spi-der-y
spiel
  spiel-er
spi-er
spiff-y
  spiff-i-er
  spiff-i-est
spig-ot
spike
  spiked
  spik-ing
  spik-y

spik-i-er
spik-i-est
spill
spilled
spill-ing
spil-lage
spill-way
spin
spun
spin-ning
spin-ach
spi-nal
spi-nal-ly
spin-dle
spin-dled
spin-dling
spin-dle-legs
spin-dle-leg-ged
spin-dly
spin-dli-er
spin-dli-est
spine-less
spin-et
spin-na-ker
spin-ner
spin-ning wheel
spin--off
spi-nose
spi-nous
spin-ster
spin-y
spin-i-ness
spi-ra-cle
spi-ral
spi-raled
spi-ral-ing
spi-ral-ly
spire
spired
spir-ing
spir-it
spir-it-ed
spir-it-ism
spir-ir-ist
spir-it-less
spir-it-les-ness
spir-i-tous
spir-it-u-al
spir-it-u-al-ly
spir-it-u-al-ism
spir-it-u-al-ist
spir-it-u-al-is-tic
spir-it-u-al-i-ty

spir-it-u-al-i-ties
spir-it-u-al-ize
spir-it-u-al-ized
spir-it-u-al-iz-ing
spir-it-u-al-i-za-tion
spir-it-u-ous
spir-it-u-os-i-ty
spi-ro-chete
spit
spat
spit-ting
spit-ter
spite
spit-ed
spit-ing
spite-ful
spit-fire
spit-tle
spit-toon
splash
splash-er
splashy
splash-i-er
splash-i-est
splash-i-ly
splash-board
splash-down
splat-ter
splay-foot
splay-feet
splay-foot-ed
spleen
spleen-ful
splen-did
splen-dif-er-ous
sple-net-ic
splice
spliced
splic-ing
splic-er
splin-ter
splin-tery
split
split-ting
split-a-ble
split-ter
split--lev-el
split--sec-ond
splotch
splotch-y
splotch-i-er
splotch-i-est
splurge

splurged
splurg-ing
splut-ter
splut-ter-er
spoil
spoil-ed
spoil-ing
spoil-age
spoil-er
spoil-sport
spoke
spoked
spok-ing
spo-ken
spokes-man
spokes-men
spokes-wom-an
spokes-wom-en
sponge
sponged
spong-ing
spong-er
spon-gy
spon-gi-er
spon-gi-est
spon-gi-ness
spon-sor
spon-sor-ship
spon-ta-ne-i-ty
spon-ta-ne-i-ties
spon-ta-ne-ous
spon-ta-ne-ous-ly
spon-ta-ne-ous-ness
spook
spook-ish
spook-y
spook-i-er
spook-i-est
spook-i-ly
spoon-er-ism
spoon-er-is-tic
spoon--fed
spoon--feed
spoon--feed-ing
spoon-ful
spoon-fuls
spo-rad-ic
spo-rad-i-cal
spo-rad-i-cal-ly
spo-ran-gi-um
spo-ran-gia
spore
spored

spor-ing
sport
sport-ing
sport-ing-ly
spor-tive
sports-cast
sports-cast-er
sports-man
sports-wear
sports-writ-er
sport-y
sport-i-er
sport-i-est
sport-i-ly
spot
spot-ted
spot-ting
spot-less
spot-less-ly
spot-light
spot-ted
spot-ted fe-ver
spot-ter
spot-ty
spot-ti-er
spot-ti-est
spot-ti-ly
spouse
spout
spout-er
sprain
sprawl
spray
spray-er
spread
spread-ing
spread--ea-gle
spread--ea-gled
spread--ea-gling
spread-er
sprig
sprigged
sprig-ging
spright-ly
spright-li-er
spright-li-est
spring
spring-ing
spring-board
spring--clean-ing
spring-time
spring-y
spring-i-er

spring-i-est
spring-i-ly
sprin-kle
sprin-kled
sprin-kling
sprink-ler
sprint
sprint-er
sprock-et
spruce
spruc-er
spruc-est
spruced
spruc-ing
spry
spry-er
spry-est
spry-ly
spue
spued
spu-ing
spume
spumed
spum-ing
spum-ous
spunk-y
spunk-i-er
spunk-i-est
spunk-i-ly
spunk-i-ness
spur
spurred
spur-ring
spu-ri-ous
spu-ri-ous-ness
spurner
spurt
spurt-er
spur-tive
sput-nik
sput-ter
sput-ter-er
spu-tum
spu-ta
spy
spies
spied
spy-ing
spy-glass
squad-ron
squal-id
squal-id-ly
squal-id-ness

squall
squally
squall-i-er
squall-i-est
squal-or
squan-der
squan-der-er
square
squared
squar-ing
square-ly
square-ness
square-dance
square-danced
square-danc-ing
squar-ish
squar-ish-ly
squash
squash-er
squash-es
squash-y
squash-i-er
squash-i-est
squat
squat-ted
squat-ting
squat-ly
squat-ter
squat-ty
squat-ti-er
squat-ti-est
squawk
squawk-er
sqauwk-y
squawk-i-er
squawk-i-est
squeak
squeal
squeal-er
squeam-ish
squeam-ish-ly
squeam-ish-ness
squee-gee
squeeze
squeez-ed
squeez-ing
squeez-er
squelch
squelch-er
squib
squid
squig-gle
squig-gled

squig-gling
squint--eyed
squire
squired
squir-ing
squirm
squirmy
squirm-i-er
squirm-i-est
squir-rel
squirt
squirt-er
stab
stabbed
stab-bing
stab-ber
sta-bil-i-ty
sta-bil-i-ties
sta-bi-lize
sta-bi-lized
sta-bi-liz-ing
sta-bi-li-za-tion
sta-bi-liz-er
sta-ble
sta-bled
sta-bling
stac-ca-to
stack-er
sta-di-um
staff-er
stag
stagged
stag-ging
stage-coach
stage-hand
stage--struck
stag-ger
stag-ger-er
stag-ger-ing
stag-nant
stag-nan-cy
stag-nate
stag-nat-ed
stag-nat-ing
stag-na-tion
stag-y
stag-i-er
stag-i-est
stag-i-ly
stag-i-ness
stain
stain-a-ble
stained

stain-er
stained glass
stain-less
stair-case
stair-way
stair-well
stake
staked
stak-ing
stake-hold-er
sta-lac-tite
sta-lag-mite
stalk
stalled
stal-lion
stal-wart
stal-wart-ness
sta-men
sta-mens
stam-i-na
stam-mer
stam-mer-ing-ly
stamp-er
stance
stand
stand-ing
stand-er
stand-ard
stand-ard-ize
stand-ard-ized
stand-ard-iz-ing
stand-ard-i-za-tion
stand-by
stnad-ee
stand--in
stand--off-ish
stand--off-ish-ness
stand-out
stand-pipe
stand-point
stand-still
sta-nine
stan-za
stan-za-ic
staph-y-lo-coc-cus
sta-ple
sta-pled
sta-pling
sta-pler
star
star-board
star-dom
stare

stared
star-ing
star-er
star-fish
star-gaze
star-gazed
star-gaz-ing
star-let
star-light
star-ling
star-ry
star-ri-er
star-ri-est
star-ri-ly
star-ry--eyed
star-span-gled
start-er
star-tle
star-tled
star-tling
star-tling-ly
star-va-tion
starve
starved
starv-ing
sta-sis
state
stat-ed
stat-ing
stat-a-ble
state-craft
state-hood
state-less
state-less-ness
state-ly
state-li-er
state-li-est
state-ment
state-room
state-side
states-man
states-men
states-man-like
states-man-ship
stat-ic
stat-ics
sta-tion
sta-tion-ar-y
ssta-tion-er
sta-tion-er-y
stat-ism
stat-ist
sta-tic-tic

196

sta-tis-ti-cal
sta-tic-ti-cal-ly
stat-is-ti-cian
sta-tis-tics
sta-tor
stat-u-ar-y
stat-u-ar-ies
stat-ue
stat-u-esque
stat-u-ette
stat-ure
sta-tus
stat-ute
staunch
stave
 staved
 stav-ing
stay
 stay-ed
 stay-ing
 stay-er
stead-fast
 stead-fast-ly
stead-y
steam-boat
steam-er
steam-fit-ter
 steam-fit-ting
steam-roll-er
steam-ship
steam-y
 steam-i-er
 steam-i-est
 steam-i-ly
ste-a-tite
sted-fast
steel-head
steel-works
 steel-work-er
steel-y
 steel-i-er
steel-yard
steep
 steep-ly
steep-en
stee-ple
stee-ple-chase
 stee-ple-chas-er
stee-ple-jack
steer
 steer-a-ble
 steer-er
steer-age

stein
stel-lar
stem
 stemmed
stem-ware
stem-wind-er
 stem-wind-ing
sten-cil
 sten-ciled
 sten-cil-ing
ste-nog-ra-pher
ste-nog-ra-phy
 sten-o-graph-ic
 sten-o-raph-i-cal-ly
sten-to-ri-an
step
 stepped
 step-ping
step-broth-er
step-child
 step-child-ren
step-daugh-ter
step-fa-ther
step-lad-der
step-moth-er
step-par-ent
stepped-up
step-sis-ter
step-son
ster-e-o
 ster-e-os
ster-e-o-phon-ic
 ster-e-o-phon-i-cal-ly
ster-e-o-scope
 ster-e-o-scop-ic
ster-e-o-type
 ster-e-o-typed
 ster-e-o-typ-ing
ster-ile
 ste-ril-i-ty
ster-i-lize
 ster-i-lized
 ster-i-liz-ing
 ster-i-li-za-tion
 ster-i-li-zer
ster-ling
stern
 stern-ly
 stern-ness
ster-num
 ster-na
 ster-nums
stern-wheel-er

ster-oid
steth-o-scope
 steth-o-scop-ic
ste-ve-dore
 ste-ve-dored
 ste-ve-dor-ing
ste-ward
stew-ard-ness
stick-er
stick-ing
stick-le-back
stick-ler
stick-pin
stick-up
stick-y
 stick-i-er
 stick-i-est
stiff
 stiff-ly
 stiff-ness
stiff-en
 stiff-en-er
stiff--necked
sti-fle
 sti-fled
 sti-fling
 sti-fler
 sti-fling-ly
stig-ma
 stig-mas
 stig-ma-ta
 stig-ma-tic
 stig-mat-i-cal-ly
stig-ma-tize
 stig-ma-tized
 stig-ma-tiz-ing
 stig-ma-ti-za-tion
sti-let-to
 sti-let-tos
 sti-let-toes
still-birth
 still-born
still life
still-ness
stilt-ed
 stilt-ed-ly
stim-u-lant
stim-u-late
 stim-u-lat-ed
 stim-u-lat-ing
 stim-u-la-tion
 stim-u-la-tive
stim-u-lus

stim-u-li
sting
  sting-ing
  sting-er
  sting-ing-ly
stin-gy
  stin-gi-er
  stin-gi-est
  stin-gi-ly
  stin-gi-ness
stink
  stink-ing
  stink-er
  stink-y
  stink-i-er
  stink-i-est
stint-er
sti-pend
stip-ple
  stip-pled
  stip-pling
stip-u-late
  stip-u-lat-ed
  stip-u-lat-ing
  stip-u-la-tion
  stip-u-la-to-ry
stir
  stirred
  stir-ring
  stri-ring-ly
stir-rup
stitch
  stitch-er
stock-ade
  stock-ad-ed
  stock-ad-ing
stock-brok-er
stock-hold-er
Stock-holm
stock-ing
stock-yard
stodg-y
  stodg-i-er
  stodg-i-est
  stodg-i-ly
sto-ic
sto-i-cal
stoke
  stoked
  stok-ing
  stok-er
stol-id
  sto-lid-i-ty

  stol-id-ly
sto-ma
  sto-ma-ta
  sto-mas
stom-ach
stom-ach-er
stone-ma-son
  stone-ma-son-ry
stone-wall
ston-y
  ston-i-er
  ston-i-est
  ston-i-ly
stop
  stopped
  stop-ping
stop-gap
stop-light
stop-o-ver
stop-page
stop-per
stop-watch
stor-age
store
  stored
  stor-ing
store-house
store-keep-er
store-room
sto-ried
storm-y
  storm-i-er
  storm-i-est
  storm-i-ly
  storm-i-ness
sto-ry
  sto-ries
  sto-ry-ing
sto-ry-book
sto-ry-tell-er
  stor-y-tell-ing
stout
  stout-ly
  stout-ness
stout--heart-ed
stove
  stoved
  stov-ing
stove-pipe
stow-age
stow-a-way
stra-bis-mus
strad-dle

strad-dled
strad-dling
strad-dler
strafe
  strafed
  straf-ing
strag-gle
  strag-gled
  strag-gling
  strag-gler
strag-gly
  strag-gli-er
  strag-gli-est
straight-en
  straight-en-er
straight-for-ward
  straight-for-ward-ly
straight-way
strain-er
strait-en
strait-jack-et
strait-laced
strange
  strang-er
  strang-est
  strang-ly
  strange-ness
stran-ger
stran-gu-la-tion
  strn-gu-late
  stran-gu-lat-ed
  stran-gu-lat-ing
strap
  srapped
  strap-ping
  strap-less
stra-te-gic
  str-te-gi-cal-ly
strat-e-gy
  strat-e-gies
  strat-e-gist
strat-i-fi-ca-tion
strat-i-fy
  strat-i-fied
  strat-i-fy-ing
stra-to-cu-mu-lus
strat-o-sphere
  strat-o-spher-ic
stra-tum
  stra-ta
  stra-tums
stra-tus
  stra-ti

straw-ber-ry
  straw-ber-ries
stream-er
stream-line
  stream-lined
  stream-lin-ing
street-car
street-walk-er
  street-walk-ing
strength-en
  strength-en-er
stren-u-ous
  stren-u-os-i-ty
  stren-u-ous-ly
strep-to-coc-cus
  strep-to-coc-ci
  strep-to-coc-cal
  strep-to-coc-cic
strep-to-my-cin
stress
  stress-ful
  stress-ful-ly
  stress-ful-ness
stretch
  stretch-a-bil-i-ty
  stretch-a-ble
stri-a
  stri-ae
stri-ate
  stri-at-ed
  stri-at-ing
strick-en
strict
  strict-ly
  strict-ness
stric-ture
stride
  strid-den
  strid-ding
stri-dent
strid-u-la-tion
strife
  strife-ful
  strife-less
string
  strung
  string-ing
strin-gent
  strin-gen-cy
  strin-gent-ly
string-y
  string-i-er
  string-i-est

strip
  stripped
  strip-ping
stripe
  striped
  strip-ing
strip-ling
strip-per
strip-tease
  strip-teas-er
stro-bo-scope
  stro-bo-scop-ic
  stro-bo-scop-i-cal-ly
stroke
  stroked
  strok-ing
stroll-er
strong
  strong-ish
  strong-ly
strong--arm
strong-box
strong-hold
strong-mind-ed
  strong-mind-ed-ly
  strong-mind-ed-ness
stron-ti-um
  stron-tic
strop
  stropped
  strop-ping
struc-tur-al
  struc-tur-al-ly
struc-ture
  struc-tured
  struc-tur-ing
  struc-ture-less
strug-gle
  strug-gled
  strug-gling
  strug-gler
strum
  strum-mer
strum-pet
strut
  strut-ted
  strut-ting
strych-nine
  strych-nia
  strych-nic
stub-born
  stub-born-ly
  stub-born-ness

stuck--up
stud
  stud-ded
  stud-ding
stu-dent
stud-ied
  stud-ied-ly
  stud-ied-ness
stu-di-o
  stu-di-os
stu-di-ous
  stu-di-ous-ly
  stu-di-ous-ness
stud-y
  stud-ies
  stud-ied
  stud-y-ing
stuff-er
stuff-ing
stuff-y
stul-ti-fy
  stul-ti-fied
  stul-ti-fy-ing
  stul-ti-fi-ca-tion
  stul-ti-fi-er
stum-ble
stump
  stump-er
  stumpy
stun-ning
stunt
  stunt-ed
  stunt-ed-ness
stu-pe-fy
  stu-pe-fied
  stu-pe-fy-ing
stu-pen-dous
  stu-pen-dous-ly
stu-por
  stu-por-ous
stur-dy
  stur-di-er
  stur-di-est
  stur-geon
stut-ter
  stut-ter-er
  stut-ter-ing-ly
style
  styled
  styl-ing
  styl-er
styl-ish
  styl-ish-ly

styl-ish-ness
sty-lus
  sty-lus-es
  sty-li
sty-mie
  sty-mies
  sty-mied
  sty-mie-ing
styp-tic
  styp-ti-cal
  styp-tic-i-ty
sub
  subbed
  sub-bing
sub-al-tern
sub-arc-tic
sub-as-sem-bly
  sub-as-sem-blies
  sub-as-sem-bler
sub-base-ment
sub-chas-er
sub-class
sub-com-mit-tee
sub-con-scious
  sub-con-scious-ly
sub-con-ti-nent
  sub-con-ti-nen-tal
sub-con-tract
  sub-con-trac-tor
sub-cul-ture
  sub-cul-tur-al
sub-cu-ta-ne-ous
  sub-cu-ta-ne-ous-ly
sub-ded-u-tante
sub-di-vide
  sub-di-vid-ed
  sub-di-vid-ing
  sub-di-vid-a-ble
  sub-di-vid-er
sub-di-vi-sion
  sub-di-vi-sion-al
sub-due
  sub-dued
sub-en-try
  sub-en-tries
sub-freez-ing
sub-group
sub-head
sub-hu-man
sub-ject
  sub-jec-tion
sub-jec-tive
  sub-jec-tive-ly

sub-jec-tive-ness
sub-jec-tiv-i-ty
sub-join
sub-ju-gate
  sub-ju-gat-ed
  sub-ju-gat-ing
  sub-ju-ga-tion
  sub-ju-ga-tor
sub-junc-tive
sub-lease
  sub-leased
  sub-leas-ing
sub-let
  sub-let-ting
sub-li-mate
  sub-li-mat-ed
  sub-li-mat-ing
  sub-li-ma-tion
sub-lime
sub-lim-i-nal
  sub-lim-i-nal-ly
sub-lim-i-ty
  sub-lim-i-ties
sub-ma-chine gun
sub-mar-gin-al
sub-ma-rine
sub-merge
  sub-merged
  sub-mer-gi-ble
sub-merse
  sub-mersed
  sub-mer-sion
sub-mers-i-ble
sub-mi-cro-scop-ic
sub-mis-sion
sub-mis-sive
  sub-mis-sive-ly
  sub-mis-sive-ness
sub-mit
  sub-mit-ted
  sub-mit-ting
sub-nor-mal
  sub-nor-mal-i-ty
sub-or-di-nate
  sub-or-di-nat-ed
  sub-or-di-na-tive
sub-orn
  sub-or-na-tion
  sub-orn-er
sub-poe-na
  sub-poe-naed
  sub-poe-na-ing
sub-scribe

sub-scribed
sub-scrib-ing
sub-scrib-er
sub-scrip-tion
sub-se-quent
  sub-se-quence
  sub-se-quent-ly
sub-ser-vi-ent
  sub-ser-vi-ence
  sub-ser-vi-en-cy
sub-side
  sub-sid-ed
  sub-sid-ing
  sub-sid-ence
sub-sid-i-ar-y
  sub-sid-i-ar-ies
sub-si-dize
  sub-si-dized
  sub-si-diz-ing
sub-si-dy
  sub-si-dies
sub-sist
sub-sist-ence
sub-soil
sub-son-ic
sub-stance
sub-stand-ard
sub-stan-tial
  sub-stan-ti-al-i-ty
  sub-stan-tial-ly
sub-stan-tive
  sub-stan-ti-val
  sub-stan-ti-val-ly
  sub-stan-tive-ly
sub-sti-tute
  sub-sti-tut-ed
  sub-sti-tut-ing
  sub-sti-tu-tion
sub-stra-tum
  sub-stra-ta
  sub-stra-tums
sub-struc-ture
sub-teen
sub-tend
sub-ter-fuge
sub-ter-ra-ne-an
  sub-ter-ra-ne-ous
  sub-ter-ra-ne-an-ly
  sub-ter-ra-ne-ous-ly
sub-ti-tle
sub-tle
  sub-tle-ness
  sub-tle-ty

sub-tle-ties
sub-tly
sub-tra-hend
sub-trop-i-cal
sub-trop-ic
sub-trop-ics
sub-ur-bia
sub-ver-sion
sub-ver-sion-ary
sub-ver-sive
sub-ver-sive-ly
sub-ver-sive-ness
sub-vert
sub-vert-er
sub-way
suc-ceed
suc-ceed-er
suc-ces-sion
suc-ces-sion-al
suc-ces-sion-al-ly
suc-ces-sive
suc-ces-sive-ly
suc-ces-sive-ness
suc-ces-sor
suc-cinct
suc-cinct-ly
suc-cinct-ness
suc-cor
suc-cor-er
suc-co-tash
suc-co-bus
suc-cu-bi
suc-cu-lent
suc-cu-lence
suc-cu-len-cy
suc-cu-lent-ly
suc-cumb
suck-er
suck-le
suck-led
suck-ling
su-crose
suc-tion
sud-den-ly
sud-den-less
suds-y
suds-i-er
suds-i-est
sue
sued
su-ing
su-er
suede

su-et
su-ety
suf-fer-ance
suf-fice
suf-ficed
suf-fic-ing
suf-fic-er
suf-fi-cien-cy
suf-fi-cien-cies
suf-fi-cient
suf-fi-cient-ly
suf-fix
suf-fo-cate
suf-fo-cat-ed
suf-fo-cat-ing
suf-frage
suf-fra-gette
suf-fuse
suf-fused
suf-fus-ing
sug-ar-coat
sug-gest
sug-gest-er
sug-gest-i-ble
sug-ges-tion
sug-ges-tive
sug-ges-tive-ly
sug-ges-tive-ness
su-i-cide
su-i-cid-ed
su-i-cid-ing
su-i-cid-al
suit-a-ble
suit-a-bil-i-ty
suit-case
suite
suit-ing
suit-or
sul-fa
sul-fa-nil-a-mide
sul-fate
sul-fide
sul-fur
sul-fu-ric
sul-fur-ous
sul-fur-ous-ly
sulk-y
sul-ly
sul-lied
sul-ly-ing
sul-tan
sul-tan-ic
sul-tan-a

sul-tan-ess
sul-tan-ate
sul-try
sul-tri-er
sul-tri-est
sum
su-mac
sum-ma-rize
sum-ma-rized
sum-ma-ry
sum-ma-ries
sum-mar-i-ly
sum-ma-tion
sum-ma-tion-al
sum-mer
sum-mery
sum-mer-house
sum-mit
sum-mon
sum-mon-er
sum-mons
sum-mons-es
sump-tu-ar-y
sump-tu-ous
sump-tu-ous-ly
sun
sunned
sun-ning
sun-bathe
sun-bon-net
sun-burn
sun-burned
sun-burnt
sun-dae
sun-der
sun-der-ance
sun-di-al
sun-dries
sun-dry
sunk-en
sun-light
sun-rise
sun-shine
sun-shiny
sun-spot
sun-stroke
sun-up
sup
supped
su-per
su-per-a-bun-dant
su-per-a-bun-dance
su-per-an-nu-ate

201

su-perb
su-perb-ly
su-per-car-go
su-per-car-goes
su-per-charge
su-per-charg-er
su-per-cil-i-ous
su-per-cil-i-ous-ly
su-per-e-go
su-per-e-rog-a-to-ry
su-per-fi-cial
su-per-fi-ci-al-i-ty
su-per-fi-ci-al-i-ties
su-per-high-way
su-per-hu-man
su-per-hu-man-i-ty
su-per-hu-man-ly
su-per-im-pose
su-per-im-posed
su-per-im-pos-ing
su-per-in-tend
su-per-in-tend-en-cy
su-per-in-tend-ent
su-pe-ri-or
su-pe-ri-or-i-ty
su-pe-ri-or-ly
su-per-la-tive
su-per-la-tive-ly
su-per-man
su-per-mar-ket
su-per-nal
su-per-nal-ly
su-per-nat-u-ral
su-per-nu-mer-ar-y
su-per-nu-mer-ar-ies
su-per-pow-er
su-per-scribe
su-per-scib-ing
su-per-scrip-tion
su-per-script
su-per-sede
su-per-sed-ed
su-per-sed-ing
su-per-son-ic
su-per-son-i-cal-ly
su-per-star
su-per-sti-tion
su-per-sti-tious
su-per-sti-tious-ly
su-per-struc-ture
su-per-vene
su-per-vened
su-per-ven-ing

su-per-ven-tion
su-per-vise
su-per-vised
su-per-vis-ing
su-per-vi-sion
su-pine
su-pine-ly
sup-per
sup-plant
sup-plan-ta-tion
sup-plant-er
sup-ple
sup-pler
sup-plest
sup-ple-ment
sup-ple-men-tal
sup-pli-ant
sup-pli-ant-ly
sup-pli-cant
sup-ply
sup-port
sup-port-a-ble
sup-port-er
sup-por-tive
sup-pose
sup-po-si-tion
sup-po-si-tion-al
sup-pos-i-to-ry
sup-press
sup-pres-sion
sup-pres-sor
su-pra-re-nal gland
su-prem-a-cy
su-prem-a-cies
su-prem-a-cist
su-preme
su-preme-ly
sur-cease
sur-charge
sur-charged
sur-charg-ing
sur-cin-gle
sure
sur-er
sur-est
sure-ly
sure--fire
sure--foot-ed
sure--foot-ed-ly
sure-ty
sure-ties
sure-ty-ship
surf

surfy
surf-i-er
sur-face
sur-faced
sur-fac-ing
surf-board
surf-board-er
sur-feit
sur-feit-er
sur-geon
sur-ger-y
sur-ger-ies
sur-gi-cal
sur-ly
sur-mise
sur-mised
sur-mis-ing
sur-mount
sur-mount-a-ble
sur-name
sur-pass
sur-pass-a-ble
sur-pass-ing
sur-plice
sur-plus
sur-plus-age
sur-prise
sur-prised
sur-pris-ing
sur-re-al-ism
sur-re-al-ist
sur-re-al-is-tic
sur-ren-der
sur-rep-ti-tious
sur-rep-ti-tious-ly
sur-rey
sur-reys
sur-ro-gate
sur-ro-gat-ed
sur-ro-gat-ing
sur-round
sur-round-er
sur-round-ing
sur-tax
sur-veil-lance
sur-veil-lant
sur-vey
sur-vey-ing
sur-vey-or
sur-viv-al
sur-vive
sur-vived
sur-viv-ing

sur-vi-vor
sus-cep-ti-ble
  sus-cep-ti-bil-i-ty
  sus-cep-ti-bly
sus-pect
sus-pend
sus-pend-er
sus-pense
  sus-pense-ful
sus-pen-sion
sus-pi-cious
  sus-pi-cious-ly
sus-tain
  sus-tain-a-ble
  sus-tain-er
  sus-tain-ment
sus-te-nance
su-ture
su-ze-rain
  su-ze-rain-ly
svelte
  svelte-ly
swad-dle
  swad-dled
  swad-dling
swain
  swain-ish
swal-low
  swal-low-er
swal-low-tail
swa-mi
  swa-mis
swamp
  swampy
swank
  swank-i-ly
swan's--down
swap
  swapped
  swap-ping
sward
swarth-y
  swarth-i-er
  swarth-i-est
swat
swathe
  swathed
  swath-ing
swat
  sway-a-ble
  sway-er
sway-back
  sway-backed

swear-word
sweat
sweat-er
sweat-shop
sweep
  swept
  sweep-ing
  sweep-er
sweep-stakes
sweet
  sweet-ish
  sweet-ly
sweet-heart
sweet-meat
sweet-talk
swell-head
swel-ter
  swel-ter-ing
swerve
  swerved
  swerv-ing
swift
  swift-ly
swim-ming
swim-ming-ly
swin-dle
  swin-dled
  swin-dling
  swin-dler
swipe
  swiped
  swip-ing
swirl
swish
  swish-er
switch
  switch-er
switch-blade
switch-board
switch--hit-ter
swiv-el
  swiv-el-ed
  swiv-el-ing
swiz-zle
sword
sword-fish
sword-play
  sword-play-er
swords-man
  swords-man
  swords-man-ship
syc-a-more
syc-o-phant

syc-o-phan-cy
syc-o-phan-tic
syl-lab-bic
syl-lab-i-cate
  syl-lab-i-cat-ed
  syl-lab-i-cat-ing
  syl-lab-i-ca-tion
syl-la-bus
  syl-la-bus-es
  syl-la-bi
syl-lo-gism
  sul-lo-gis-tic
sylph-like
syl-van
sym-bi-o-sis
  sym-bi-ot-ic
  sym-bi-ot-i-cal-ly
sym-bol
  sym-bol-ic
  sym-bol-i-cal
sym-bol-ism
  sym-bol-ist
sym-me-try
  sym-me-tries
sym-pa-thize
  sym-pa-thized
  sym-pa-thiz-ing
  sym-pa-thiz-er
sym-pa-thy
  sym-pa-thies
sym-pho-ny
  sym-pho-nies
  sym-phon-ic
sym-po-si-um
  sym-po-sia
  sym-po-si-ums
symp-tom
syn-a-gogue
  syn-gog-al
  syn-gog-i-cal
syn-apse
sync
  synced
  sync-ing
syn-chro-nism
  syn-chro-nis-tic
  syn-chro-nis-ti-cal
  syn-chro-nis-ti-cal-ly
syn-chro-nize
  syn-chro-nized
  syn-chro-niz-ing
  syn-chro-ni-za-tion
syn-chro-nous

syn-chro-nous-ly
syn-di-cate
  syn-di-cat-ed
  syn-di-cat-ing
syn-drome
  syn-drom-ic
syn-od
  syn-od-al
syn-o-nym
  syn-no-nym-ic
  syn-no-nym-i-cal
  syn-no-nym-i-ty
syn-on-y-mous
  syn-on-y-mous-ly
syn-on-y-my
  syn-on-y-mies
syn-op-sis
  syn-op-ses
  syn-op-ti-cal
syn-tac-tic
  syn-tac-ti-cal
  syn-tac-ti-cal-ly
syn-tax
syn-the-sis
  syn-the-ses
  syn-the-sist
syn-the-size
  syn-the-sized
  syn-the-siz-ing
syn-the-ic
  syn-thet-i-cal
  syn-thet-i-cal-ly
syph-i-lis
syph-i-lit-ic
sy-ringe
  sy-ringed
  sy-ring-ing
syr-up
  syr-upy
  syr-up-i-er
  syr-up-i-est
sys-tem
sys-tem-at-ic
  sys-tem-at-i-cal
sys-tem-a-tize
  sys-tem-a-tized
  sys-tem-a-tiz-ing
  sys-tem-a-ti-za-tion
  sys-tem-a-tiz-er
sys-tem-ic
  sys-tem-i-cal-ly
sys-to-le
  sys-tol-ic

tap
tab-er-na-cle
ta-ble
ta-ble-spoon
tab-leau
tab-let
tab-loid
ta-boo
tab-u-lar
  tab-u-lar-ly
ta-chom-e-ter
tac-it
  tac-it-ly
tack
  tack-er
tack claw
tacki-ness
tack-le
ta-co
tact
  tact-ful
tac-tic
  tac-tic-al
  tac-tic-ian
tad
tad-pole
taf-fe-ta
  taf-fet-ized
taff-rail
tag
  tag-ger
tail
tail-gate
tai-lor
taint
take
talc
tale
tal-ent
  tal-ent-ed
tal-ent scout
tall
  tall-ish
tal-low
  tal-low
tal-ly
tal-on
  tal-on-ed
tam-bou-rine
tame
  tame-ly
tam-per
tan

tan-dem
tang
  tangy
tan-gent
  tan-gen-cy
  tan-gen-tial
tan-ger-ine
tan-gi-ble
  tan-gi-bil-ity
tan-gle
  tanglement
tan-go
tank
  tank-ful
tan-kard
tan-ta-lize
  tan-ta-lizer
  tan-ta-liz-ingly
tan-ta-lum
tan-trum
tap
tape
ta-per
tap-es-try
tap-i-o-ca
taps
tar-dy
  tar-di-ness
tar-get
tar-iff
tar-nish
  tar-nish-able
tar-ot
tar-pau-lin
tar-ry
tart
  tart-ly
  tart-ness
tar-tan
tar-tar
  tar-tar-ic
task
tas-sel
taste
  taste-ful
  taste-less
tat-ter
tat-tle
  tat-tler
tattle-tale
tat-too
  tat-too
  tat-too-er

taught
taut
  taut-ly
  taut-ness
tau-tol-o-gy
tav-ern
  tav-ern-er
tax
  tax-able
  tax-a-tion
tax--ex-empt
tax shel-ter
tax-i
taxi-cab
tax-i-der-my
  tax-i-derm-ist
tea
teach
  teach-ing
  teach-able
  teach-er
team
team-ster
tear
  teary
tease
  teaser
tech-ne-tium
tech-ni-cal
  tech-ni-cal-ly
tech-nique
tech-nol-o-gy
te-dious
  te-dious-ly
tee
teem
teens
teeth
tele-cast
tele-graph
  tele-graph-er
  tele-graph-ic
te-lep-a-thy
  te-lep-a-thic
  te-lep-a-thist
tele-phone
  tele-phoner
tele-pho-to
  tele-pho-to-graph
tele-scope
  tele-scopic
tele-thon
tele-vi-sion

tel-ex
tell
  tell-able
  tell-ing
  tell-er
tel-lu-ri-um
tem-per
  tem-per-able
tem-per-a-ment
  tem-per-a-ment-al
tem-per-ance
tem-per-ate
  tem-per-ate-ly
tem-per-a-ture
tem-pest
tem-ple
tem-po
tem-po-rary
tempt
  tempt-er
ten
te-na-cious
  te-na-cious-ly
ten-ant
tend
ten-den-cy
ten-der
  ten-der-ly
  ten-der-ness
ten-der-loin
ten-don
ten-dril
  ten-dril-ed
ten-nis
ten-or
tense
ten-sion
  ten-sion-al
tent
ten-ta-cle
ten-ta-tive
  ten-ta-tive-ly
ten-ure
te-pee
tep-id
  tep-id-ly
ter-bi-um
ter-cen-ten-a-ry
term
ter-mi-nal
ter-mi-nate
  ter-mi-nation
ter-mite

ter-race
ter-rain
ter-ra-pin
ter-res-tri-al
ter-ri-ble
  ter-ri-bly
ter-ri-er
ter-rif-ic
  ter-rif-ical-ly
ter-ri-fy
  ter-ri-fied
  ter-ri-fying
ter-ri-to-ry
  ter-ri-to-rial
  ter-ri-to-rial-ly
ter-ror
ter-ror-ism
terse
test
  test-er
tes-ta-ment
  tes-ta-ment-ary
tes-tate
tes-ti-fy
  tes-ti-fier
tes-ti-mo-ni-al
tes-ti-mo-ny
tes-tis
test tube
test--tube baby
tet-a-nus
teth-er
text
text-book
tex-tile
tex-ture
  tex-tural
  tex-tural-ly
thal-li-um
than
thank
thank-ful
  thank-ful-ly
  thank-ful-ness
  thank-less
thanks
that
thatch
thaw
the
the-atre
the-at-ri-cal
  the-at-ri-cals

theft
their
the-ism
them
theme
  the-matic
them-selves
then
thence
  thence-forth
  thence-for-ward
the-oc-ra-cy
  the-oc-rat
the-ol-o-gy
  the-ol-o-gian
the-o-rize
  the-o-re-ti-cian
  the-o-ri-za-tion
  the-o-rist
the-o-ry
  ther-a-peu-tics
  ther-a-peu-tist
ther-a-py
  ther-a-pist
there
  there-abouts
  there-after
  there-by
  there-fore
  there-from
  there-in
ther-mal
ther-mom-e-ter
  ther-mom-e-tric
ther-mo-plas-tic
ther-mo-stat
  ther-mo-stat-ic
the-sau-rus
these
the-sis
they
they'd
they'll
they're
they've
thick
  thick-ly
  thick-ness
  thick-en
thief
thieve
thigh
thim-ble

thim-ble-ful
thin
  thin-ly
  thin-ness
thing
think
  think-able
  think-er
third
thirst
  thirst-y
thir-teen
this
this-tle
thith-er
thong
tho-rax
  tho-racic
tho-ri-um
thorn
  thorn-y
thor-ough
  thor-ough-ness
  thor-ough-ly
thor-ough-bred
thor-ough-fare
those
though
thought
  thought-ful
  thought-less
thou-sand
thrash
  thrash-er
thread
  thread-y
thread-bare
threat
  threat-en
three
thresh
thresh-old
threw
thrice
thrift
  thrift-i-ly
  thrift-i-ness
  thrift-y
thrill
  thrill-ing
  thrill-ing-ly
thrive
throat

throb
throm-bo-sis
throng
throt-tle
through
through-out
throw
thru
thrush
thrust
thru-way
thud
thug
  thug-gish
thumb
thump
thun-der
thun-der-bolt
thun-der-cloud
thun-der-show-er
thus
thwack
thwart
thy
thyme
thy-roid
thy-rox-ine
ti-ara
tick
tick-et
tick-le
  tick-ler
tidal wave
tid-bit
tide
tid-ings
ti-dy
  ti-di-ly
  ti-di-ness
tie
tier
  tier-ed
ti-ger
tiger-eye
tight
tight-en
  tight-en-er
tight-rope
tights
tile
till
  till-er
tilt

tim-ber
time
time--shar-ing
time tri-al
tim-id
tinc-ture
tin-der
tin-der-box
tine
tinge
tin-gle
 tin-gly
tink-er
tin-ny
tin-sel
tint
ti-ny
tip
tip-ple
tip-sy
 tip-si-ness
ti-rade
tire
tire-less
 tire-less-ly
tis-sue
ti-ta-ni-um
tithe
 tither
tit-il-late
 tit-il-lat-ing
ti-tle
toad
 toad-stool
toast
 toast-y
toast-er
to-bac-co
to-bog-gan
 to-bog-gan-ist
to-day
tod-dle
 tod-dler
tod-dy
toe
tof-fee
to-geth-er
 to-geth-er-ness
toil
 toil-some
toi-let
toi-lette
to-ken

tol-er-ate
 tol-er-a-tion
 tol-er-ance
 tol-er-ant
toll
tom-a-hawk
to-ma-to
tom-boy
 tom-boy-ish
tomb-stone
tom-cat
to-mor-row
ton
tone
tongs
tongue
ton-ic
ton-sil
ton-sil-lec-to-my
tool
tooth
 tooth-ed
 tooth-less
top
to-paz
top-coat
top-ic
top-most
to-pog-ra-phy
top-ple
top-sy--tur-vy
torch
tor-ment
 tor-ment-ing-ly
 tor-ment-or
tor-na-do
tor-pe-do
tor-pid
 tor-pid-ity
 tor-pid-ly
tor-rent
 tor-rent-ial
tor-rid
 tor-rid-ly
tor-sion
 tor-sion-al
tor-so
tort
tor-toise
tor-tu-ous
 tor-tu-ous-ness
to-tal
 to-tal-ly

to-tal-i-tar-i-an
 to-tal-i-tar-i-an
tote
to-tem
tot-ter
tou-can
touch
 touch-able
tough
 tough-ly
 tough-ness
tou-pee
tour
 tour-ism
 tour-ist
tour-na-ment
tour-ni-quet
tou-sle
tout
 tout-er
tow
to-ward
tow-el
tow-er
 tow-er-ing
town
town-ship
tox-e-mi-a
tox-ic
tox-in
toy
trace
 trace-able
 trace-ably
 trac-er
track
 track-able
 track-er
tract
trac-tion
trac-tor
trade
 trade-able
trade-mark
trade--off
tra-di-tion
 tra-di-tion-al
 tra-di-tion-al-ly
tra-duce
 tra-duce-ment
 tra-ducer
traf-fic
trag-e-dy

trail
trail-er
trait
trai-tor
tra-jec-to-ry
tram-mel
  tram-mel-er
tramp
tram-ple
  tram-pler
tram-po-line
  tram-po-lin-ist
trance
tran-quil
  tran-quil-lity
  tran-quil-ly
  tran-quil-ize
tran-scend
  tran-scend-ent
  tran-scend-ence
tran-scribe
tran-script
tran-scrip-tion
trans-fer
  trans-fer-able
  trans-fer-ence
trans-fig-ure
  trans-fig-ura-tion
trans-fix
  trans-fix-ion
trans-form
  trans-for-mable
  trans-for-ma-tion
  trans-for-mer
trans-fuse
  trans-fus-ion
  trans-fus-er
trans-gress
  trans-gress-ion
  trans-gress-or
  trans-gres-sive
tran-sient
  tran-sient-ly
tran-sit
trans-late
  trans-la-tion
  tran-sla-tor
trans-lu-cent
trans-mis-sion
trans-mit
  trans-miss-ible,
  trans-mitt-able
  trans-mitt-er

trans-mute
  trans-mu-ta-tion
tran-som
trans-par-ent
  trans-par-ency
  trans-par-ent-ly
tran-spire
trans-plant
  trans-plant-able
trans-pose
trans-sex-u-al
trap
tra-peze
trap-shoot-ing
trau-ma
tra-vail
trav-el
  trav-el-er
tra-verse
  tra-vers-able
  tra-ver-sal
  tra-ver-ser
trawl
tray
treach-er-ous
  treach-er-ous-ly
  treach-ery
tread
trea-son
  trea-son-able
  trea-son-ous
treas-ure
treas-ur-er
treas-ur-y
treat
  treat-able
  treat-er
treat-ment
treb-le
tre-foil
trek
trel-lis
trem-ble
  trem-bler
  trem-bly
tre-men-dous
trem-or
trench
  trench-er
trend
  trend-set-ter
tres-pass
tri-al

tri-an-gle
  tri-an-gu-lar-i-ty
tribe
trib-u-la-tion
trib-un-al
trib-ute
tri-ceps
trick
  trick-y
trick-er-y
trick-le
tri-col-or
  tri-col-or-ed
tri-cy-cle
tri-dent
tried
tri-en-ni-al
  tri-en-ni-al-ly
trill
tril-lion
trim
tri-ni-tro-tol-u-ene
trin-ket
tri-o
tripe
trip-le
trip-let
trip-li-cate
tri-pod
trite
tri-umph
  tri-umph-ant
  tri-umph-ant-ly
triv-i-al
trol-ley
trom-bone
troop
  troop-er
tro-phy
trop-ic
trop-i-cal
  trop-i-cal-ly
tro-pism
tro-po-sphere
trot
troth
trou-ble
  trou-bler
  trou-bling-ly
trough
trounce
troupe
trout

trow-el
  trow-el-er
tru-ant
truce
truck
  truck-er
trudge
true
  true-ness
trump
trum-pet
trunk
truss
trust
  trust-er
  trust-less
truth
  truth-ful
  truth-ful-ly
  truth-ful-ness
try
  try-ing
tryst
tsu-na-mi
tub
tu-ba
tube
tu-ber
tu-ber-cu-lo-sis
tuck
tuft
tug
tu-i-tion
tu-lip
tum-ble
  tum-bler
tu-mult
tu-mul-tu-ous
tu-na
tun-dra
tune
tune-ful
tung-sten
tu-nic
tun-nel
tur-ban
tur-bine
tur-bu-lent
  tur-bu-lent-ly
tu-reen
turf
tur-key
tur-moil

tur-nip
turn-key
turn-off
turn-over
tur-pen-tine
tur-quoise
tur-ret
tur-tle
tur-tle-neck
tusk
tus-sle
tu-tor
tut-ti--frut-ti
tu-tu
tux-e-do
twain
tweed
twee-zers
twelve
twen-ty
twice
twid-dle
twig
twi-light
twill
twin
twine
twinge
  twing-ed
twin-kle
twirl
twist
  twist-er
twit
twitch
twit-ter
  twit-ter-y
two-fold
ty-coon
tyke
type
type-face
type-writ-er
ty-phoid
ty-phoon
typ-i-cal
  typ-i-cal-ly
typ-i-fy
  typ-i-fy-ing
typ-ist
ty-po
ty-ran-no-sau-rus
tyr-an-ny

U

ubiq-ui-tous
  ubiq-ui-tary
  ubiq-ui-tous-ly
  ubiq-ui-ty
ud-der
ug-ly
  ug-li-er
  ug-li-est
ukase
uku-le-le
ul-cer
  ul-cer-ous
ul-cer-ate
  ul-cer-at-ed
ul-na
  ul-nae
ul-ster
ul-te-ri-or
  ul-te-ri-or-ly
ul-ti-mate
  ul-ti-mate-ly
ul-ti-ma-tum
  ul-ti-ma-tums
  ul-ti-ma-ta
ul-tra
ul-tra-con-serv-a-tive
ul-tra-high
ul-tra-ma-rine
ul-tra-son-ic
ul-tra-vi-o-let
ul-u-late
  ul-u-lat-ed
  ul-u-lat-ing
um-ber
um-bil-i-cal
um-bra
  um-bras
  um-brae
um-brage
  um-bra-geous
um-brel-la
umi-ak
um-laut
um-pire
  um-pired
  um-pir-ing
ump-teen
  ump-teenth
un-a-bashed
  un-a-bash-ed-ly
un-a-ble
un-a-bridged
un-ac-cep-t-able

un-ac-cept-ed
un-ac-com-pa-nied
un-ac-count-able
un-ac-count-a-bly
un-ac-cus-tomed
un-ac-quaint-ed
un-a-dorned
un-a-dul-ter-at-ed
un-a-dul-ter-at-ed-ly
un-ad-vised
un-ad-vis-ed-ly
un-af-fect-ed
un-af-fect-ed-ly
un-a-fraid
un--Amer-i-can
unan-i-mous
una-nim-i-ty
unan-i-mous-ly
un-an-swer-able
un-an-swered
un-ap-pe-tiz-ing
un-ap-pre-ci-at-ed
un-ap-pre-ci-a-tive
un-armed
un-a-shamed
un-asked
un-a-spir-ing
un-as-sail-able
un-as-sail-ably
un-as-sailed
un-at-tached
un-at-tain-able
un-at-tained
un-at-tend-ed
un-au-thor-ized
un-a-vail-a-ble
un-a-vail-a-bil-i-ty
un-a-vail-a-bly
un-a-void-a-ble
un-a-void-a-bil-i-ty
un-a-void-ably
un-a-ware
un-backed
un-bal-anced
un-bar
un-barred
un-bar-ring
un-bear-able
un-bear-ably
un-beat-en
un-beat-able
un-be-com-ing
un-be-com-ing-ly

un-be-lief
un-be-liev-able
un-be-liev-ably
un-be-liev-er
un-be-liev-ing
un-be-liev-ing-ly
un-bend
un-bend-ing
un-bi-ased
un-bi-ased-ly
un-bid-den
un-bind
un-bound
un-bind-ing
un-blem-ished
un-bolt
un-bolt-ed
un-born
un-bos-om
un-bound
un-bound-ed-ly
un-bowed
un-bread-able
un-bri-dle
un-bri-dled
un-bri-dling
un-bro-ken
un-bro-ken-ly
un-buck-le
un-buck-led
un-bur-den
un-but-ton
un-but-toned
un--called--for
un-can-ny
un-can-ni-er
un-can-ni-est
un-can-ni-ly
un-cap
un-capped
un-cap-ping
un-ceas-ing
un-ceas-ing-ly
un-cer-e-mo-ni-ous
un-cer-e-mo-ni-ous-ly
un-cer-tain
un-cer-tain-ly
un-cer-tain-ty
un-cer-tain-ties
un-chal-lenged
un-change-able
un-change-ably
un-changed

un-chang-ing
un-char-i-ta-ble
un-char-i-ta-bly
un-chart-ed
un-chris-tian
un-cir-cum-cised
un-civ-il
un-civ-il-ly
un-civ-i-lized
un-class-i-fi-able
un-clas-si-fied
un-cle
un-clean
un-clean-ly
un-clear
un-cloak
un-clut-tered
un-coil
un-com-fort-able
un-com-fort-ably
un-com-mit-ted
un-com-mon
un-com-mon-ly
un-com-mu-ni-ca-tive
un-com-pre-hend-ing
un-com-pro-mis-ing
un-com-pro-mised
un-con-cern
un-con-cerned
un-con-di-tion-al
un-con-di-tion-al-ly
un-con-firmed
un-con-nect-ed
un-con-nect-ed-ly
un-con-quer-a-ble
un-con-quered
un-con-scion-able
un-con-scion-ably
un-con-scious
un-con-scious-ly
un-con-scious-ness
un-con-sti-tui-tion-al
un-con-strained
un-con-test-ed
un-con-trol-la-ble
un-con-trol-la-bly
un-con-trolled
un-con-ven-tion-al
un-con-ven-tion-al-ly
un-count-ed
un-cou-ple
un-cou-pled
un-cou-pling

un-couth
un-couth-ly
un-cov-er
un-cov-ered
unc-tion
unc-tu-ous
unc-tu-os-i-ty
unc-tu-ous-ly
un-curl
un-cut
un-daunt-ed
un-daunt-ed-ly
un-de-ceive
un-de-ceived
un-de-ceiv-ing
un-de-ceiv-a-ble
un-de-cid-ed
un-de-cid-ed-ly
un-de-cid-ed-ness
un-de-fined
un-de-fin-a-ble
un-de-mon-stra-tive
un-de-ni-a-ble
un-de-ni-a-bly
un-de-nied
un-de-pend-able
un-de-pend-a-bil-i-ty
un-der
un-der-a-chiev-er
un-der-a-chiev-ment
un-der-act
un-der-age
un-der-arm
un-der-bel-ly
un-der-car-riage
un-der-charge
un-der-charged
un-der-charg-ing
un-der-class-man
un-der-class-men
un-der-clothes
un-der-coast
un-der-cur-rent
un-der-cut
un-der-cut-ting
un-der-de-vel-oped
un-der-de-vel-op-ing
un-der-dog
un-der-done
un-der-es-ti-mate
un-der-es-ti-mat-ed
un-der-es-ti-mat-ing
un-der-es-ti-ma-tion

un-der-foot
un-der-gar-ment
un-der-go
un-der-went
un-der-gone
un-der-grad-u-ate
un-der-ground
un-der-growth
un-der-lie
un-der-lay
un-der-lain
un-der-ly-ing
un-der-line
un-der-lined
un-der-lin-ing
un-der-ling
un-der-mine
un-der-mined
un-der-min-ing
un-der-min-er
un-der-most
un-der-neath
un-der-priv-i-leged
un-der-rate
un-der-rat-ed
un-der-rat-ing
un-der-score
un-der-scored
un-der-scor-ing
un-der-sea
un-der-sec-re-tary
un-der-sec-re-tar-ies
un-der-sell
un-der-sold
un-der-ell-ing
un-der-sell-er
un-der-shirt
un-der-shot
un-der-side
un-der-signed
un-der-stand
un-der-stood
un-der-stand-ing
un-der-stand-a-ble
un-der-stand-a-bly
un-der-state
un-der-stat-ed
un-der-stat-ing
un-der-state-ment
un-der-stood
un-der-study
un-der-stud-ied
un-der-stud-y-ing

un-der-stud-ies
un-der-take
un-der-took
un-der-tak-en
un-der-tak-ing
un-der-tak-er
un-der-the-coun-ter
un-der-tone
un-der-tow
un-der-wa-ter
un-der-weight
un-der-write
un-der-wrote
un-der-writ-ten
un-der-writ-er
un-de-sir-a-ble
un-de-sir-a-bil-i-ty
un-de-sir-a-bly
un-de-ter-mined
un-dies
un-dip-lo-mat-ic
un-dip-lo-mat-i-cal-ly
un-dis-ci-plined
un-dis-closed
un-dis-posed
un-dis-tin-guished
un-di-vid-ed
un-doubt-ed
un-doubt-ed-ly
un-doubt-ing
un-due
un-du-lant
un-du-late
un-du-lat-ed
un-du-lat-ing
un-du-la-tion
un-du-ly
un-dy-ing
un-earth
un-earth-ly
un-easy
un-eas-i-er
un-eas-i-est
un-ease
un-eas-i-ly
un-eas-i-ness
un-em-ployed
un-em-ploy-ment
un-e-qual
un-e-qual-ly
un-e-qual-ed
un-e-quiv-o-cal
un-e-quiv-o-cal-ly

un-err-ing
un-err-ing-ly
un-eth-i-cal
un-eth-i-cal-ly
un-e-ven
un-e-ven-ly
un-e-ven-ness
un-ex-cep-tion-able
un-ex-pect-ed
un-ex-pect-ed-ly
un-fail-ing
un-fail-ing-ly
un-faith-ful
un-faith-ful-ly
un-faith-ful-ness
un-fa-mil-iar
un-fa-mil-i-ar-i-ty
un-fa-mil-iar-ly
un-fast-en
un-fas-ten-a-ble
un-fas-ten-er
un-fath-om-a-ble
un-fa-vor-a-ble
un-fa-vor-a-bly
un-feel-ing
un-feel-ing-ly
un-feigned
un-feign-ed-ly
un-fet-ter
un-fet-tered
un-fin-ished
un-fit
un-fit-ly
un-fit-ness
un-fit-ting
un-flat-ter-ing
un-flinch-ing
un-flinch-ing-ly
un-fold
un-for-get-ta-ble
un-for-get-ta-bly
un-for-giv-a-ble
un-for-tu-nate
un-for-tu-nate-ly
un-found-ed
un-found-ed-ness
un-friend-ly
un-friend-li-er
un-friend-li-est
un-friend-li-ness
un-frock
un-furl
un-gain-ly

un-gain-li-ness
un-gird
un-gird-ed
un-gird-ing
un-glazed
un-god-ly
un-god-li-er
un-god-li-est
un-god-li-ness
un-gov-ern-able
un-gov-ern-ably
un-gra-cious
un-gra-cious-ly
un-gra-cious-ness
un-gram-mat-i-cal
un-gram-mat-i-cal-ly
un-grate-ful
un-grate-ful-ly
un-grate-ful-ness
un-guard-ed
un-guard-ed-ly
un-guent
un-gu-late
un-ham-pered
un-hand
un-handy
un-hand-i-er
un-hand-i-est
un-hap-py
un-hap-pi-er
un-hap-pi-est
un-hap-pi-ly
un-hap-pi-ness
un-harmed
un-healthy
un-health-i-er
un-health-i-ly
un-heard
un-heed-ed
un-heed-ful
un-heed-ing
un-hinge
un-hinged
un-hing-ing
un-hitch
un-ho-ly
un-ho-li-er
un-ho-li-est
un-hol-li-ly
un-ho-li-ness
un-hook
un-horse
un-horsed

un-hors-ing
un-hur-ried
un-hurt
uni-cam-er-al
uni-cam-er-al-ly
uni-cel-lu-lar
uni-corn
uni-fi-ca-tion
uni-form
uni-formed
uni-form-i-ty
uni-form-ly
uni-fy
uni-fied
uni-fy-ing
uni-fi-er
uni-lat-er-al
uni-lat-er-al-ism
uni-lat-er-al-ly
un-imag-in-able
un-im-pair-ed
un-im-peach-able
un-im-peach-a-bly
un-im-por-tance
un-im-por-tant
un-im-proved
un-in-hib-it-ed
un-in-hib-it-ed-ly
un-in-ter-est-ed
un-in-ter-est-ing
un-ion
un-ion-ism
un-ion-ist
un-ion-ize
un-ion-ized
un-ion-iz-ing
un-ion-i-za-tion
unique
unique-ly
unique-ness
uni-son
unit
unite
unit-ed
unit-ing
unit-er
uni-ty
uni-ties
uni-valve
uni-valved
uni-val-vu-lar
uni-ver-sal
uni-ver-sal-i-ty

uni-ver-sal-ly
uni-ver-sal-ness
uni-ver-sal-ize
uni-ver-sal-ized
uni-ver-sal-iz-ing
uni-verse
uni-ver-si-ty
uni-ver-si-ties
un-just
un-just-ly
un-kempt
un-kind
un-kind-ness
un-kind-ly
un-known
un-law-ful
un-law-ful-ly
un-law-ful-ness
un-learn
un-learned
un-learn-ing
un-learn-ed
un-learn-ed-ly
un-leash
un-less
un-let-ter-ed
un-like
un-like-ness
un-like-ly
un-like-li-er
un-like-li-est
un-like-li-ness
un-lim-ber
un-lim-it-ed
un-load
un-load-er
un-lock
un-looked--for
un-loose
un-loosed
un-loos-ing
un-loos-en
un-lucky
un-luck-i-er
un-luck-i-est
un-luck-i-ly
un-make
un-made
un-mak-ing
un-mak-er
un-man
un-manned
un-man-ning

un-mask
un-mean-ing
un-mean-ing-ly
un-men-tion-able
un-mer-ci-ful
un-mer-ci-ful-ly
un-mis-tak-able
un-mis-tak-a-bly
un-mit-i-gat-ed
un-mit-i-gat-ed-ly
un-nat-u-ral
un-nat-u-ral-ly
un-nat-u-ral-ness
un-nec-es-sary
un-nec-es-sar-i-ly
un-nerve
un-nerved
un-nerv-ing
un-num-bered
un-ob-jec-tion-able
un-or-gan-ized
un-pack
un-par-al-leled
un-par-don-able
un-pleas-ant
un-pleas-ant-ly
un-pleas-ant-ness
un-plumbed
un-pop-u-lar
un-pop-u-lar-i-ty
un-pop-u-lar-ly
un-prec-e-dent-ed
un-prec-e-dent-ed-ly
un-prin-ci-pled
un-print-able
un-pro-fes-sion-al
un-pro-fes-sion-al-ly
un-qual-i-fied
un-qual-i-fied-ly
un-ques-tion-able
un-ques-tion-ably
un-ques-tioned
un-quote
un-quot-ed
un-quot-ing
un-rav-el
un-rav-eled
un-rav-el-ing
un-rav-el-ment
un-read
un-re-al
un-rea-son-able
un-rea-son-ably

un-rea-son-ing
un-re-fined
un-re-gen-er-ate
un-re-lat-ed
un-re-lent-ing
un-re-lent-ing-ly
un-remit-ting
un-re-serve
un-re-served
un-re-serv-ed-ly
un-rest
un-ri-valed
un-roll
un-ruf-fled
un-ru-ly
un-ruy-li-er
un-ru-li-est
un-sad-dle
un-sad-dled
un-sad-dling
un-said
un-sa-vory
un-say
un-say-ing
un-scathed
un-schooled
un-scram-ble
un-scram-bled
un-scram-bling
un-screw
un-scru-pu-lous
un-scru-pu-lous-ly
un-seal
un-sea-son-able
un-sea-son-ably
un-seat
un-seem-ly
un-set-tle
un-set-tled
un-set-tling
un-sheathe
un-sheathed
un-sheath-ing
un-shod
un-sight-ly
un-sight-li-er
un-sight-li-est
un-skilled
un-skill-ful
un-skill-ful-ly
un-snap
un-snapped
un-snap-ping

un-snarl
un-so-phis-ti-cat-ed
  un-so-phis-ti-cat-ed-ly
  un-so-phis-ti-ca-tion
un-sound
  un-sound-ly
un-spar-ing
  un-spar-ing-ly
un-speak-a-ble
  un-speak-a-bly
un-sta-ble
  un-sta-bly
un-steady
  un-stead-i-er
  un-stead-i-est
  un-stead-i-ly
un-stop
  un-stopped
  un-stop-ping
un-strung
un-stud-ied
un-sung
un-tan-gle
  un-tan-gled
  un-tan-gling
un-taught
un-think-able
  un-think-ing
  un-think-ing-ly
un-ti-dy
un-tie
  un-tied
  un-ty-ing
un-til
un-time-ly
  un-time-li-ness
un-to
un-told
  un-touch-a-ble
  un-touch-a-bly
un-to-ward
  un-to-ward-ly
un-truth
un-tu-tored
un-used
un-u-su-al
  un-u-su-al-ly
  un-u-su-al-ness
un-ut-ter-able
  un-ut-ter-ably
un-var-nished
un-veil
un-wary

un-war-i-ly
un-well
un-whole-some
  un-whole-some-ly
un-wieldy
  un-wield-i-ness
un-will-ing
  un-will-ing-ly
  un-will-ing-ness
un-wind
  un-wound
  un-wind-ing
un-wise
  un-wise-ly
un-wit-ting
  un-wit-ting-ly
un-wont-ed
  un-wont-ed-ly
un-wor-thy
  un-wor-thi-ly
  un-wor-thi-ness
un-wrap
  un-wrapped
  un-wrap-ping
un-yield-ing
up-beat
up-braid
  up-braid-er
  up-braid-ing
up-com-ing
up-coun-try
up-date
  up-dat-ed
  up-dat-ing
up-end
up-grade
  up-grad-ed
  up-grad-ing
up-heav-al
up-heave
  up-heaved
  up-heav-ing
up-hill
up-hold
  up-held
  up-hold-ing
up-hol-ster
  up-hol-ster-er
  up-hol-stery
up-keep
up-land
up-lift
up-most

up-on
up-per
up-per--class
up-per-cut
  up-per-cut-ting
up-per-most
up-pish
  up-pish-ly
up-pi-ty
up-raise
  up-raised
  up-rais-ing
up-rear
up-right
  up-right-ly
  up-right-ness
up-ris-ing
up-roar
  up-roar-i-ous
up-set
  up-set-ting
up-shot
up-side
up-stage
  up-staged
  up-stag-ing
up-stairs
up-stand-ing
up-start
up-take
up-to-date
up-town
up-trend
up-turn
up-ward
  up-ward-ly
ura-ni-um
ur-ban
ur-bane
  ur-bane-ly
  ur-ban-i-ty
ur-ban-ize
  ur-ban-ized
  ur-ban-iz-ing
  ur-ban-i-za-tion
ur-chin
urea
  ure-al
ure-ter
ure-thra
  ure-thrae
  ure-thras
  ure-thral

ur-gent
  ur-gen-cy
  ur-gen-cies
  ur-gent-ly
uric
uri-nal
uri-nal-y-sis
  uri-nal-y-ses
uri-nary
  uri-nar-ies
uri-nate
urine
urol-o-gy
  uro-log-ic
  uro-log-i-cal
  urol-o-gist
us-able
  us-ably
  us-abil-i-ty
us-age
use
use-ful
  use-ful-ly
ush-er
usu-al
  usu-al-ly
usurp
  usur-pa-tion
  usurp-er
usu-ry
  usu-ries
  usu-ri-ous
uten-sil
uter-us
  ut-eri
util-i-tar-ian
util-i-ty
  util-i-ties
uti-lize
  uti-lized
  uti-liz-ing
  uti-li-za-tion
ut-most
ut-ter
  ut-ter-a-ble
  ut-ter-er
ut-ter-ance
ut-ter-most
uvu-la
  uvu-las
  uvu-lae
ux-o-ri-ous
  ux-o-ri-ous-ly

V

va-can-cy
  va-can-cies
va-cant
  va-cant-ly
va-cate
  va-cat-ed
  va-cat-ing
va-ca-tion
vac-ci-nate
  vac-ci-nat-ed
  vac-ci-nat-ing
  vac-ci-na-tion
vac-cine
vac-il-late
  vac-il-lat-ed
  vac-il-lat-ing
  vac-il-la-tion
  vac-il-la-tor
va-cu-i-ty
  va-cu-i-ties
vac-u-ous
  vac-u-ous-ly
vac-u-um
  vac-u-ums
  vac-ua
vac-u-um--packed
va-gi-na
  va-gi-nas
  va-gi-nae
  vag-i-nal
va-grant
  va-gran-cy
  va-gran-cies
  va-grant-ly
vague
  vague-ly
vain
  vain-ly
  vain-ness
vain-glo-ry
  vain-glo-ries
  vain-glo-ri-ous
val-ance
  val-anced
val-e-dic-tion
  val-e-dic-to-ri-an
val-e-dic-to-ry
  val-e-dic-to-ries
va-lence
  va-len-cy
val-en-tine
va-let
val-iant

val-iant-ly
val-id
  val-id-ly
val-i-date
  val-i-dat-ed
  val-i-dat-ig
  val-i-da-tion
va-lid-i-ty
  va-lid-i-ties
va-lise
val-ley
  val-leys
val-or
  val-or-ous
  val-or-ous-ly
val-u-able
  val-u-ably
val-u-a-tion
  val-u-a-tion-al
val-ue
  val-ued
  val-u-ing
  val-ue-less
valve
  valve-less
  val-vu-lar
va-moose
vam-pire
  vam-pir-ic
  vam-pir-ism
va-na-di-um
van-dal
  van-dal-ism
  van-dal-ize
  van-dal-ized
  van-dal-iz-ing
vane
  vaned
  vane-less
van-guard
va-nil-la
van-ish
  van-ish-er
van-i-ty
  van-i-ties
van-quish
  van-quish-a-ble
  van-quish-er
van-tage
vap-id
  va-pid-i-ty
  vap-id-ly
va-por

va-por-er
va-por-ish
va-por-ize
va-por-ized
va-por-iz-ing
va-por-i-za-tion
va-por-iz-er
va-por-ous
va-por-opus-ly
va-que-ro
va-que-ros
var-i-able
var-i-abil-i-ty
var-i-ably
var-i-ance
var-i-ant
var-i-a-tion
var-i-a-tion-al
var-i-a-tion-al-ly
var-i-col-ored
var-i-cose
var-ied
var-ied-ness
var-ie-gate
var-ie-gat-ed
var-ie-gat-ing
var-ie-ga-tion
var-ie-ga-tor
va-ri-etal
va-ri-etal-ly
va-ri-ety
va-ri-e-ties
var-i-ous
var-i-ous-ly
var-nish
var-nish-er
var-si-ty
var-si-ties
vary
var-ied
vary-ing
var-i-er
vary-ing-ly
vas-cu-lar
vas-cu-lar-i-ty
va-sec-to-my
va-sec-to-mies
vas-o-mo-tor
vas-sal
vas-sal-age
vast-ness
vat
vat-ted

vat-ting
vaude-ville
vault
vault-ed
vault-er
vault-ing
vaunt
vaunt-er
vaunt-ing-ly
vec-tor
vec-to-ri-al
veer-ing
veg-e-ta-ble
veg-e-tal
veg-e-tar-i-an
veg-e-tar-i-an-ism
veg-e-tate
veg-e-tat-ed
veg-e-tat-ing
veg-e-ta-tion
veg-e-ta-tion-al
veg-e-ta-tive
ve-he-ment
ve-he-mence
ve-he-men-cy
ve-hi-cle
ve-hic-u-lar
veil
veiled
veil-ing
vein
veiny
vein-i-er
vein-i-est
vein-ing
vel-lum
ve-loc-i-ty
ve-loc-i-ties
vel-our
ve-lum
ve-la
vel-vet
vel-vet-ed
vel-ve-teen
vel-vety
vel-vet-i-er
vel-vet-i-est
ve-nal
ve-nal-i-ty
ve-nal-ly
ve-na-tion
ve-na-tion-al
vend-er

vend-or
ven-det-ta
vend-i-ble
vend-i-bil-i-ty
ve-neer
ve-neer-er
ve-neer-ig
ven-er-able
ven-er-abil-i-ty
ven-er-ably
ven-er-ate
ven-er-a-tion
ven-er-a-tor
ve-ne-re-ai
venge-ance
venge-ful
venge-ful-ness
ve-ni-al
ve-ni-al-i-ty
ve-ni-al-ness
ve-ni-al-ly
ven-i-son
ven-om
ven-om-ous
ve-nous
ve-nous-ly
vent
vent-ed
vent-ing
ven-ti-late
ven-ti-lat-ed
ven-ti-lat-ing
ven-ti-la-tion
ven-ti-la-tor
ven-tral
ven-tral-ly
ven-tri-cle
ven-tril-o-quism
ven-tri-lo-qui-al
ven-tril-o-quist
ven-tril-o-quize
ven-tril-o-quized
ven-tril-o-quiz-ing
ven-ture
ven-ture-some
ven-tur-ous
ve-ra-cious
ve-rac-i-ty
ve-rac-i-ties
ve-ran-da
ver-bal
ver-bal-ly
ver-bal-ize

ver-bal-ized
ver-bal-iz-ing
ver-bal-i-za-tion
ver-bal-iz-er
ver-ba-tim
ver-bi-age
ver-bose
ver-bose-ness
ver-bos-i-ty
ver-bo-ten
ver-dant
ver-dan-cy
ver-dict
ver-di-gris
ver-dure
ver-dured
ver-dur-ous
verge
verged
verg-ing
ver-i-fi-ca-tion
ver-i-fy
ver-i-fied
ver-i-fy-ing
ver-i-fi-abil-i-ty
ver-i-fi-able
ver-i-fi-er
veri-si-mil-i-tude
veri-ta-ble
veri-ta-bly
ver-i-ty
ver-i-ties
ver-meil
ver-mic-u-lar
ver-mic-u-late
ver-mic-u-lat-ed
ver-mi-fuge
ver-mil-ion
ver-min
ver-min-ous
ver-mouth
ver-nac-u-lar
ver-nac-u-lar-ism
ver-nal
ver-nal-ly
ver-sa-tile
ver-sa-til-i-ty
versed
ver-si-fy
ver-si-fied
ver-si-fy-ing
ver-si-fi-er
ver-si-fi-ca-tion

ver-sion
ver-sion-al
ver-sus
ver-te-bra
ver-te-brae
ver-te-bral
ver-te-bral-ly
ver-te-brate
ver-tex
ver-tex-es
ver-ti-ces
ver-ti-cal
ver-ti-cal-i-ty
ver-ti-cal-ly
ver-ti-go
ver-ti-goes
ver-tig-i-nes
ves-i-cant
ves-i-ca-to-ry
ves-i-ca-to-ries
ves-i-cate
ves-i-cat-ed
ves-i-cat-ing
ves-i-ca-tion
ves-i-cle
ve-sic-u-lar
ves-pers
ves-sel
ves-tal
vest-ed
ves-ti-bule
ves-ti-buled
ves-ti-bul-ing
ves-tib-u-lar
ves-tige
ves-tig-i-al
ves-tig-i-al-ly
vest-ment
vest-pock-et
ves-try
ves-tries
vet
vet-ted
vet-ting
vet-er-an
vet-er-i-nar-i-an
vet-er-i-nary
ve-to
vex
vex-er
vex-ing-ly
vex-a-tion
vex-a-tious

vexed
via
vi-a-ble
vi-a-bil-i-ty
vi-a-bly
vi-a-duct
vi-al
vi-and
vi-brant
vi-bran-cy
vi-brate
vi-brat-ed
vi-brat-ing
vi-bra-tion
vi-bra-to
vi-bra-tos
vi-bra-tor
vi-bra-to-ry
vi-bur-num
vic-ar
vic-ar-ship
vic-ar-age
vi-car-i-ous
vi-car-i-ous-ly
vice ad-mi-ral
vice--con-sul
vice--pres-i-dent
vice-roy
vice-roy-al
vice ver-sa
vi-cin-i-ty
vi-cin-i-ties
vi-cious
vi-cious-ly
vi-cis-si-tude
vic-tim
vic-tim-ize
vic-tim-ized
vic-tim-iz-ing
vic-tim-iz-er
vic-tor
vic-to-ri-ous
vic-to-ri-ous-ly
vic-to-ry
vic-to-ries
vict-ual
vid-eo
view-er
view-less
view-point
vig-il
vig-i-lance
vig-i-lant

vig-i-lan-te
vi-gnette
vig-or
vig-or-ous
vig-or-ous-ly
vi-king
vile
vil-i-fy
vil-i-fied
vil-i-fy-ing
vil-i-fi-ca-tion
vil-la
vil-lain
vil-lain-ous
vil-lainy
vil-lain-ies
vil-lein
vil-lous
vil-lus
vil-li
vin-ci-ble
vin-ci-bil-i-ty
vin-di-cate
vin-di-cat-ed
vin-di-cat-ing
vin-dic-tive
vin-dic-tive-ly
vin-dic-tive-ness
vin-e-gar
vin-e-gary
vine-yard
vi-nous
vin-tage
vint-ner
vi-nyl
vi-ol
vi-o-la
vi-o-list
vi-o-la-ble
vi-o-la-bil-i-ty
vi-o-late
vi-o-lat-ed
vi-o-la-tion
vi-o-lence
vi-o-lent
vi-o-let
vi-o-lin
vi-o-lin-ist
vi-o-lon-cel-lo
vi-o-lon-cel-list
vi-per
vi-ra-go
vi-ral

vir-eo
vir-e-os
vir-gin
vir-gin-al
vir-gin-i-ty
vir-gule
vir-ile
vi-ril-i-ty
vi-rol-o-gy
vi-rol-o-gist
vir-tu-al
vir-tue
vir-tu-os-i-ty
vir-tu-os-i-ties
vir-tu-o-so
vir-tu-ous
vir-tu-ous-ly
vir-u-lence
vir-u-len-cy
vir-u-lent
vi-rus
vi-rus-es
vi-sa
vis-age
vis-cera
vis-cer-al
vis-cid
vis-cid-ly
vis-cos-i-ty
vis-cos-i-ties
vis-count
vis-count-cy
vis-count-ship
vis-count-ess
vis-cous
vis-i-bil-i-ty
vis-i-bil-i-ties
vis-i-ble
vi-sion
vi-sion-ary
vi-sion-ar-ies
vis-it
vis-i-tant
vis-it-a-tion
vis-it-ing
vis-i-tor
vi-sor
vis-ta
vi-tal
vi-tal-i-ty
vi-tal-i-ties
vi-tal-ize
vi-tal-ized

vi-tal-iz-ing
vi-tal-i-za-tion
vi-tals
vi-ta-min
vi-ti-ate
vit-re-ous
vit-re-os-i-ty
vit-ri-fy
vit-ri-fied
vit-ri-fy-ing
vit-ri-fi-a-ble
vit-ri-fi-ca-tion
vit-ri-ol
vit-ri-ol-ic
vi-tu-per-ate
vi-tu-per-at-ed
vi-tu-per-at-ing
vi-tu-per-a-tion
vi-va
vi-va-cious
vi-vac-i-ty
vi-vac-i-ties
viv-id
viv-i-fy
viv-i-fied
viv-i-fy-ing
vi-vip-ar-ous
vivi-sec-tion
vix-en
vi-zier
vi-zor
vo-cab-u-lar-y
vo-cab-u-lar-ies
vo-cal
vo-ca-tion
vo-ca-tion-al
vo-cif-er-ous
vod-ka
voice-print
void-able
vol-a-tile
vol-a-til-i-ty
vol-can-ic
vol-can-i-cal-ly
vol-ca-no
vol-ca-noes
vol-ca-nos
vo-li-tion
vol-ley
vol-leys
vol-ley-ball
volt-age
vol-ta-ic

volt-me-ter
vol-u-ble
  vol-u-bly
  vol-u-bil-i-ty
vol-ume
vo-lu-mi-nous
  vo-lu-mi-nous-ly
vol-un-tary
  vol-un-tar-i-ly
vol-un-teer
vo-lup-tu-ary
  vo-lup-tu-ar-ies
vo-lup-tu-ous
vom-it
voo-doo
vo-ra-cious
vo-rac-i-ty
vor-tex
  vor-tex-es
  vor-ti-ces
vo-ta-ry
  vor-ta-ries
vot-er
vo-tive
vouch-er
vouch-safe
  vouch-safed
  vouch-saf-ing
vow-el
voy-age
  voy-aged
  voy-ag-ing
  voy-ag-er
vo-ya-geur
vo-yeur
  vo-yeur-ism
  voy-eur-is-tic
vul-can-ite
vul-gar
  vul-gar-ism
vul-gar-i-ty
  vul-gar-i-ties
vul-gar-ize
  vul-gar-ized
  vul-gar-iz-ing
vul-gate
vul-ner-a-ble
  vul-ner-a-bly
vul-pine
vul-ture
vul-va
  vul-vae
  vul-vas

W

wab-ble
  wab-bled
  wab-bling
wacky
  wack-i-er
  wack-i-est
  wack-i-ly
wad
  wad-ded
  wad-ding
wade
  wad-ed
  wad-ing
wad-er
waf-er
waf-fle
wag
  wagged
  wag-ging
  wag-ger
  wag-gish
wage
  waged
  wag-ing
wa-ger
  wag-gery
  wag-ger-ies
wag-gle
  wag-gled
  wag-gling
wag-on
  wag-on-er
wain-scot
  wain-scot-ing
wain-wright
waist-band
waist-coat
waist-line
wait-er
wait-ing
wait-ress
waive
  waived
  waiv-ing
  waiv-er
wake
  waked
  wok-en
  wak-ing
wake-ful
  wake-ful-ly
wak-en
wale

waled
wal-ing
walk-a-way
walk-er
walk-ie-talk-ie
walk-out
walk-o-ver
walk-up
walk-way
wal-al-by
  wal-la-bies
wall-board
wal-let
wall-eye
  wall-eyed
wall-flow-er
wal-lop
wall-to-wall
wal-nut
wal-rus
  wal-rus-es
wam-pum
wan
  wan-ner
  wan-nest
  wan-ness
wan-der
  wan-der-lust
wane
  waned
  wan-ing
wan-gle
  wan-gled
  wan-gling
  wan-gler
want-ing
wan-ton
wa-pi-ti
  wa-pi-ties
war
  warred
  war-ring
war-ble
  war-bled
  war-bling
war-bler
war-den
  war-den-ship
ward-er
ward-robe
ware-house
war-fare
war-head

war-horse
war-like
war-lock
warm
  warm-er
  warm-est
warm--blood-ed
warm-heart-ed
war-mon-ger
warmth
warn-ing
war-path
war-rant
  war-ran-ty
  war-ran-ties
war-ren
war-ri-or
war-ship
war-time
wary
  war-i-er
  war-i-est
  war-i-ly
wash-able
wash-ba-sin
wash-board
wash-bowl
wash-cloth
wash-er
wash-ing
wash-out
wash-room
wash-stand
wash-tub
wasn't
wasp
  wasp-ish
  wasp-ish-ly
was-sail
wast-age
waste
  wast-ed
  wast-ing
  waste-ful
  waste-ful-ly
  waste-ful-ness
waste-bas-ket
waste-land
waste-pa-per
wast-er
wast-rel
watch-dog
watch-ful

watch-man
  watch-men
watch-tow-er
watch-word
wa-ter
wat-er-buck
wa-ter-col-or
wa-ter-course
wa-ter-cress
wa-ter-fall
wa-ter-foul
wa-ter-front
wa-ter-less
wa-ter lev-el
wa-ter lily
  wa-ter lil-ies
wa-ter line
wa-ter-llogged
Wa-ter-loo
wa-ter main
wa-ter-man
  wa-ter-men
wa-ter-mark
wa-ter-mel-on
wa-ter moc-ca-sin
wa-ter-proof
wa-ter-re-pel-lent
wa-ter-shed
wa-ter-side
wa-ter ski
  wa-ter-skied
  wa-ter-ski-ing
wa-ter-spout
wa-ter-tight
wa-ter-way
wa-ter-works
wa-tery
watt-age
watt-hour
wat-tle
  wat-tled
  wat-tling
wave
  waved
  wav-ing
wave-length
wave-let
wa-ver
wav-y
  wav-i-er
  wav-i-est
  wav-i-ly
wax

waxed
wax-ing
wax-en
wax-wing
wax-work
waxy
  wax-i-er
  wax-i-est
way-far-er
  way-far-ing
way-lay
  way-laid
  way-lay-ing
way-side
way-ward
weak-en
weak-kneed
weak-ling
weak-ly
  weak-li-er
  weak-li-est
weak-mind-ed
weak-ness
wealthy
  wealth-i-er
  wealth-i-est
  wealth-i-ly
wean
weap-on
  weap-on-ry
wear
  wear-ing
wea-ri-some
wea-ry
  wea-ri-er
  wea-ri-est
  wea-ried
  wea-ry-ing
  wea-ri-ly
wea-sel
weath-er
weath-er--beat-en
weath-er-cock
weath-er-glass
weath-er-ing
weath-er-man
  weath-er-men
weath-er-proof
weather vane
weave
  weaved
  wov-en
  weav-ing

weav-er
web
 webbed
 web-bing
web-foot
 web-foot-ed
wed-ding
wedge
 wedged
 wedg-ing
wed-lock
weedy
 weed-i-er
 weed-i-est
week-day
week-end
week-ly
weep-ing
wee-vil
weigh
weight
weighty
 weight-i-er
 weight-i-est
 weight-i-ly
weird
 weird-er
 weird-est
wel-come
 wel-comed
 wel-com-ing
wel-fare
well--be-ing
well-born
well--bred
well--dis-posed
well--done
well--found-ed
well--groomed
well--ground-ed
well--known
well--mean-ing
well--nigh
well--off
well--read
well--spo-ken
well-spring
well--thought--of
well--timed
well--to--do
well--wish-er
well--worn
wel-ter

wel-ter-weight
were-wolf
 were-wolves
west-bound
west-er-ly
west-ern
 west-ern-er
west-ern-ize
 west-ern-ized
 west-ern-iz-ing
 west-ern-i-za-tion
west-ern-most
west-ward
wet
 wet-ter
 wet-test
wet-back
whale
 whaled
 whal-ing
whale-boat
whale-bone
whal-er
wharf
 wharves
what-ev-er
what-not
what-so-ev-er
wheat
wheat-en
whee-dle
 whee-dled
 whee-dling
 whee-dler
wheel and ax-le
wheel-bar-row
wheel-chair
wheeled
wheel-house
wheel-wright
wheeze
 wheezed
 wheez-ing
wheezy
 wheez-i-er
 wheez-i-est
 wheez-i-ly
whelm
whelp
whence-so-ev-er
where-abouts
where-as
where-by

where-fore
where-in
where-on
where-so-ev-er
where-to
where-up-on
wher-ev-er
where-with
where-with-al
wher-ry
 wher-ries
whet
 whet-ted
 whet-ting
wheth-er
whet-stone
whch-ev-er
whim-per
whim-si-cal
whim-sy
 whim-sies
whine
 whined
 whin-ing
whin-ny
 whin-nied
 whin-nying
 whin-nies
whip
 whipped
 whip-ping
whip-lash
whip-per-snap-per
whip-pet
whip-poor-will
whir
 whirred
 whir-ring
whirl-i-gig
whirl-pool
whirl-wind
whisk-er
whis-key
whis-ky
 whis-keys
 whis-kies
whis-per
whist
whis-tle
 whis-tled
 whis-tling
whis-tler
white

whit-er
whit-est
whit-ish
white--col-lar
white-fish
whit-en
white-wash
white water
whith-er
whit-ing
whit-tle
whit-tled
whit-tling
whit-tler
whiz
whizzed
whiz-zing
whiz-zes
whoa
who-ev-er
whole-heart-ed
whole-sale
whole-saled
whole-sal-ing
whole-sal-er
whole-some
whole-wheat
whol-ly
whom-ev-er
whom-so-ev-er
whoop-ing
whop-per
whop-ping
whorled
whose-so-ev-er
who-so-ev-er
wick-ed
wick-er
wick-er-work
wick-et
wide
wid-er
wid-est
wide--awake
wide--eyed
wid-en
wide-spread
wid-geon
wid-ow
wid-ow-er
wid-ow-hood
width
wield-er

wieldy
wie-ner
wig-gle
wig-gled
wig-gling
wig-gly
wig-gli-er
wig-gler
wig-wag
wig-wagged
wig-wag-ging
wig-wam
wild-cat
wild-cat-ted
wild-cat-ting
wild-cat strike
wil-der-ness
wild-fire
wild-fowl
wild--goose chase
wild-life
wild-wood
wile
wiled
wil-ing
wil-i-ly
wil-i-ness
willed
will-ful
wil-lies
will-ing
will--o'--the--wisp
wil-low
wil-lowy
wil-ly--nil-ly
wim-ble
wim-ple
win
win-ning
wince
winced
winc-ing
wind
wound
wind-ing
wind-bag
wind-break
wind-ed
wind-fall
wind-flow-er
win-dow
wind-row
wind-shield

wind-storm
wind-up
wind-ward
windy
wind-i-er
wind-i-est
wine
wined
win-ing
win-ery
win-er-ies
wine-skin
winged
win-ner
win-ning
win-some
win-ter
win-ter-gree
win-ter-ize
win-ter-ized
win-ter-iz-ing
win-ter-i-za-tion
win-try
wipe
wiped
wip-ing
wire-haired
wire-les
wire-tap
wiry
wir-i-er
wir-i-est
wis-dom
wise
wis-er
wis-est
wise-acre
wise-crack
wish-bone
wish-ful
wishy-washy
wisp
wispy
wis-ter-ia
wist-ful
witch-craft
witch-ery
witch-er-ies
witch-ing
with-draw
with-er
with-ered
with-er-ing

with-hold
  with-held
  with-hold-ing
with-in
with-out
with-stand
  with-stood
  with-stand-ing
wit-less
wit-ness
wit-ted
wit-ti-cism
wit-ting
  wit-ting-ly
wiz-ard
  wi-zard-ly
  wi-zard-ry
wiz-en
  wiz-ened
wob-ble
woe-be-gone
woe-ful
wolf-hound
wolf-ram
wol-ver-ine
wom-an
  wom-en
  wom-an-ly
  wom-an-hood
womb
wom-bat
wom-en-folk
won-der
won-der-ful
won-der-land
won-der-ment
won-drous
wont-ed
wood-bine
wood-cut-ter
wood-ed
wood-en
wood-land
wood-man
  wood-men
wood-peck-er
wood-shed
woods-man
  woods-men
wood-wind
wood-work
woody
  wood-i-er

  wood-i-est
woof-er
wool-en
wool-gath-er-ing
wool-ly
  wool-li-er
  wool-li-est
wool-ly-head-ed
woozy
  wooz-i-er
  wooz-i-est
word-book
word-ing
word-less
  word-less-ly
work-a-ble
  work-a-bil-i-ty
  work-a-day
work-bench
work-book
work-day
worked-up
work-er
work-horse
work-house
work-ing
work-ing-man
  work-ing-men
work-man
  work-men
work-man-like
work-man-ship
work-ta-ble
world-ly
  world-li-er
  world-li-est
world-ly--wise
world-wide
worm--eat-en
worm-wood
wormy
  worm-i-er
  worm-i-est
worn--out
wor-ri-some
wor-ry
  wor-ried
  wor-ry-ing
  wor-ries
  wor-ry-wart
wors-en
wor-ship
  wor-ship-ful

wor-sted
worth-less
worth-while
wor-thy
  wor-thi-er
  wor-thi-est
  wor-thi-ness
would--be
wouldn't
wound-ed
wraith
wran-gle
  wran-gled
  wran-gling
  wran-gler
wrath-ful
wreak
wreath
wreathe
  wreathed
  wreath-ing
wreck-age
wreck-er
wrench
wres-tle
  wres-tled
  wres-tling
wretch-ed
wrig-gle
  wrig-gled
wrin-kle
  wrin-kled
  wrin-kling
wrist-band
write
  wrote
  writ-ten
  writ-ing
write-in
writ-er
writhe
  writhed
  writh-ing
wrong-do-er
  wrong-do-ing
wronged
wrong-ful
wrong-head-ed
wrought
wry
  wri-er
  wri-est
  wry-ly

X

X chro-mo-some
xe-bec
xe-non
xen-o-pho-bia
X-ray
x-sec-tion
xy-lem
xy-lo-phone
xy-lose

Y

yacht
  yacht-ing
  yachts-man
  yachts-men
yak
yam
yank
Yan-kee
yap
  yapped
  yap-ping
yard-age
yard-arm
yard-mas-ter
yard-stick
yarn
yar-row
yawn
year
year-book
year-ling
year-long
year-ly
yearn
  yearn-ing
year--round
yeast
yeasty
  yeast-i-er
  yeast-i-est

yel-low
  yel-low-ish
yel-low-bird
yel-low fe-ver
yel-low-ham-mer
yel-low jack-et
yelp
yen
  yenned
  yen-ning
yeo-man
  yeo-men
ye-shi-va
  ye-shi-vas
yes-ter-day
yes-ter-year
ye-ti
yew
yield
yield-ing
yip
  yipped
  yip-ping
yo-del
  yo-deled
  yo-del-ing
  yo-del-er
yo-ga
  yo-gic
yo-gi
  yo-gis
yo-gurt
yoke
  yoked
  yok-ing
yo-kel
yolk
yon-der
yore
young
young-ling
young-ster
your-self
  your-selves
youth-ful
yowl
yt-ter-bi-um
yt-tri-um
yuc-ca
yule-tide
yum-my
  yum-mi-er
  yum-mi-est

Z

za-ny
  za-nies
  za-ni-er
  za-n-est
  za-ni-ly
  za-ni-ness
zeal-ot
zeal-ous
ze-bra
  ze-bras
ze-bu
ze-nith
zeph-yr
zep-pe-lin
ze-ro
  ze-ros
  ze-roes
zest
  zesty
  zest-i-er
  zest-i-est
zig-zag
  zig-zagged
  zig-zag-ging
zinc
zing
zin-nia
zip
  zipped
  zip-ping
zip-per
zip-py
  zip-pi-er
  zip-pi-est
zir-con
zir-con-ni-um
zith-er
zo-di-ac
  zo-di-a-cal
zom-bie
  zom-bi
zon-al
zone
  zoned
  zon-ing
zoo
  zoos
zo-ol-o-gy
  zo-o-log-i-cal
  zo-o-log-i-cal-ly
  zo-ol-o-gist
zuc-chi-ni
zwie-back